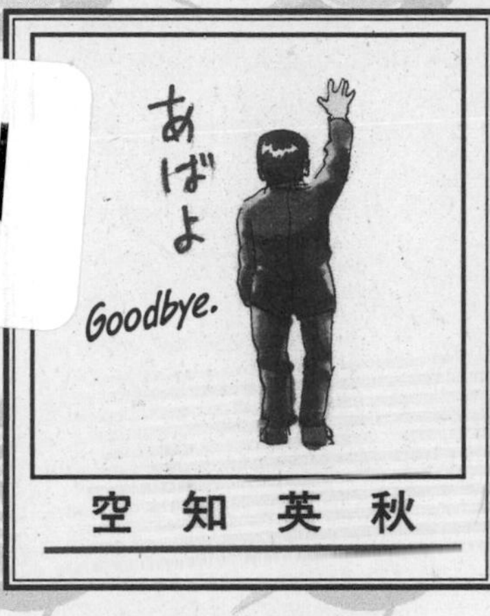
あばよ
Goodbye.
空知英秋

Hideaki Sorachi

We're changing editors at *Gin Tama*. Mr. Oonishi, the man who found this hopeless punk of a manga artist in Hokkaido, is leaving. So I'd like to dedicate this volume to him.

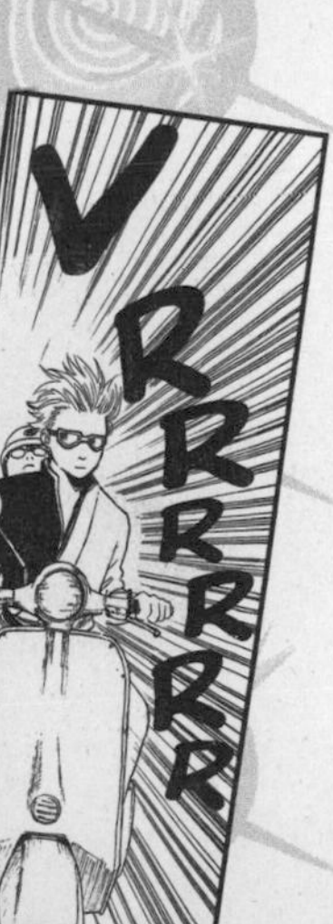
VRRRRRR

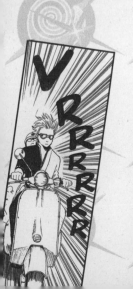

Hideaki Sorachi was born on May 25, 1979, and grew up in Hokkaido, Japan. His ongoing series, ***GIN TAMA***, became a huge hit when it began running in the pages of Japan's ***Weekly Shonen Jump*** in 2004. A ***GIN TAMA*** animated series followed soon after, premiering on Japanese TV in April 2006. Sorachi made his manga debut with the one-shot story ***DANDELION***.

GIN TAMA VOL. 21
SHONEN JUMP ADVANCED Manga Edition

STORY & ART BY HIDEAKI SORACHI

Translation/Kyoko Shapiro, Honyaku Center Inc.
English Adaptation/Lance Caselman
Touch-up Art & Lettering/Avril Averill
Design/Ronnie Casson
Editor/Mike Montesa

Published by VIZ Media, LLC
P.O. Box 77010
San Francisco, CA 94107

10 9 8 7 6 5 4 3 2 1
First printing, February 2011

www.viz.com

THE WORLD'S MOST
CUTTING-EDGE MANGA

SHONEN JUMP
ADVANCED
www.shonenjump.com

GIN TAMA

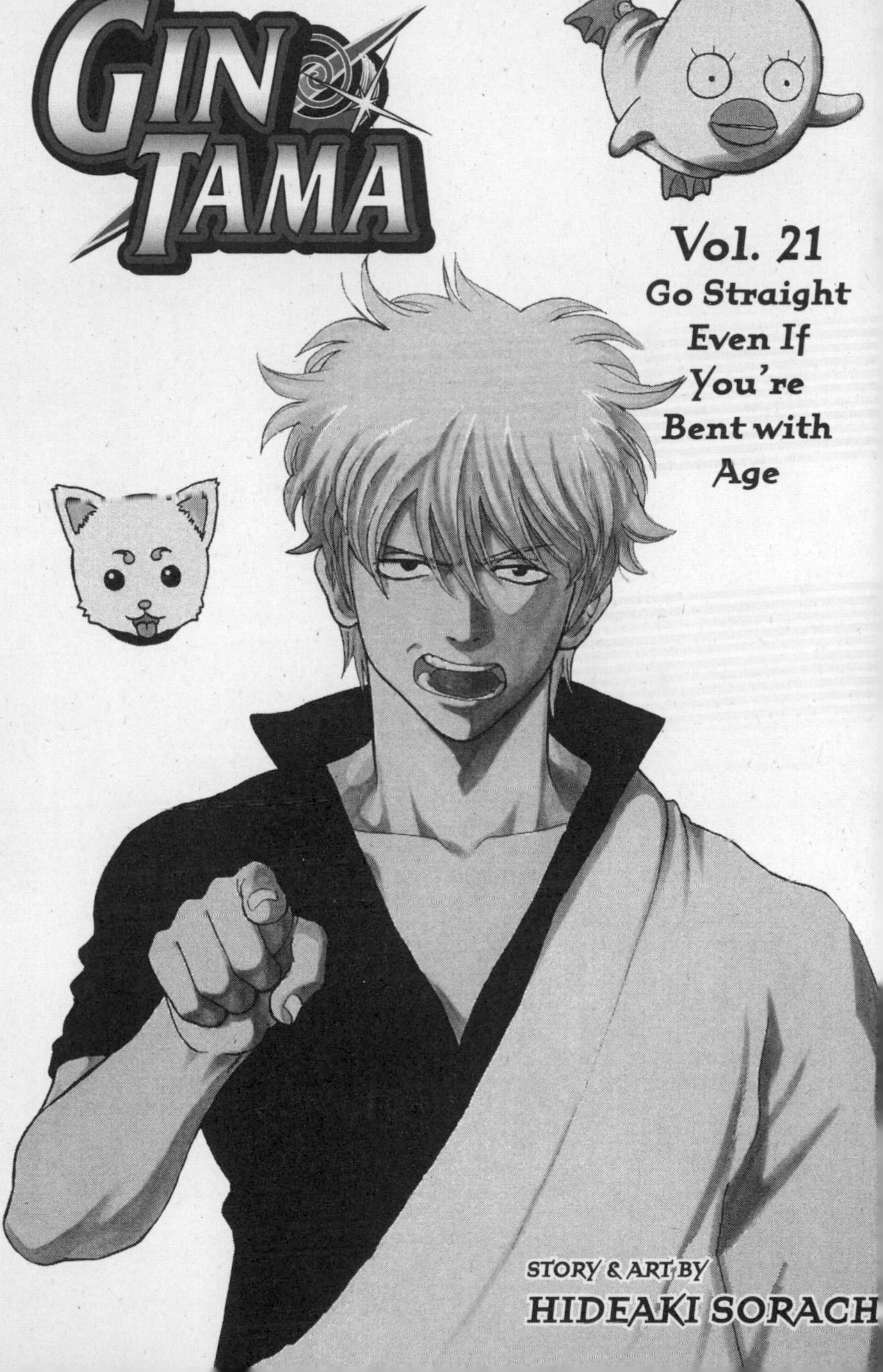

Vol. 21

Go Straight Even If You're Bent with Age

STORY & ART BY
HIDEAKI SORACHI

Yorozuya Members

Shinpachi Shimura

Works under Gintoki in an attempt to learn about the samurai spirit but has often come to regret his decision recently. President of the Tsu Terakado Fan Club.

Gintoki Sakata

The hero of our story. If he doesn't eat something sweet periodically he gets cranky—really cranky. He boasts a powerful sword arm, but he's one step away from diabetes. A former member of the exclusionist faction that seeks to expel the space aliens and protect the nation.

Kagura

A member of the Yato Clan, the most powerful warrior race in the universe. Her voracious appetite and alien worldview lead frequently to laughter...and sometimes contusions.

Sadaharu

A giant space creature turned office pet. Likes to bite people (especially Gin).

Shinsengumi Members

Okita

The Shinsengumi's most formidable swordsman. Behind a facade of amiability, he tirelessly schemes to eliminate Hijikata and usurp his position.

Hijikata

Vice chief of the Shinsengumi, Edo's elite counter-terrorist police unit. His air of detached cool transforms into hot rage the instant he draws his sword...or when someone disparages mayonnaise.

Kondo

The trusted chief of the Shinsengumi (and the remorseless stalker of Shinpachi's older sister Otae).

Other Characters

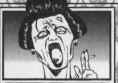

Otose-san

Gin's landlady and proprietor of the pub below the Yorozuya hideout. She has a lot of difficulty collecting the rent.

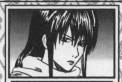

Kotaro Katsura

The last surviving holdout of the exclusionist rebels, and Gintoki's pal. Nickname: Zura.

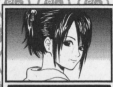

Otae Shimura

Her demure manner hides the heart of a lion. Though employed at a hostess bar, she ruthlessly guards her virtue and plots to revive the family fortunes.

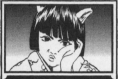

Catherine

A space alien thief who mended her ways and now works at the Otose Snack House.

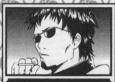

Taizo Hasegawa

Formerly a high official in the Bakufu government, his life has become one long slide into despair.

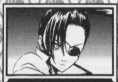

Kyube Yagyu

Crown prince of the famous Yagyu family of swordsmen and Otae's former fiancé. Only this prince has no scepter.

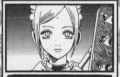

Tama

A robot housekeeper who works at the Otose Snack House. Circumstances have made her a fugitive from the Bakufu government.

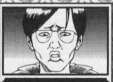

Kamenashi

A turtle-man caught secretly filming girls at the beach who offered to take Gin and his friends to the Dragon Palace.

The story thus far

In an alternate-universe Edo (Tokyo), extraterrestrials land in Japan, and the new government issues an order outlawing swords. The samurai, who have reached the pinnacle of power and prosperity, fall into rapid decline.

Twenty years hence, only one samurai has managed to hold on to his fighting spirit: a somewhat eccentric fellow named Gintoki "Odd Jobs Gin" Sakata. A lover of sweets and near diabetic, our hero sets up shop as a *yorozuya*—an expert at managing trouble and handling the oddest of jobs.

Joining Gin in his business is Shinpachi Shimura, whose sister Gin saved from the clutches of nefarious debt collectors. After a series of unexpected circumstances, the trio meet a powerful alien named Kagura, who becomes—after some arm-twisting—a part-time team member.

Gin helps the Shinsengumi overcome a major threat; he gives advice to a dispirited *Shonen Jump* editor; the great Umibozu becomes the savior of a devastated planet; Kagura displays her femininity, and Yamazaki seeks to infiltrate the Exclusionist ronin. Now while accompanying a turtle-man to the mythical Dragon Palace, Gin and the others find themselves stranded on a desert island!

WHAT THIS MANGA'S FULL OF
vol. 21

Lesson 176

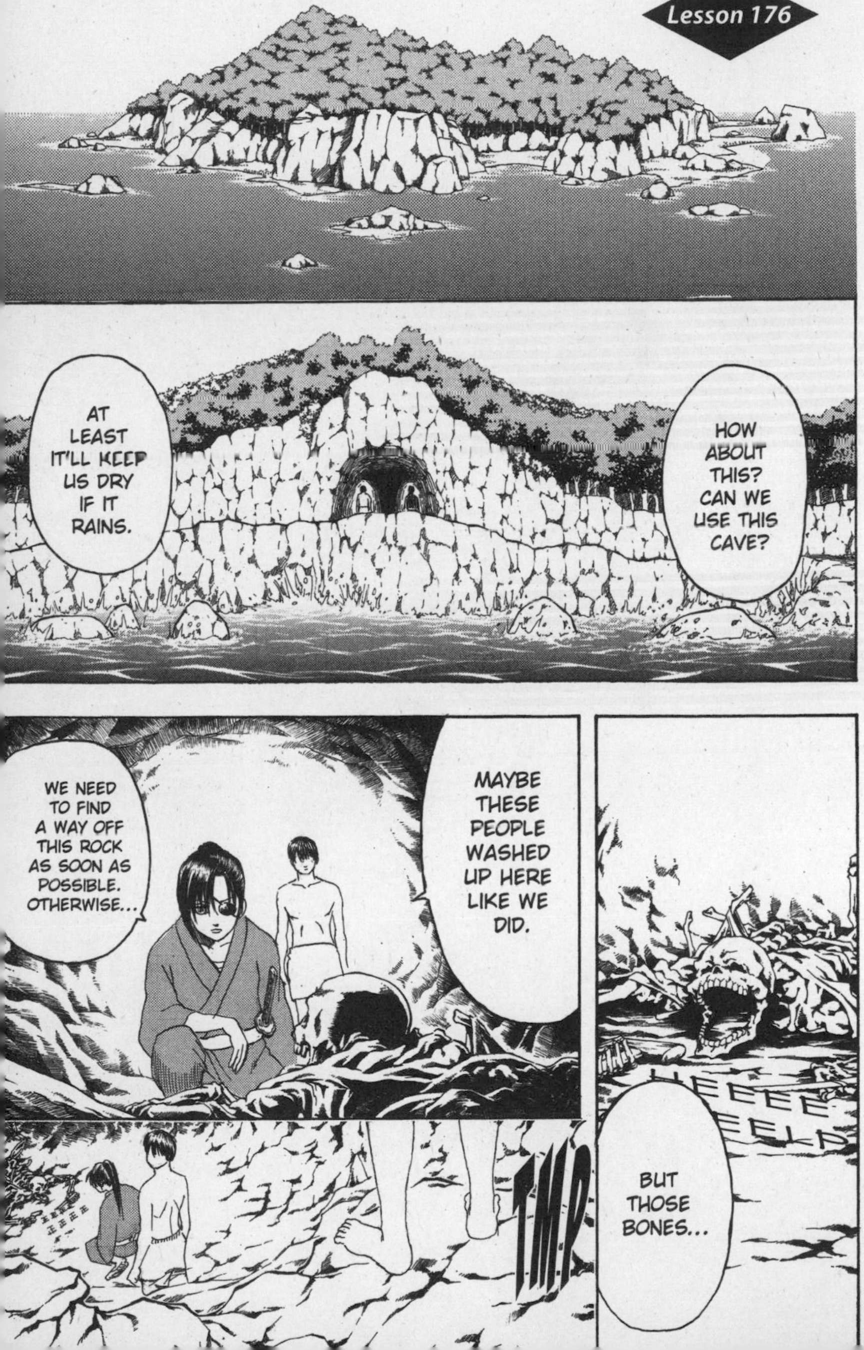

HOW ABOUT THIS? CAN WE USE THIS CAVE?
AT LEAST IT'LL KEEP US DRY IF IT RAINS.
BUT THOSE BONES...
MAYBE THESE PEOPLE WASHED UP HERE LIKE WE DID.
WE NEED TO FIND A WAY OFF THIS ROCK AS SOON AS POSSIBLE. OTHERWISE...
TMP

Lesson 176: Age Brings Wisdom

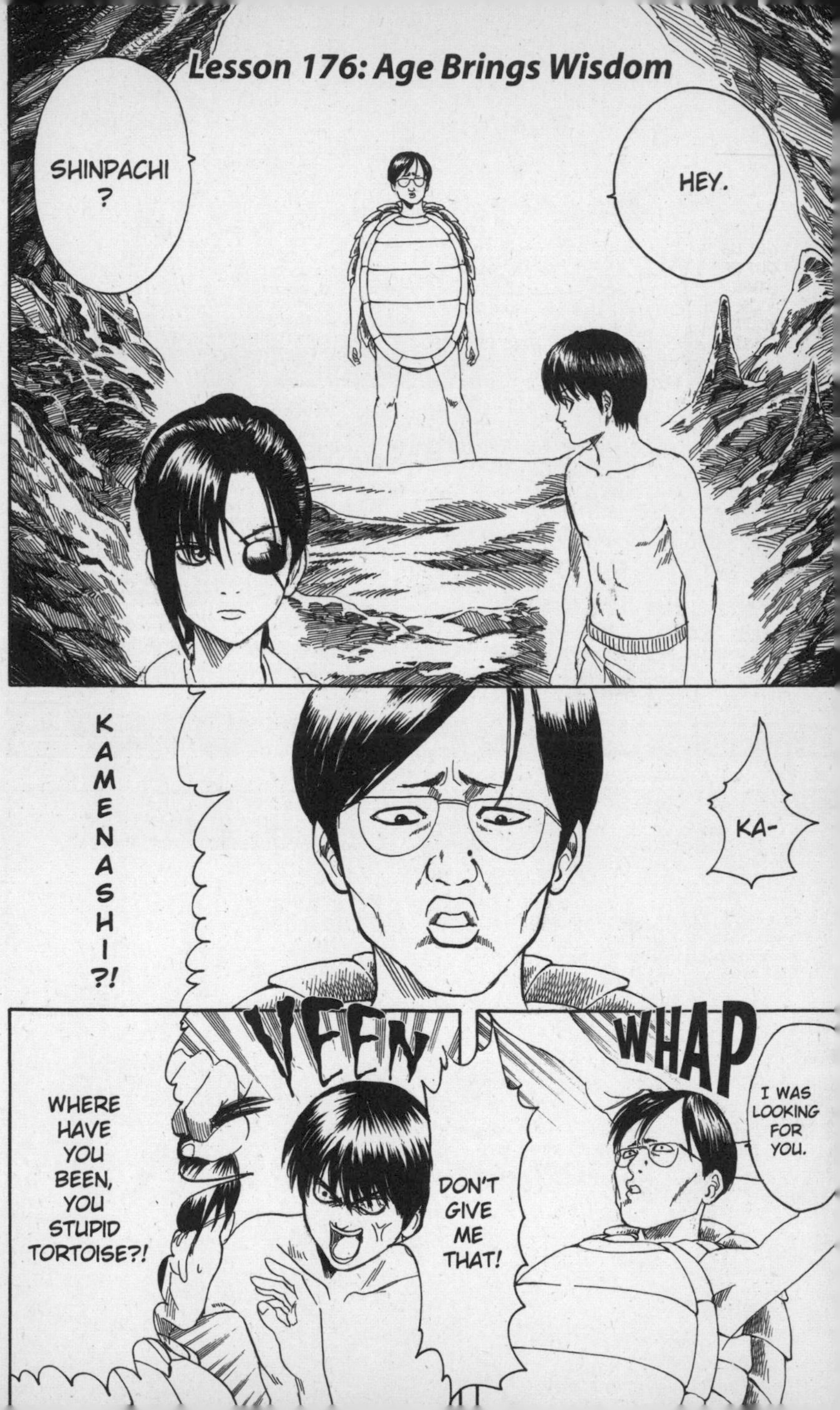
HEY.
SHINPACHI ?
KA-
KAMENASHI?!
WHAP
I WAS LOOKING FOR YOU.
VEEN
DON'T GIVE ME THAT!
WHERE HAVE YOU BEEN, YOU STUPID TORTOISE?!

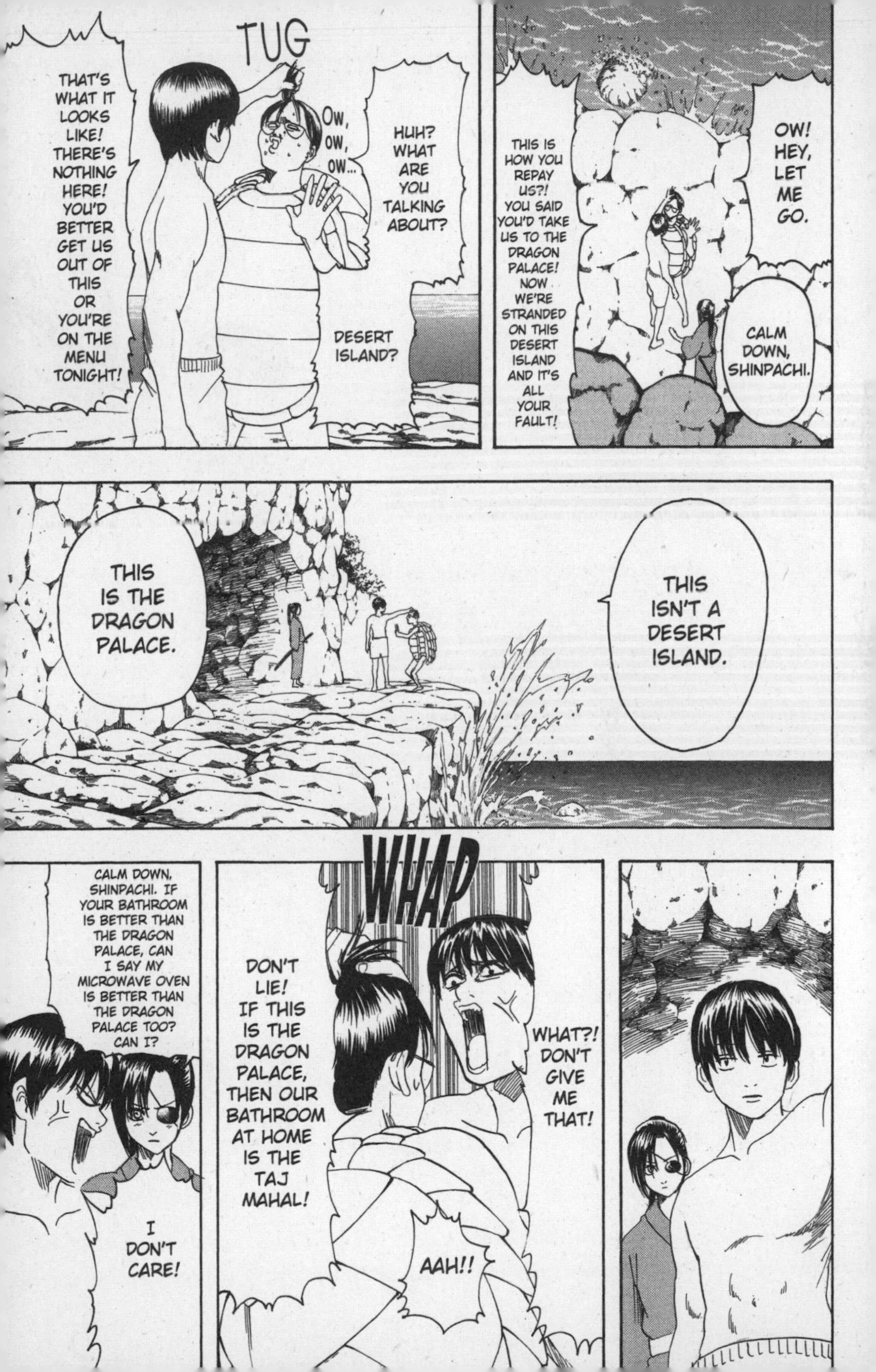
OW! HEY, LET ME GO.
THIS IS HOW YOU REPAY US?! YOU SAID YOU'D TAKE US TO THE DRAGON PALACE! NOW WE'RE STRANDED ON THIS DESERT ISLAND AND IT'S ALL YOUR FAULT!
CALM DOWN, SHINPACHI.
TUG
HUH? WHAT ARE YOU TALKING ABOUT?
DESERT ISLAND?
OW, OW, OW...
THAT'S WHAT IT LOOKS LIKE! THERE'S NOTHING HERE! YOU'D BETTER GET US OUT OF THIS OR YOU'RE ON THE MENU TONIGHT!
THIS ISN'T A DESERT ISLAND.
THIS IS THE DRAGON PALACE.
WHAP
WHAT?! DON'T GIVE ME THAT!
DON'T LIE! IF THIS IS THE DRAGON PALACE, THEN OUR BATHROOM AT HOME IS THE TAJ MAHAL!
AAH!!
CALM DOWN, SHINPACHI. IF YOUR BATHROOM IS BETTER THAN THE DRAGON PALACE, CAN I SAY MY MICROWAVE OVEN IS BETTER THAN THE DRAGON PALACE TOO? CAN I?
I DON'T CARE!

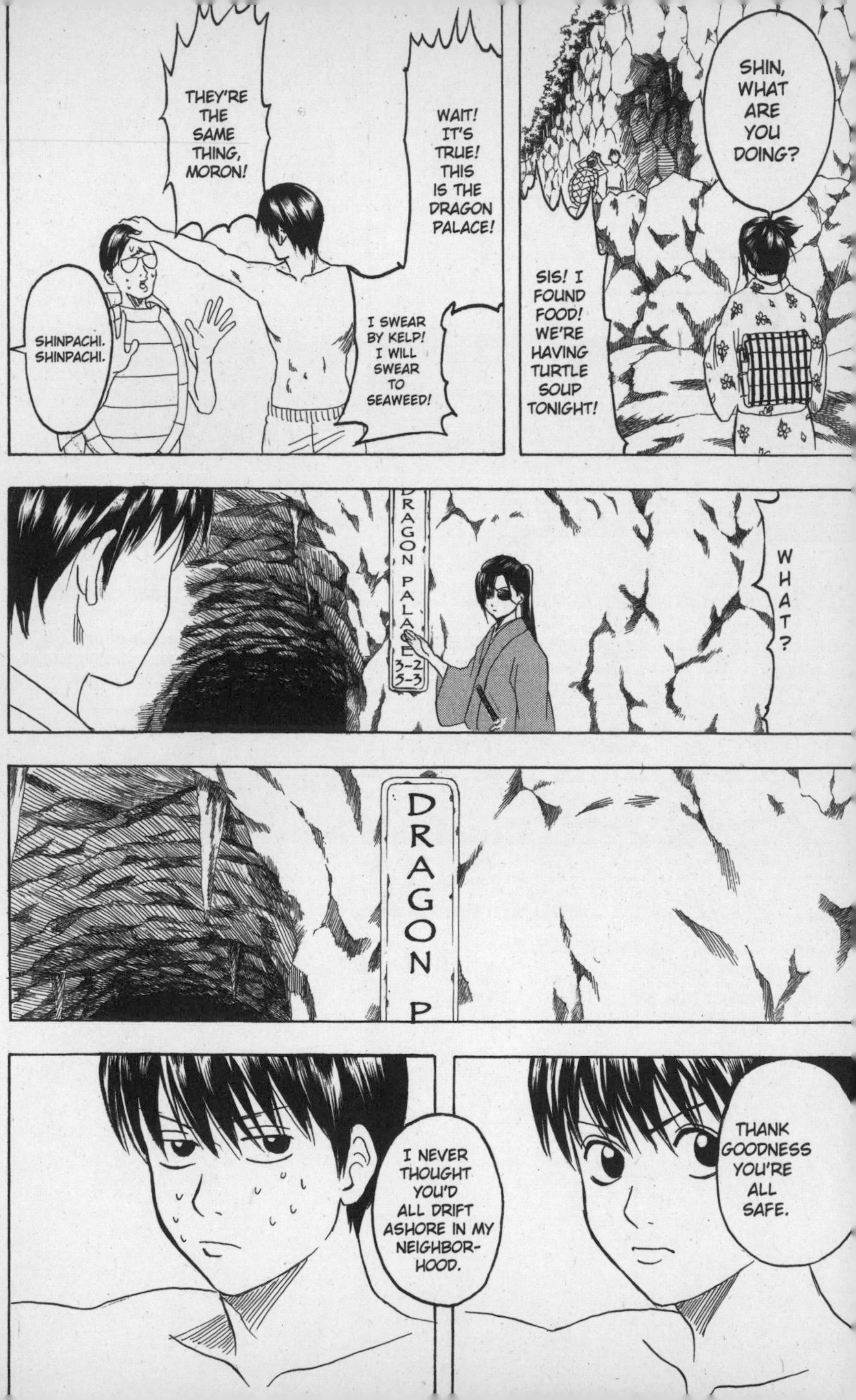
SHIN, WHAT ARE YOU DOING?
SIS! I FOUND FOOD! WE'RE HAVING TURTLE SOUP TONIGHT!
WAIT! IT'S TRUE! THIS IS THE DRAGON PALACE!
I SWEAR BY KELP! I WILL SWEAR TO SEAWEED!
THEY'RE THE SAME THING, MORON!
SHINPACHI. SHINPACHI.
WHAT?
DRAGON PALACE 3-2 3-3
DRAGON P
THANK GOODNESS YOU'RE ALL SAFE.
I NEVER THOUGHT YOU'D ALL DRIFT ASHORE IN MY NEIGHBOR-HOOD.

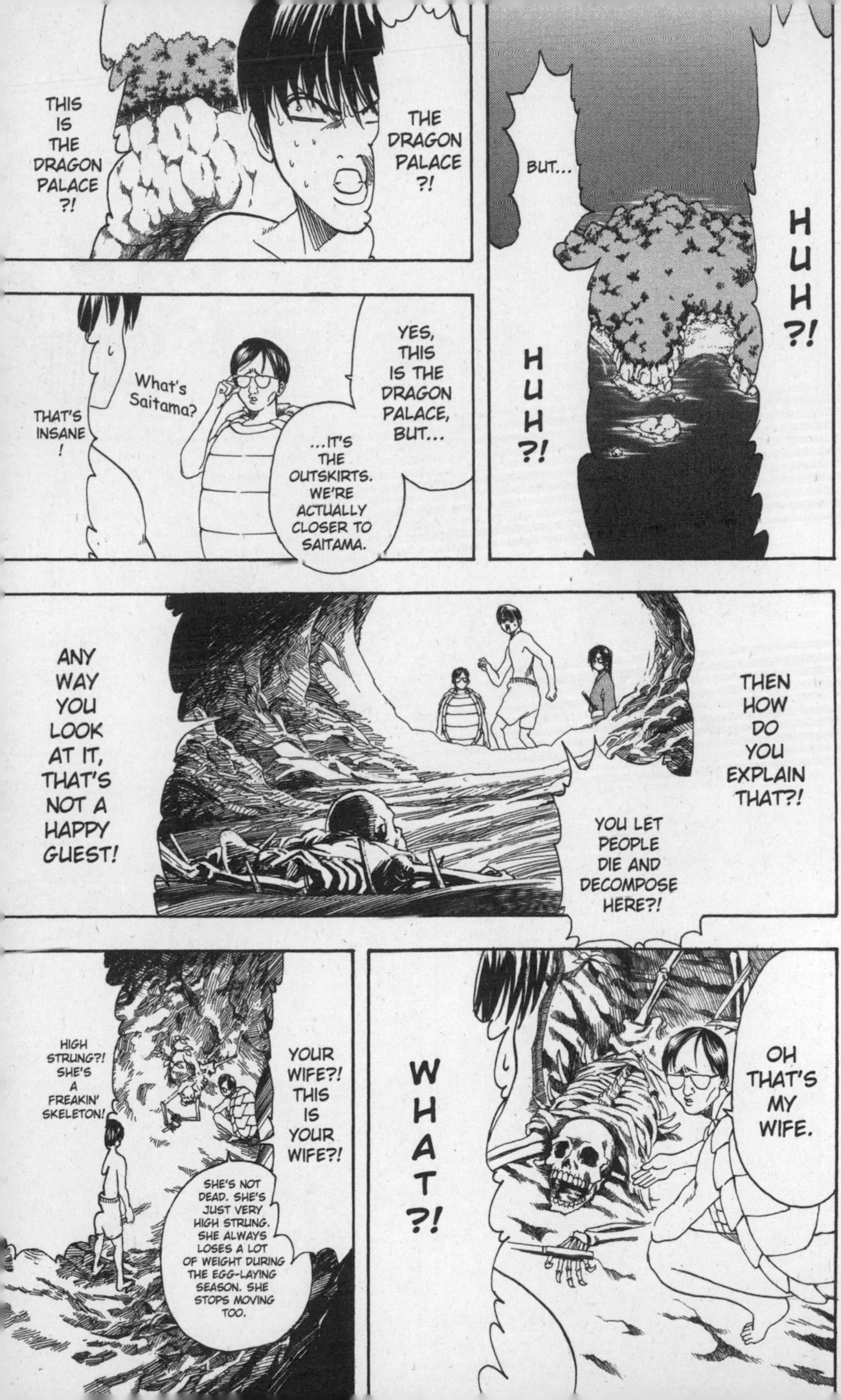
BUT...
HUH?!
HUH?!
THE DRAGON PALACE?!
THIS IS THE DRAGON PALACE?!
YES, THIS IS THE DRAGON PALACE, BUT...
...IT'S THE OUTSKIRTS. WE'RE ACTUALLY CLOSER TO SAITAMA.
What's Saitama?
THAT'S INSANE!
THEN HOW DO YOU EXPLAIN THAT?!
YOU LET PEOPLE DIE AND DECOMPOSE HERE?!
ANY WAY YOU LOOK AT IT, THAT'S NOT A HAPPY GUEST!
OH THAT'S MY WIFE.
WHAT?!
YOUR WIFE?! THIS IS YOUR WIFE?!
SHE'S NOT DEAD. SHE'S JUST VERY HIGH STRUNG. SHE ALWAYS LOSES A LOT OF WEIGHT DURING THE EGG-LAYING SEASON. SHE STOPS MOVING TOO.
HIGH STRUNG?! SHE'S A FREAKIN' SKELETON!

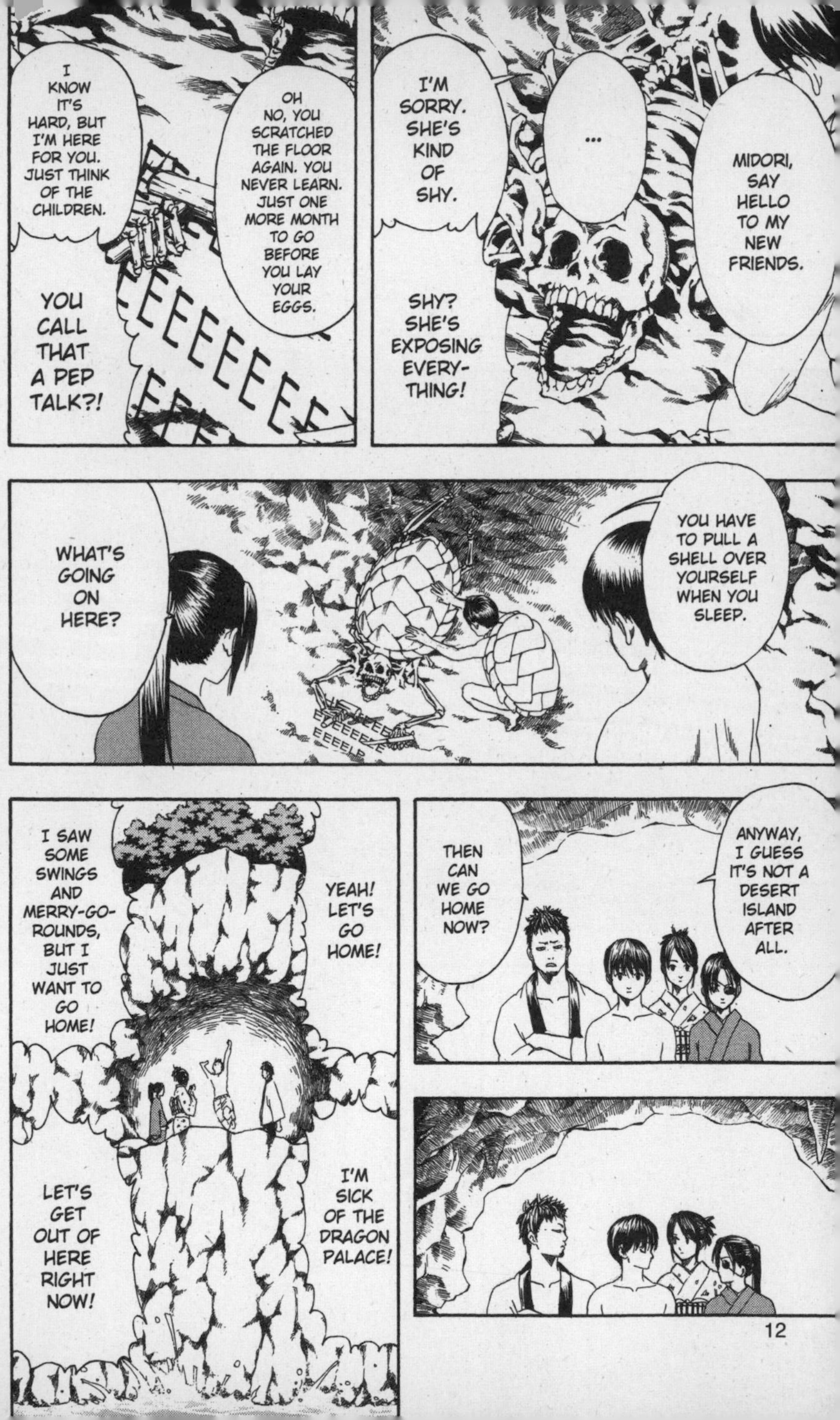
MIDORI, SAY HELLO TO MY NEW FRIENDS.
...
I'M SORRY. SHE'S KIND OF SHY.
SHY? SHE'S EXPOSING EVERY-THING!
OH NO, YOU SCRATCHED THE FLOOR AGAIN. YOU NEVER LEARN. JUST ONE MORE MONTH TO GO BEFORE YOU LAY YOUR EGGS.
I KNOW IT'S HARD, BUT I'M HERE FOR YOU. JUST THINK OF THE CHILDREN.
YOU CALL THAT A PEP TALK?!
YOU HAVE TO PULL A SHELL OVER YOURSELF WHEN YOU SLEEP.
WHAT'S GOING ON HERE?
ANYWAY, I GUESS IT'S NOT A DESERT ISLAND AFTER ALL.
THEN CAN WE GO HOME NOW?
YEAH! LET'S GO HOME!
I SAW SOME SWINGS AND MERRY-GO-ROUNDS, BUT I JUST WANT TO GO HOME!
I'M SICK OF THE DRAGON PALACE!
LET'S GET OUT OF HERE RIGHT NOW!

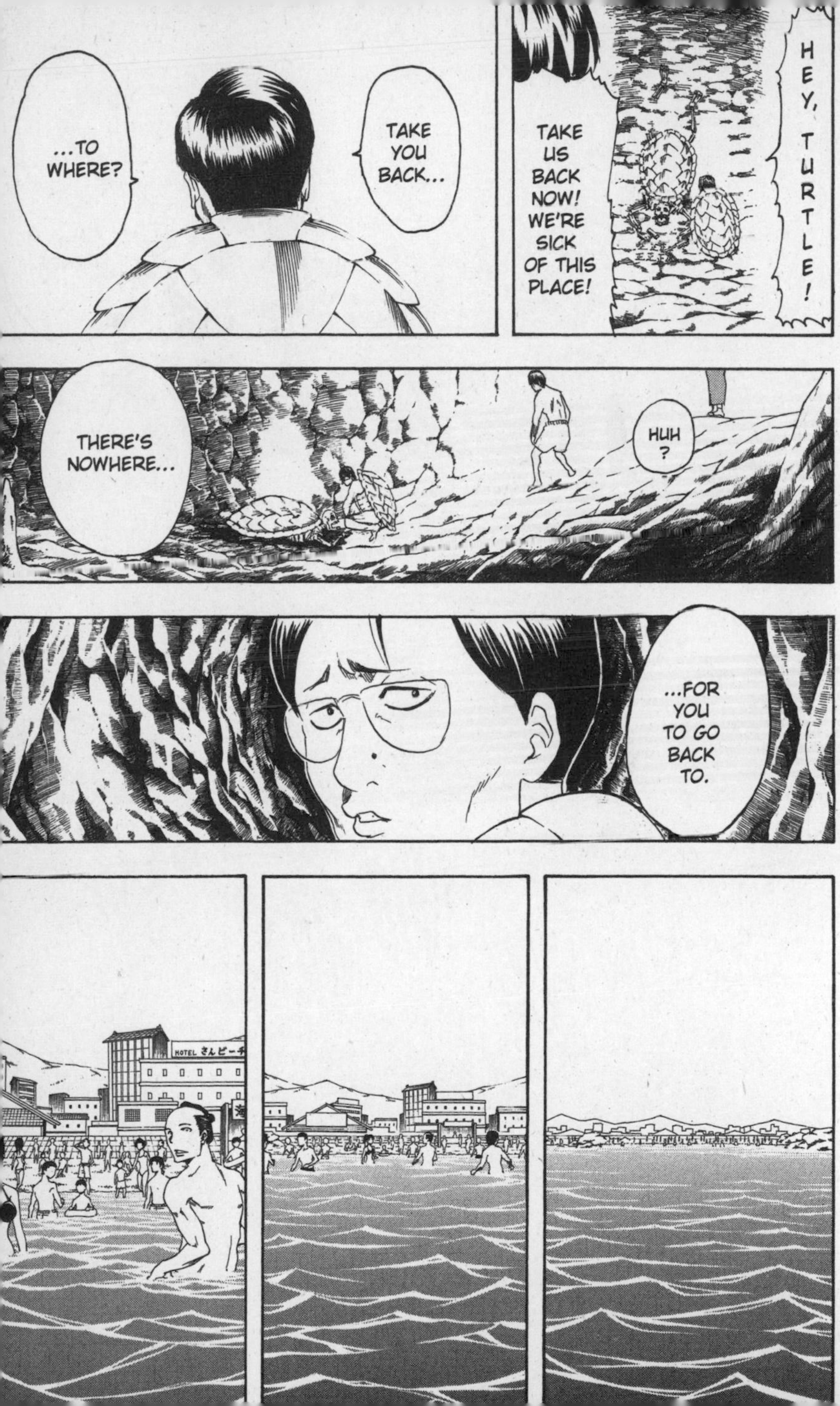
HEY, TURTLE!
TAKE US BACK NOW! WE'RE SICK OF THIS PLACE!
TAKE YOU BACK...
...TO WHERE?
HUH?
THERE'S NOWHERE...
...FOR YOU TO GO BACK TO.
HOTEL さんビーチ

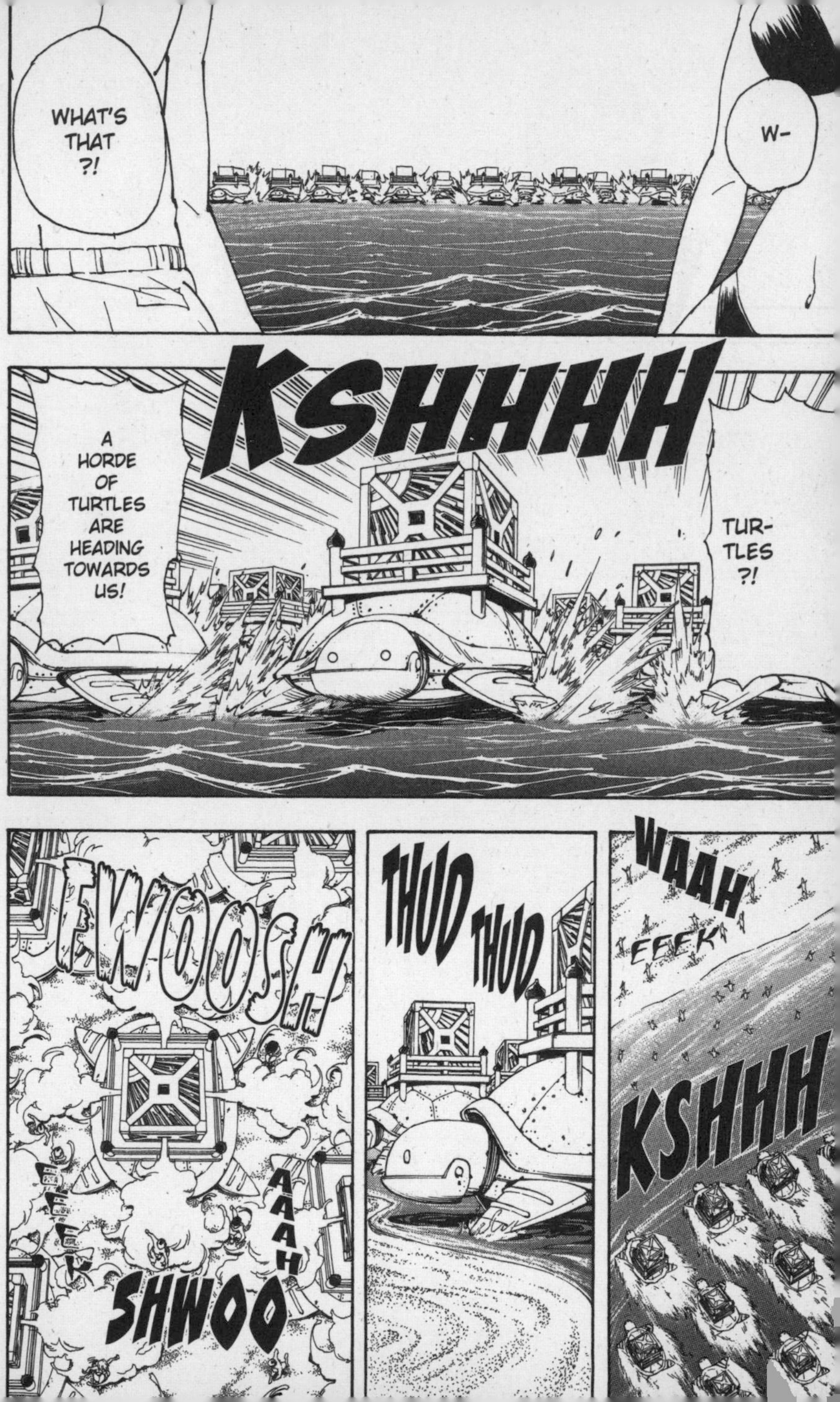
W-
WHAT'S THAT ?!
KSHHHH
TUR-TLES ?!
A HORDE OF TURTLES ARE HEADING TOWARDS US!
WAAH
EEEK
KSHHH
THUD
THUD
FWOOSH
AAAAH
SHWOO

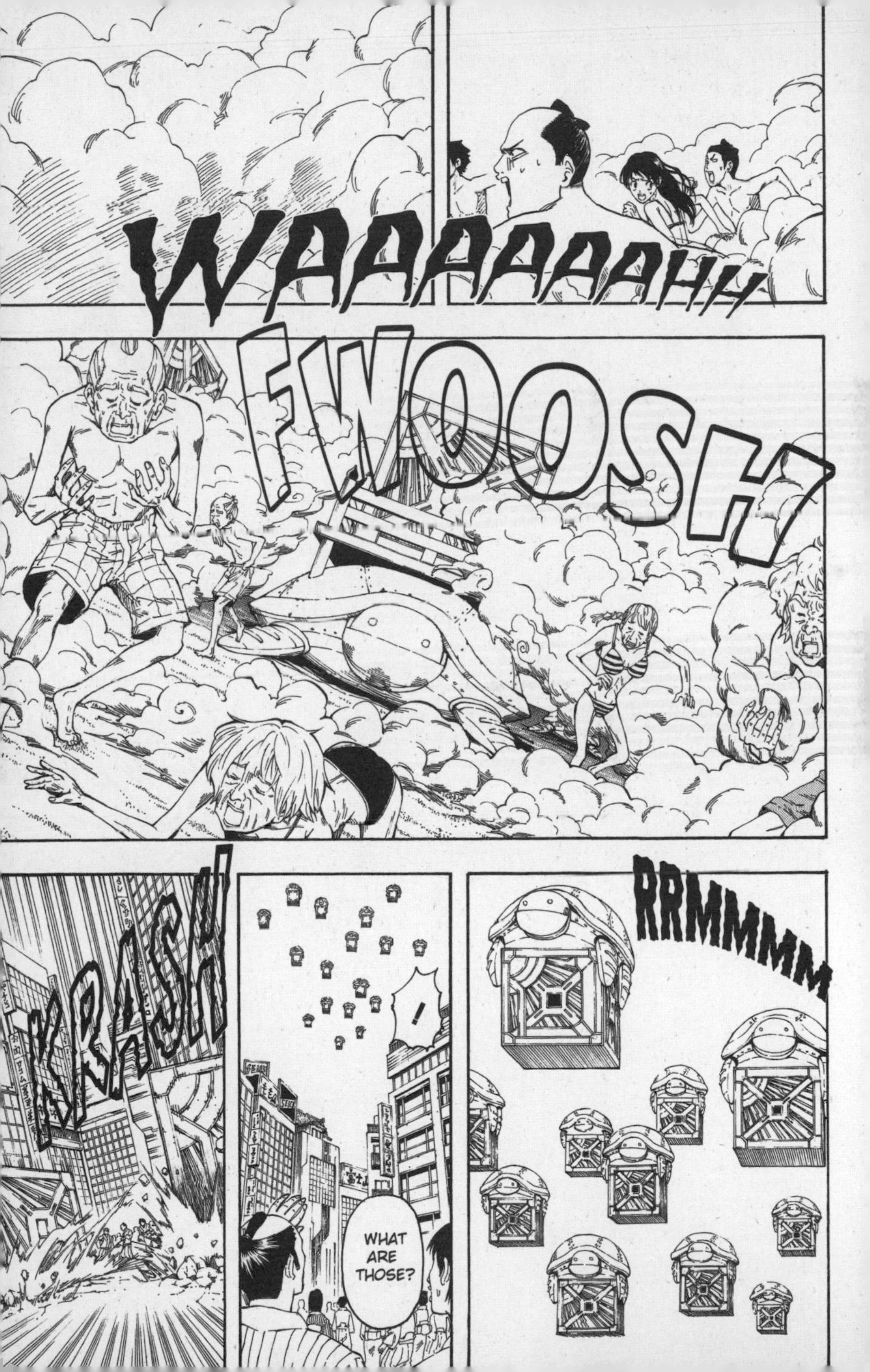
WAAAAAAAHH
FWOOSH
RRMMMMM
!
WHAT ARE THOSE?
KRASH!

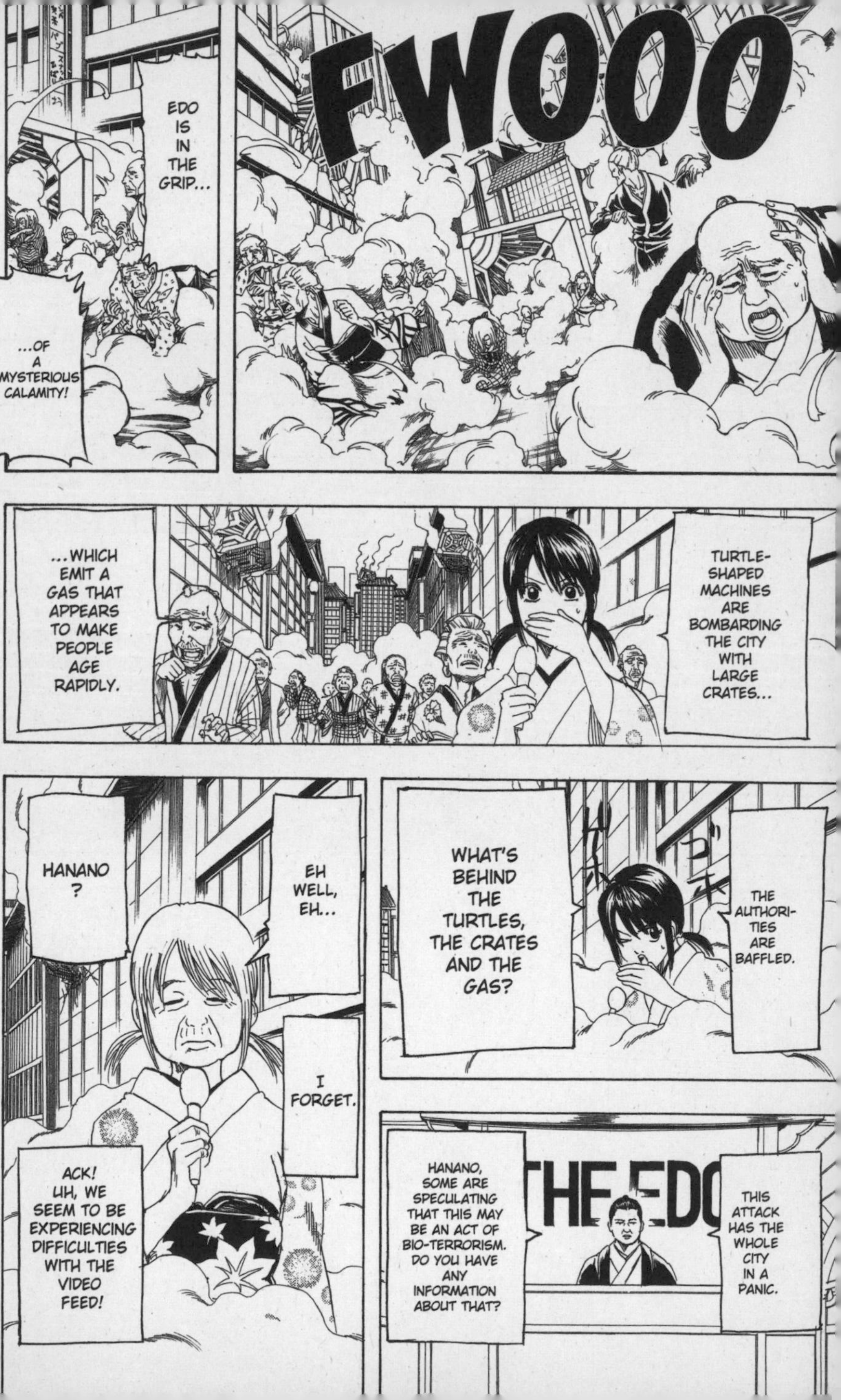
FWOOO
EDO IS IN THE GRIP...
...OF A MYSTERIOUS CALAMITY!
TURTLE-SHAPED MACHINES ARE BOMBARDING THE CITY WITH LARGE CRATES...
...WHICH EMIT A GAS THAT APPEARS TO MAKE PEOPLE AGE RAPIDLY.
THE AUTHORITIES ARE BAFFLED.
WHAT'S BEHIND THE TURTLES, THE CRATES AND THE GAS?
THIS ATTACK HAS THE WHOLE CITY IN A PANIC.
THE EDO
HANANO, SOME ARE SPECULATING THAT THIS MAY BE AN ACT OF BIO-TERRORISM. DO YOU HAVE ANY INFORMATION ABOUT THAT?
HANANO?
EH WELL, EH...
I FORGET.
ACK! UH, WE SEEM TO BE EXPERIENCING DIFFICULTIES WITH THE VIDEO FEED!

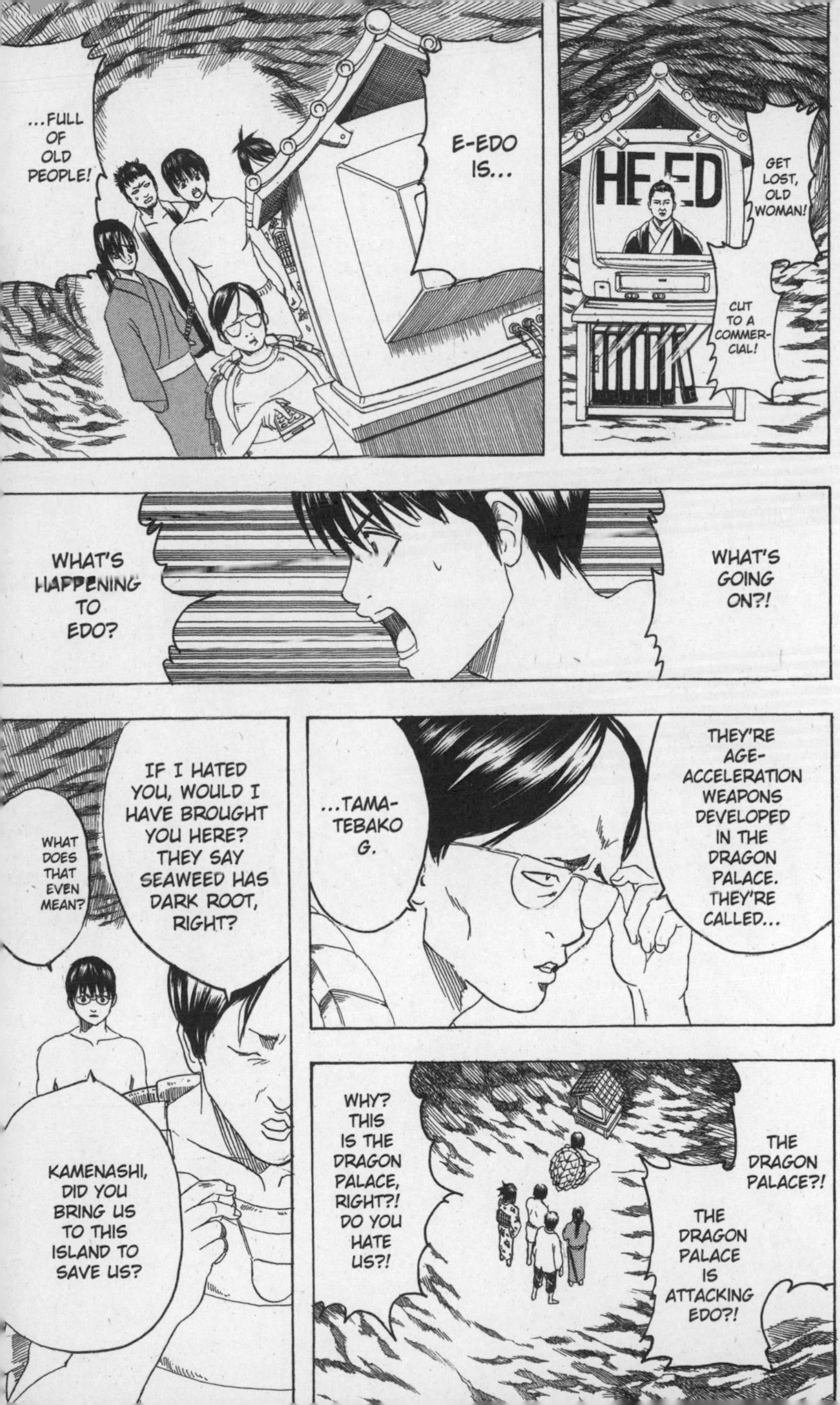

HE ED
GET LOST, OLD WOMAN!
CUT TO A COMMERCIAL!
E-EDO IS...
...FULL OF OLD PEOPLE!
WHAT'S GOING ON?!
WHAT'S HAPPENING TO EDO?
THEY'RE AGE-ACCELERATION WEAPONS DEVELOPED IN THE DRAGON PALACE. THEY'RE CALLED...
...TAMATEBAKO G.
THE DRAGON PALACE?!
THE DRAGON PALACE IS ATTACKING EDO?!
WHY? THIS IS THE DRAGON PALACE, RIGHT?! DO YOU HATE US?!
IF I HATED YOU, WOULD I HAVE BROUGHT YOU HERE? THEY SAY SEAWEED HAS DARK ROOT, RIGHT?
WHAT DOES THAT EVEN MEAN?
KAMENASHI, DID YOU BRING US TO THIS ISLAND TO SAVE US?

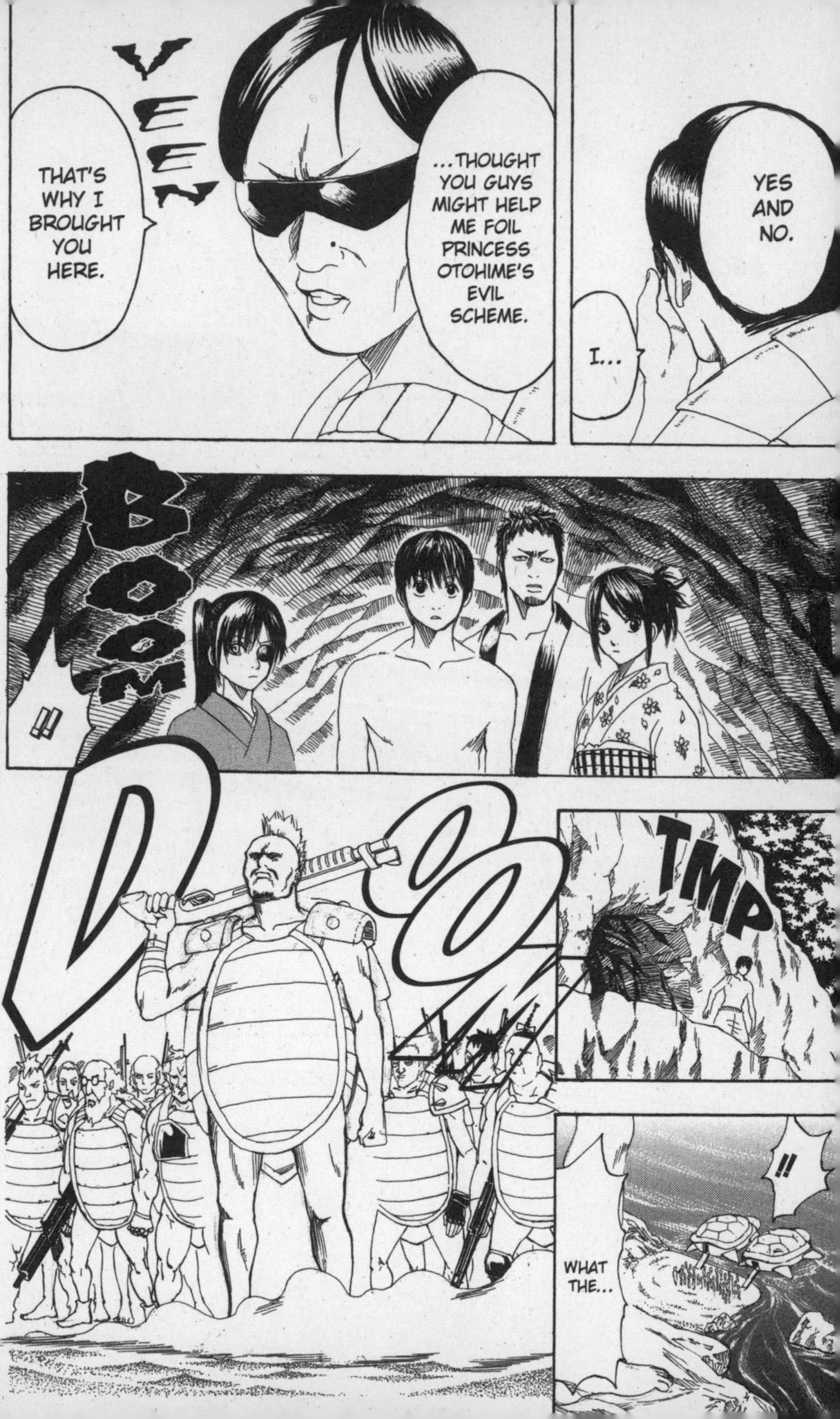
YES AND NO.
I...
...THOUGHT YOU GUYS MIGHT HELP ME FOIL PRINCESS OTOHIME'S EVIL SCHEME.
VEEN
THAT'S WHY I BROUGHT YOU HERE.
BOOM
!!
TMP
!!
WHAT THE...
DOOM

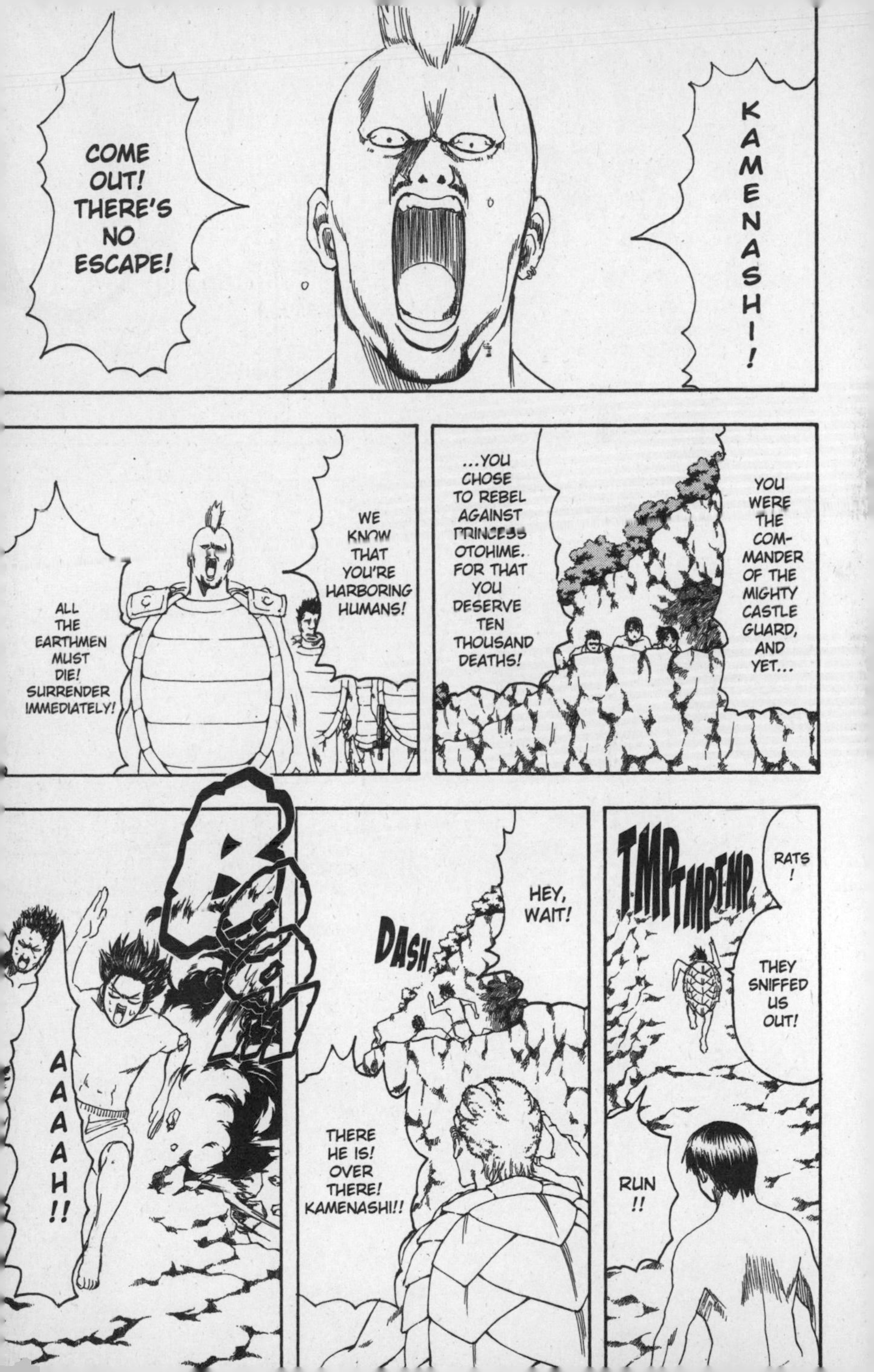
KAMENASHI!!
COME OUT! THERE'S NO ESCAPE!
YOU WERE THE COM-MANDER OF THE MIGHTY CASTLE GUARD, AND YET...
...YOU CHOSE TO REBEL AGAINST PRINCESS OTOHIME. FOR THAT YOU DESERVE TEN THOUSAND DEATHS!
WE KNOW THAT YOU'RE HARBORING HUMANS!
ALL THE EARTHMEN MUST DIE! SURRENDER IMMEDIATELY!
RATS!
THEY SNIFFED US OUT!
TMP TMP TMP
RUN!!
HEY, WAIT!
DASH
THERE HE IS! OVER THERE! KAMENASHI!!
AAAAH!!

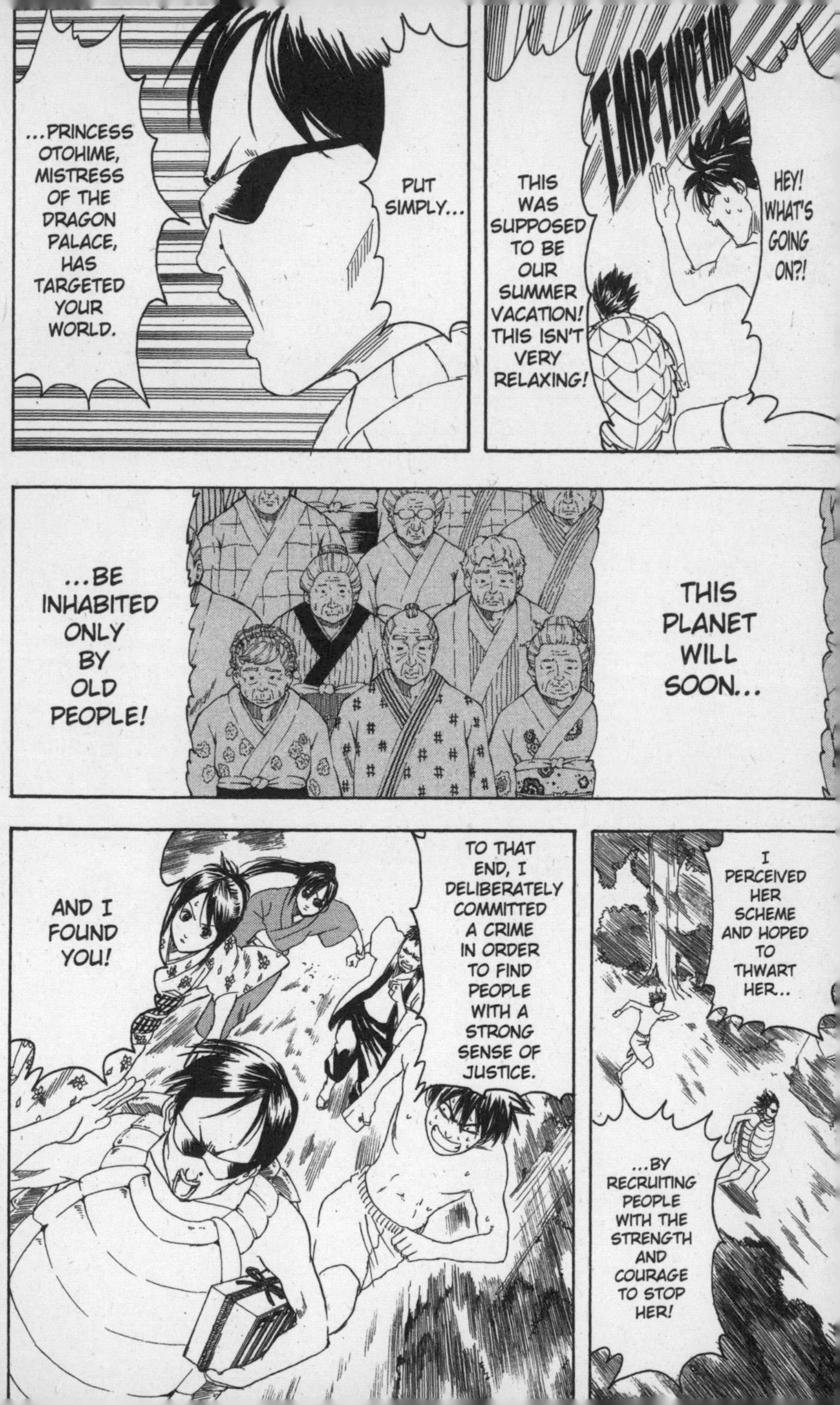
THMPTHMPTHM
HEY! WHAT'S GOING ON?!
THIS WAS SUPPOSED TO BE OUR SUMMER VACATION! THIS ISN'T VERY RELAXING!
PUT SIMPLY...
...PRINCESS OTOHIME, MISTRESS OF THE DRAGON PALACE, HAS TARGETED YOUR WORLD.
THIS PLANET WILL SOON...
...BE INHABITED ONLY BY OLD PEOPLE!
I PERCEIVED HER SCHEME AND HOPED TO THWART HER...
...BY RECRUITING PEOPLE WITH THE STRENGTH AND COURAGE TO STOP HER!
TO THAT END, I DELIBERATELY COMMITTED A CRIME IN ORDER TO FIND PEOPLE WITH A STRONG SENSE OF JUSTICE.
AND I FOUND YOU!

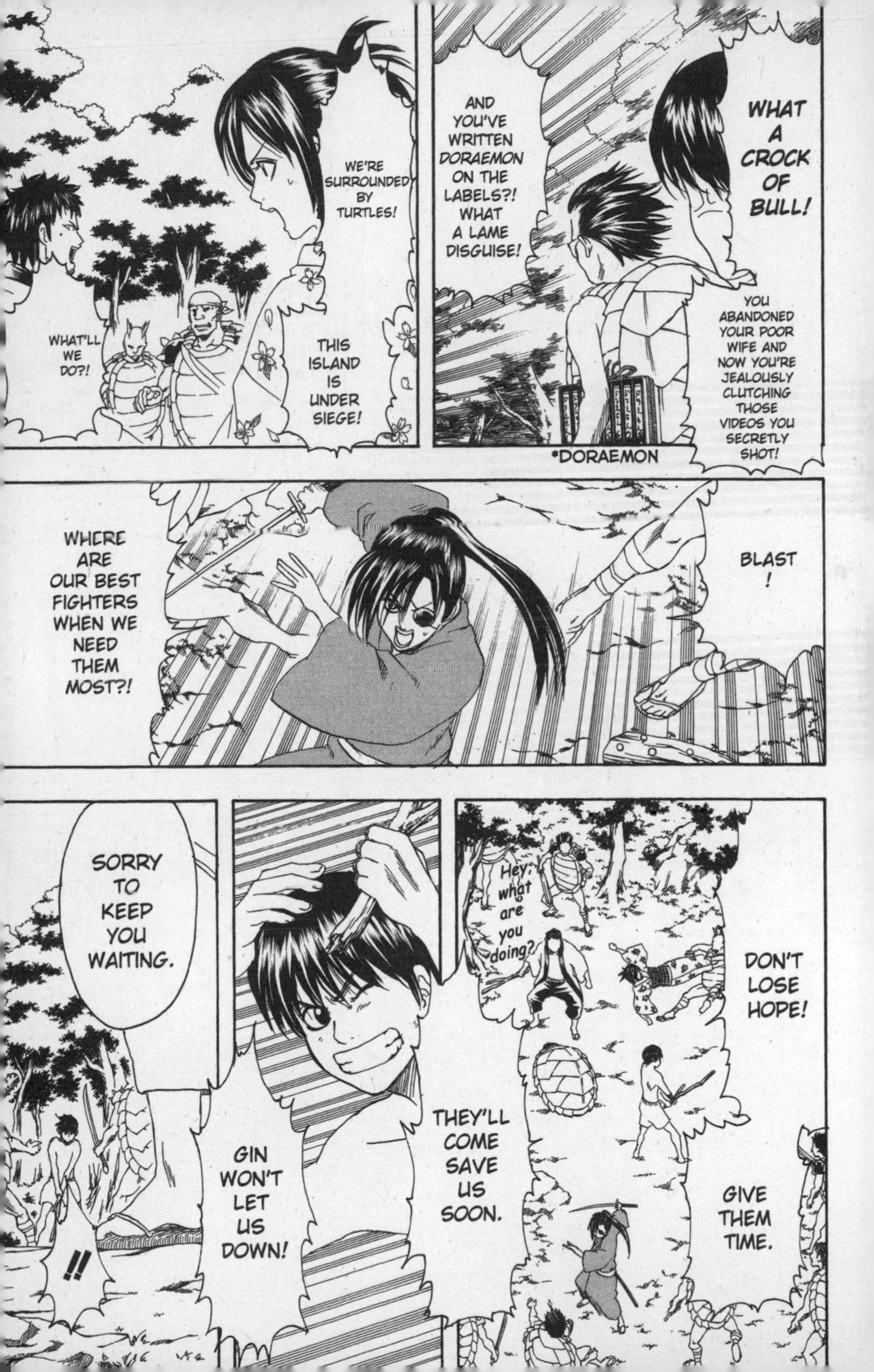
WHAT A CROCK OF BULL!
YOU ABANDONED YOUR POOR WIFE AND NOW YOU'RE JEALOUSLY CLUTCHING THOSE VIDEOS YOU SECRETLY SHOT!
AND YOU'VE WRITTEN DORAEMON ON THE LABELS?! WHAT A LAME DISGUISE!
*DORAEMON
WE'RE SURROUNDED BY TURTLES!
THIS ISLAND IS UNDER SIEGE!
WHAT'LL WE DO?!
BLAST!
WHERE ARE OUR BEST FIGHTERS WHEN WE NEED THEM MOST?!
DON'T LOSE HOPE!
Hey, what are you doing?
GIVE THEM TIME.
THEY'LL COME SAVE US SOON.
GIN WON'T LET US DOWN!
SORRY TO KEEP YOU WAITING.
!!

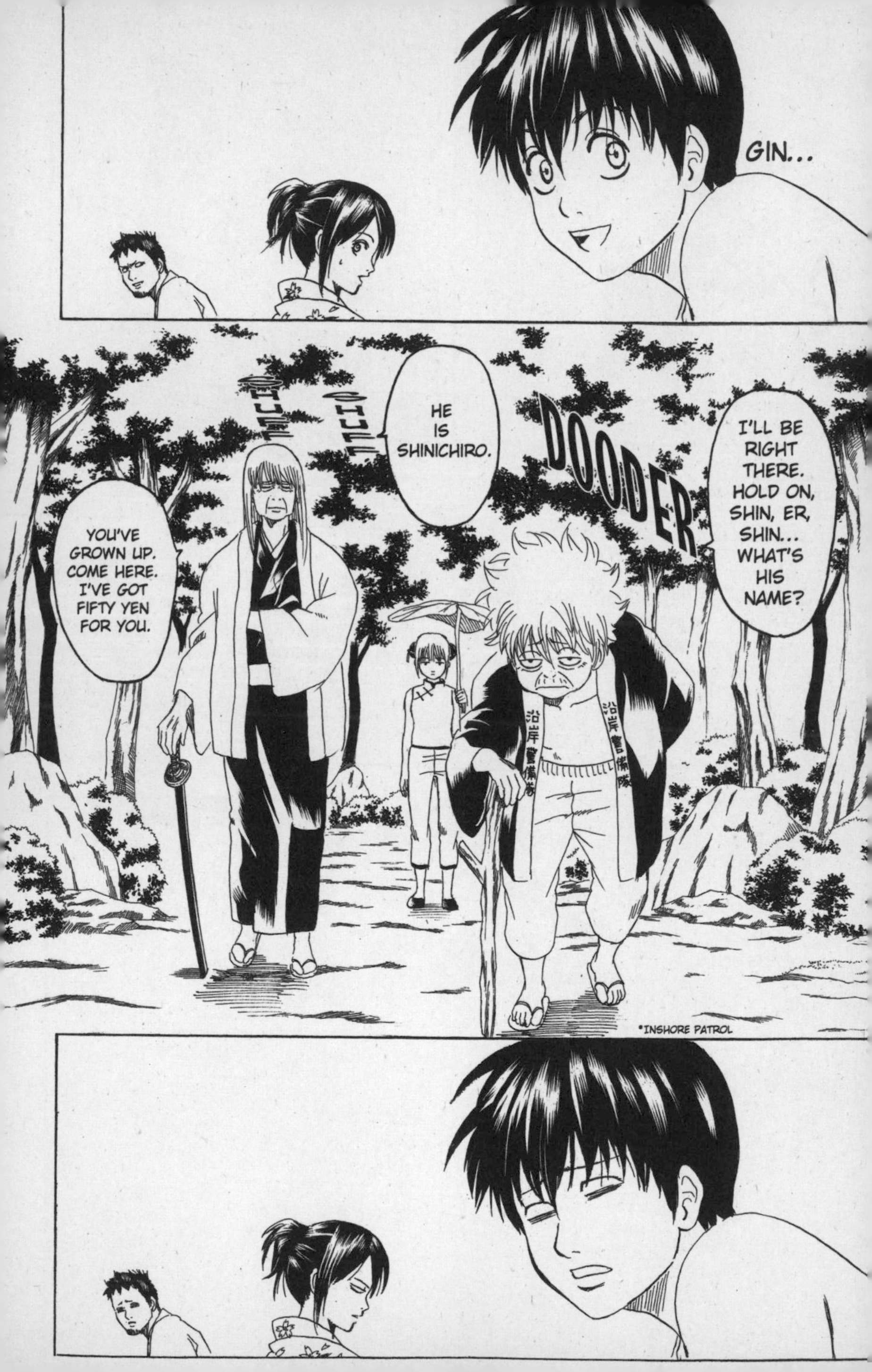
GIN...
I'LL BE RIGHT THERE. HOLD ON, SHIN, ER, SHIN... WHAT'S HIS NAME?
DOODER
HE IS SHINICHIRO.
SHUFF
SHUFF
YOU'VE GROWN UP. COME HERE. I'VE GOT FIFTY YEN FOR YOU.
*INSHORE PATROL

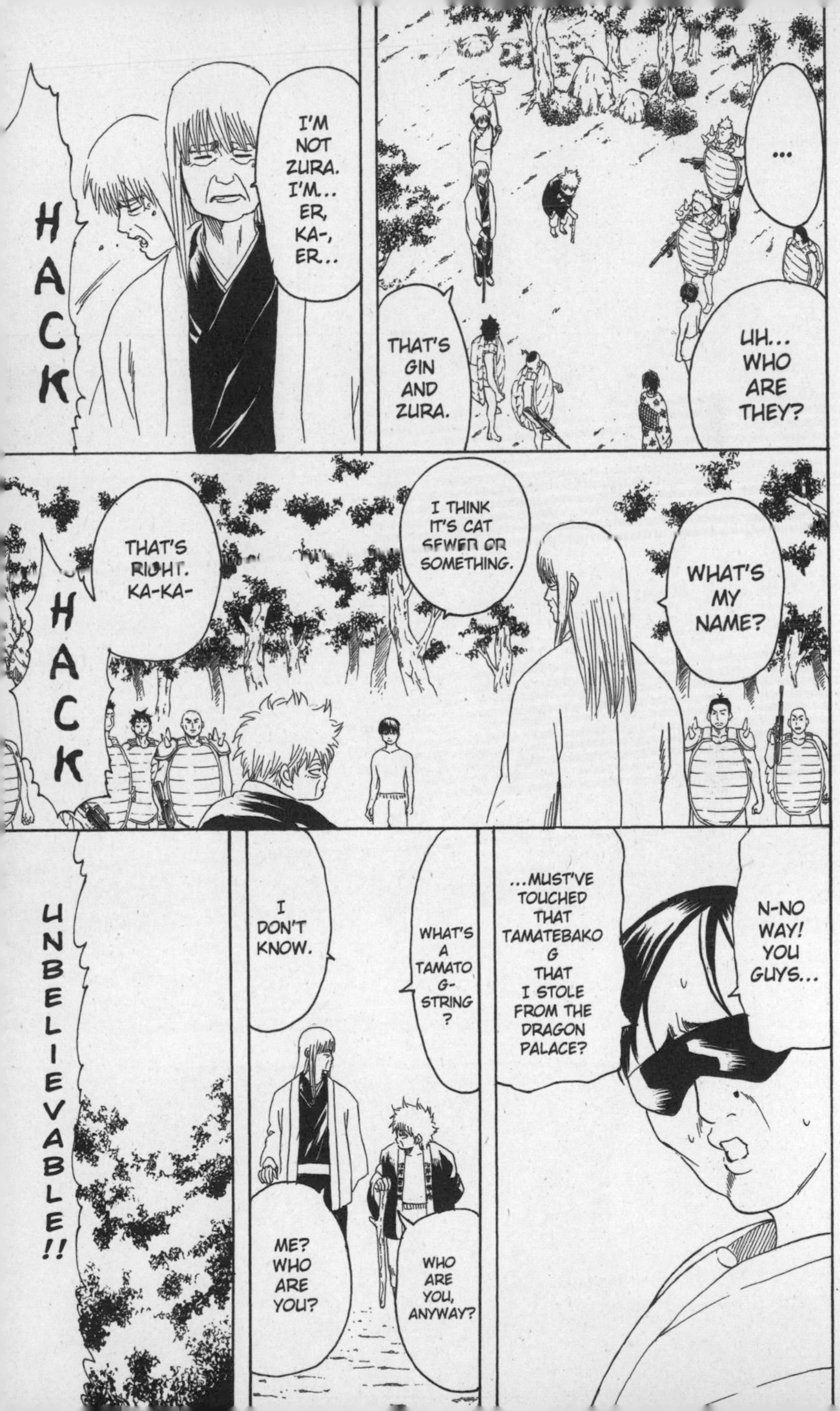
...
UH... WHO ARE THEY?
THAT'S GIN AND ZURA.
I'M NOT ZURA. I'M... ER, KA-, ER...
HACK
WHAT'S MY NAME?
I THINK IT'S CAT SEWER OR SOMETHING.
THAT'S RIGHT. KA-KA-
HACK
N-NO WAY! YOU GUYS...
...MUST'VE TOUCHED THAT TAMATEBAKO G THAT I STOLE FROM THE DRAGON PALACE?
WHAT'S A TAMATO G-STRING?
I DON'T KNOW.
WHO ARE YOU, ANYWAY?
ME? WHO ARE YOU?
UNBELIEVABLE!!

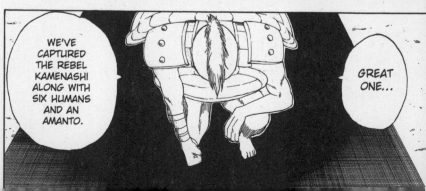

WE'VE CAPTURED THE REBEL KAMENASHI ALONG WITH SIX HUMANS AND AN AMANTO.

GREAT ONE...

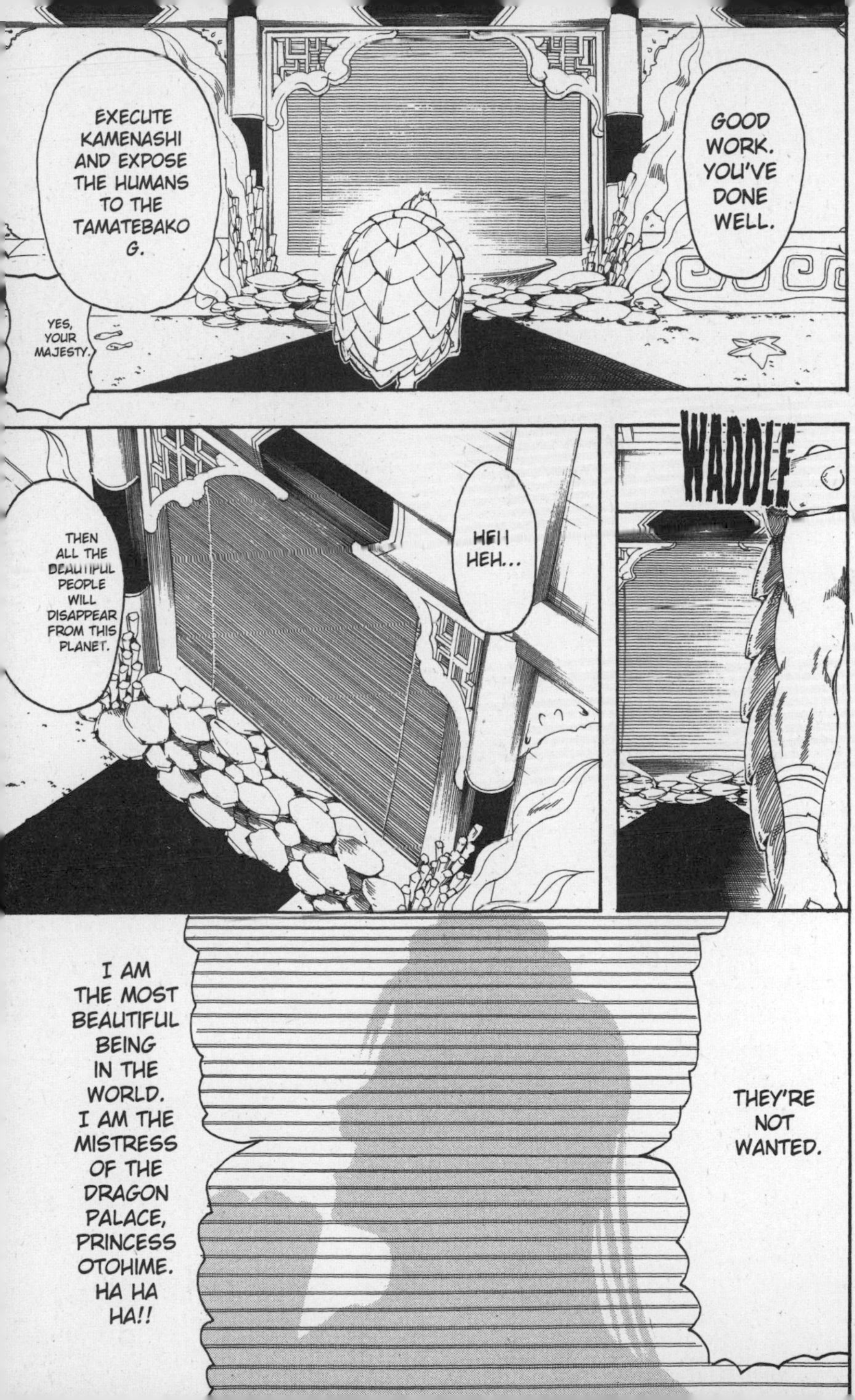
GOOD WORK. YOU'VE DONE WELL.
EXECUTE KAMENASHI AND EXPOSE THE HUMANS TO THE TAMATEBAKO G.
YES, YOUR MAJESTY.
WADDLE
HEH HEH...
THEN ALL THE BEAUTIFUL PEOPLE WILL DISAPPEAR FROM THIS PLANET.
THEY'RE NOT WANTED.
I AM THE MOST BEAUTIFUL BEING IN THE WORLD. I AM THE MISTRESS OF THE DRAGON PALACE, PRINCESS OTOHIME. HA HA HA!!

Thank you for buying *Gin Tama* volume 21. Well, there's been a change in the editorial department. The editor of *Gin Tama*, Mr. Oonishi, who I've mentioned and mocked so many times, is leaving. Even though letters have been pouring in that say, "Die, Oonishi," this brave man has worked hard as my editor for six years, and I want all my readers to see him off with a big round of applause. I've cursed him a lot, but we worked together for six years and I'll miss him a little. When I was in school, I always had a hard time getting used to new classmates when I started a new grade. I used to put my head down on my desk for a week and pretend I was sleeping so that people would think, "It's not that he doesn't have any friends. He's just sleepy." So I am scared to death about the future now. When I see my new editor, I may have to put my head on my desk and say to myself, "Hey, somebody talk to me." It makes me feel like skipping school. I don't know what I'll do if the new editor is an introvert and puts his head on his desk too. If we both have our heads on our desks, the meeting won't go very well. While I was worrying about this, I had the opportunity to discuss the future with Mr. Oonishi and my new editor, Mr. Saito, the other day...

(Continued on page 46)

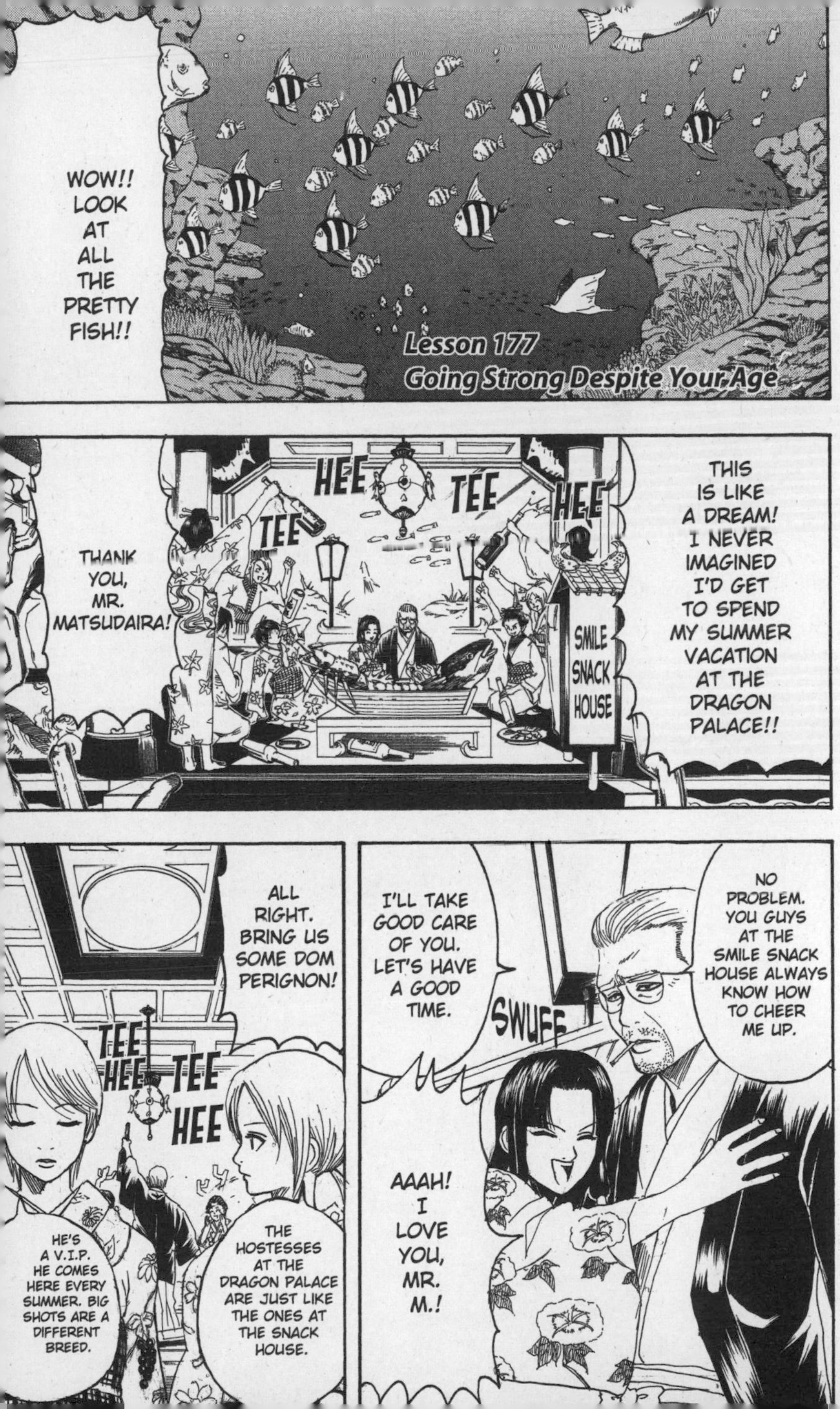
Lesson 177
Going Strong Despite Your Age
WOW!! LOOK AT ALL THE PRETTY FISH!!
THIS IS LIKE A DREAM! I NEVER IMAGINED I'D GET TO SPEND MY SUMMER VACATION AT THE DRAGON PALACE!!
SMILE SNACK HOUSE
HEE TEE HEE
TEE
THANK YOU, MR. MATSUDAIRA!
NO PROBLEM. YOU GUYS AT THE SMILE SNACK HOUSE ALWAYS KNOW HOW TO CHEER ME UP.
I'LL TAKE GOOD CARE OF YOU. LET'S HAVE A GOOD TIME.
SWUFF
AAAH! I LOVE YOU, MR. M.!
ALL RIGHT. BRING US SOME DOM PERIGNON!
TEE HEE TEE HEE
THE HOSTESSES AT THE DRAGON PALACE ARE JUST LIKE THE ONES AT THE SNACK HOUSE.
HE'S A V.I.P. HE COMES HERE EVERY SUMMER. BIG SHOTS ARE A DIFFERENT BREED.

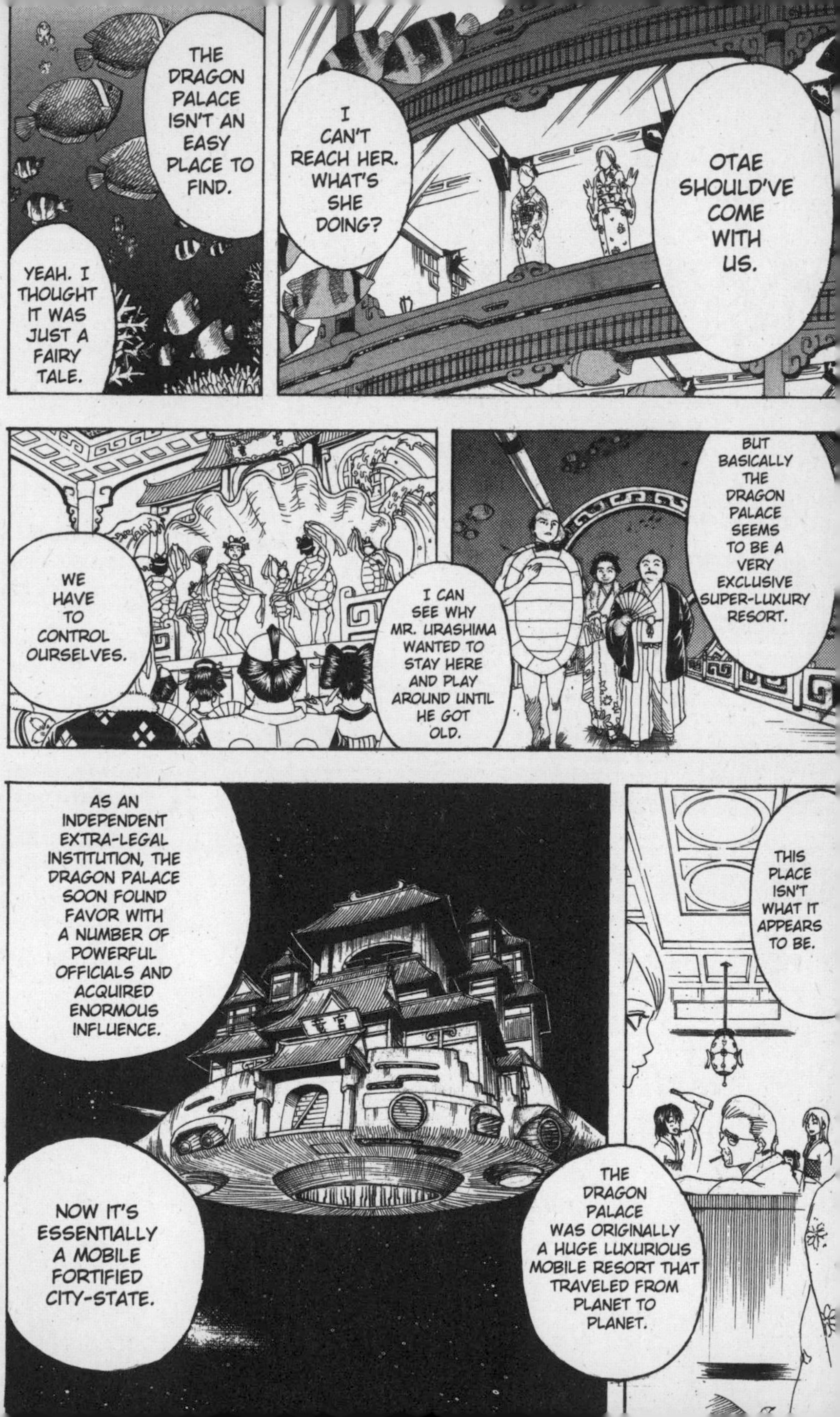
OTAE SHOULD'VE COME WITH US.
I CAN'T REACH HER. WHAT'S SHE DOING?
THE DRAGON PALACE ISN'T AN EASY PLACE TO FIND.
YEAH. I THOUGHT IT WAS JUST A FAIRY TALE.
BUT BASICALLY THE DRAGON PALACE SEEMS TO BE A VERY EXCLUSIVE SUPER-LUXURY RESORT.
I CAN SEE WHY MR. URASHIMA WANTED TO STAY HERE AND PLAY AROUND UNTIL HE GOT OLD.
WE HAVE TO CONTROL OURSELVES.
THIS PLACE ISN'T WHAT IT APPEARS TO BE.
THE DRAGON PALACE WAS ORIGINALLY A HUGE LUXURIOUS MOBILE RESORT THAT TRAVELED FROM PLANET TO PLANET.
AS AN INDEPENDENT EXTRA-LEGAL INSTITUTION, THE DRAGON PALACE SOON FOUND FAVOR WITH A NUMBER OF POWERFUL OFFICIALS AND ACQUIRED ENORMOUS INFLUENCE.
NOW IT'S ESSENTIALLY A MOBILE FORTIFIED CITY-STATE.

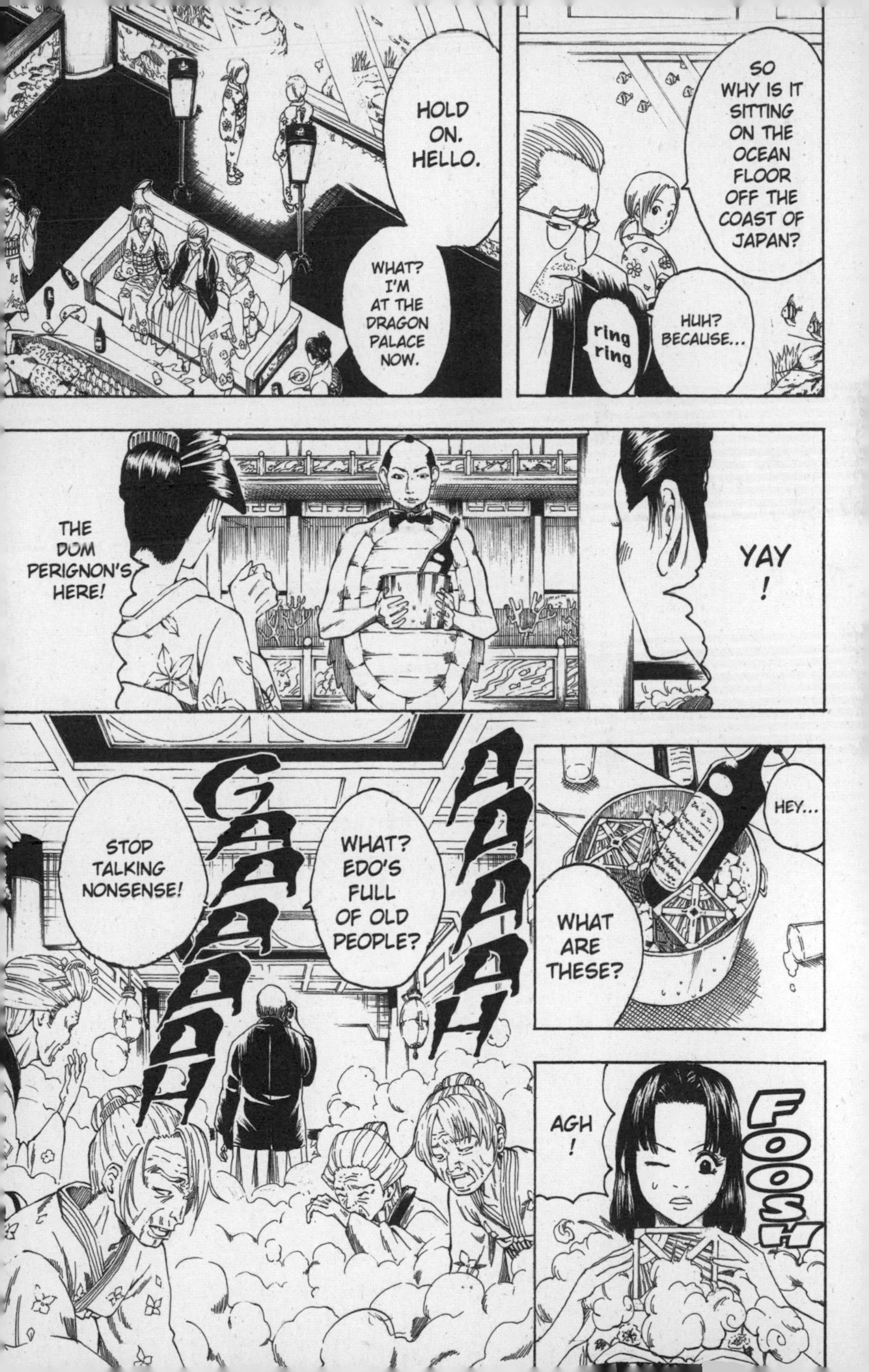
SO WHY IS IT SITTING ON THE OCEAN FLOOR OFF THE COAST OF JAPAN?
HUH? BECAUSE...
ring ring
HOLD ON. HELLO.
WHAT? I'M AT THE DRAGON PALACE NOW.
YAY!
THE DOM PERIGNON'S HERE!
HEY...
WHAT ARE THESE?
AGH!
FOOSH
WHAT? EDO'S FULL OF OLD PEOPLE?
STOP TALKING NONSENSE!

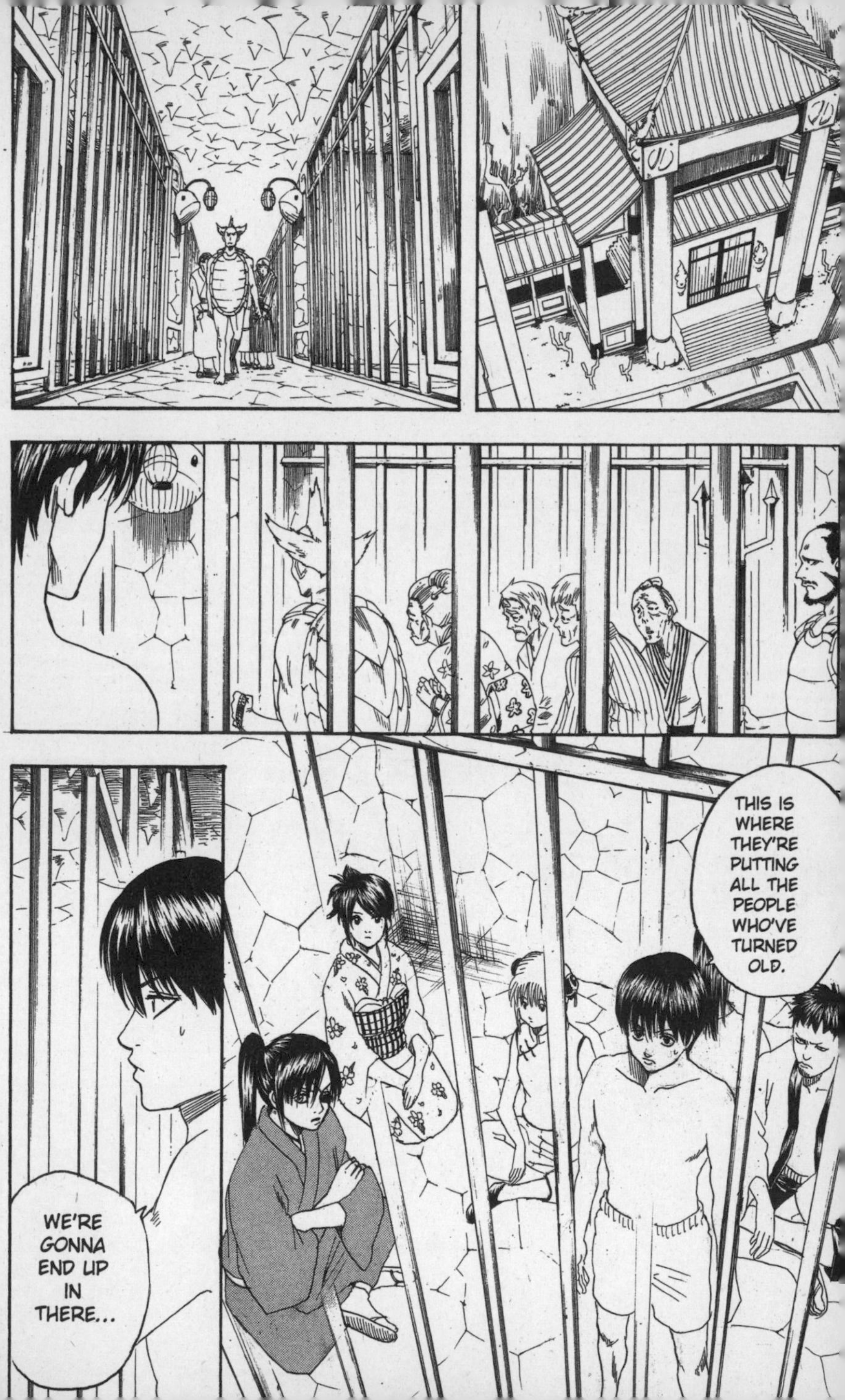
THIS IS WHERE THEY'RE PUTTING ALL THE PEOPLE WHO'VE TURNED OLD.
WE'RE GONNA END UP IN THERE...

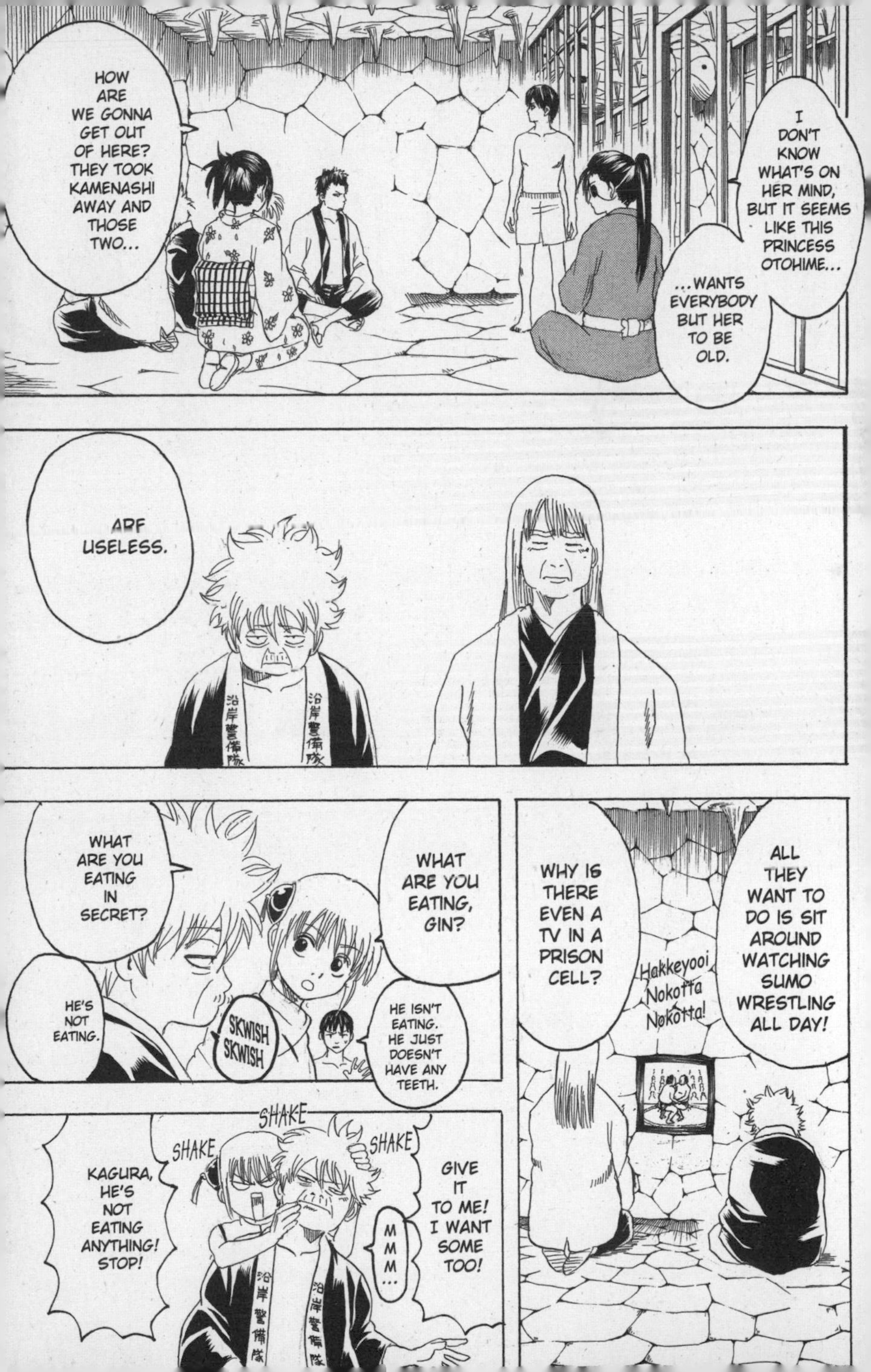

I DON'T KNOW WHAT'S ON HER MIND, BUT IT SEEMS LIKE THIS PRINCESS OTOHIME...
...WANTS EVERYBODY BUT HER TO BE OLD.
HOW ARE WE GONNA GET OUT OF HERE? THEY TOOK KAMENASHI AWAY AND THOSE TWO...
ARF USELESS.
沿岸警備隊
沿岸警備隊
ALL THEY WANT TO DO IS SIT AROUND WATCHING SUMO WRESTLING ALL DAY!
Hakkeyooi Nokotta Nokotta!
WHY IS THERE EVEN A TV IN A PRISON CELL?
WHAT ARE YOU EATING, GIN?
WHAT ARE YOU EATING IN SECRET?
HE ISN'T EATING. HE JUST DOESN'T HAVE ANY TEETH.
SKWISH SKWISH
HE'S NOT EATING.
SHAKE
GIVE IT TO ME! I WANT SOME TOO!
MMM...
SHAKE
SHAKE
KAGURA, HE'S NOT EATING ANYTHING! STOP!
沿岸警備隊
沿岸警備隊

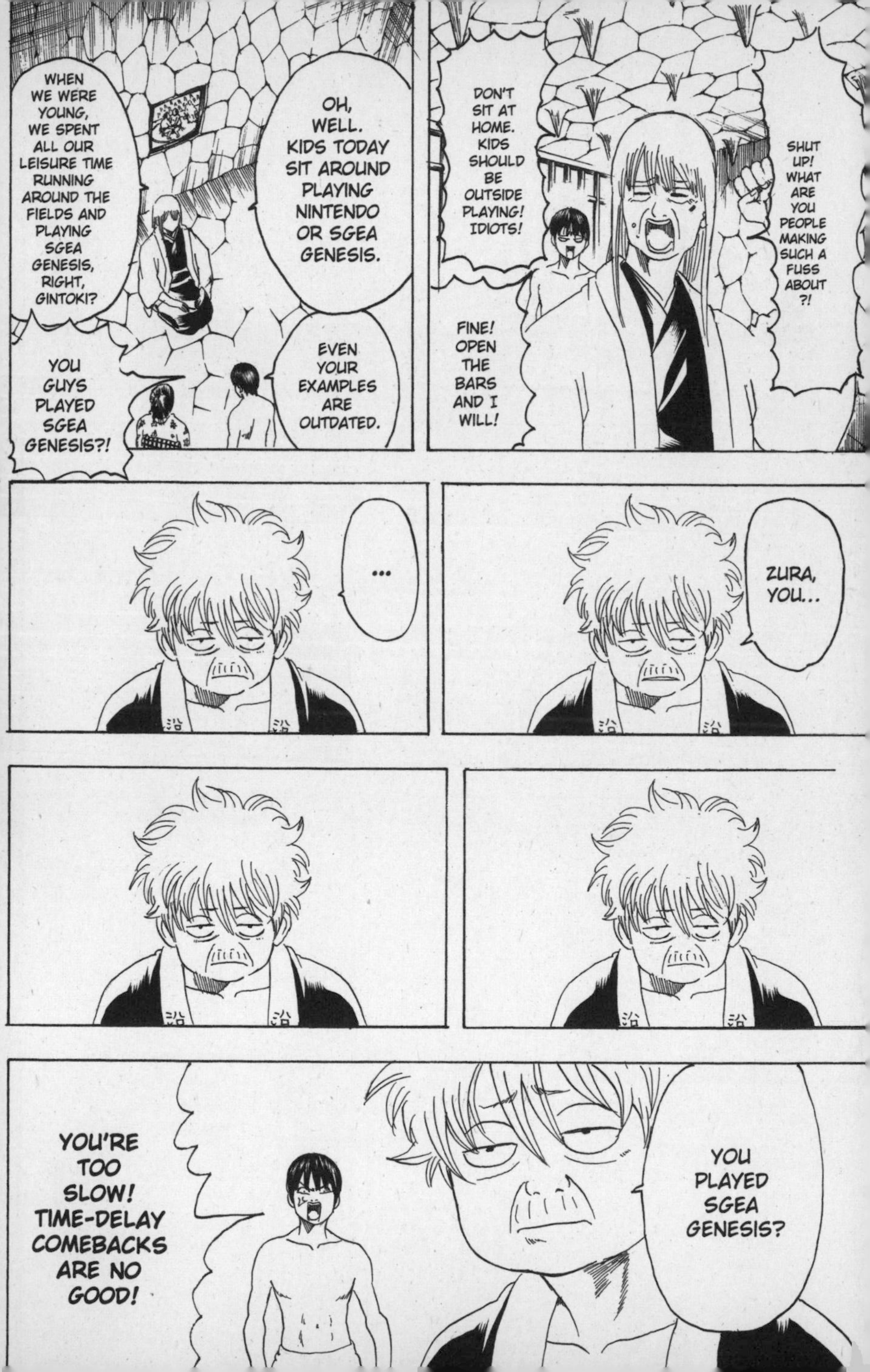
DON'T SIT AT HOME. KIDS SHOULD BE OUTSIDE PLAYING! IDIOTS!
SHUT UP! WHAT ARE YOU PEOPLE MAKING SUCH A FUSS ABOUT?!
FINE! OPEN THE BARS AND I WILL!
OH, WELL. KIDS TODAY SIT AROUND PLAYING NINTENDO OR SGEA GENESIS.
WHEN WE WERE YOUNG, WE SPENT ALL OUR LEISURE TIME RUNNING AROUND THE FIELDS AND PLAYING SGEA GENESIS, RIGHT, GINTOKI?
EVEN YOUR EXAMPLES ARE OUTDATED.
YOU GUYS PLAYED SGEA GENESIS?!
ZURA, YOU...
...
YOU PLAYED SGEA GENESIS?
YOU'RE TOO SLOW! TIME-DELAY COMEBACKS ARE NO GOOD!

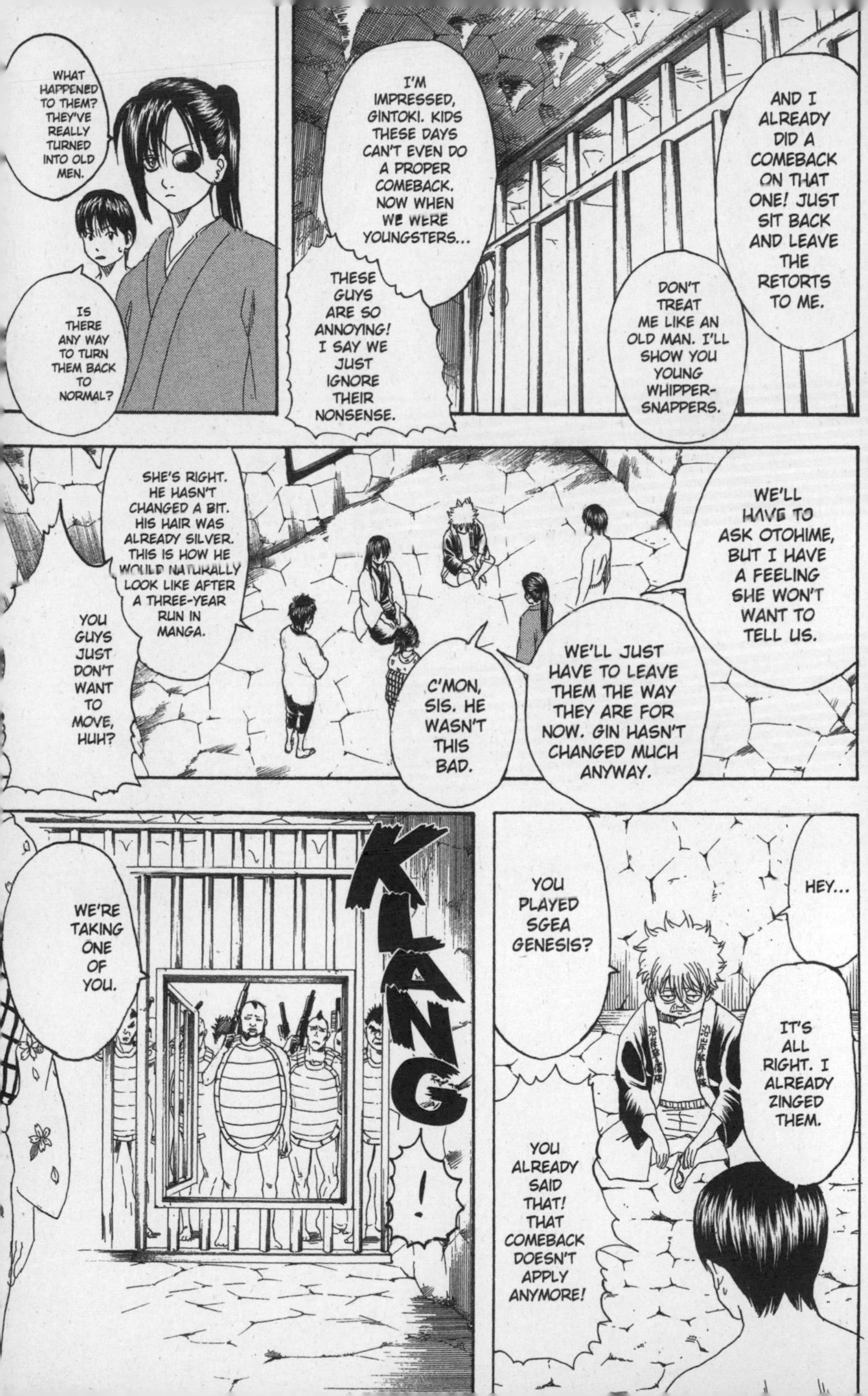
AND I ALREADY DID A COMEBACK ON THAT ONE! JUST SIT BACK AND LEAVE THE RETORTS TO ME.
I'M IMPRESSED, GINTOKI. KIDS THESE DAYS CAN'T EVEN DO A PROPER COMEBACK. NOW WHEN WE WERE YOUNGSTERS...
DON'T TREAT ME LIKE AN OLD MAN. I'LL SHOW YOU YOUNG WHIPPER-SNAPPERS.
THESE GUYS ARE SO ANNOYING! I SAY WE JUST IGNORE THEIR NONSENSE.
WHAT HAPPENED TO THEM? THEY'VE REALLY TURNED INTO OLD MEN.
IS THERE ANY WAY TO TURN THEM BACK TO NORMAL?
WE'LL HAVE TO ASK OTOHIME, BUT I HAVE A FEELING SHE WON'T WANT TO TELL US.
WE'LL JUST HAVE TO LEAVE THEM THE WAY THEY ARE FOR NOW. GIN HASN'T CHANGED MUCH ANYWAY.
SHE'S RIGHT. HE HASN'T CHANGED A BIT. HIS HAIR WAS ALREADY SILVER. THIS IS HOW HE WOULD NATURALLY LOOK LIKE AFTER A THREE-YEAR RUN IN MANGA.
C'MON, SIS. HE WASN'T THIS BAD.
YOU GUYS JUST DON'T WANT TO MOVE, HUH?
HEY...
YOU PLAYED SGEA GENESIS?
IT'S ALL RIGHT. I ALREADY ZINGED THEM.
YOU ALREADY SAID THAT! THAT COMEBACK DOESN'T APPLY ANYMORE!
KLANG!
WE'RE TAKING ONE OF YOU.

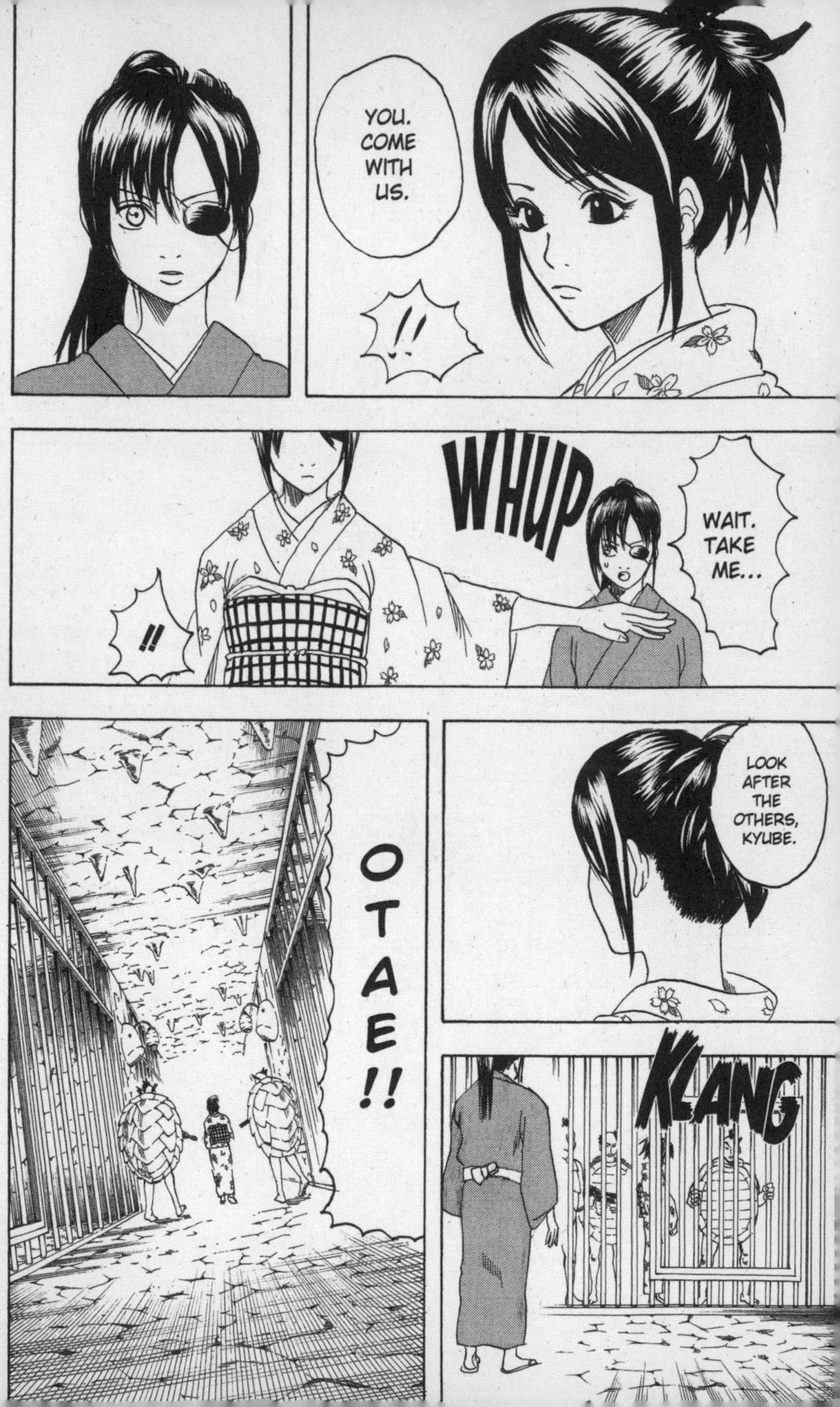
YOU. COME WITH US.
!!
WAIT. TAKE ME...
WHUP
!!
LOOK AFTER THE OTHERS, KYUBE.
KLANG
OTAE!!

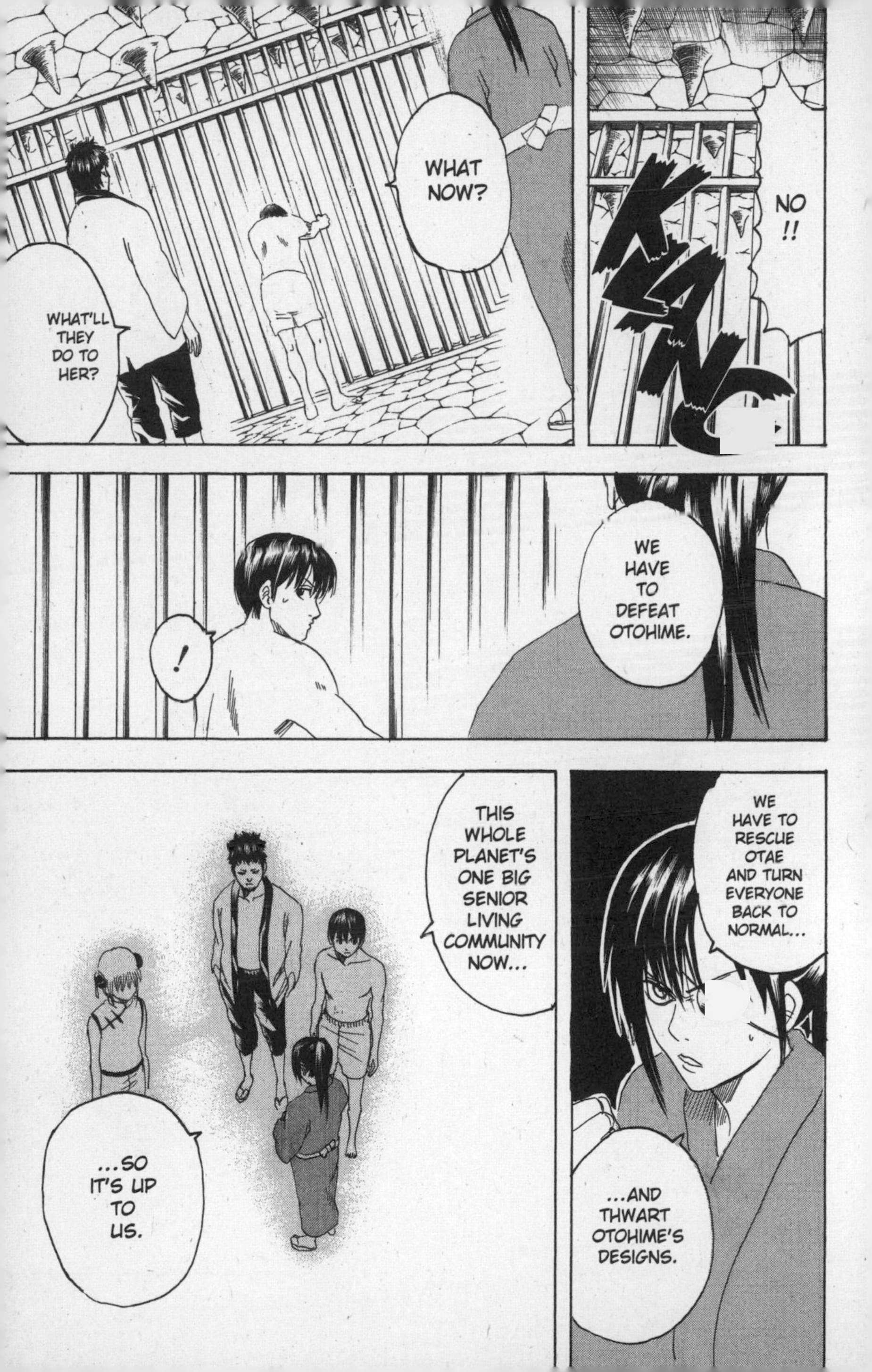
NO !!
KAN
WHAT NOW?
WHAT'LL THEY DO TO HER?
WE HAVE TO DEFEAT OTOHIME.
!
WE HAVE TO RESCUE OTAE AND TURN EVERYONE BACK TO NORMAL...
...AND THWART OTOHIME'S DESIGNS.
THIS WHOLE PLANET'S ONE BIG SENIOR LIVING COMMUNITY NOW...
...SO IT'S UP TO US.

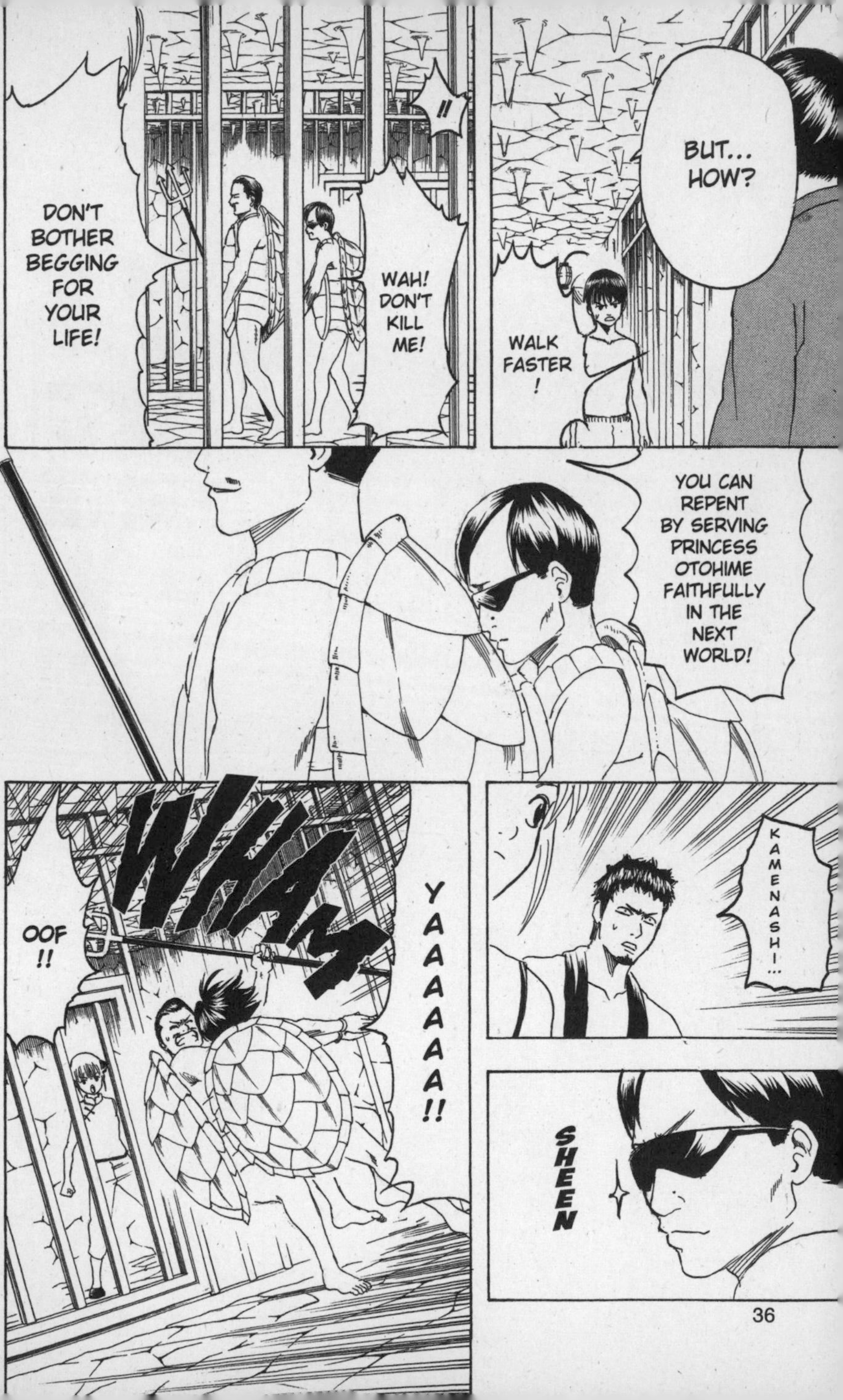
BUT... HOW?
WALK FASTER!
!!
WAH! DON'T KILL ME!
DON'T BOTHER BEGGING FOR YOUR LIFE!
YOU CAN REPENT BY SERVING PRINCESS OTOHIME FAITHFULLY IN THE NEXT WORLD!
KAMENASHI...
SHEEN
WHAM
YAAAAAAAAA!!
OOF!!

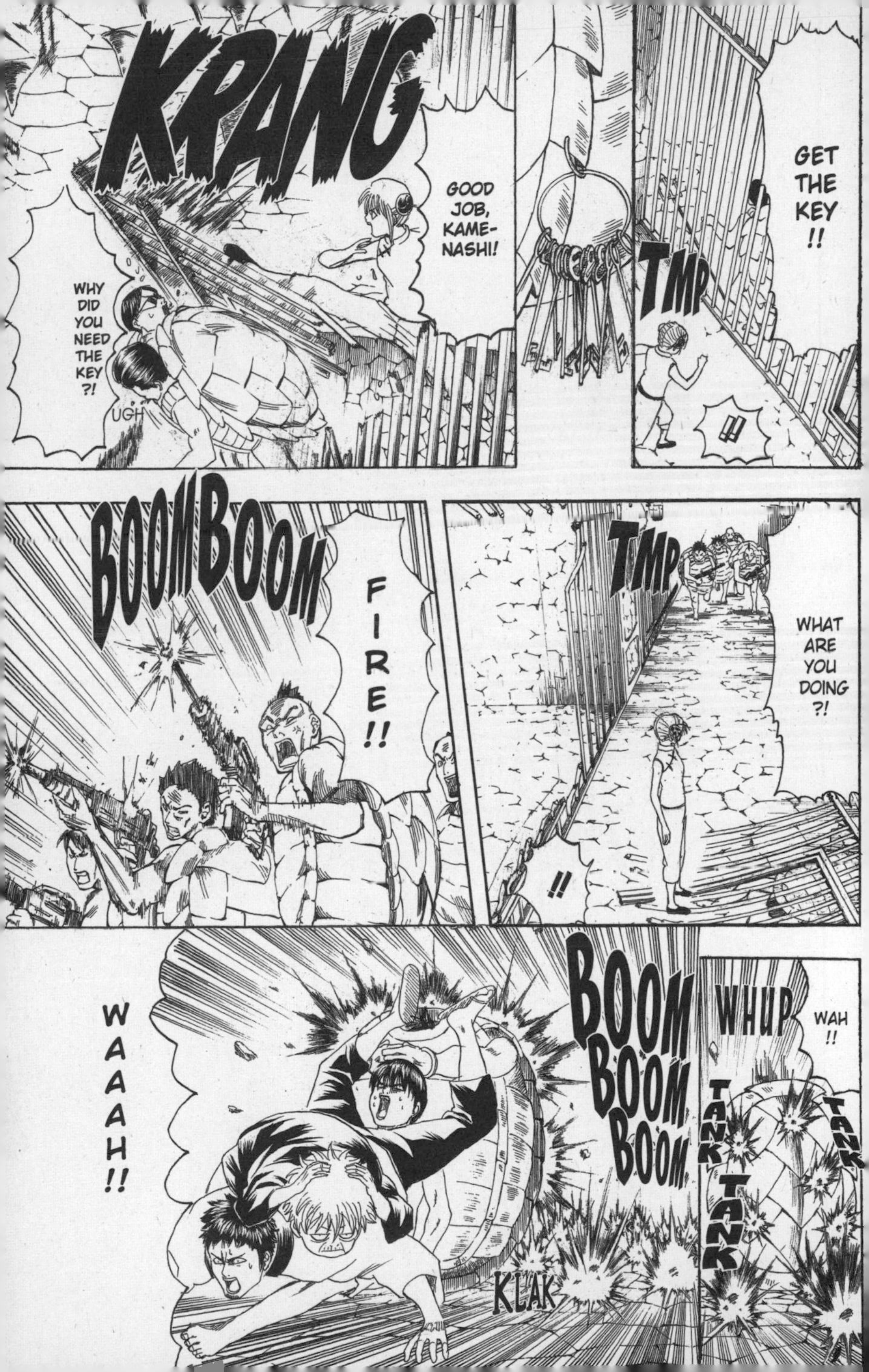
GET THE KEY !!
TMP
!!
KRANG
GOOD JOB, KAME-NASHI!
WHY DID YOU NEED THE KEY ?!
UGH
TMP
WHAT ARE YOU DOING ?!
!!
BOOMBOOM
FIRE!!
WHUP
WAH !!
TANK
TANK
TANK
BOOM BOOM BOOM
WAAAAH!!
KLAK

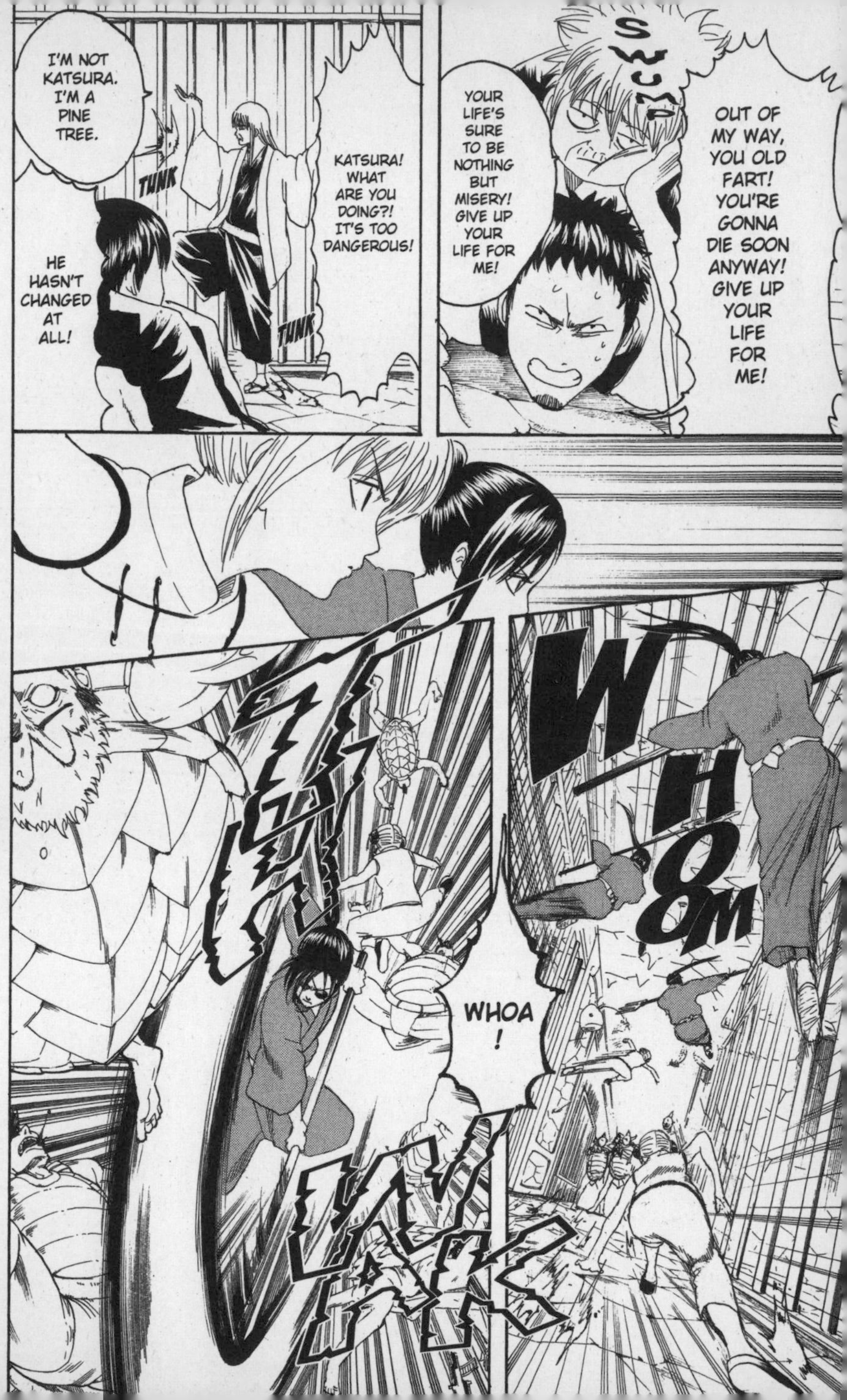
SWUMP
OUT OF MY WAY, YOU OLD FART! YOU'RE GONNA DIE SOON ANYWAY! GIVE UP YOUR LIFE FOR ME!
YOUR LIFE'S SURE TO BE NOTHING BUT MISERY! GIVE UP YOUR LIFE FOR ME!
KATSURA! WHAT ARE YOU DOING?! IT'S TOO DANGEROUS!
I'M NOT KATSURA. I'M A PINE TREE.
TUNK
TUNK
HE HASN'T CHANGED AT ALL!
WHOOM
WHOA!

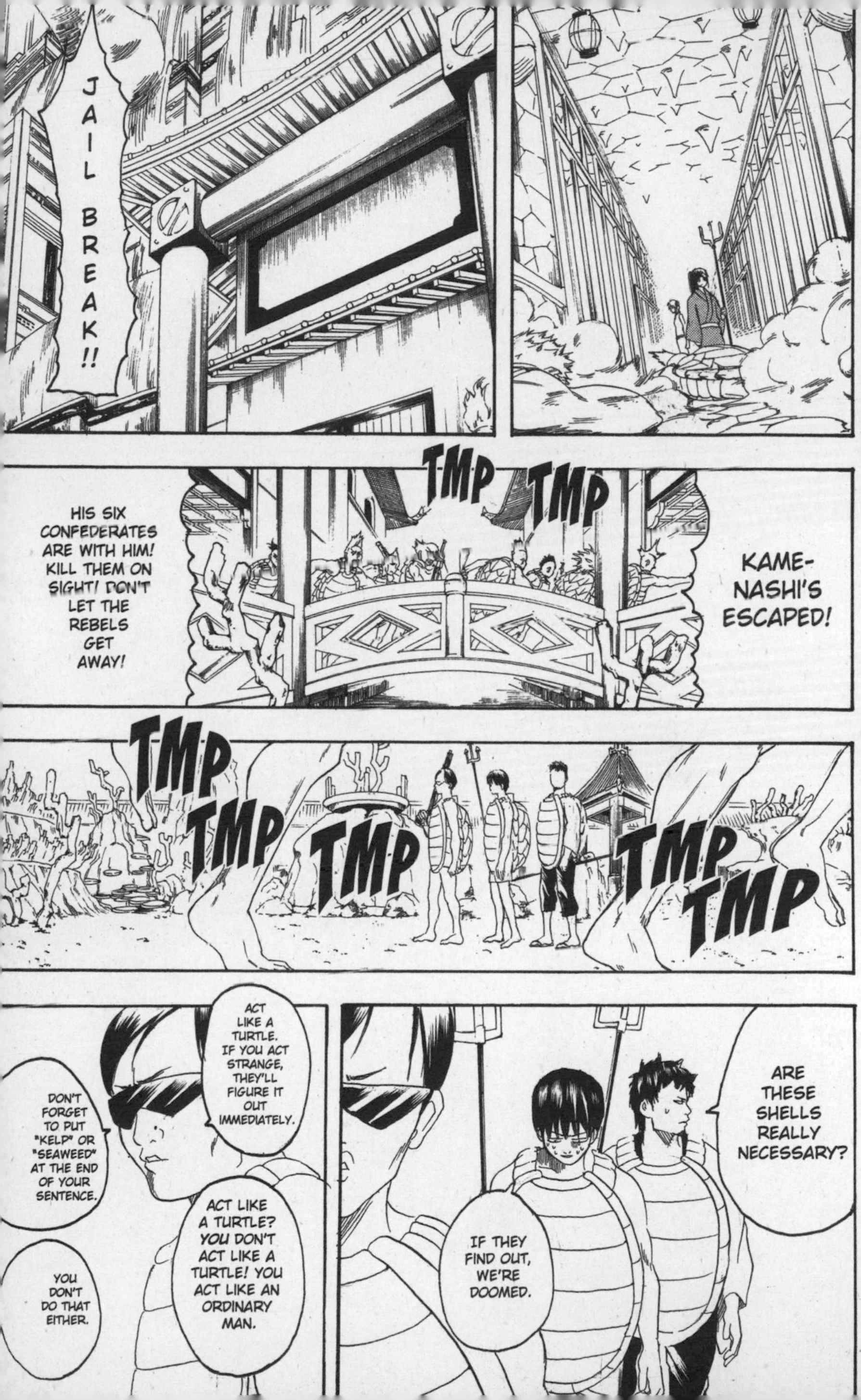
JAIL BREAK!!
TMP TMP
KAME-NASHI'S ESCAPED!
HIS SIX CONFEDERATES ARE WITH HIM! KILL THEM ON SIGHT! DON'T LET THE REBELS GET AWAY!
TMP TMP
TMP TMP
TMP TMP
ARE THESE SHELLS REALLY NECESSARY?
IF THEY FIND OUT, WE'RE DOOMED.
ACT LIKE A TURTLE. IF YOU ACT STRANGE, THEY'LL FIGURE IT OUT IMMEDIATELY.
DON'T FORGET TO PUT "KELP" OR "SEAWEED" AT THE END OF YOUR SENTENCE.
ACT LIKE A TURTLE? YOU DON'T ACT LIKE A TURTLE! YOU ACT LIKE AN ORDINARY MAN.
YOU DON'T DO THAT EITHER.

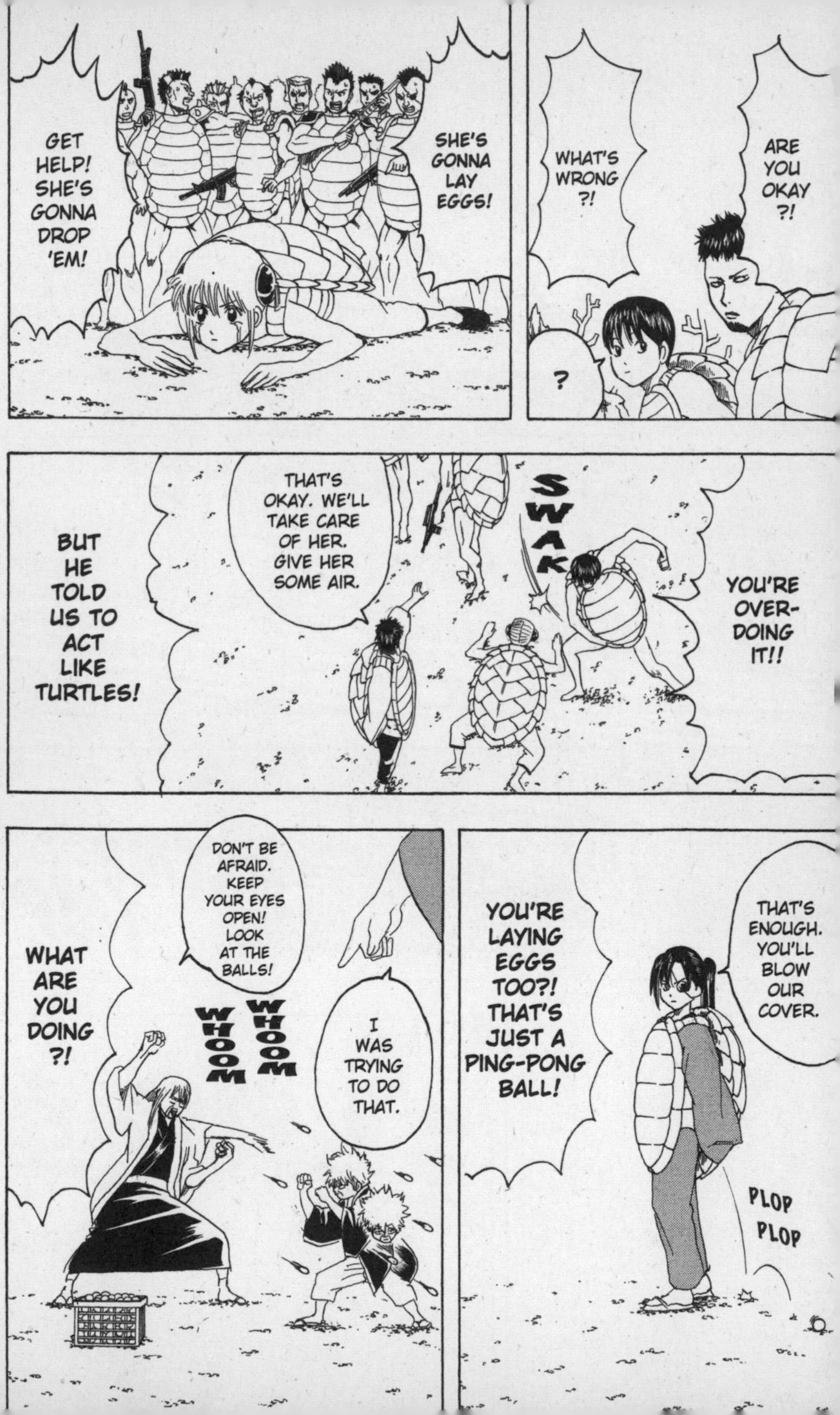
ARE YOU OKAY ?!
WHAT'S WRONG ?!
?
SHE'S GONNA LAY EGGS!
GET HELP! SHE'S GONNA DROP 'EM!
YOU'RE OVER-DOING IT!!
SWAK
THAT'S OKAY. WE'LL TAKE CARE OF HER. GIVE HER SOME AIR.
BUT HE TOLD US TO ACT LIKE TURTLES!
THAT'S ENOUGH. YOU'LL BLOW OUR COVER.
YOU'RE LAYING EGGS TOO?! THAT'S JUST A PING-PONG BALL!
PLOP
PLOP
DON'T BE AFRAID. KEEP YOUR EYES OPEN! LOOK AT THE BALLS!
WHOOM
WHOOM
I WAS TRYING TO DO THAT.
WHAT ARE YOU DOING ?!

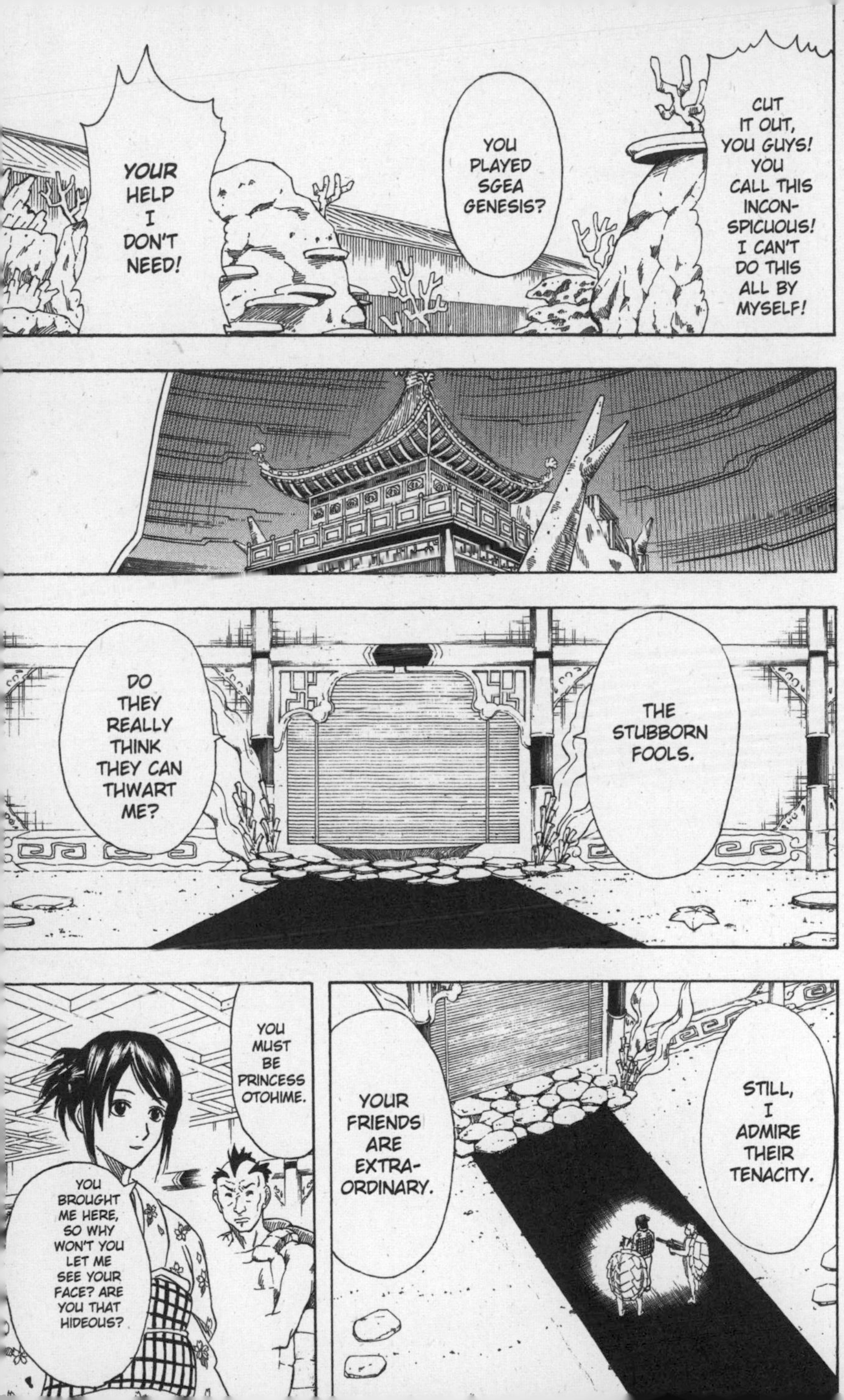
CUT IT OUT, YOU GUYS! YOU CALL THIS INCON-SPICUOUS! I CAN'T DO THIS ALL BY MYSELF!
YOU PLAYED SGEA GENESIS?
YOUR HELP I DON'T NEED!
THE STUBBORN FOOLS.
DO THEY REALLY THINK THEY CAN THWART ME?
STILL, I ADMIRE THEIR TENACITY.
YOUR FRIENDS ARE EXTRA-ORDINARY.
YOU MUST BE PRINCESS OTOHIME.
YOU BROUGHT ME HERE, SO WHY WON'T YOU LET ME SEE YOUR FACE? ARE YOU THAT HIDEOUS?

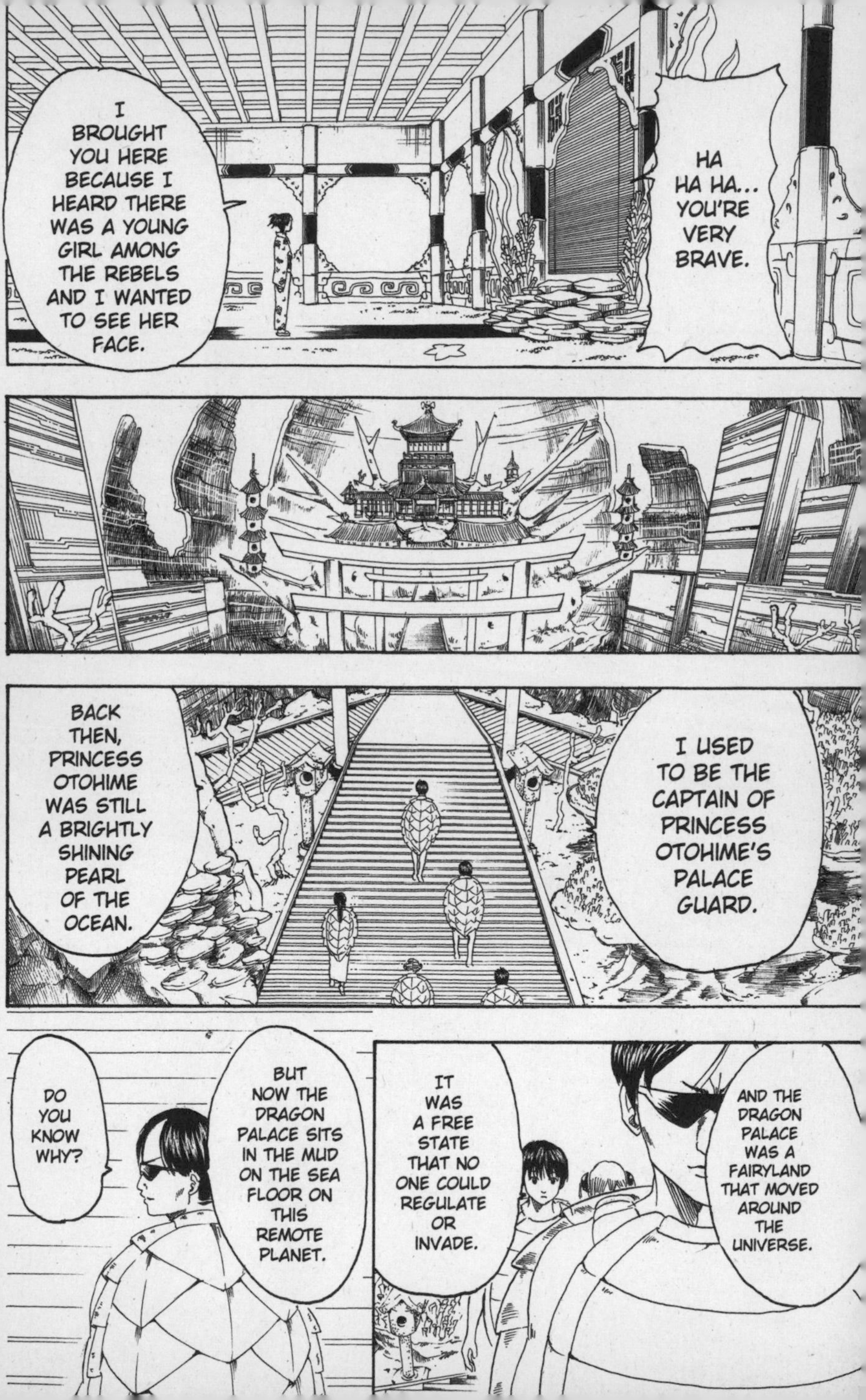
HA HA HA... YOU'RE VERY BRAVE.
I BROUGHT YOU HERE BECAUSE I HEARD THERE WAS A YOUNG GIRL AMONG THE REBELS AND I WANTED TO SEE HER FACE.
I USED TO BE THE CAPTAIN OF PRINCESS OTOHIME'S PALACE GUARD.
BACK THEN, PRINCESS OTOHIME WAS STILL A BRIGHTLY SHINING PEARL OF THE OCEAN.
AND THE DRAGON PALACE WAS A FAIRYLAND THAT MOVED AROUND THE UNIVERSE.
IT WAS A FREE STATE THAT NO ONE COULD REGULATE OR INVADE.
BUT NOW THE DRAGON PALACE SITS IN THE MUD ON THE SEA FLOOR ON THIS REMOTE PLANET.
DO YOU KNOW WHY?

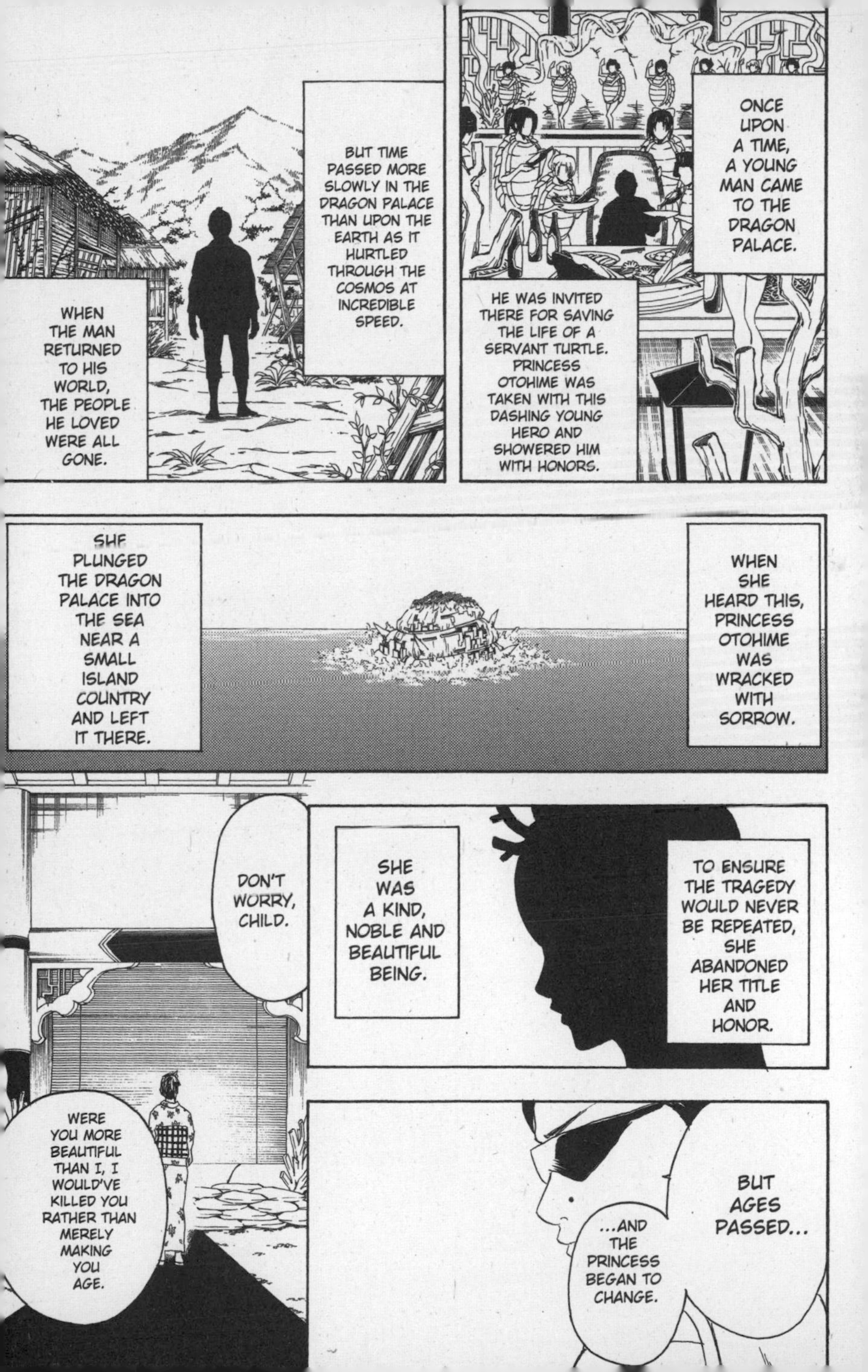
ONCE UPON A TIME, A YOUNG MAN CAME TO THE DRAGON PALACE.
HE WAS INVITED THERE FOR SAVING THE LIFE OF A SERVANT TURTLE. PRINCESS OTOHIME WAS TAKEN WITH THIS DASHING YOUNG HERO AND SHOWERED HIM WITH HONORS.
BUT TIME PASSED MORE SLOWLY IN THE DRAGON PALACE THAN UPON THE EARTH AS IT HURTLED THROUGH THE COSMOS AT INCREDIBLE SPEED.
WHEN THE MAN RETURNED TO HIS WORLD, THE PEOPLE HE LOVED WERE ALL GONE.
WHEN SHE HEARD THIS, PRINCESS OTOHIME WAS WRACKED WITH SORROW.
SHE PLUNGED THE DRAGON PALACE INTO THE SEA NEAR A SMALL ISLAND COUNTRY AND LEFT IT THERE.
TO ENSURE THE TRAGEDY WOULD NEVER BE REPEATED, SHE ABANDONED HER TITLE AND HONOR.
SHE WAS A KIND, NOBLE AND BEAUTIFUL BEING.
BUT AGES PASSED...
...AND THE PRINCESS BEGAN TO CHANGE.
DON'T WORRY, CHILD.
WERE YOU MORE BEAUTIFUL THAN I, I WOULD'VE KILLED YOU RATHER THAN MERELY MAKING YOU AGE.

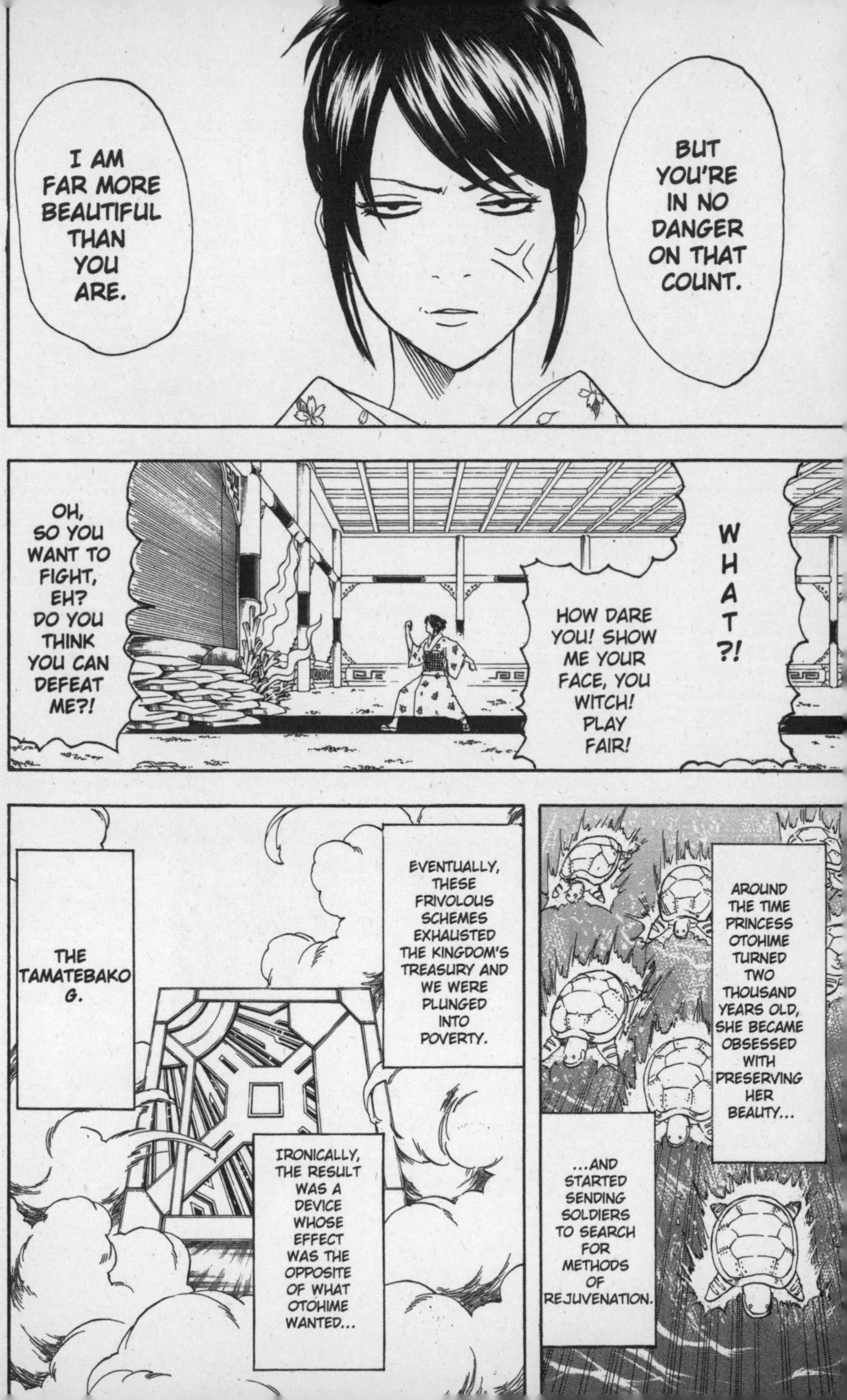
BUT YOU'RE IN NO DANGER ON THAT COUNT.
I AM FAR MORE BEAUTIFUL THAN YOU ARE.
WHAT?!
HOW DARE YOU! SHOW ME YOUR FACE, YOU WITCH! PLAY FAIR!
OH, SO YOU WANT TO FIGHT, EH? DO YOU THINK YOU CAN DEFEAT ME?!
AROUND THE TIME PRINCESS OTOHIME TURNED TWO THOUSAND YEARS OLD, SHE BECAME OBSESSED WITH PRESERVING HER BEAUTY...
...AND STARTED SENDING SOLDIERS TO SEARCH FOR METHODS OF REJUVENATION.
EVENTUALLY, THESE FRIVOLOUS SCHEMES EXHAUSTED THE KINGDOM'S TREASURY AND WE WERE PLUNGED INTO POVERTY.
IRONICALLY, THE RESULT WAS A DEVICE WHOSE EFFECT WAS THE OPPOSITE OF WHAT OTOHIME WANTED...
THE TAMATEBAKO G.

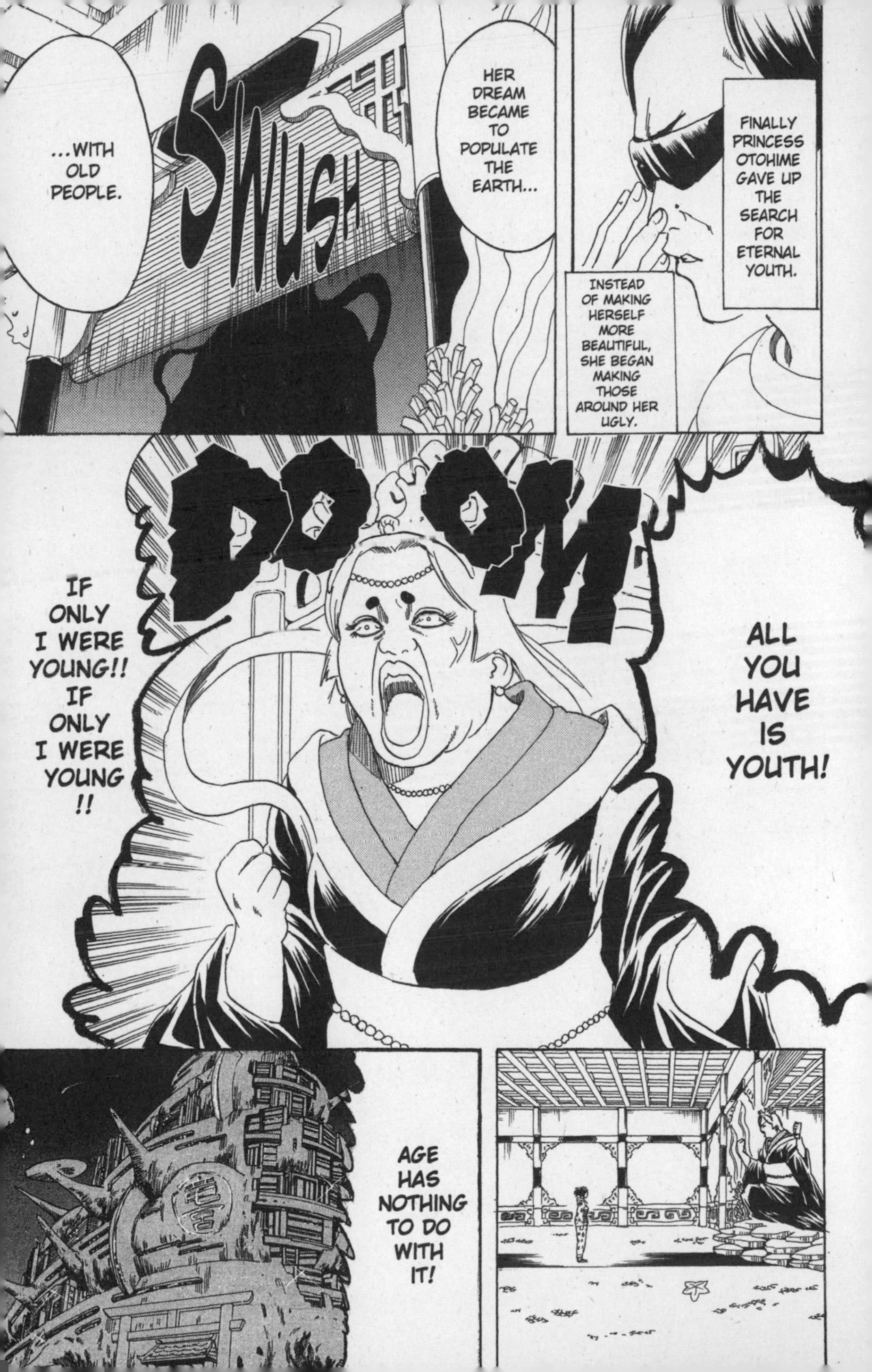
FINALLY PRINCESS OTOHIME GAVE UP THE SEARCH FOR ETERNAL YOUTH.
INSTEAD OF MAKING HERSELF MORE BEAUTIFUL, SHE BEGAN MAKING THOSE AROUND HER UGLY.
HER DREAM BECAME TO POPULATE THE EARTH...
SWUSH
...WITH OLD PEOPLE.
DOOM
ALL YOU HAVE IS YOUTH!
IF ONLY I WERE YOUNG!! IF ONLY I WERE YOUNG!!
AGE HAS NOTHING TO DO WITH IT!

My new editor, Mr. Saito, is three years younger than I am. I hear he played rugby in college and loves sports. He actually looked like a cool, short-haired athlete. He definitely didn't look like an introvert who would put his head down on his desk. "It'll be okay. If I put my head down, he'll just tackle my desk." While thoughts like that were going through my mind, he said, "I was a rugby player, but I like to read girls' manga. I came to Shueisha because I wanted to work on a women's fashion magazine." What kind of athlete is that?! According to Mr. Oonishi, Mr. Saito also likes TV shows about superheroes, anime and games. In other words, he's a girly otaku rugby player. And he's an introvert like me. In fact, whether it was because he was nervous or out of habit, he was picking his nose throughout our meeting. He was digging like a miner. That's got to be a sign of an introverted nature, right? He digs into himself.

But I thought his fondness for anime might be good because we sometimes work with the people at Sunrise Inc. who produce the *Gin Tama* anime. They like to make references to *Gundam* in casual conversation, so I thought Mr. Saito would fit right in. I forced myself to say this to him and he said, "I like anime, but I never watched *Gundam*. I'm a fan of *Hiiragi Aoi*." He is totally useless!

(Continued on page 66)

Lesson 178
When the Kids' Summer Vacation Begins, Adults Get Excited Too

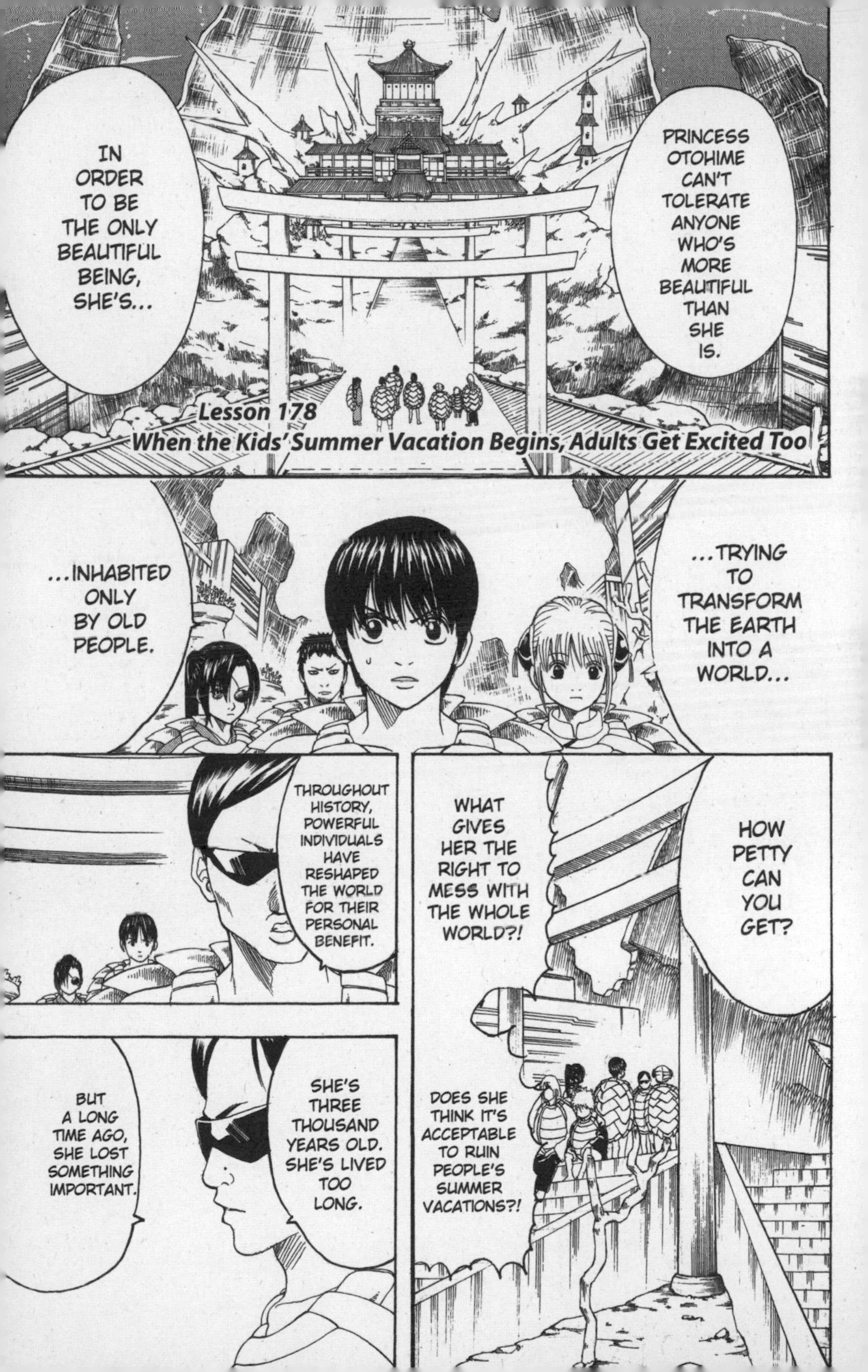
PRINCESS OTOHIME CAN'T TOLERATE ANYONE WHO'S MORE BEAUTIFUL THAN SHE IS.
IN ORDER TO BE THE ONLY BEAUTIFUL BEING, SHE'S...
...TRYING TO TRANSFORM THE EARTH INTO A WORLD...
...INHABITED ONLY BY OLD PEOPLE.
HOW PETTY CAN YOU GET?
WHAT GIVES HER THE RIGHT TO MESS WITH THE WHOLE WORLD?!
THROUGHOUT HISTORY, POWERFUL INDIVIDUALS HAVE RESHAPED THE WORLD FOR THEIR PERSONAL BENEFIT.
DOES SHE THINK IT'S ACCEPTABLE TO RUIN PEOPLE'S SUMMER VACATIONS?!
SHE'S THREE THOUSAND YEARS OLD. SHE'S LIVED TOO LONG.
BUT A LONG TIME AGO, SHE LOST SOMETHING IMPORTANT.

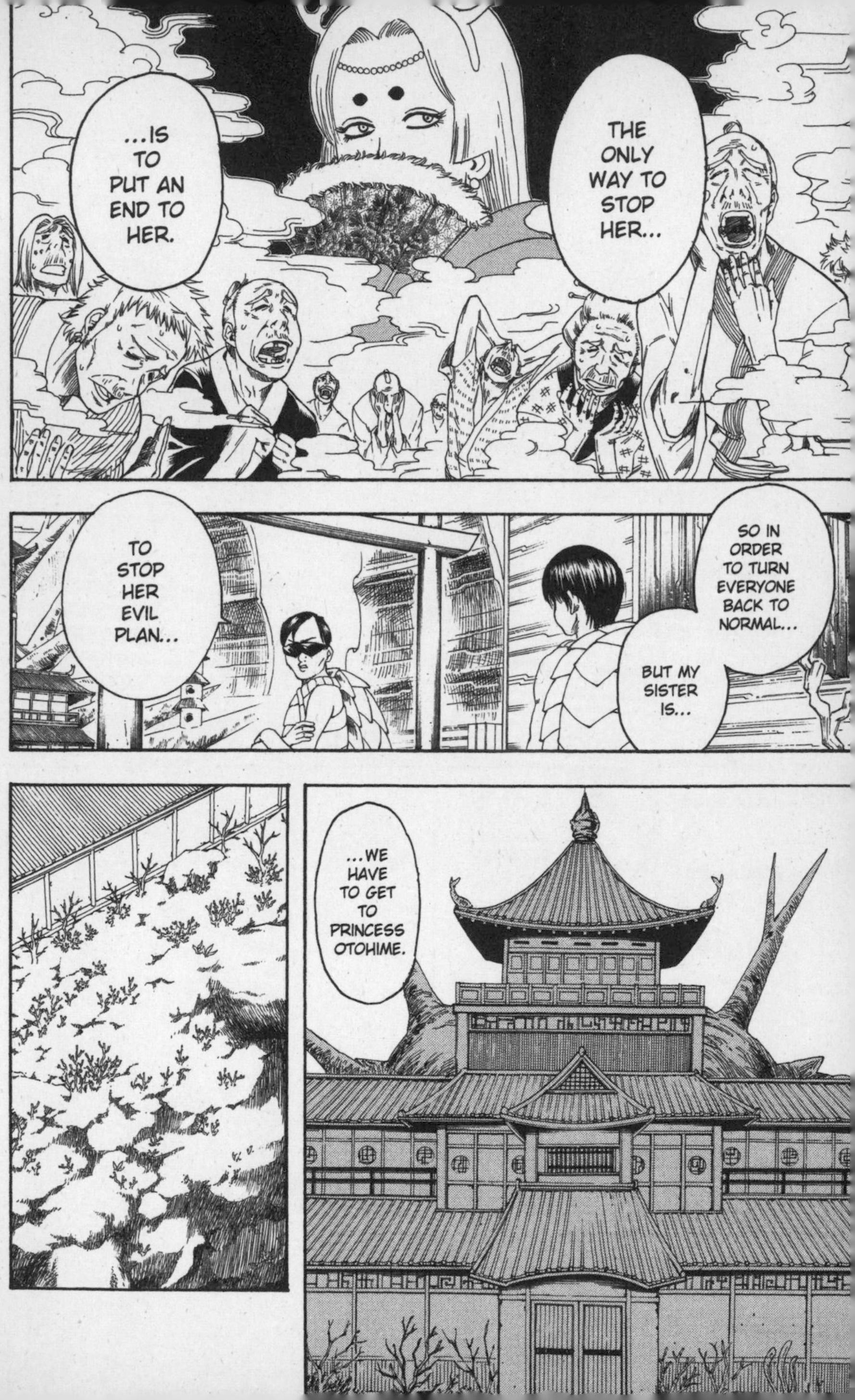
THE ONLY WAY TO STOP HER...
...IS TO PUT AN END TO HER.
SO IN ORDER TO TURN EVERYONE BACK TO NORMAL...
BUT MY SISTER IS...
TO STOP HER EVIL PLAN...
...WE HAVE TO GET TO PRINCESS OTOHIME.

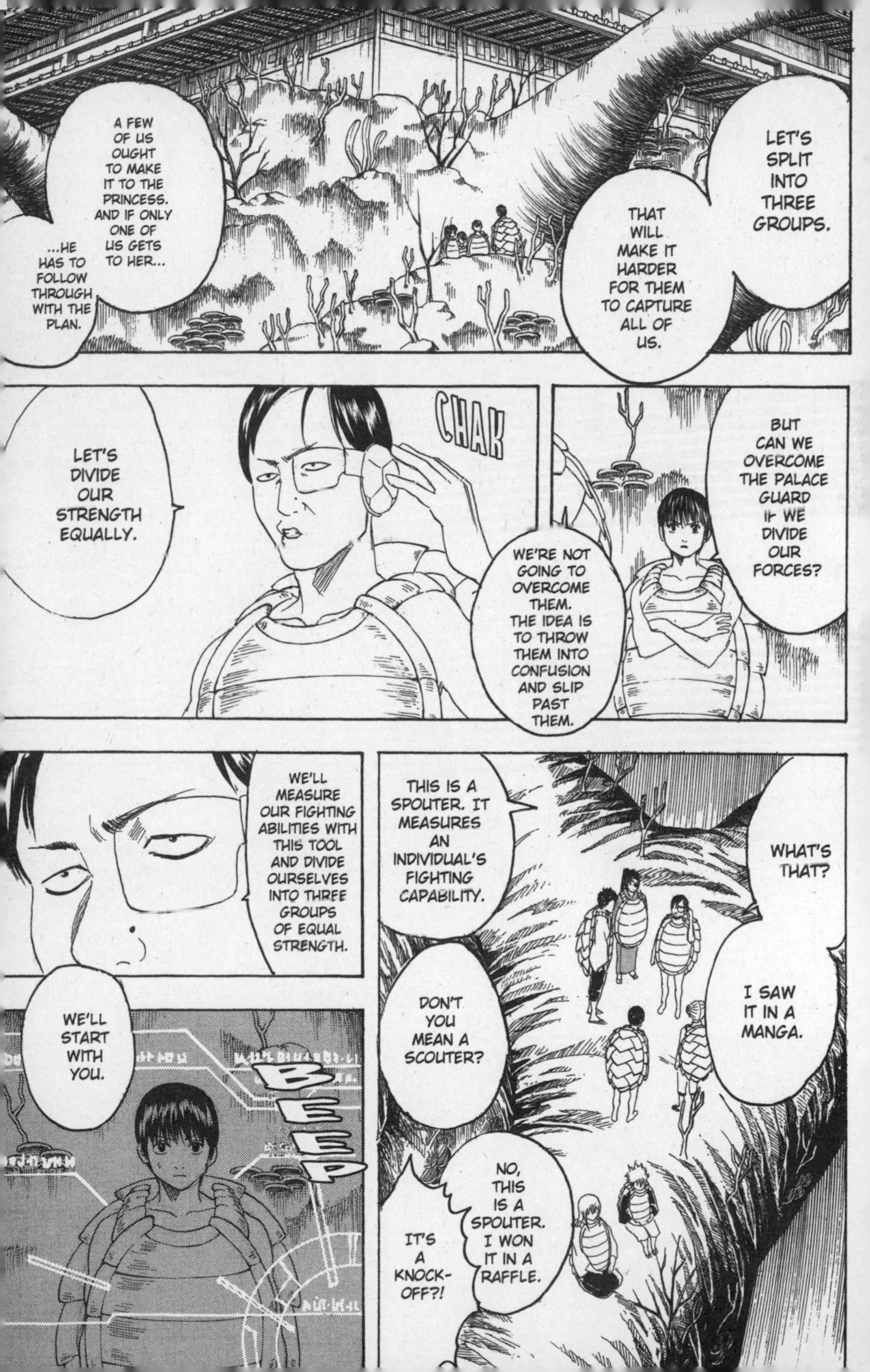
LET'S SPLIT INTO THREE GROUPS.
THAT WILL MAKE IT HARDER FOR THEM TO CAPTURE ALL OF US.
A FEW OF US OUGHT TO MAKE IT TO THE PRINCESS. AND IF ONLY ONE OF US GETS TO HER...
...HE HAS TO FOLLOW THROUGH WITH THE PLAN.
BUT CAN WE OVERCOME THE PALACE GUARD IF WE DIVIDE OUR FORCES?
WE'RE NOT GOING TO OVERCOME THEM. THE IDEA IS TO THROW THEM INTO CONFUSION AND SLIP PAST THEM.
CHAK
LET'S DIVIDE OUR STRENGTH EQUALLY.
WHAT'S THAT?
THIS IS A SPOUTER. IT MEASURES AN INDIVIDUAL'S FIGHTING CAPABILITY.
I SAW IT IN A MANGA.
DON'T YOU MEAN A SCOUTER?
NO, THIS IS A SPOUTER. I WON IT IN A RAFFLE.
IT'S A KNOCK-OFF?!
WE'LL MEASURE OUR FIGHTING ABILITIES WITH THIS TOOL AND DIVIDE OURSELVES INTO THREE GROUPS OF EQUAL STRENGTH.
WE'LL START WITH YOU.
BEEP

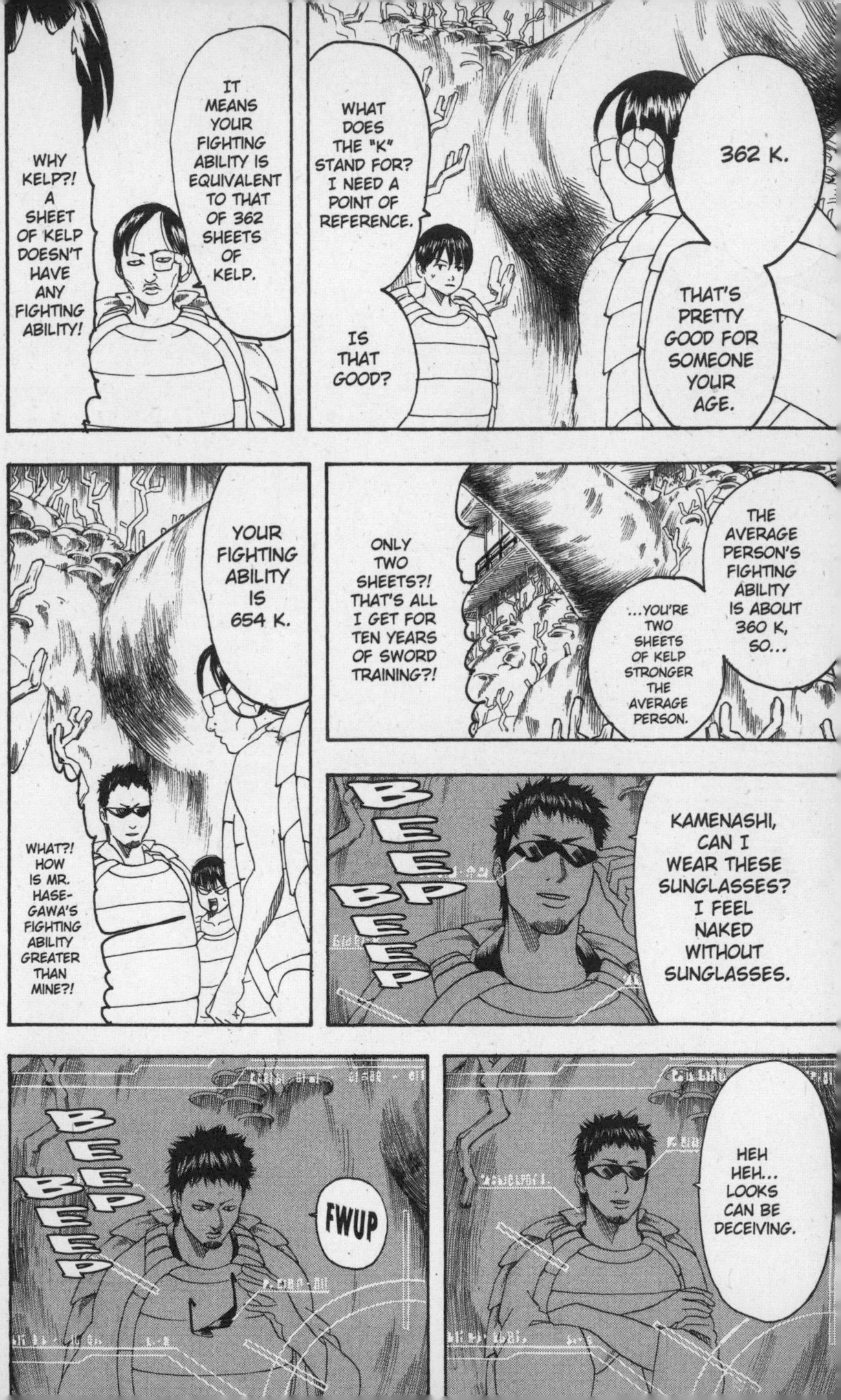
362 K.
THAT'S PRETTY GOOD FOR SOMEONE YOUR AGE.
WHAT DOES THE "K" STAND FOR? I NEED A POINT OF REFERENCE.
IS THAT GOOD?
IT MEANS YOUR FIGHTING ABILITY IS EQUIVALENT TO THAT OF 362 SHEETS OF KELP.
WHY KELP?! A SHEET OF KELP DOESN'T HAVE ANY FIGHTING ABILITY!
THE AVERAGE PERSON'S FIGHTING ABILITY IS ABOUT 360 K, SO...
...YOU'RE TWO SHEETS OF KELP STRONGER THE AVERAGE PERSON.
ONLY TWO SHEETS?! THAT'S ALL I GET FOR TEN YEARS OF SWORD TRAINING?!
KAMENASHI, CAN I WEAR THESE SUNGLASSES? I FEEL NAKED WITHOUT SUNGLASSES.
YOUR FIGHTING ABILITY IS 654 K.
WHAT?! HOW IS MR. HASE-GAWA'S FIGHTING ABILITY GREATER THAN MINE?!
HEH HEH... LOOKS CAN BE DECEIVING.
FWUP

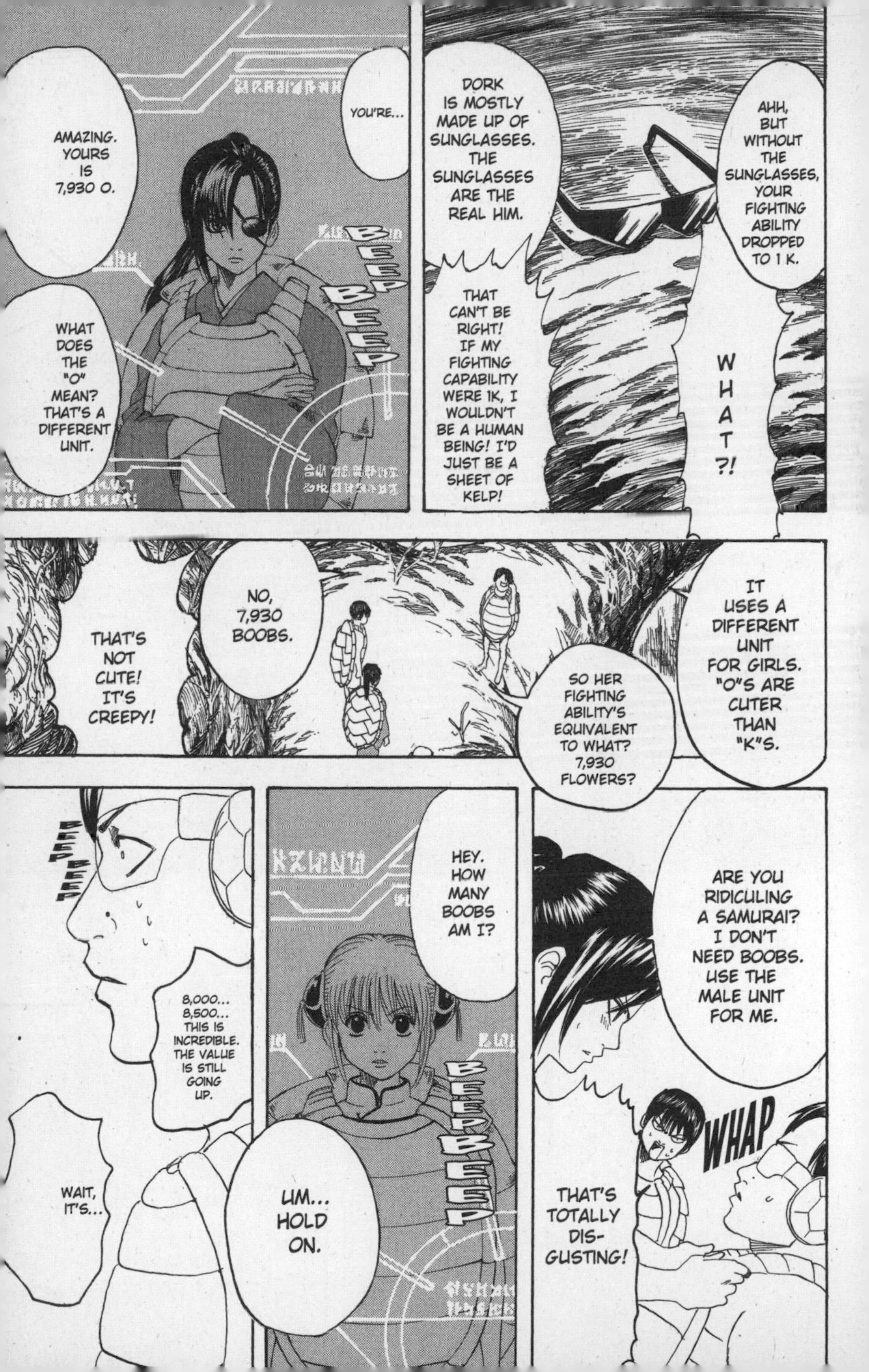

AHH, BUT WITHOUT THE SUNGLASSES, YOUR FIGHTING ABILITY DROPPED TO 1 K.
DORK IS MOSTLY MADE UP OF SUNGLASSES. THE SUNGLASSES ARE THE REAL HIM.
WHAT?!
THAT CAN'T BE RIGHT! IF MY FIGHTING CAPABILITY WERE 1K, I WOULDN'T BE A HUMAN BEING! I'D JUST BE A SHEET OF KELP!
YOU'RE...
AMAZING. YOURS IS 7,930 O.
BEEP BEEP
WHAT DOES THE "O" MEAN? THAT'S A DIFFERENT UNIT.
IT USES A DIFFERENT UNIT FOR GIRLS. "O"S ARE CUTER THAN "K"S.
SO HER FIGHTING ABILITY'S EQUIVALENT TO WHAT? 7,930 FLOWERS?
NO, 7,930 BOOBS.
THAT'S NOT CUTE! IT'S CREEPY!
ARE YOU RIDICULING A SAMURAI? I DON'T NEED BOOBS. USE THE MALE UNIT FOR ME.
WHAP
THAT'S TOTALLY DIS-GUSTING!
HEY. HOW MANY BOOBS AM I?
BEEP BEEP
UM... HOLD ON.
BEEP BEEP
8,000... 8,500... THIS IS INCREDIBLE. THE VALUE IS STILL GOING UP.
WAIT, IT'S...

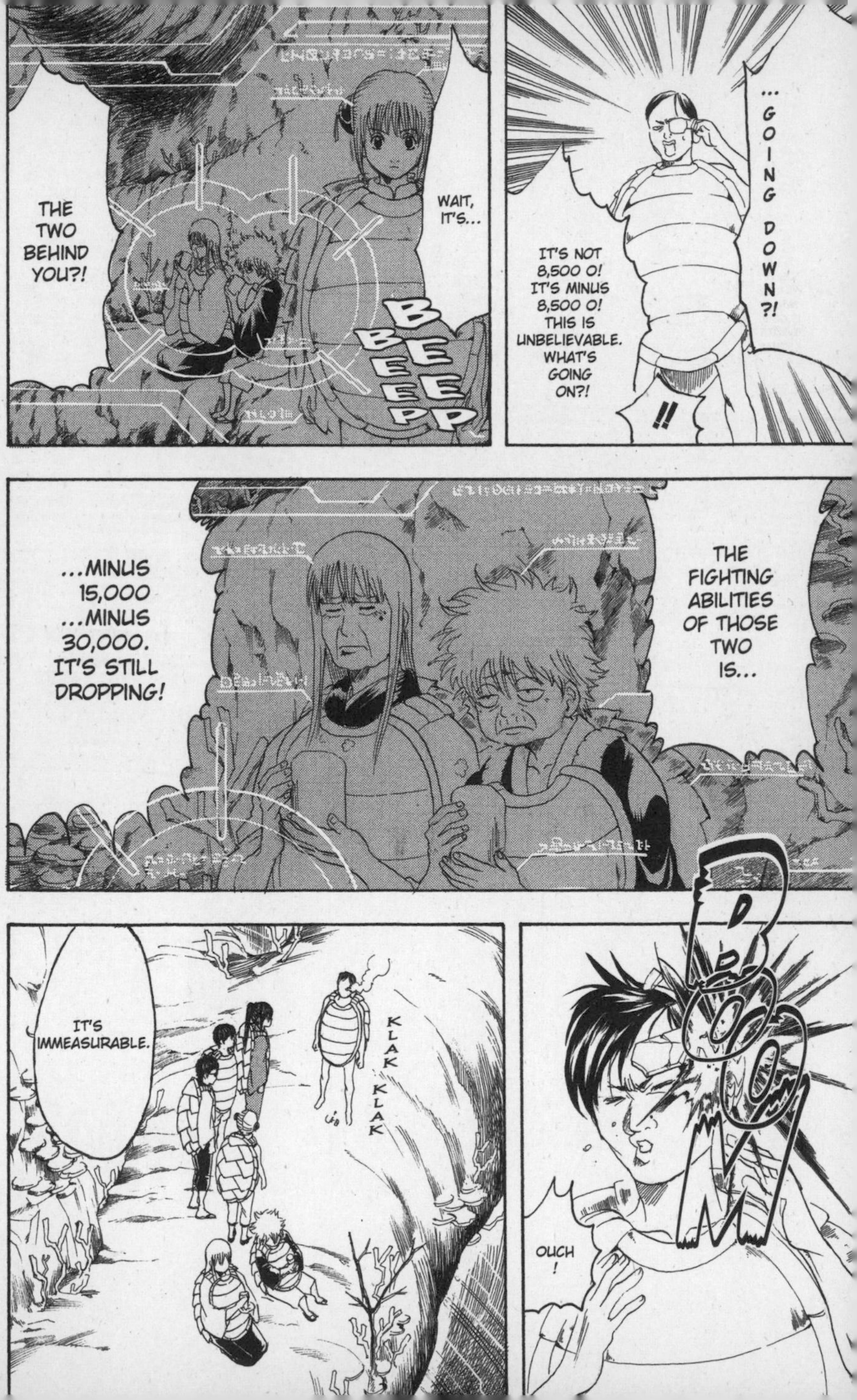
...GOING DOWN?!
IT'S NOT 8,500 O! IT'S MINUS 8,500 O! THIS IS UNBELIEVABLE. WHAT'S GOING ON?!
!!
WAIT, IT'S...
THE TWO BEHIND YOU?!
BEEEEPP
THE FIGHTING ABILITIES OF THOSE TWO IS...
...MINUS 15,000 ...MINUS 30,000. IT'S STILL DROPPING!
BOOOM
OUCH!
IT'S IMMEASURABLE.
KLAK KLAK

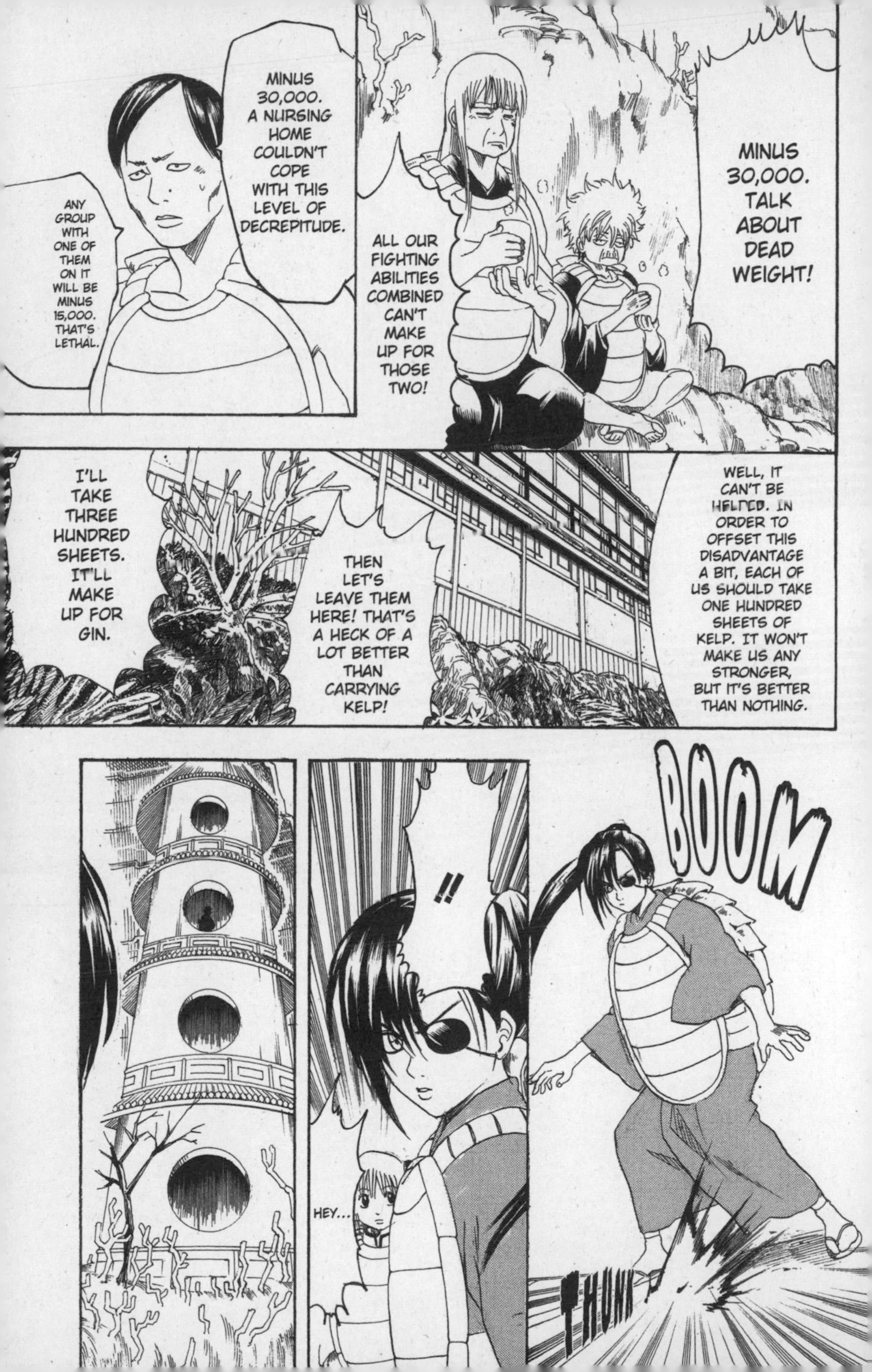
MINUS 30,000. TALK ABOUT DEAD WEIGHT!
ALL OUR FIGHTING ABILITIES COMBINED CAN'T MAKE UP FOR THOSE TWO!
MINUS 30,000. A NURSING HOME COULDN'T COPE WITH THIS LEVEL OF DECREPITUDE.
ANY GROUP WITH ONE OF THEM ON IT WILL BE MINUS 15,000. THAT'S LETHAL.
WELL, IT CAN'T BE HELPED. IN ORDER TO OFFSET THIS DISADVANTAGE A BIT, EACH OF US SHOULD TAKE ONE HUNDRED SHEETS OF KELP. IT WON'T MAKE US ANY STRONGER, BUT IT'S BETTER THAN NOTHING.
THEN LET'S LEAVE THEM HERE! THAT'S A HECK OF A LOT BETTER THAN CARRYING KELP!
I'LL TAKE THREE HUNDRED SHEETS. IT'LL MAKE UP FOR GIN.
BOOM
THUNK
!!
HEY...

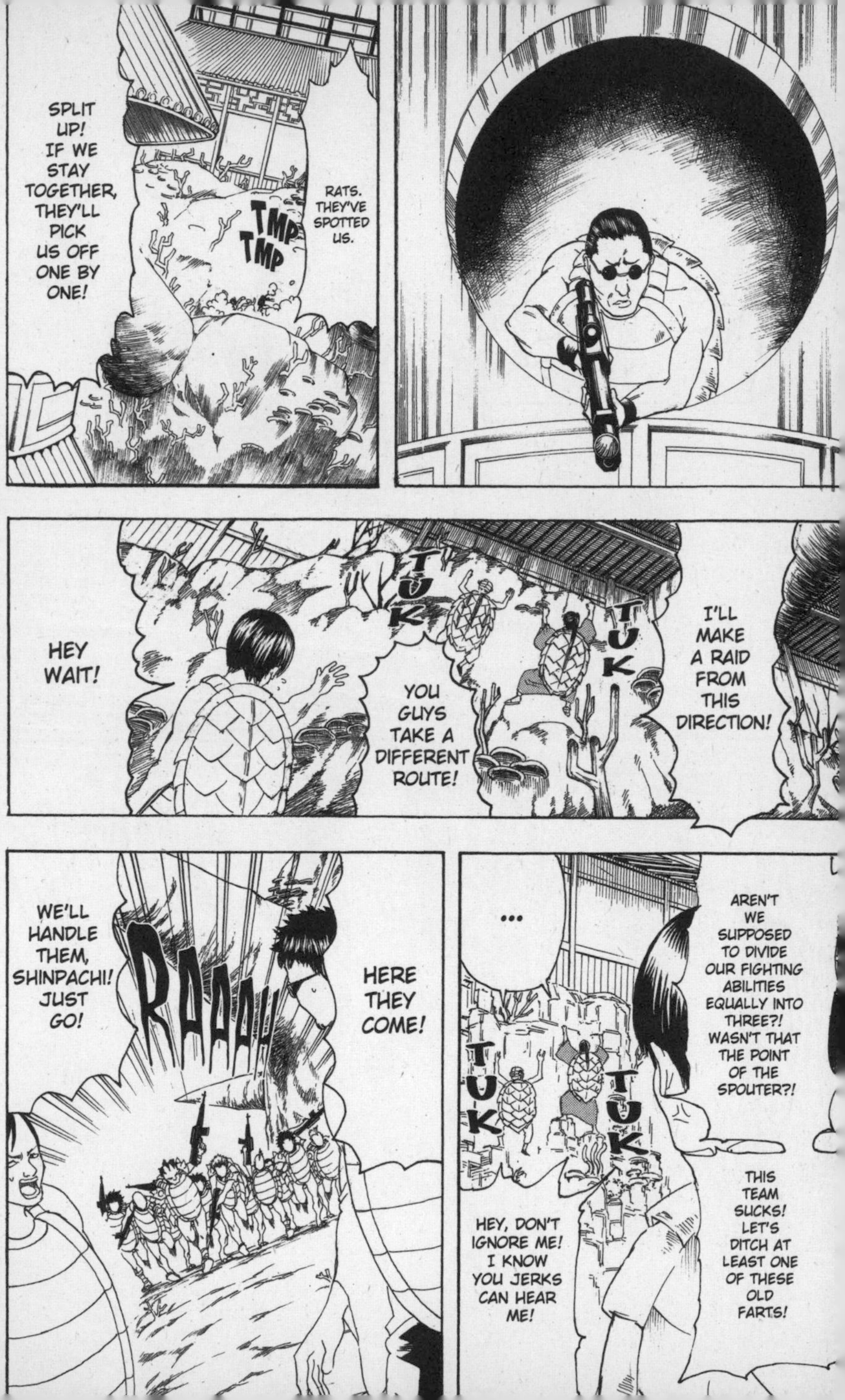
RATS. THEY'VE SPOTTED US.
TMP TMP
SPLIT UP! IF WE STAY TOGETHER, THEY'LL PICK US OFF ONE BY ONE!
I'LL MAKE A RAID FROM THIS DIRECTION!
TUK
TUK
YOU GUYS TAKE A DIFFERENT ROUTE!
HEY WAIT!
AREN'T WE SUPPOSED TO DIVIDE OUR FIGHTING ABILITIES EQUALLY INTO THREE?! WASN'T THAT THE POINT OF THE SPOUTER?!
...
TUK
TUK
THIS TEAM SUCKS! LET'S DITCH AT LEAST ONE OF THESE OLD FARTS!
HEY, DON'T IGNORE ME! I KNOW YOU JERKS CAN HEAR ME!
HERE THEY COME!
RAAAH
WE'LL HANDLE THEM, SHINPACHI! JUST GO!

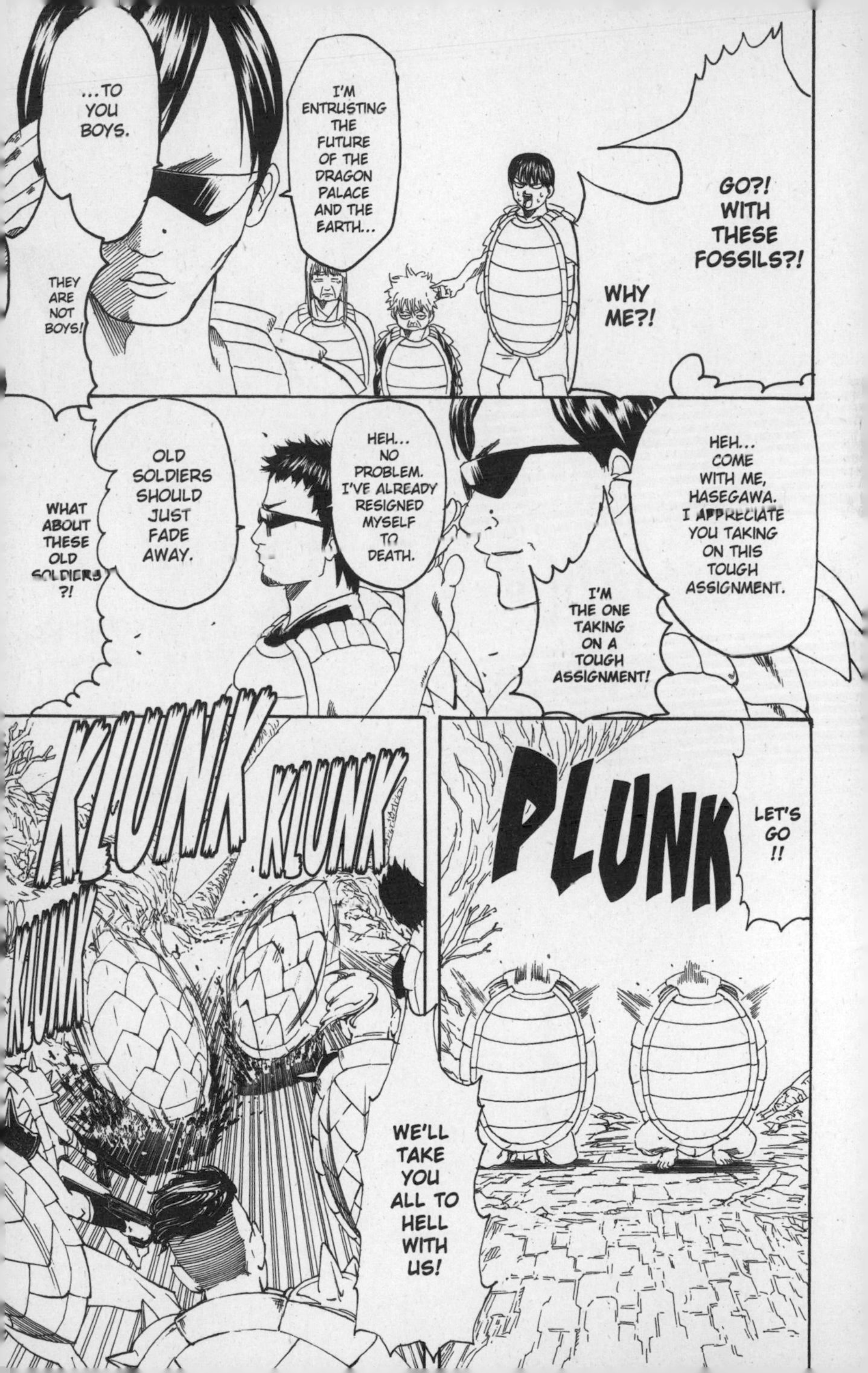
GO?! WITH THESE FOSSILS?!
WHY ME?!
I'M ENTRUSTING THE FUTURE OF THE DRAGON PALACE AND THE EARTH...
...TO YOU BOYS.
THEY ARE NOT BOYS!
HEH... COME WITH ME, HASEGAWA. I APPRECIATE YOU TAKING ON THIS TOUGH ASSIGNMENT.
I'M THE ONE TAKING ON A TOUGH ASSIGNMENT!
HEH... NO PROBLEM. I'VE ALREADY RESIGNED MYSELF TO DEATH.
OLD SOLDIERS SHOULD JUST FADE AWAY.
WHAT ABOUT THESE OLD SOLDIERS?!
PLUNK
LET'S GO!!
WE'LL TAKE YOU ALL TO HELL WITH US!
KLUNK
KLUNK
KLUNK

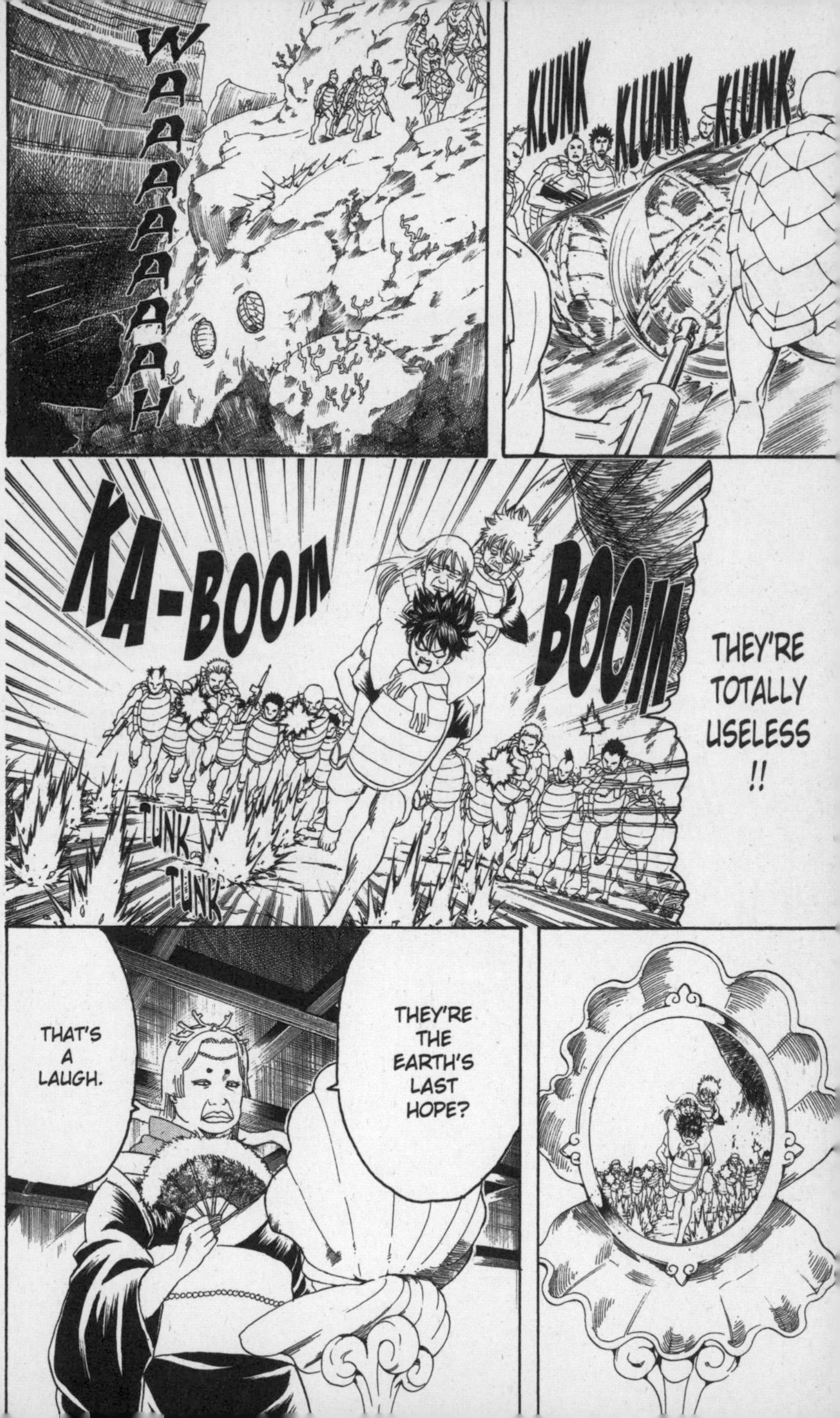
KLUNK KLUNK KLUNK
WAAAAAAAAH
KA-BOOM
BOOM
THEY'RE TOTALLY USELESS!!
TUNK TUNK
THEY'RE THE EARTH'S LAST HOPE?
THAT'S A LAUGH.

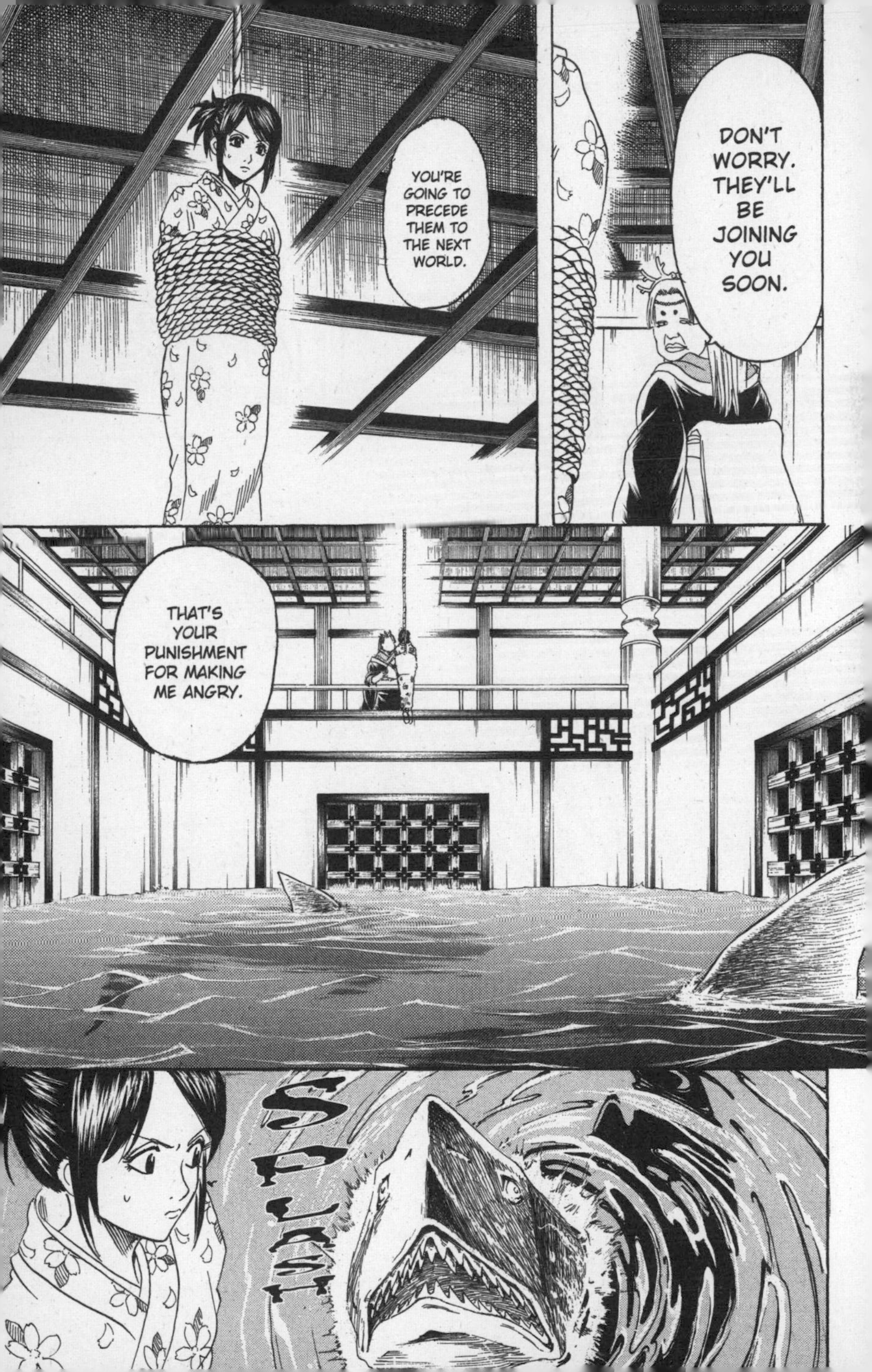
DON'T WORRY. THEY'LL BE JOINING YOU SOON.
YOU'RE GOING TO PRECEDE THEM TO THE NEXT WORLD.
THAT'S YOUR PUNISHMENT FOR MAKING ME ANGRY.
SPLASH

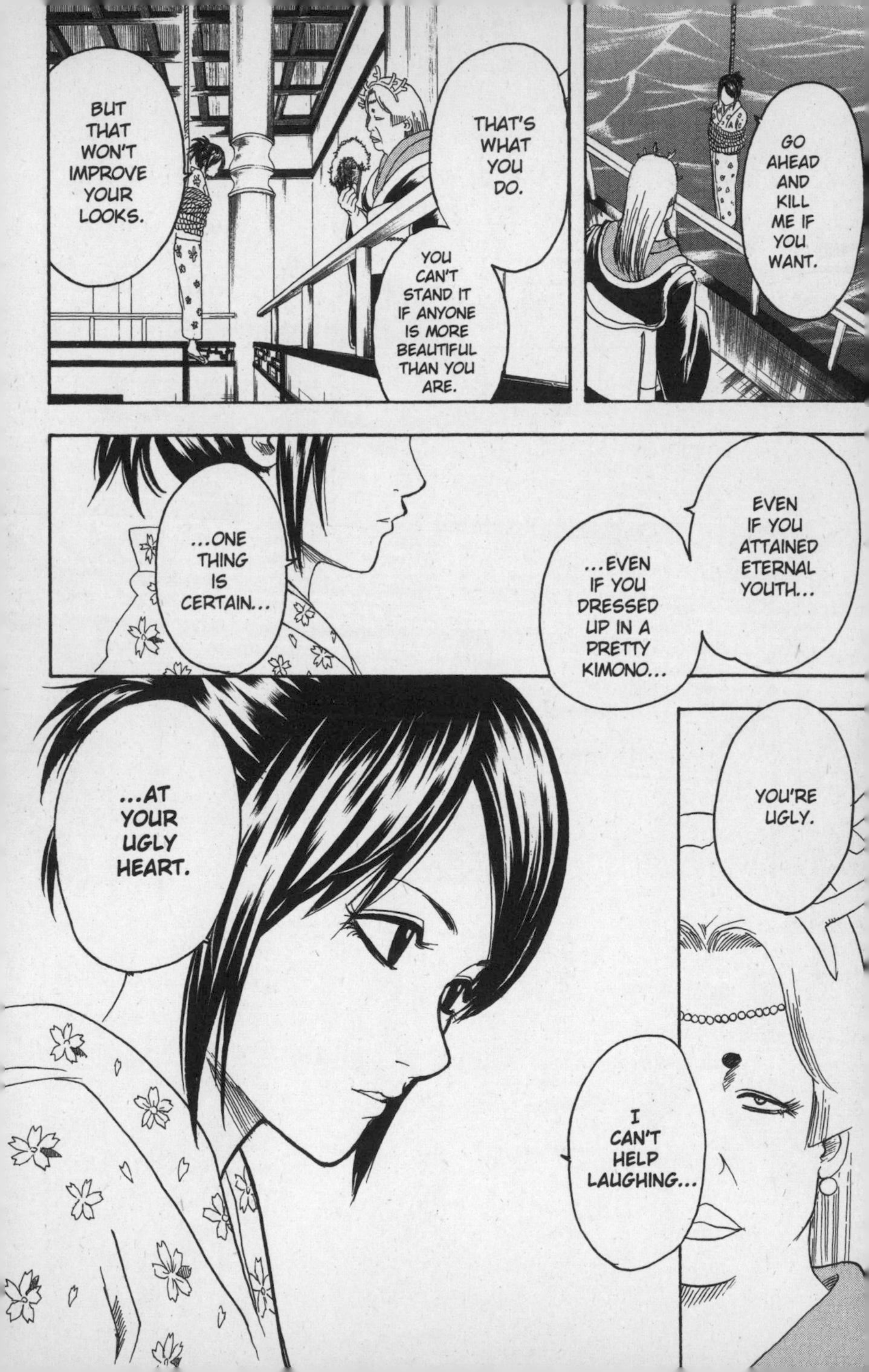
GO AHEAD AND KILL ME IF YOU WANT.
THAT'S WHAT YOU DO.
YOU CAN'T STAND IT IF ANYONE IS MORE BEAUTIFUL THAN YOU ARE.
BUT THAT WON'T IMPROVE YOUR LOOKS.
EVEN IF YOU ATTAINED ETERNAL YOUTH...
...EVEN IF YOU DRESSED UP IN A PRETTY KIMONO...
...ONE THING IS CERTAIN...
YOU'RE UGLY.
I CAN'T HELP LAUGHING...
...AT YOUR UGLY HEART.

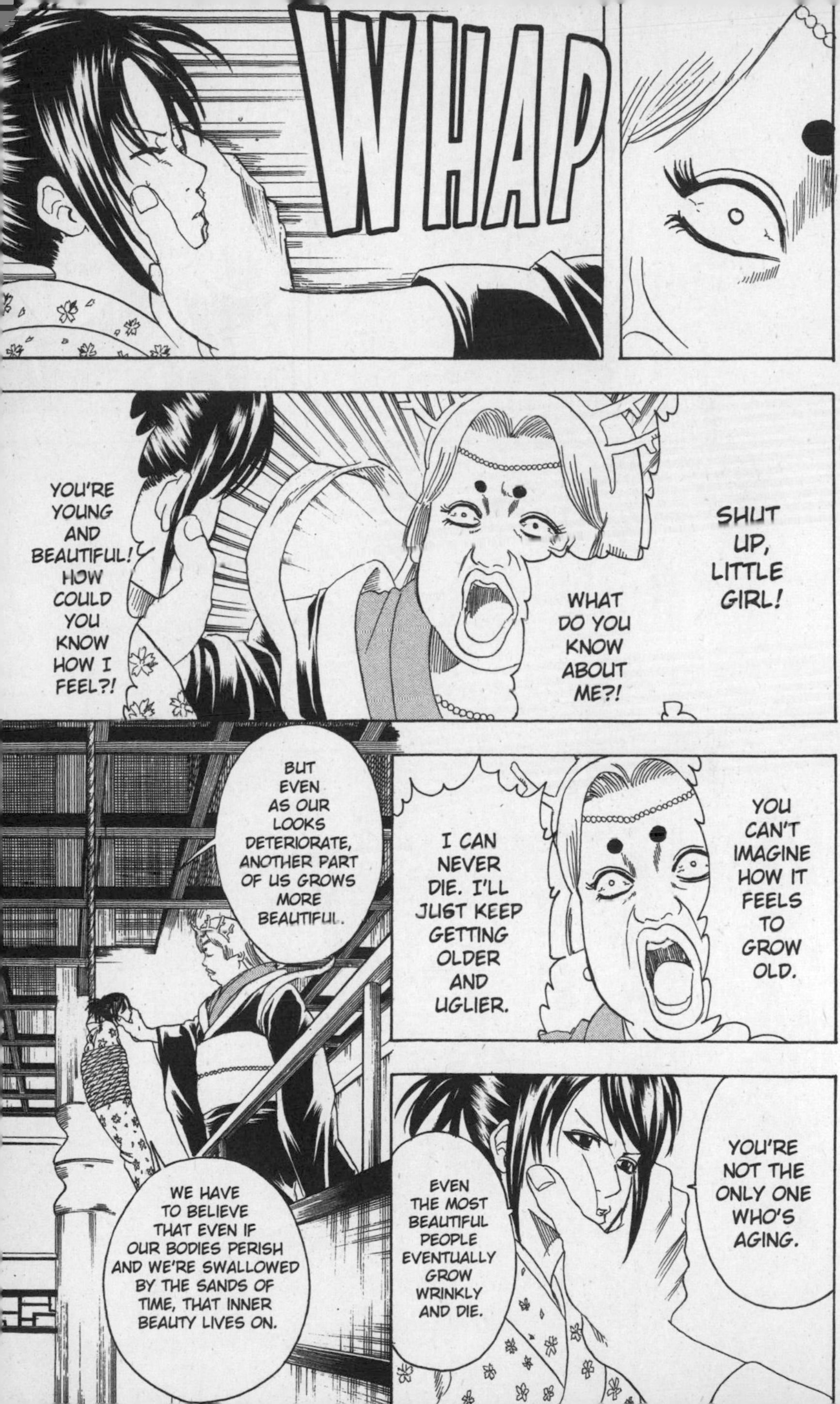
WHAP
SHUT UP, LITTLE GIRL!
WHAT DO YOU KNOW ABOUT ME?!
YOU'RE YOUNG AND BEAUTIFUL! HOW COULD YOU KNOW HOW I FEEL?!
YOU CAN'T IMAGINE HOW IT FEELS TO GROW OLD.
I CAN NEVER DIE. I'LL JUST KEEP GETTING OLDER AND UGLIER.
YOU'RE NOT THE ONLY ONE WHO'S AGING.
EVEN THE MOST BEAUTIFUL PEOPLE EVENTUALLY GROW WRINKLY AND DIE.
BUT EVEN AS OUR LOOKS DETERIORATE, ANOTHER PART OF US GROWS MORE BEAUTIFUL.
WE HAVE TO BELIEVE THAT EVEN IF OUR BODIES PERISH AND WE'RE SWALLOWED BY THE SANDS OF TIME, THAT INNER BEAUTY LIVES ON.

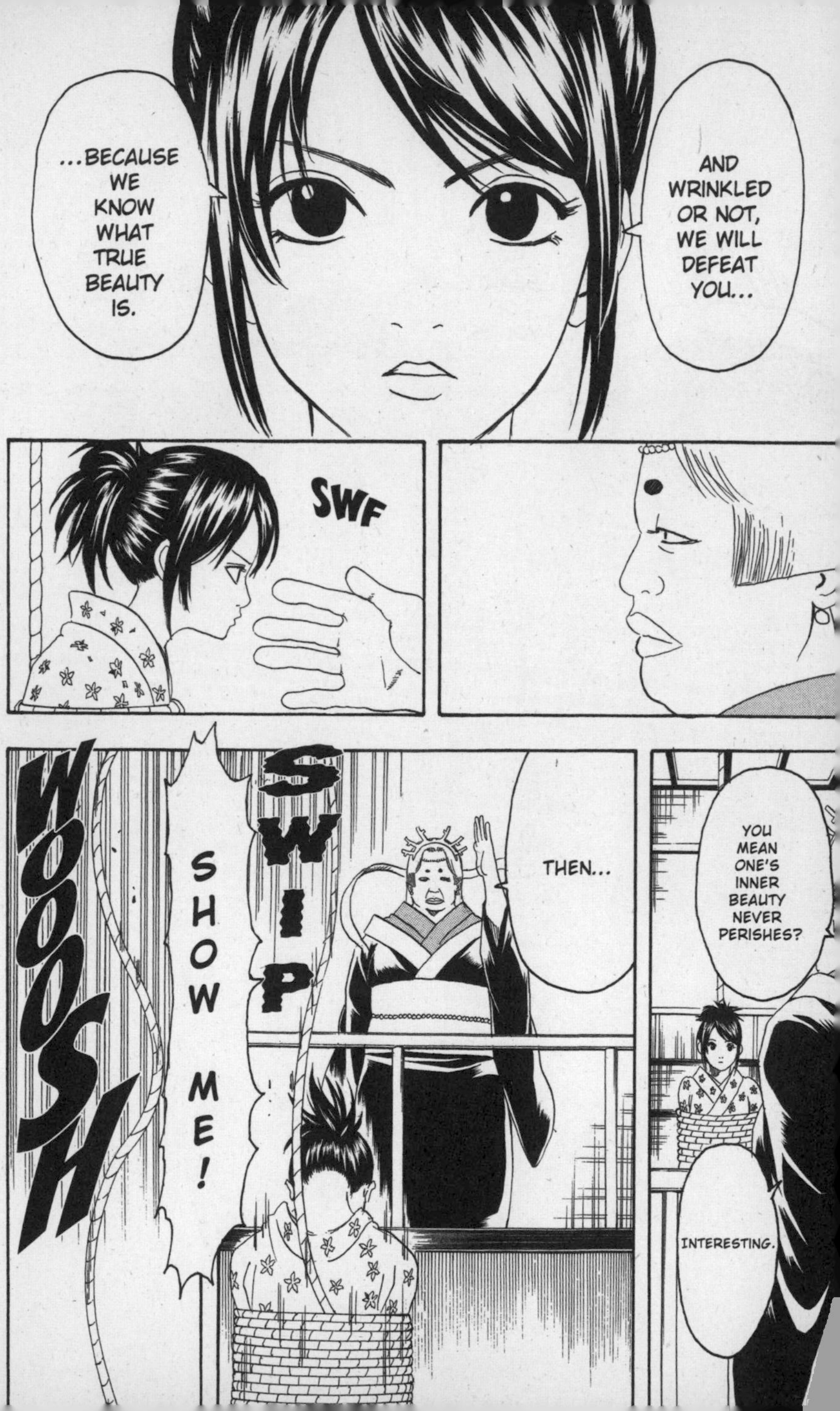
AND WRINKLED OR NOT, WE WILL DEFEAT YOU...
...BECAUSE WE KNOW WHAT TRUE BEAUTY IS.
SWF
YOU MEAN ONE'S INNER BEAUTY NEVER PERISHES?
INTERESTING.
THEN...
SWIP
SHOW ME!
WOOOSH

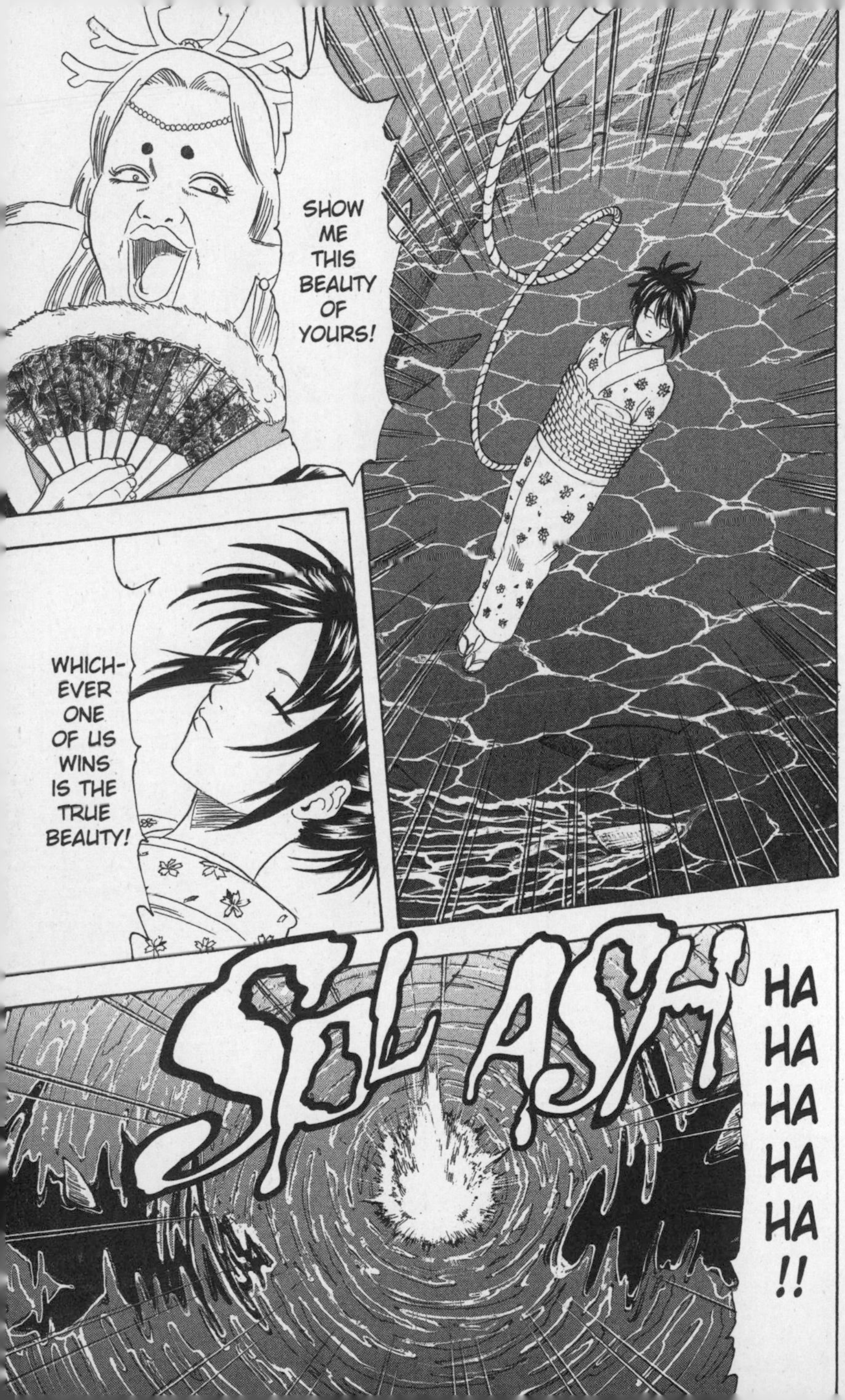
SHOW ME THIS BEAUTY OF YOURS!
WHICH-EVER ONE OF US WINS IS THE TRUE BEAUTY!
SPLASH
HA HA HA HA HA!!

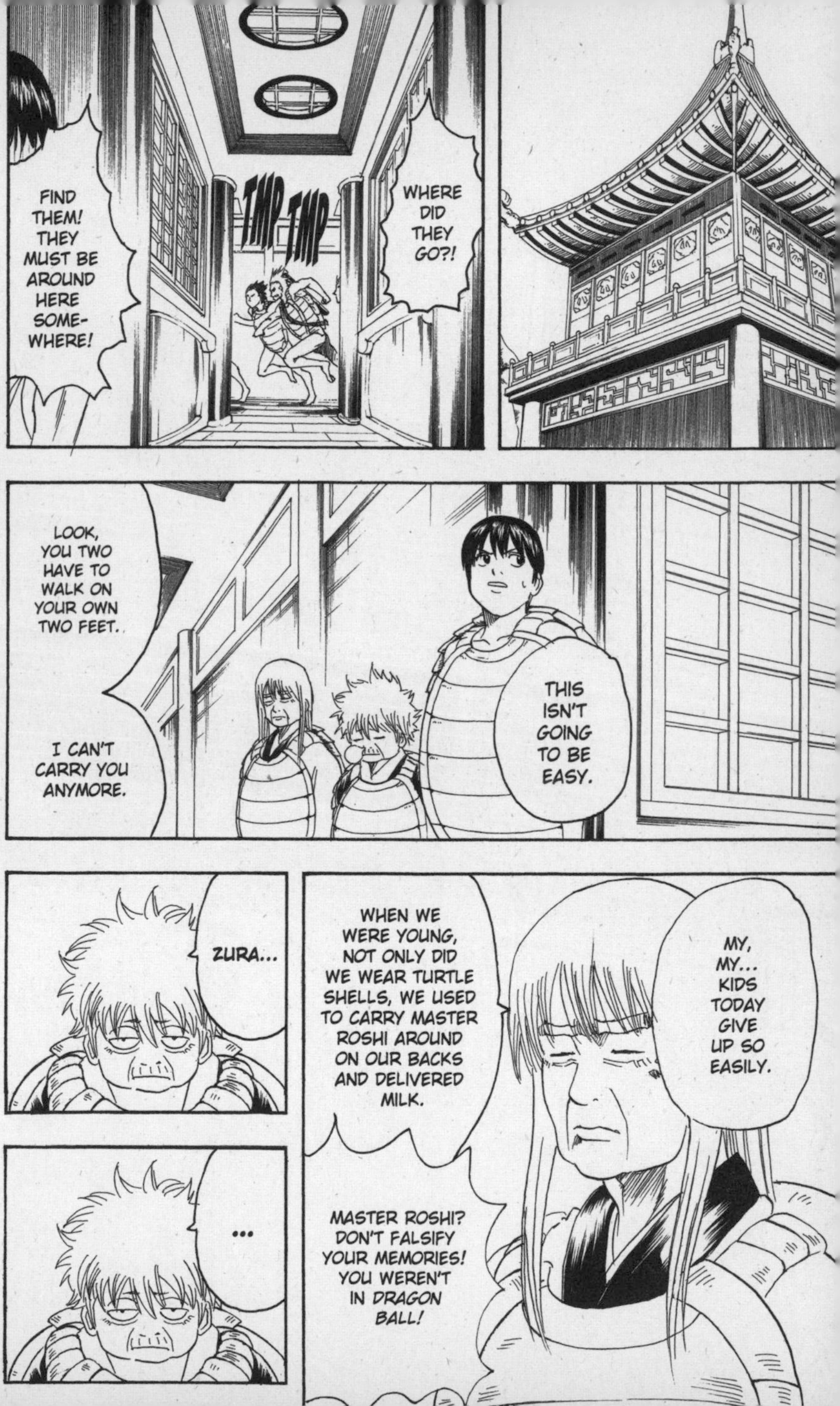
WHERE DID THEY GO?!
TMP TMP
FIND THEM! THEY MUST BE AROUND HERE SOME-WHERE!
THIS ISN'T GOING TO BE EASY.
LOOK, YOU TWO HAVE TO WALK ON YOUR OWN TWO FEET.
I CAN'T CARRY YOU ANYMORE.
MY, MY... KIDS TODAY GIVE UP SO EASILY.
WHEN WE WERE YOUNG, NOT ONLY DID WE WEAR TURTLE SHELLS, WE USED TO CARRY MASTER ROSHI AROUND ON OUR BACKS AND DELIVERED MILK.
MASTER ROSHI? DON'T FALSIFY YOUR MEMORIES! YOU WEREN'T IN *DRAGON BALL*!
ZURA...
...

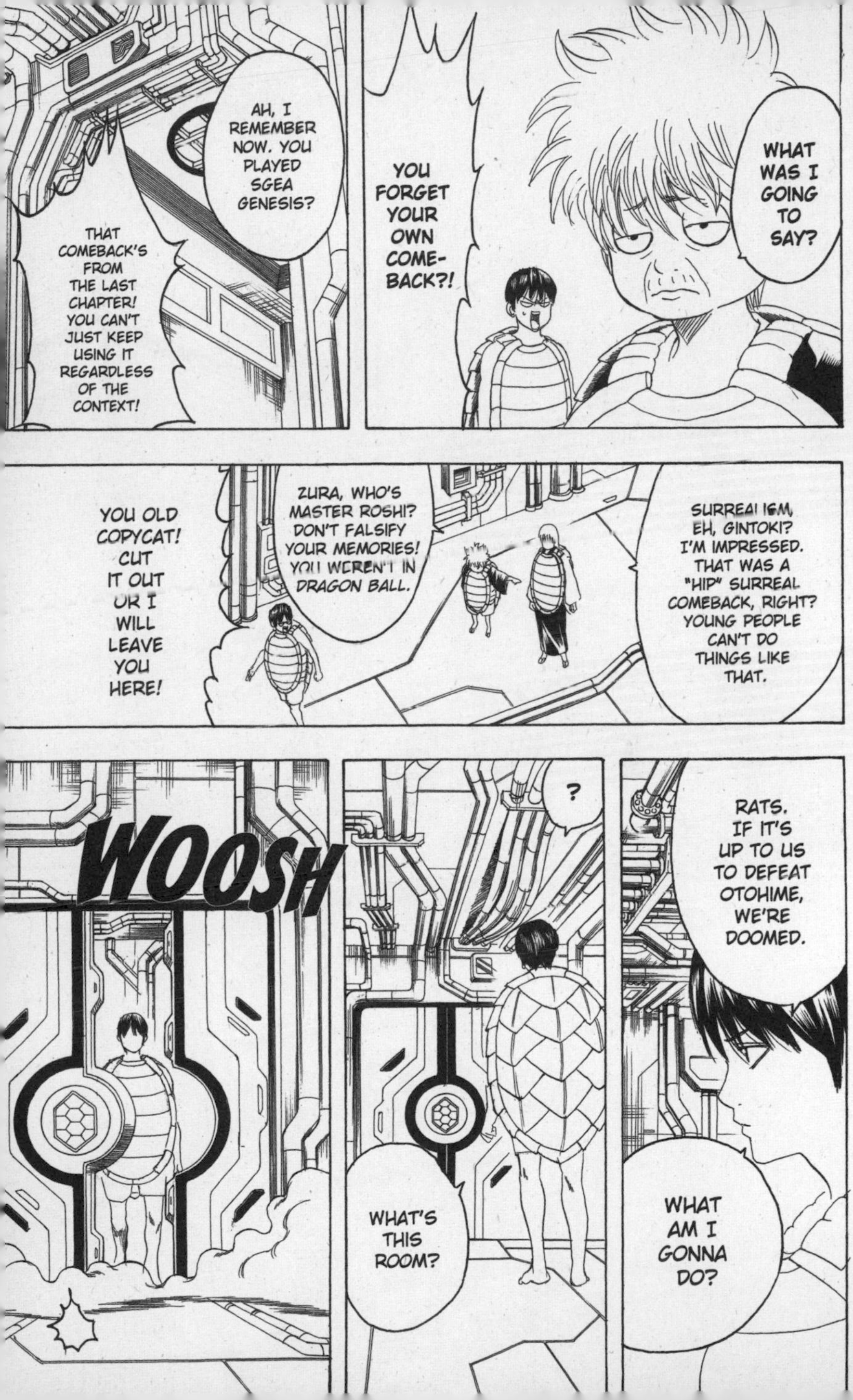
WHAT WAS I GOING TO SAY?
YOU FORGET YOUR OWN COME-BACK?!
AH, I REMEMBER NOW. YOU PLAYED SGEA GENESIS?
THAT COMEBACK'S FROM THE LAST CHAPTER! YOU CAN'T JUST KEEP USING IT REGARDLESS OF THE CONTEXT!
SURREALISM, EH, GINTOKI? I'M IMPRESSED. THAT WAS A "HIP" SURREAL COMEBACK, RIGHT? YOUNG PEOPLE CAN'T DO THINGS LIKE THAT.
ZURA, WHO'S MASTER ROSHI? DON'T FALSIFY YOUR MEMORIES! YOU WEREN'T IN DRAGON BALL.
YOU OLD COPYCAT! CUT IT OUT OR I WILL LEAVE YOU HERE!
RATS. IF IT'S UP TO US TO DEFEAT OTOHIME, WE'RE DOOMED.
WHAT AM I GONNA DO?
?
WHAT'S THIS ROOM?
WOOSH

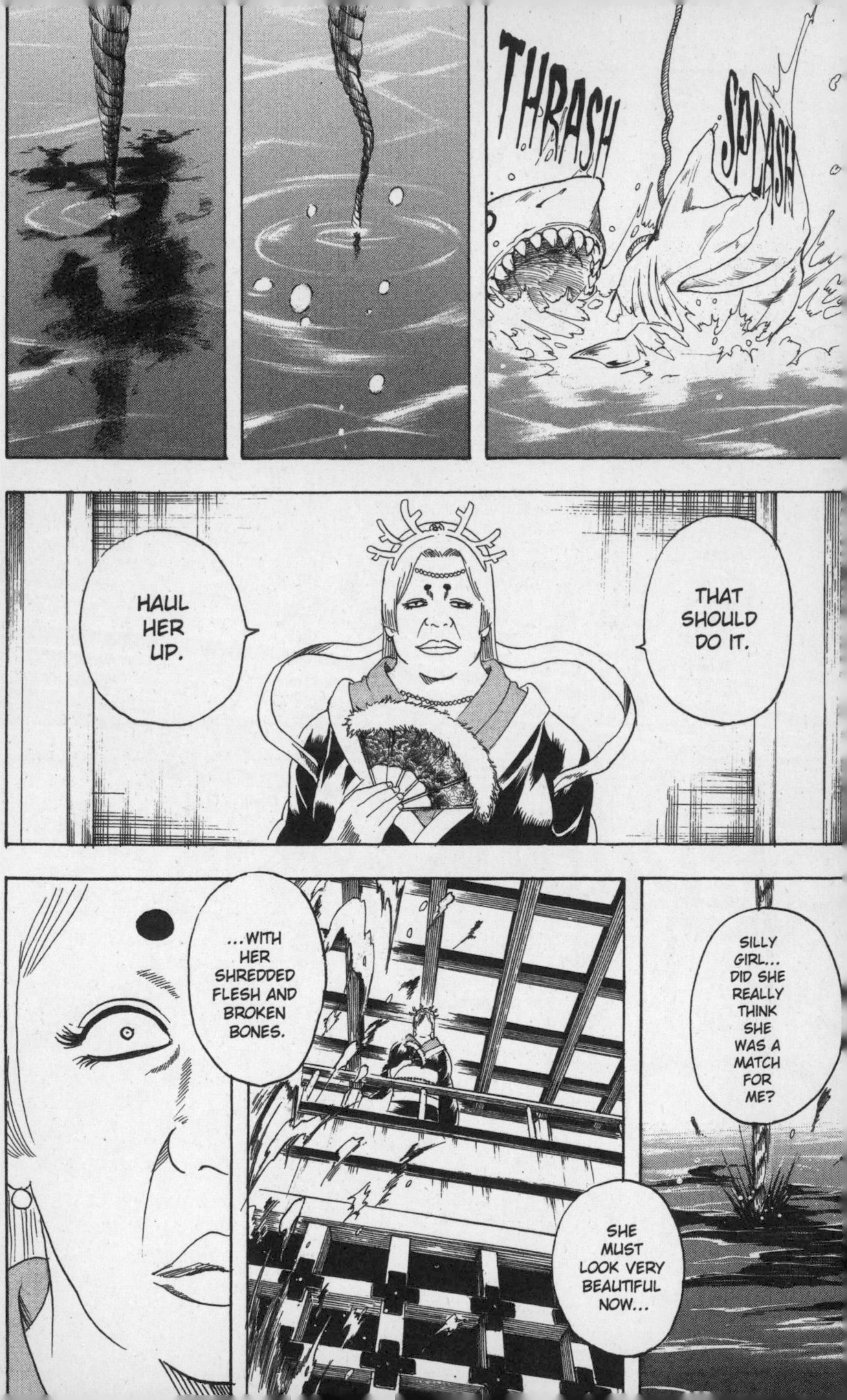
THRASH
SPLASH
THAT SHOULD DO IT.
HAUL HER UP.
SILLY GIRL... DID SHE REALLY THINK SHE WAS A MATCH FOR ME?
SHE MUST LOOK VERY BEAUTIFUL NOW...
...WITH HER SHREDDED FLESH AND BROKEN BONES.

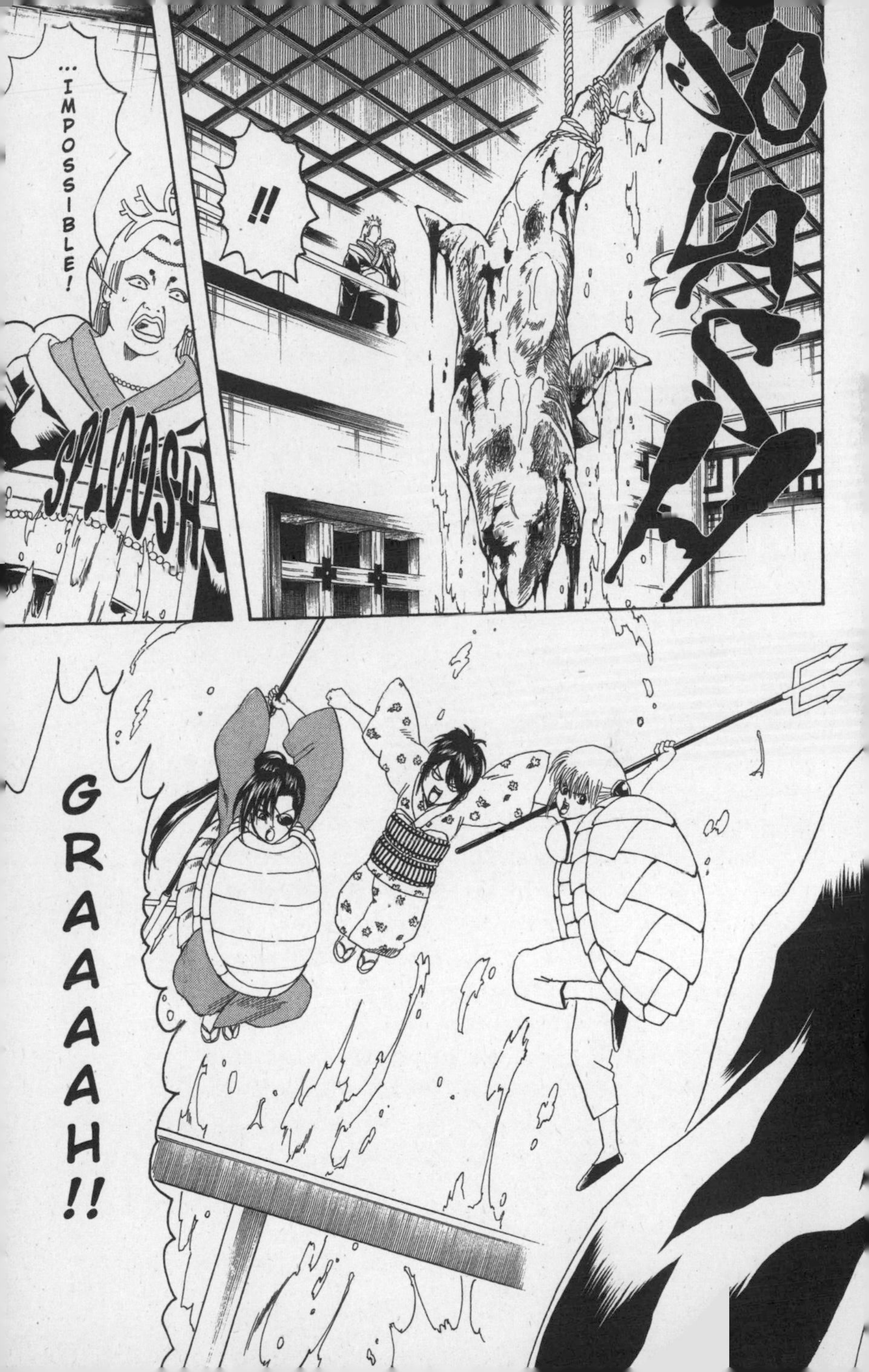
!!
...IMPOSSIBLE!
SPLOOSH
GRAAAAH!!

So, I'm worried about my future. But I'm not the only one who's worried, Mr. Oonishi is too. He's editing **One Piece** now. In our last meeting, Mr. Oonishi was very quiet and he looked deathly pale. His lips were dry too. He's a nervous wreck and he hasn't even met Oda Sensei yet. Well, I can understand how he feels. I was so afraid of Oda Sensei that it took me three years to talk to him. At the New Year's party my first year here, I spotted Oda Sensei across the room and Mr. Oonishi told me to go say hello to him. But Oda Sensei's aura was overwhelming. The power of his spirit made me faint, so I made an excuse. "I'm sure he's never heard of **Gin Tama**. It'll probably end soon anyway," I said. Fortunately, **Gin Tama** has survived, and I had another opportunity to meet Oda Sensei the next year at Jump Festa. Mr. Oonishi said, "You have to go say hello to him this time." But I said, "Wait. If I say hello to him this year, he'll be offended that I didn't say hello to him last year." And Mr. Oonishi said, "By that logic you'll never be able to say hello to him." While we were still arguing like this, Oda Sensei casually walked past me in the hallway, so I said hello to him, almost in a falsetto. He just said, "Oh, hi." He completely mistook me for one of the backstage staff (Ha). He walked on without stopping. Finally, this year, at the tenth year anniversary celebration for **One Piece**, I managed to tell him, "Congratulations!"

(Continued on page 86)

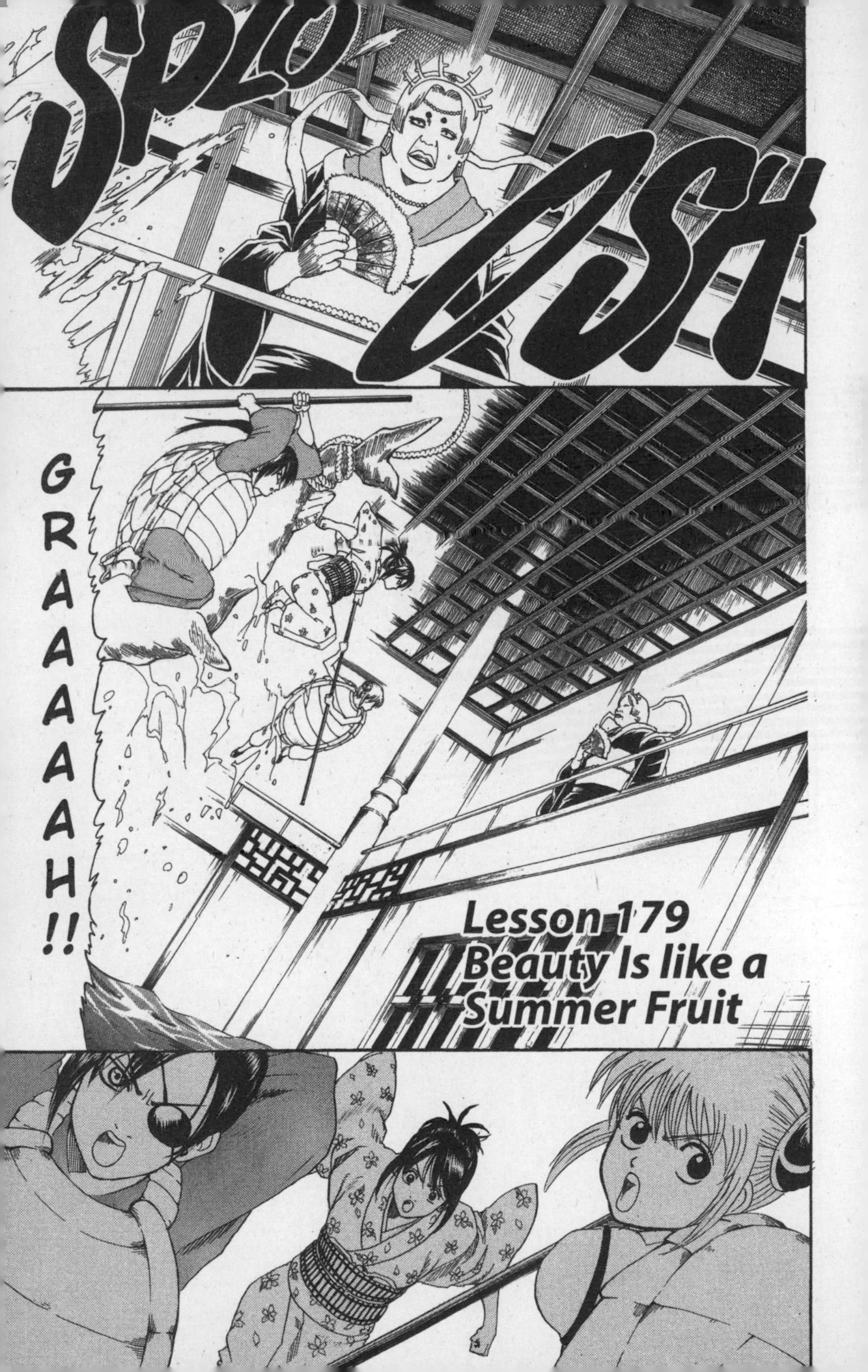
SPLOOSH
GRAAAAAAH!!
Lesson 179
Beauty Is like a Summer Fruit

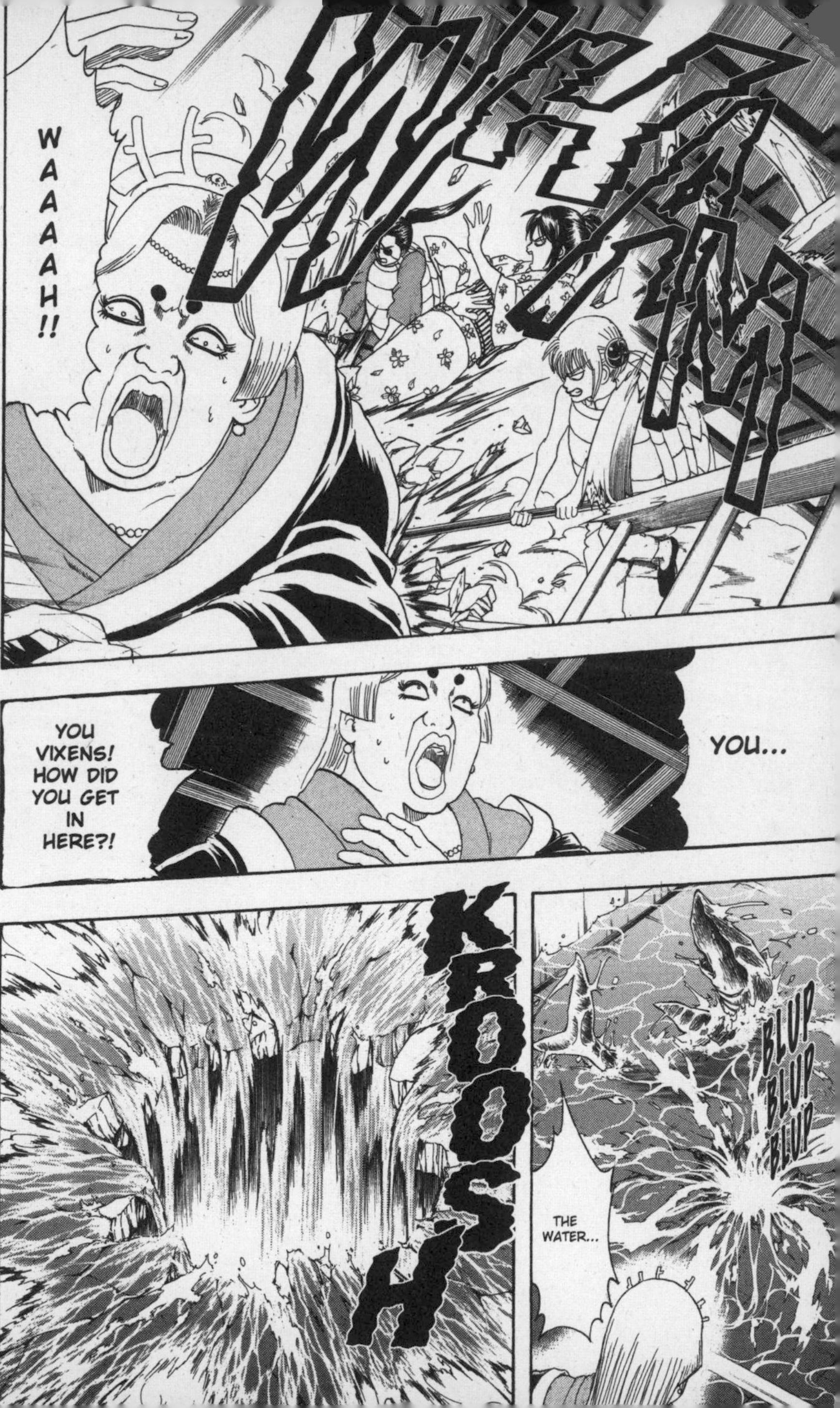
WAAAAAAH!!
YOU...
YOU VIXENS! HOW DID YOU GET IN HERE?!
BLUP BLUP BLUP
THE WATER...
KROOSH

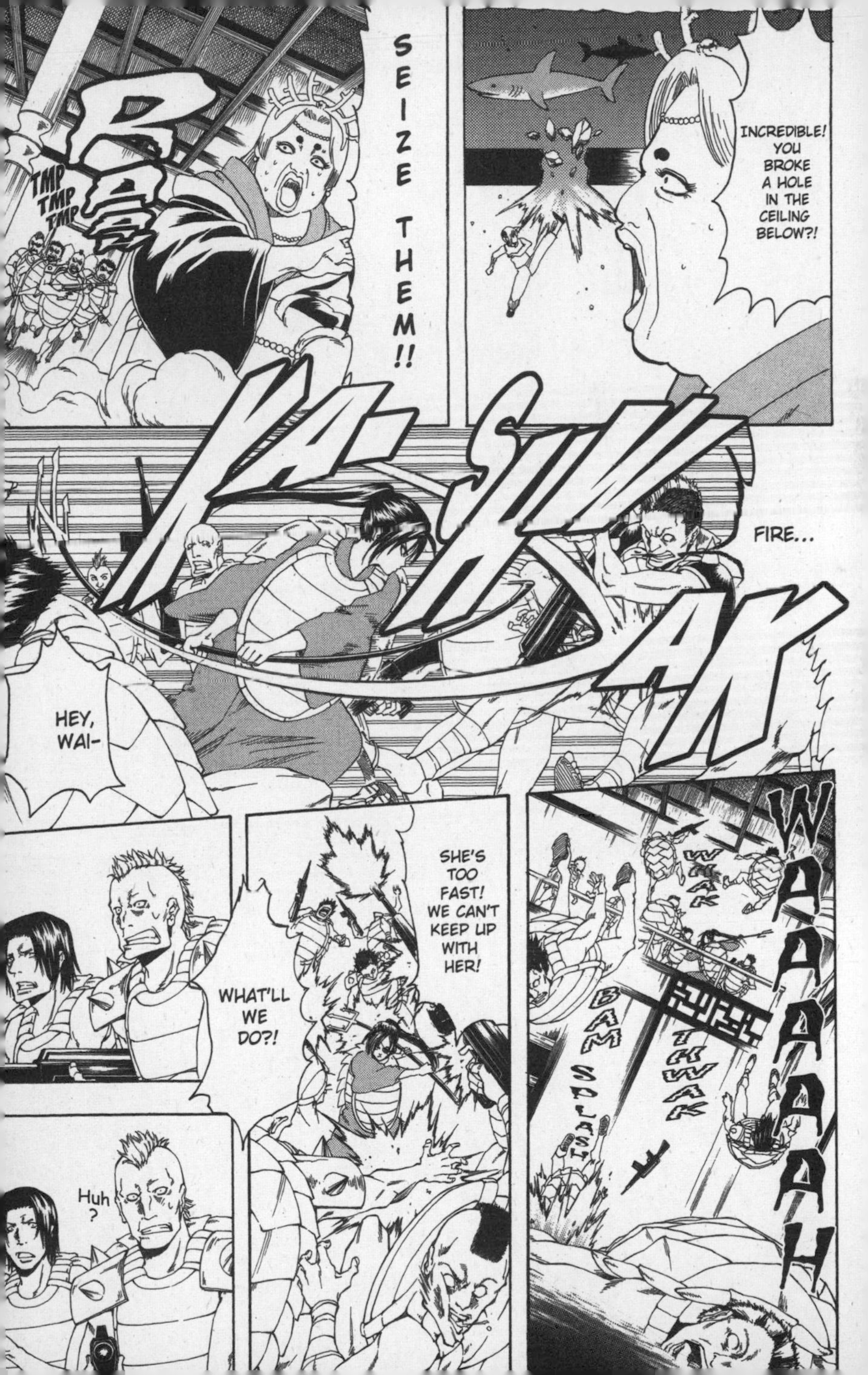
INCREDIBLE! YOU BROKE A HOLE IN THE CEILING BELOW?!
SEIZE THEM!!
TMP TMP TMP
FIRE...
HEY, WAI-
WAAAAAAAH
THWAK
BAM SPLASH
SHE'S TOO FAST! WE CAN'T KEEP UP WITH HER!
WHAT'LL WE DO?!
Huh?

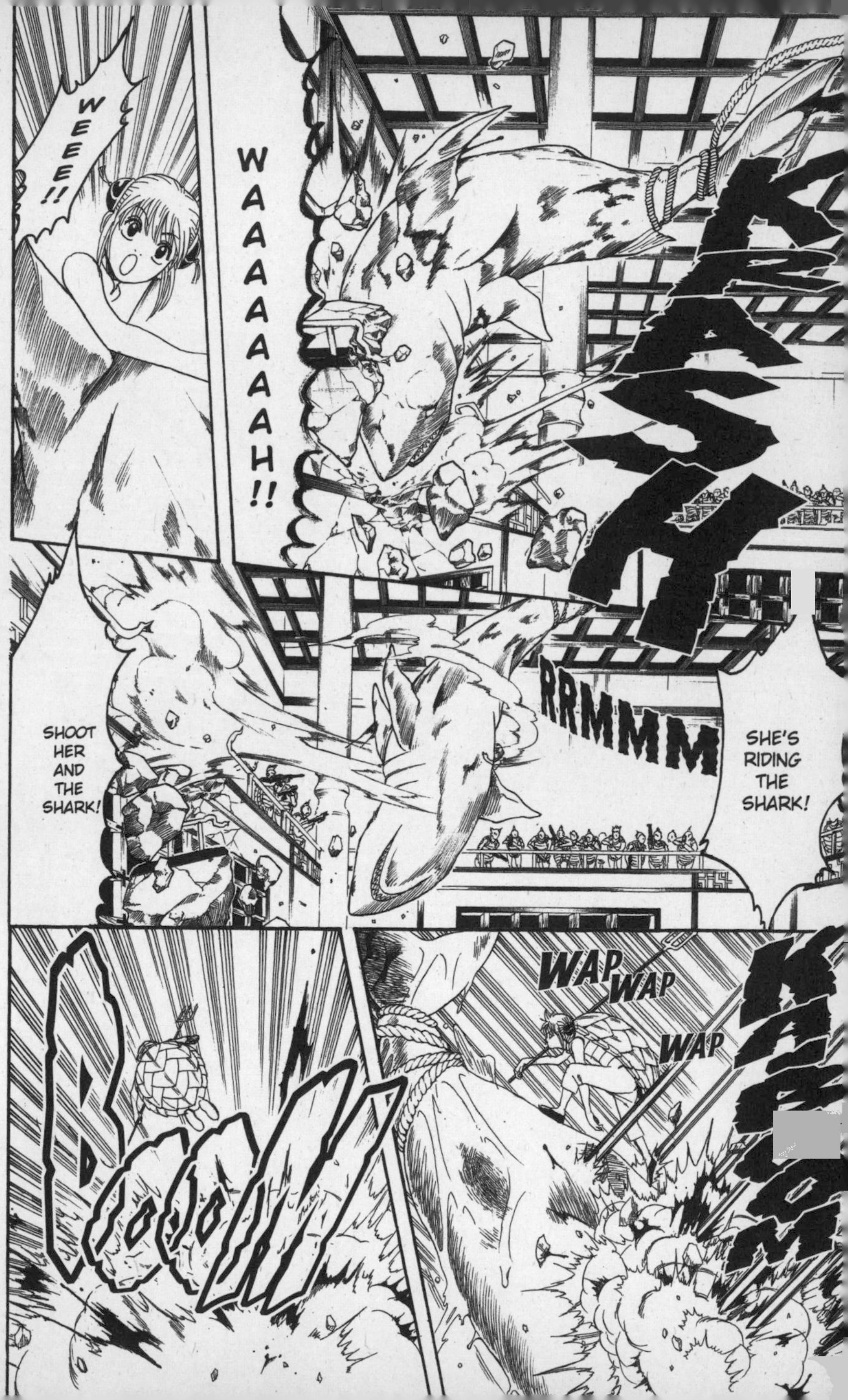
KRASH
WAAAAAAAAAH!!
WEEEE!!
SHE'S RIDING THE SHARK!
RRMMMM
SHOOT HER AND THE SHARK!
WAP WAP
WAP

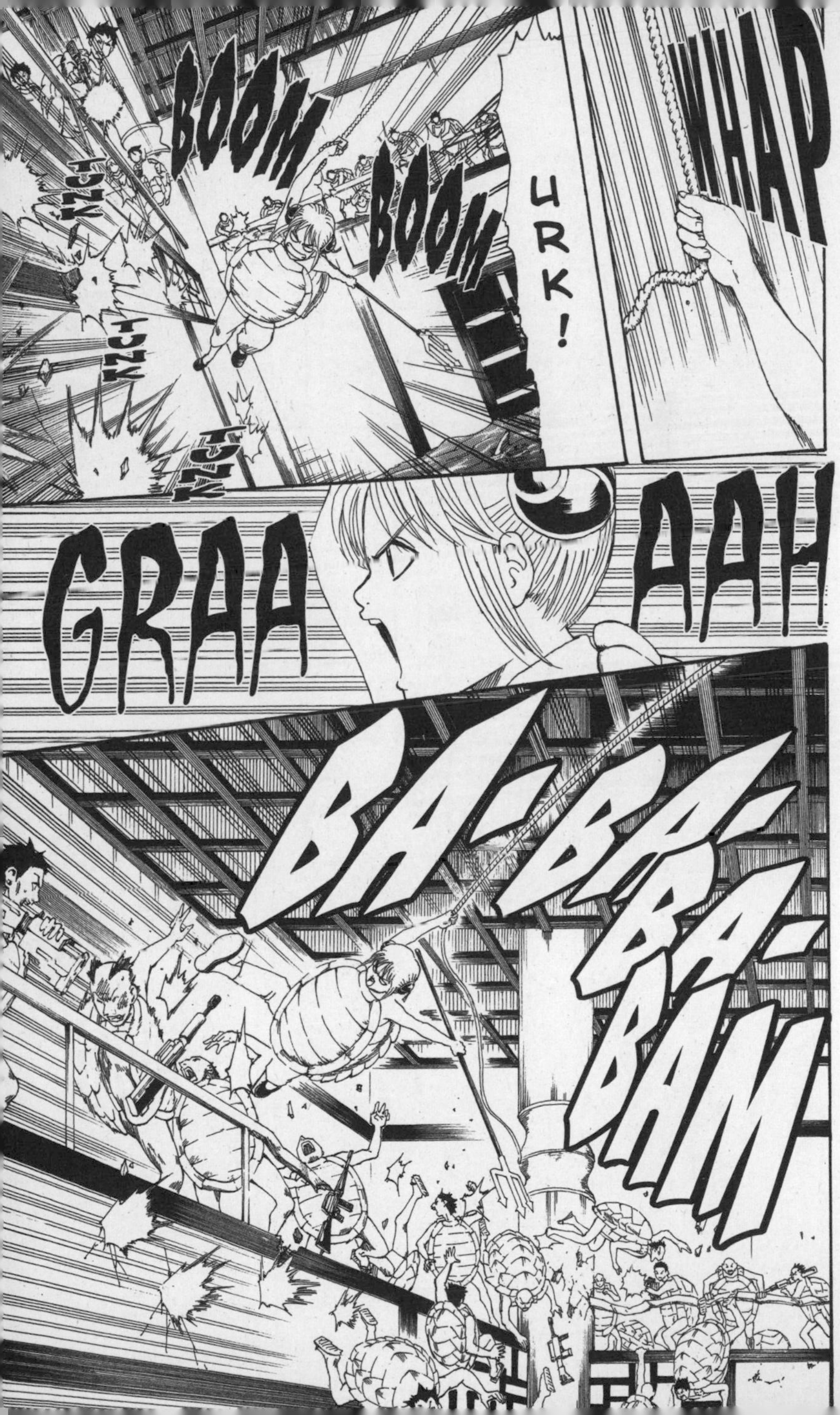
WHAP
URK!
BOOM
BOOM
BOOM
TUNK
TUNK
TUNK
GRAAAAH
BA-BA-BA-BAM

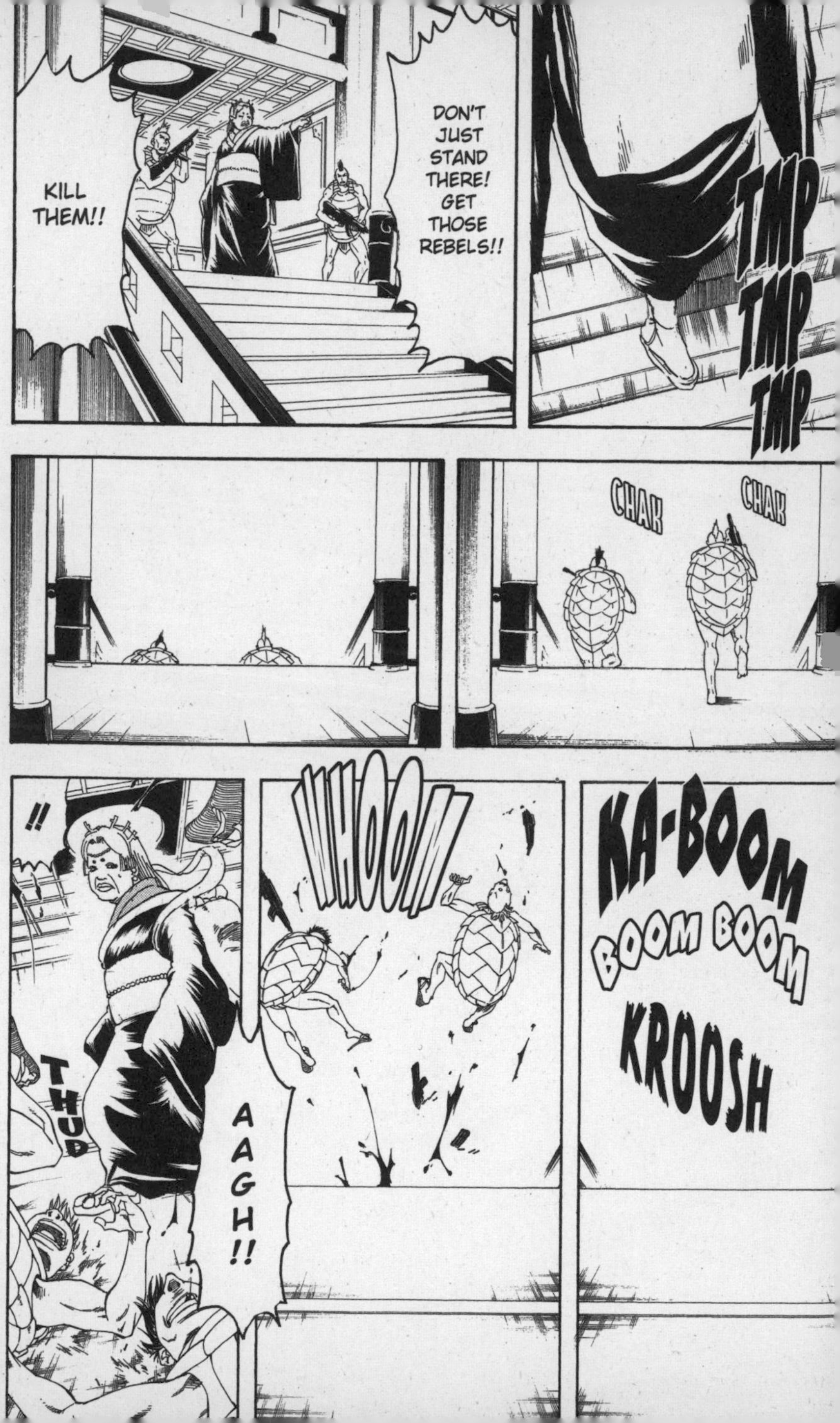
TMP TMP TMP
DON'T JUST STAND THERE! GET THOSE REBELS!!
KILL THEM!!
CHAK
CHAK
KA-BOOM
BOOM BOOM
KROOSH
WHOOM
!!
AAGH!!
THUD

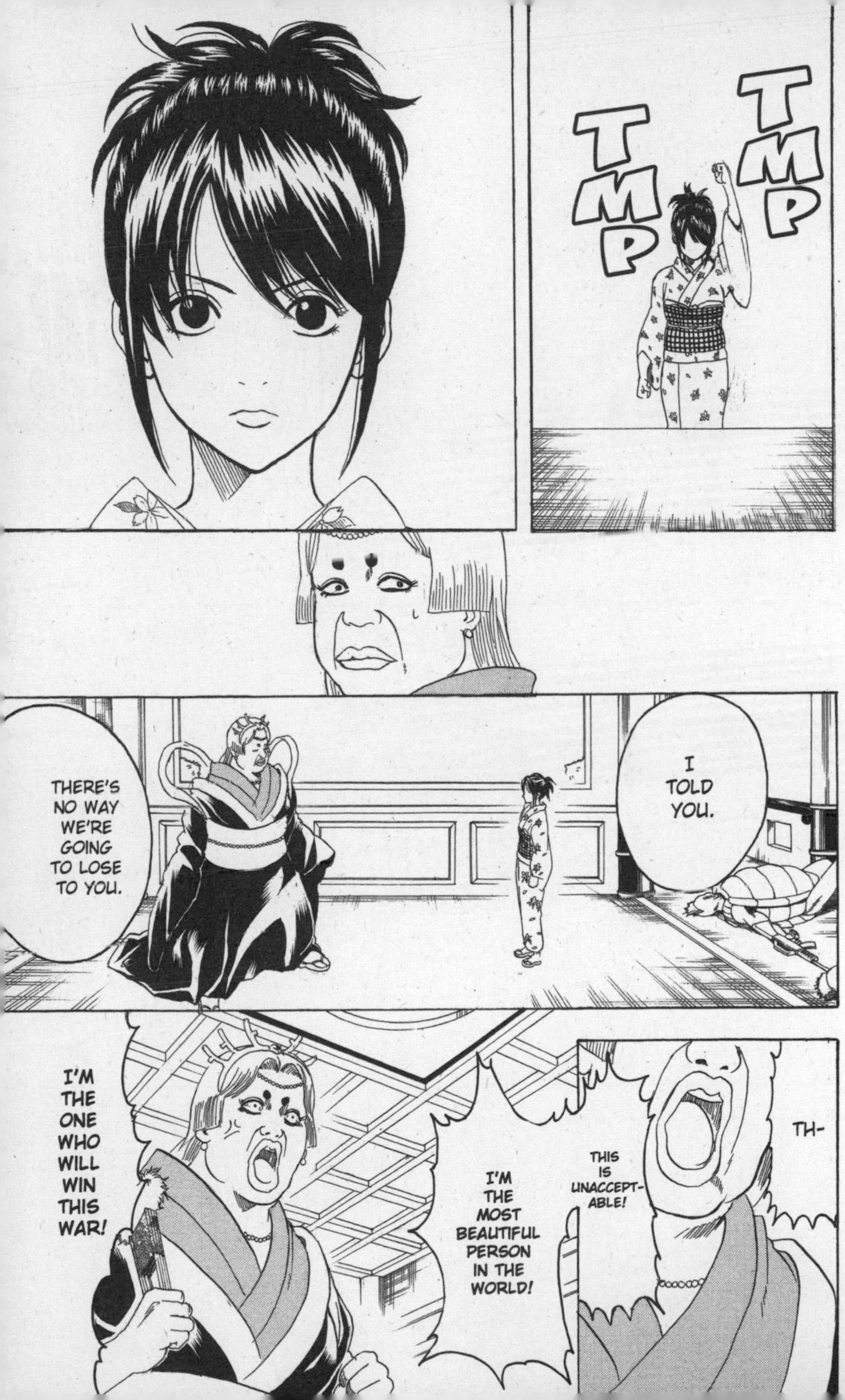
TMP
TMP
I TOLD YOU.
THERE'S NO WAY WE'RE GOING TO LOSE TO YOU.
TH-
THIS IS UNACCEPTABLE!
I'M THE MOST BEAUTIFUL PERSON IN THE WORLD!
I'M THE ONE WHO WILL WIN THIS WAR!

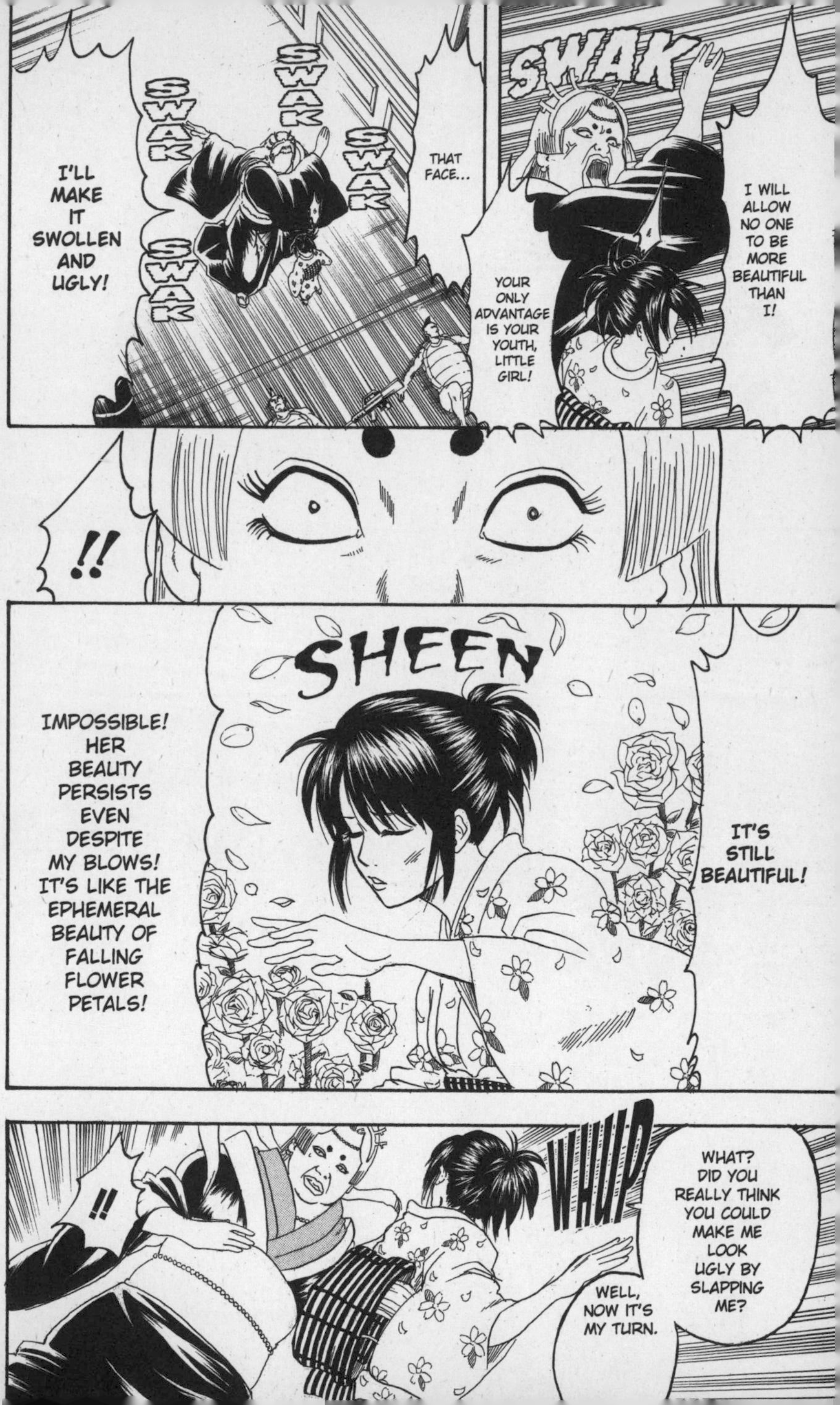
SWAK
I WILL ALLOW NO ONE TO BE MORE BEAUTIFUL THAN I!
YOUR ONLY ADVANTAGE IS YOUR YOUTH, LITTLE GIRL!
THAT FACE...
SWAK
SWAK
SWAK
SWAK
I'LL MAKE IT SWOLLEN AND UGLY!
!!
SHEEN
IT'S STILL BEAUTIFUL!
IMPOSSIBLE! HER BEAUTY PERSISTS EVEN DESPITE MY BLOWS! IT'S LIKE THE EPHEMERAL BEAUTY OF FALLING FLOWER PETALS!
WHAT? DID YOU REALLY THINK YOU COULD MAKE ME LOOK UGLY BY SLAPPING ME?
WHUP
WELL, NOW IT'S MY TURN.
!!

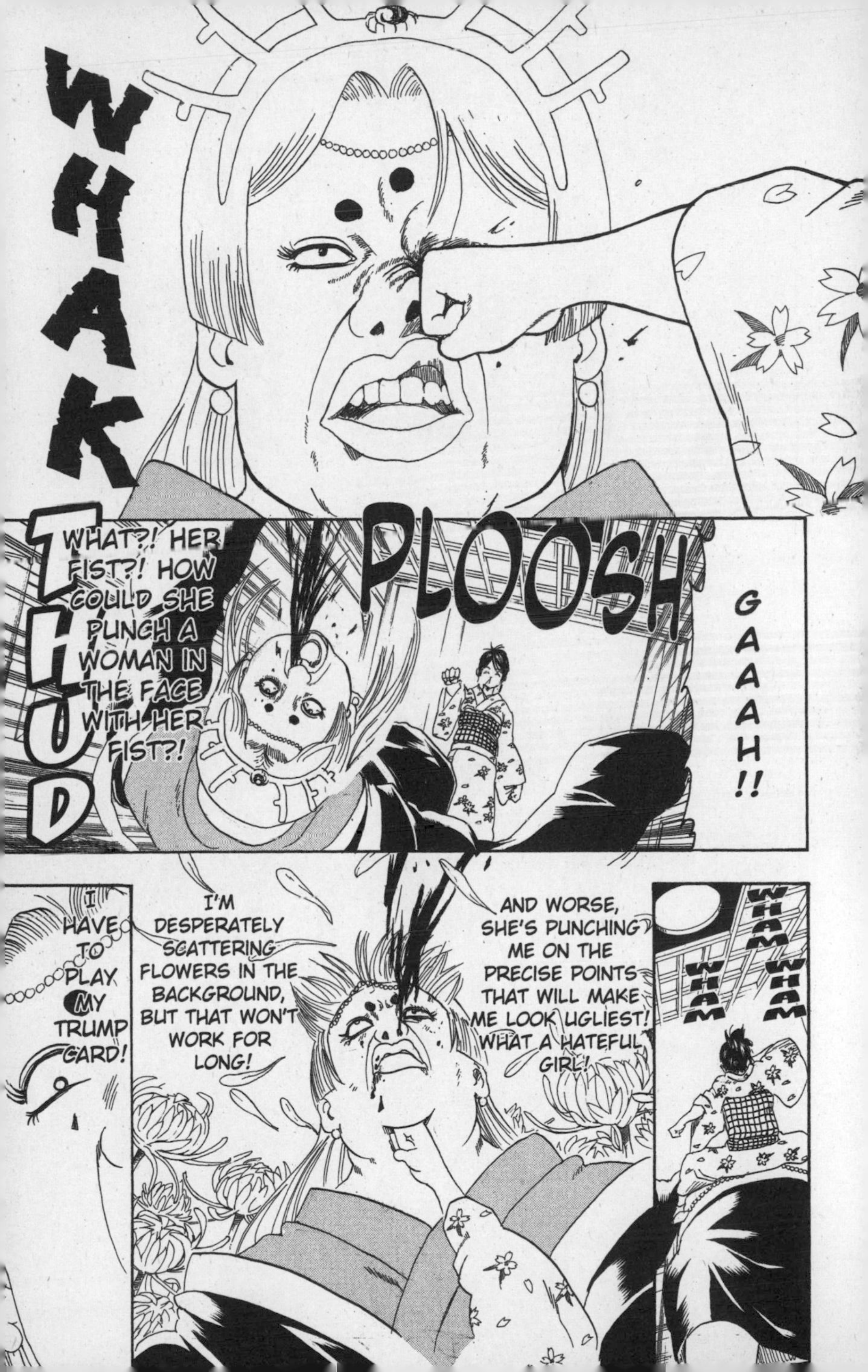
WHAK
GAAAH!!
PLOOSH
WHAT?! HER FIST?! HOW COULD SHE PUNCH A WOMAN IN THE FACE WITH HER FIST?!
THUD
WHAM WHAM
WHAM
AND WORSE, SHE'S PUNCHING ME ON THE PRECISE POINTS THAT WILL MAKE ME LOOK UGLIEST! WHAT A HATEFUL GIRL!
I'M DESPERATELY SCATTERING FLOWERS IN THE BACKGROUND, BUT THAT WON'T WORK FOR LONG!
I HAVE TO PLAY MY TRUMP CARD!

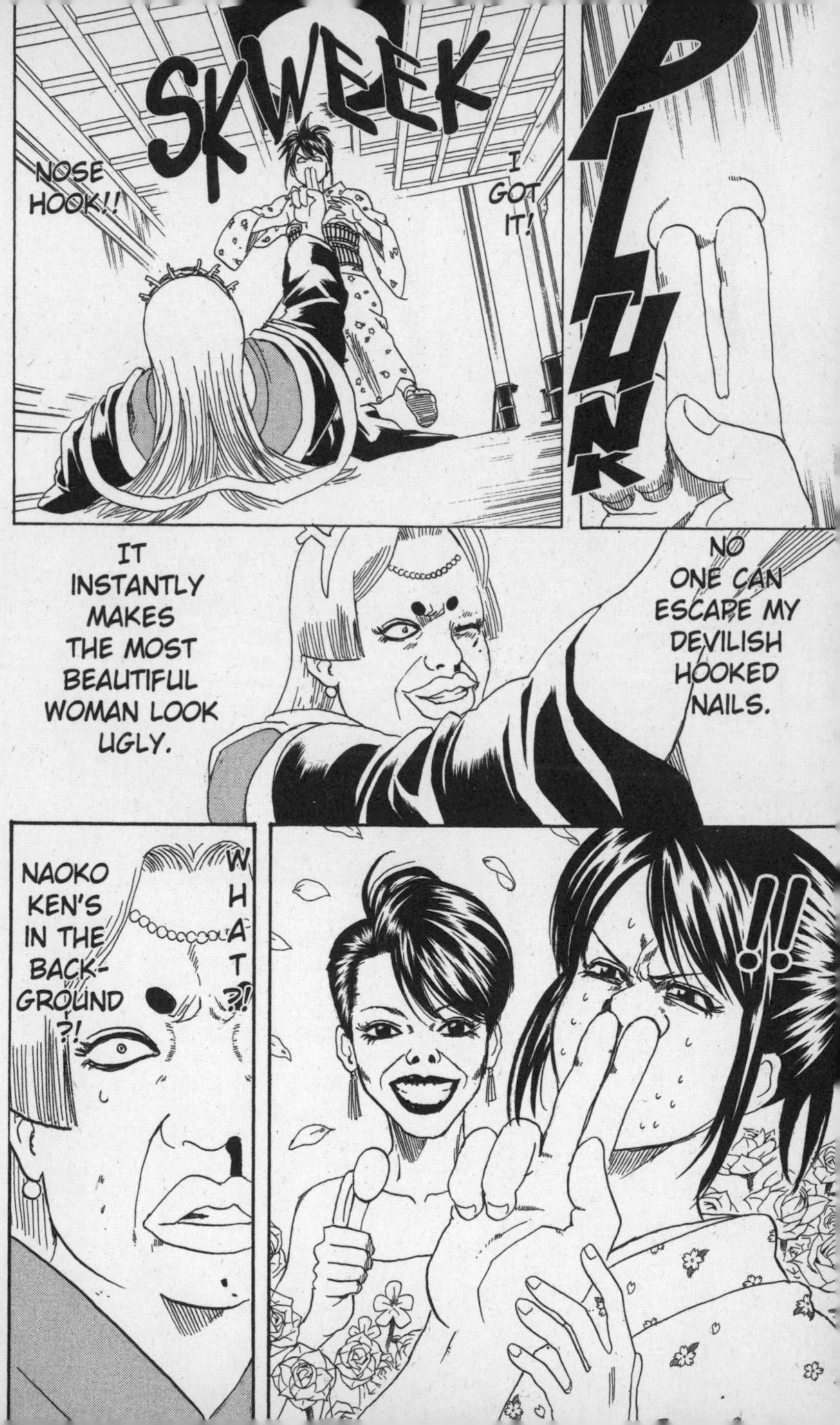
PLLUNK
SKWEEK
I GOT IT!
NOSE HOOK!!
NO ONE CAN ESCAPE MY DEVILISH HOOKED NAILS.
IT INSTANTLY MAKES THE MOST BEAUTIFUL WOMAN LOOK UGLY.
!!
WHAT?!
NAOKO KEN'S IN THE BACK-GROUND?!

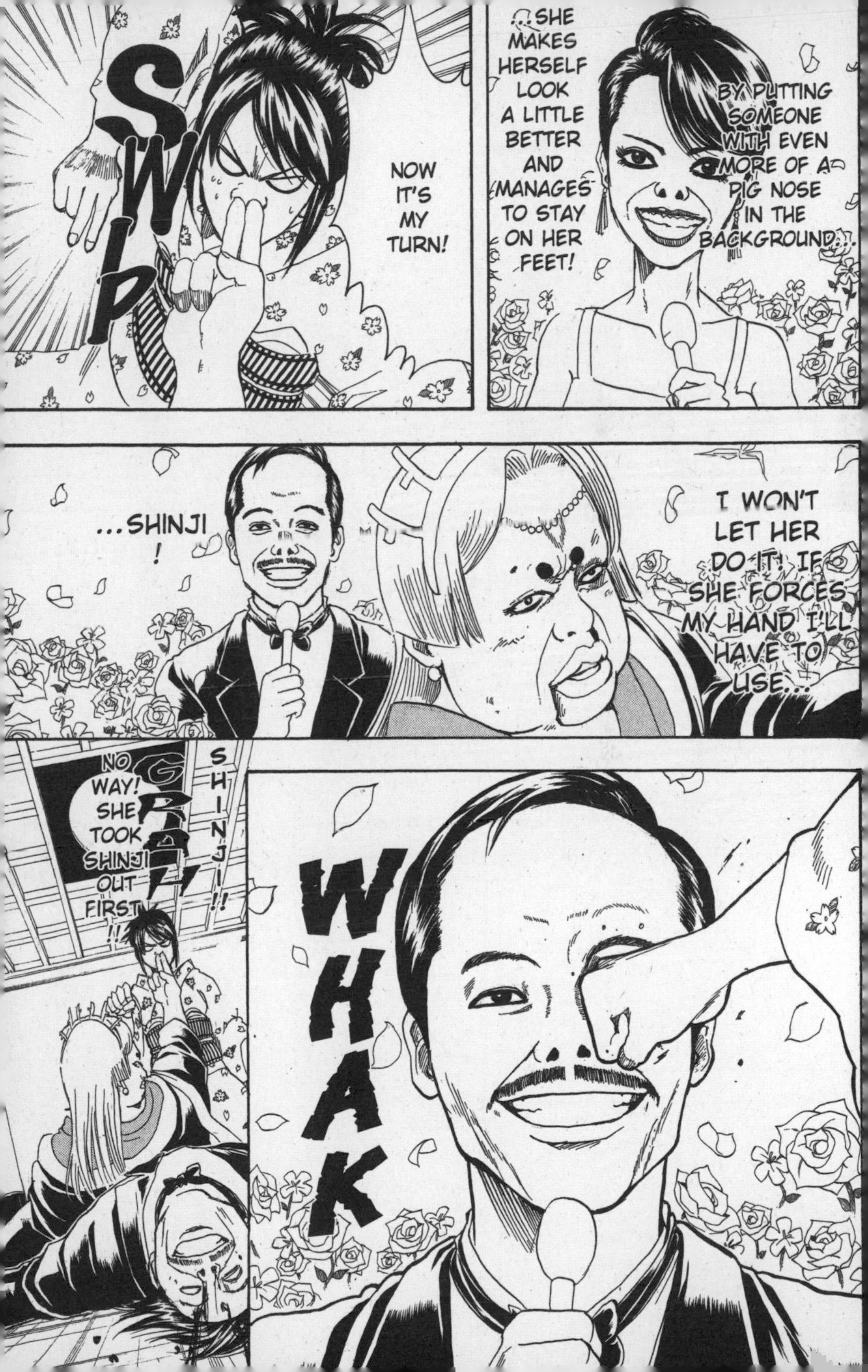
...SHE MAKES HERSELF LOOK A LITTLE BETTER AND MANAGES TO STAY ON HER FEET!
BY PUTTING SOMEONE WITH EVEN MORE OF A PIG NOSE IN THE BACKGROUND...
SWIP
NOW IT'S MY TURN!
I WON'T LET HER DO IT! IF SHE FORCES MY HAND I'LL HAVE TO USE...
...SHINJI!
WHAK
SHINJI!!
GRAH
NO WAY! SHE TOOK SHINJI OUT FIRST!!

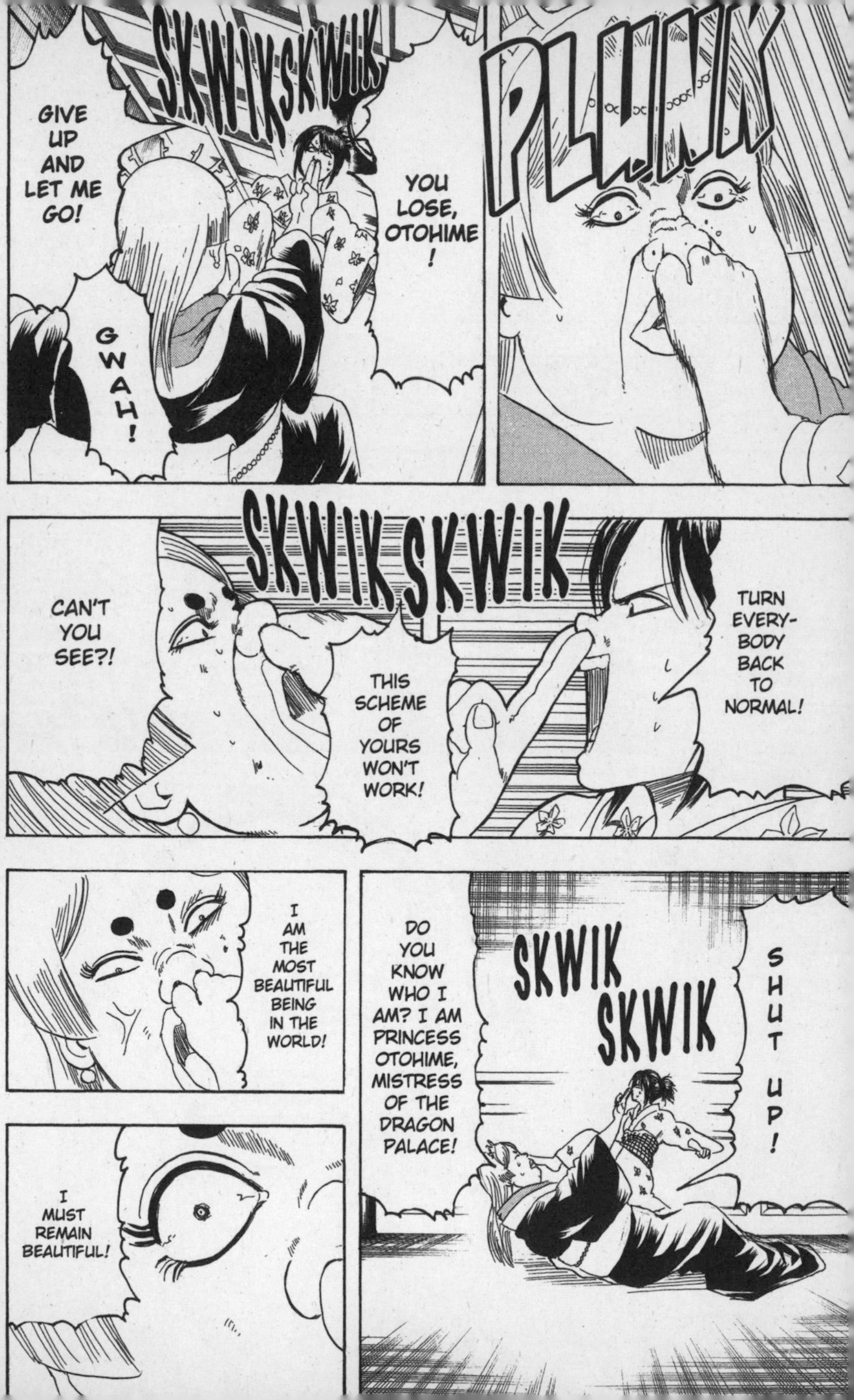
PLUNK
SKWIK SKWIK
YOU LOSE, OTOHIME!
GIVE UP AND LET ME GO!
GWAH!
SKWIK SKWIK
TURN EVERYBODY BACK TO NORMAL!
THIS SCHEME OF YOURS WON'T WORK!
CAN'T YOU SEE?!
SHUT UP!
SKWIK SKWIK
DO YOU KNOW WHO I AM? I AM PRINCESS OTOHIME, MISTRESS OF THE DRAGON PALACE!
I AM THE MOST BEAUTIFUL BEING IN THE WORLD!
I MUST REMAIN BEAUTIFUL!

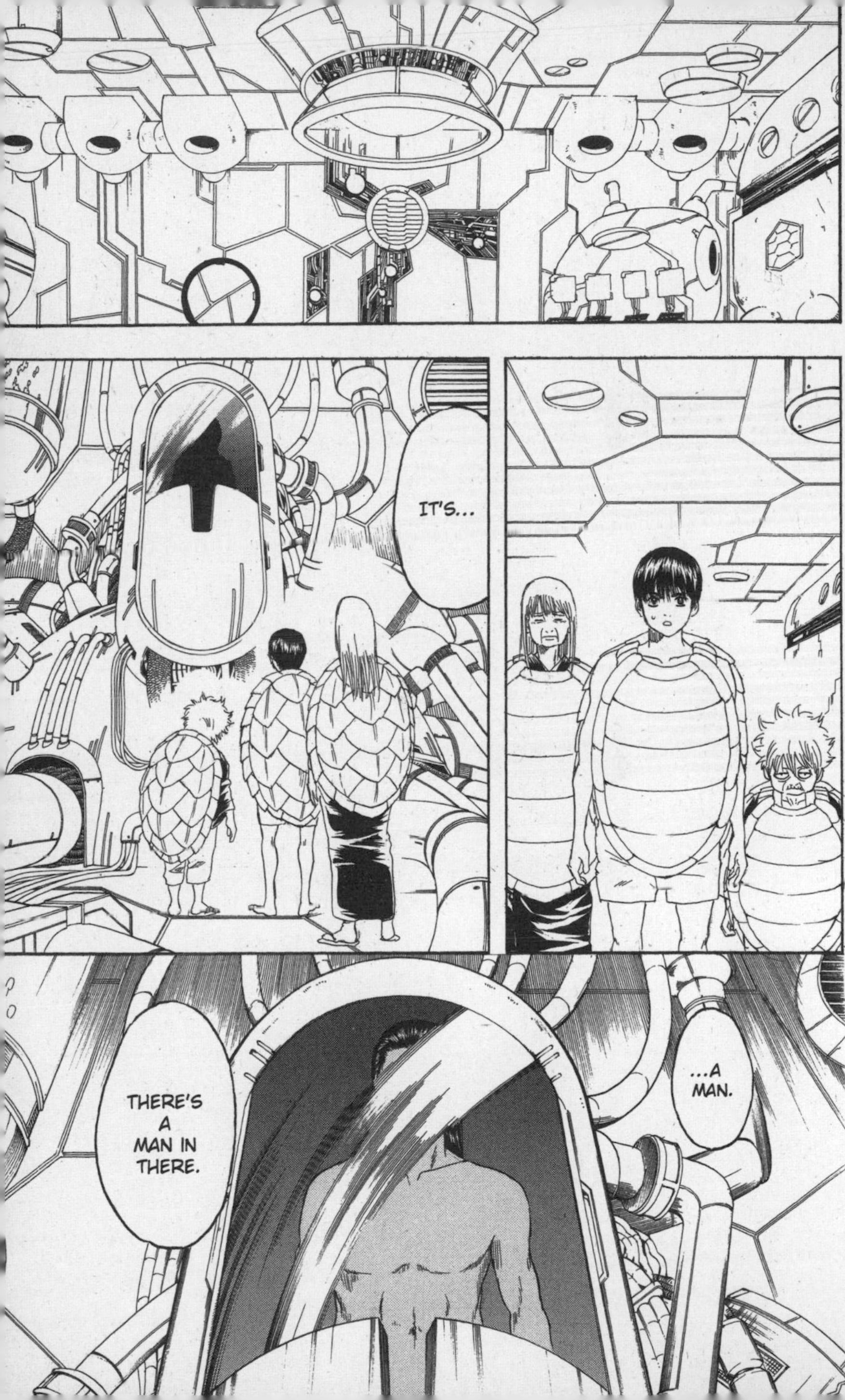
IT'S...
...A MAN.
THERE'S A MAN IN THERE.

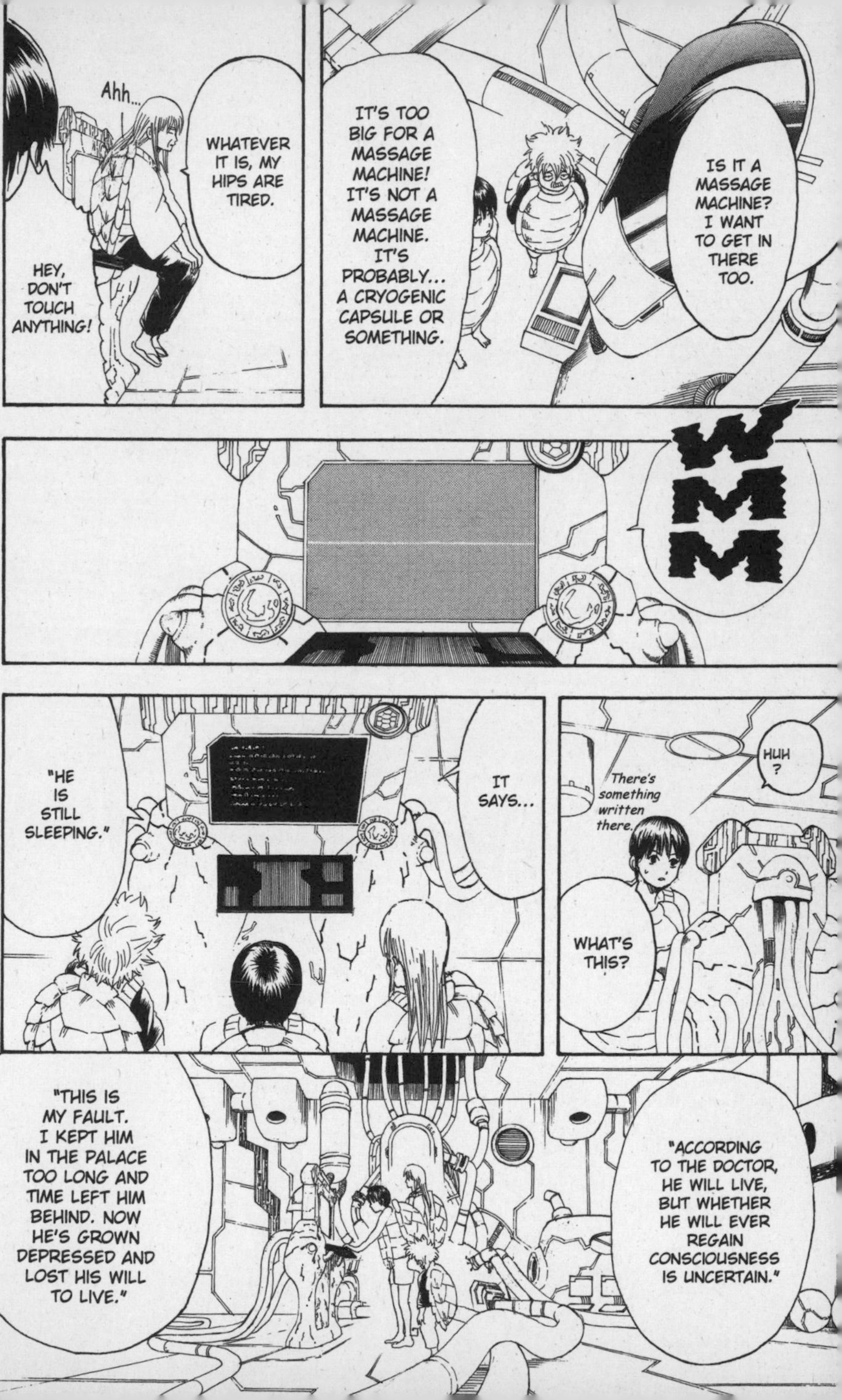
IS IT A MASSAGE MACHINE? I WANT TO GET IN THERE TOO.
IT'S TOO BIG FOR A MASSAGE MACHINE! IT'S NOT A MASSAGE MACHINE. IT'S PROBABLY... A CRYOGENIC CAPSULE OR SOMETHING.
WHATEVER IT IS, MY HIPS ARE TIRED.
Ahh...
HEY, DON'T TOUCH ANYTHING!
WMM
HUH?
There's something written there.
WHAT'S THIS?
IT SAYS...
"HE IS STILL SLEEPING."
"ACCORDING TO THE DOCTOR, HE WILL LIVE, BUT WHETHER HE WILL EVER REGAIN CONSCIOUSNESS IS UNCERTAIN."
"THIS IS MY FAULT. I KEPT HIM IN THE PALACE TOO LONG AND TIME LEFT HIM BEHIND. NOW HE'S GROWN DEPRESSED AND LOST HIS WILL TO LIVE."

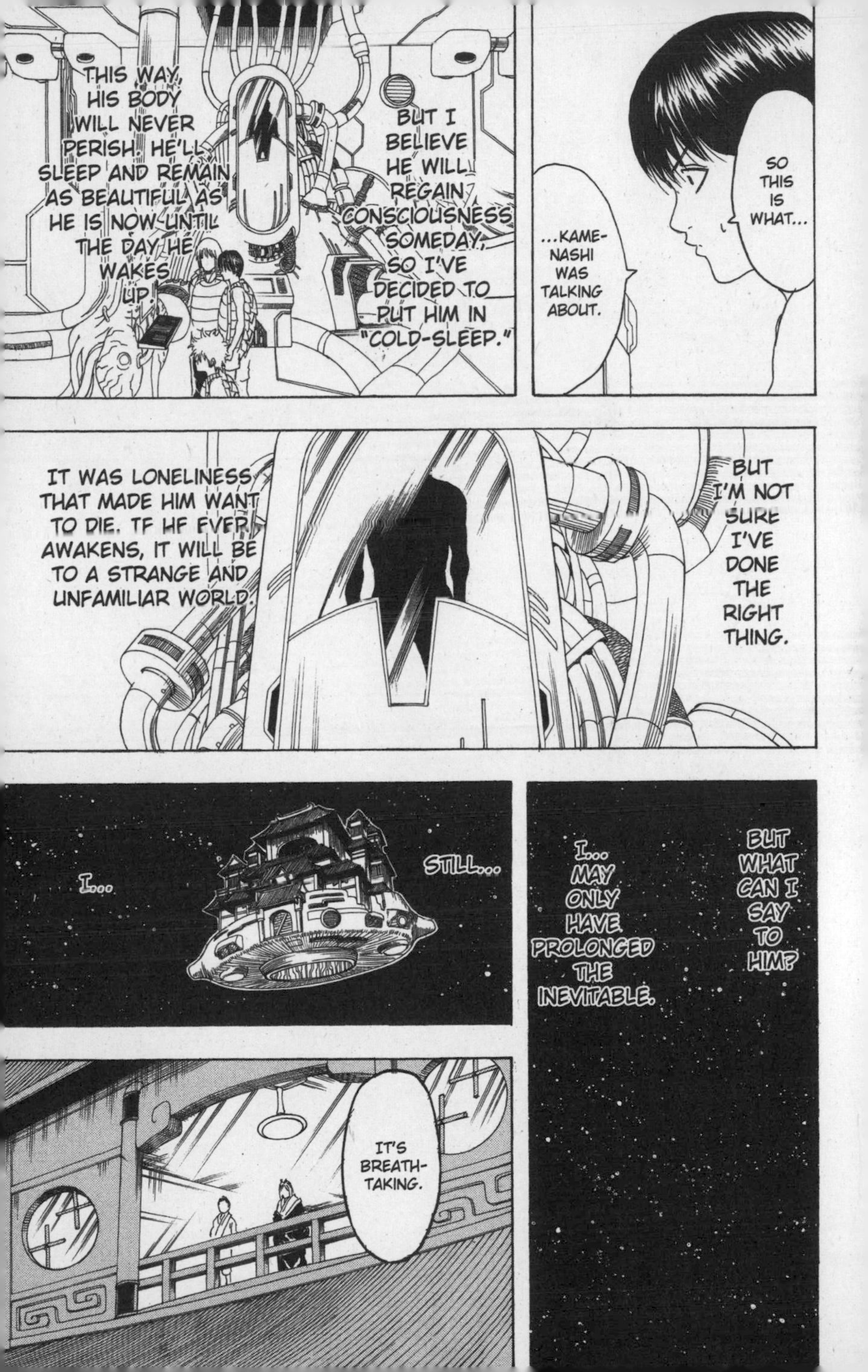
SO THIS IS WHAT...
...KAME-NASHI WAS TALKING ABOUT.
BUT I BELIEVE HE WILL REGAIN CONSCIOUSNESS SOMEDAY, SO I'VE DECIDED TO PUT HIM IN "COLD-SLEEP."
THIS WAY, HIS BODY WILL NEVER PERISH. HE'LL SLEEP AND REMAIN AS BEAUTIFUL AS HE IS NOW UNTIL THE DAY HE WAKES UP.
BUT I'M NOT SURE I'VE DONE THE RIGHT THING.
IT WAS LONELINESS THAT MADE HIM WANT TO DIE. IF HE EVER AWAKENS, IT WILL BE TO A STRANGE AND UNFAMILIAR WORLD.
BUT WHAT CAN I SAY TO HIM?
I... MAY ONLY HAVE PROLONGED THE INEVITABLE.
STILL...
I...
IT'S BREATH-TAKING.

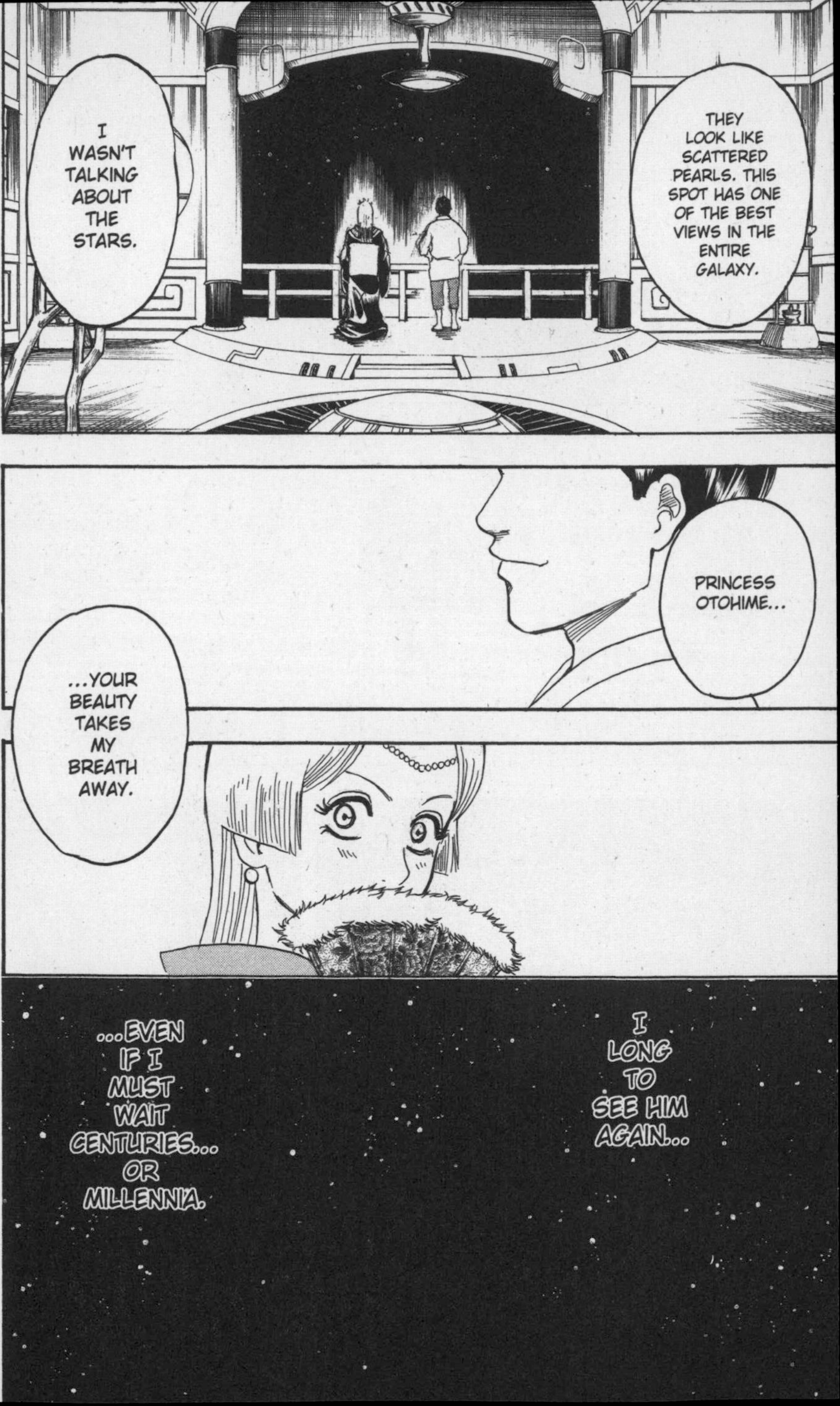
THEY LOOK LIKE SCATTERED PEARLS. THIS SPOT HAS ONE OF THE BEST VIEWS IN THE ENTIRE GALAXY.
I WASN'T TALKING ABOUT THE STARS.
PRINCESS OTOHIME...
...YOUR BEAUTY TAKES MY BREATH AWAY.
I LONG TO SEE HIM AGAIN...
...EVEN IF I MUST WAIT CENTURIES... OR MILLENNIA.

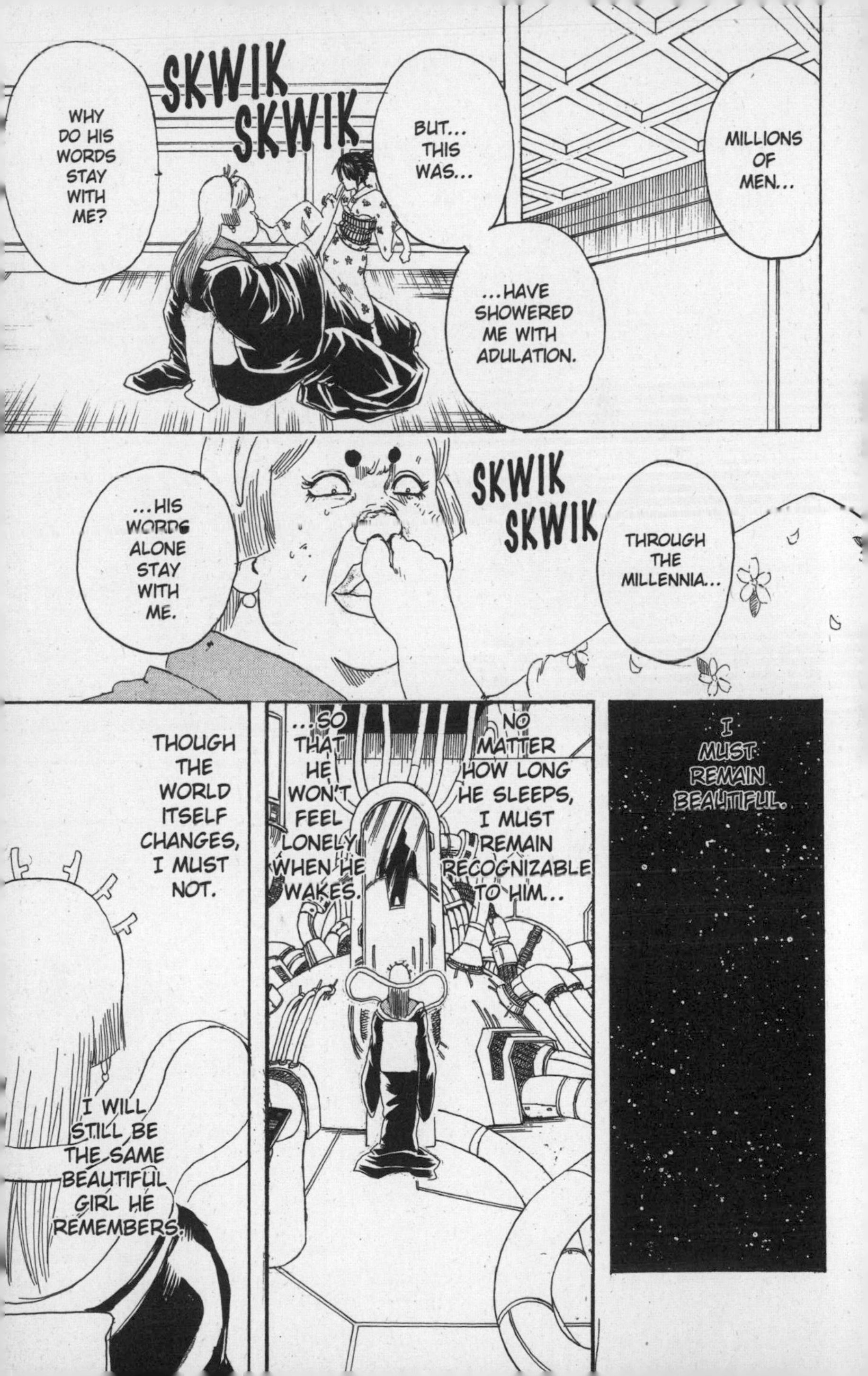
MILLIONS OF MEN...
...HAVE SHOWERED ME WITH ADULATION.
BUT... THIS WAS...
SKWIK SKWIK
WHY DO HIS WORDS STAY WITH ME?
THROUGH THE MILLENNIA...
SKWIK SKWIK
...HIS WORDS ALONE STAY WITH ME.
I MUST REMAIN BEAUTIFUL.
NO MATTER HOW LONG HE SLEEPS, I MUST REMAIN RECOGNIZABLE TO HIM...
...SO THAT HE WON'T FEEL LONELY WHEN HE WAKES.
THOUGH THE WORLD ITSELF CHANGES, I MUST NOT.
I WILL STILL BE THE SAME BEAUTIFUL GIRL HE REMEMBERS.

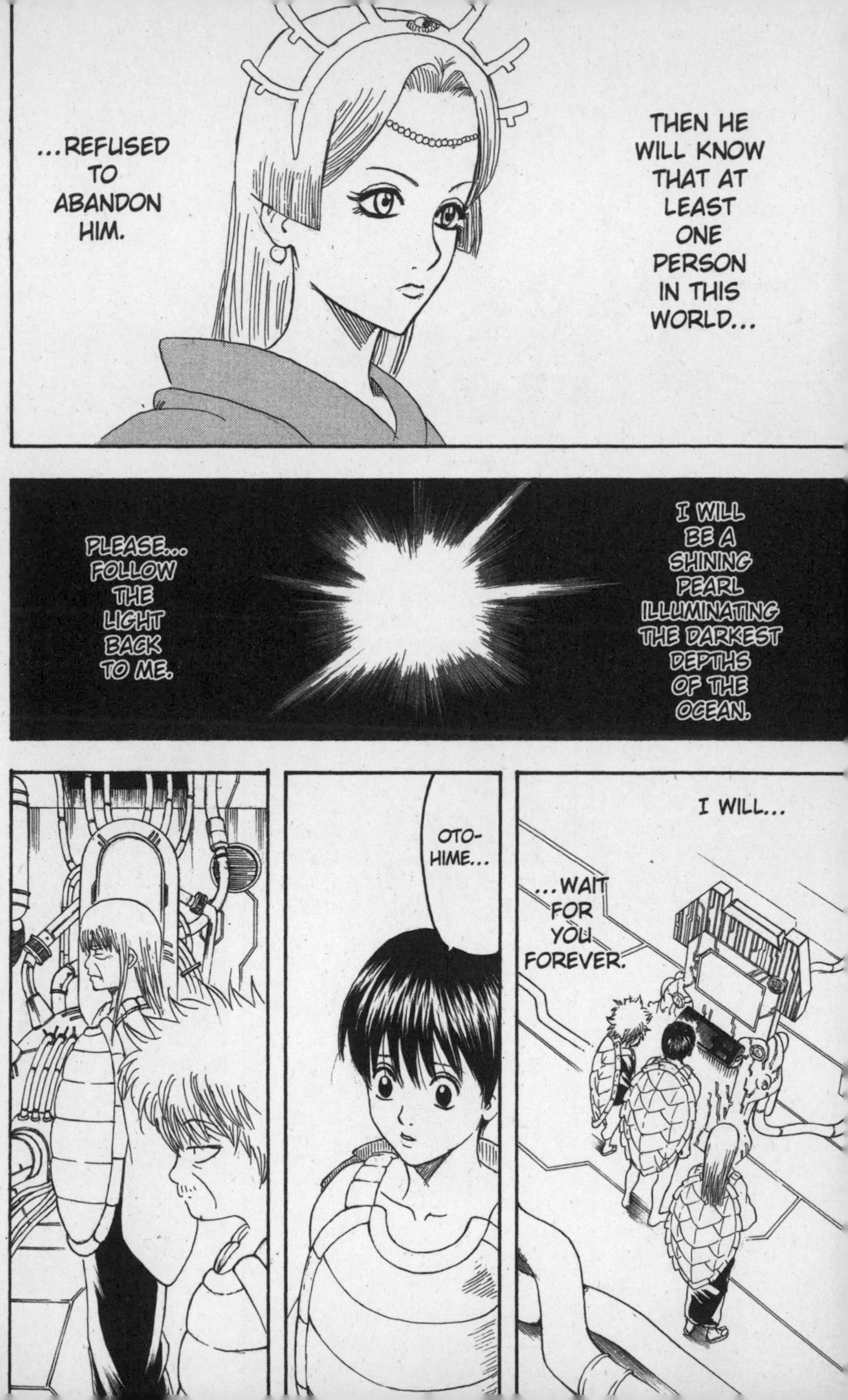
THEN HE WILL KNOW THAT AT LEAST ONE PERSON IN THIS WORLD...
...REFUSED TO ABANDON HIM.
I WILL BE A SHINING PEARL ILLUMINATING THE DARKEST DEPTHS OF THE OCEAN.
PLEASE... FOLLOW THE LIGHT BACK TO ME.
I WILL...
...WAIT FOR YOU FOREVER.
OTO-HIME...

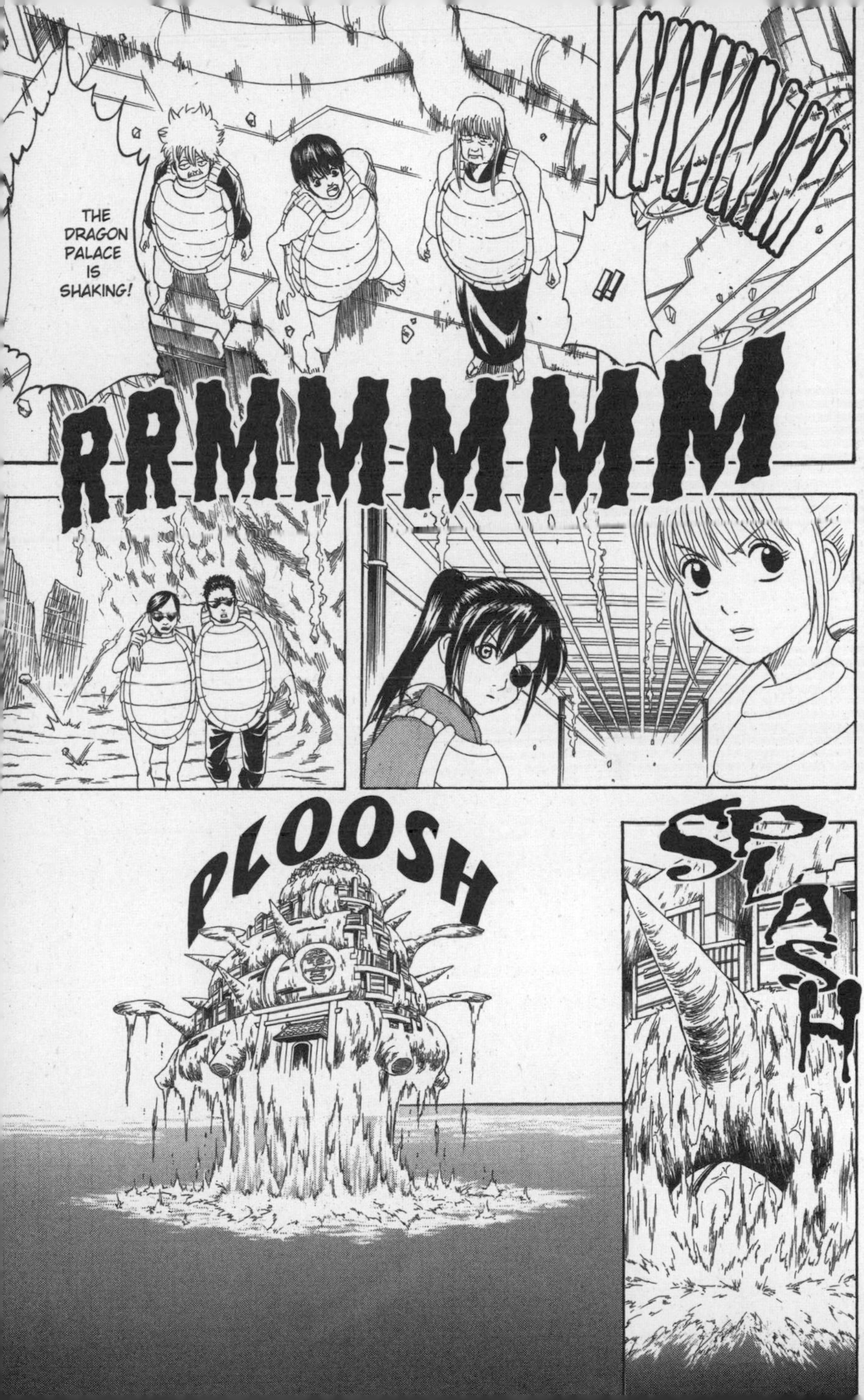
!!
THE DRAGON PALACE IS SHAKING!
RRMMMMM
SPLASH
PLOOSH

That's how I felt, so it's understandable that Mr. Oonishi was scared, but it was really terrible. It's the last job of the outgoing editor to smooth the transition for the new editor, but instead we let work slide and the second half of the meeting turned into a big pep talk for Mr. Oonishi. Mr. Saito's first job for *Gin Tama* was to encourage Mr. Oonishi. Let me be clear, Oda Sensei is a very nice person. He has a big heart, just like Luffy. But his aura is overwhelming. We worms wriggle before its fiery radiance. There's nothing wrong with Oda Sensei, but Mr. Oonishi is a mess. I couldn't help thinking that the editorial department had lost its mind. But Mr. Oonishi is leaving *Gin Tama*, so I can finally say—and I think anyone who's worked with Mr. Oonishi will verify this—that he plays with his dinger during meetings. Well, not in every meeting, but he sometimes unzips his fly, puts his hand down his pants, and fumbles around while he's talking. Whenever I ask him what he's doing, he says, "My belly itches." But he's obviously touching himself. He was doing it in the middle of a *Gin Tama* meeting! If he does that in front of Oda Sensei, he'll get worse than a Gum-Gum Punch. Another guy might be able to talk his way out of it by claiming he was just putting the car in second gear, but Mr. Oonishi isn't that quick-witted. He'll tear off his gearshift.

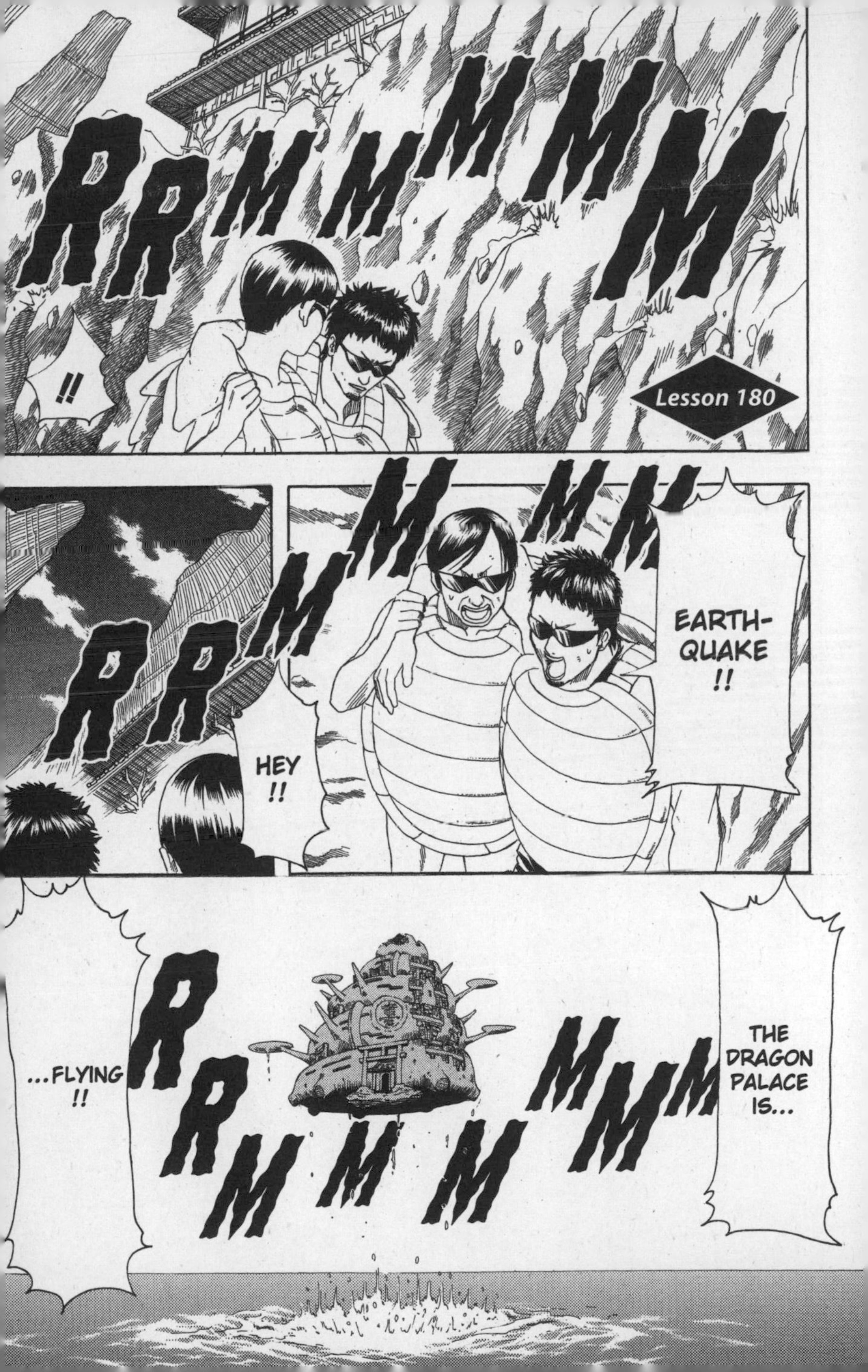
Lesson 180
RRMMMMMMM
!!
EARTH-QUAKE !!
RRMMMMMM
HEY !!
THE DRAGON PALACE IS...
RRMMMMMMM
...FLYING !!

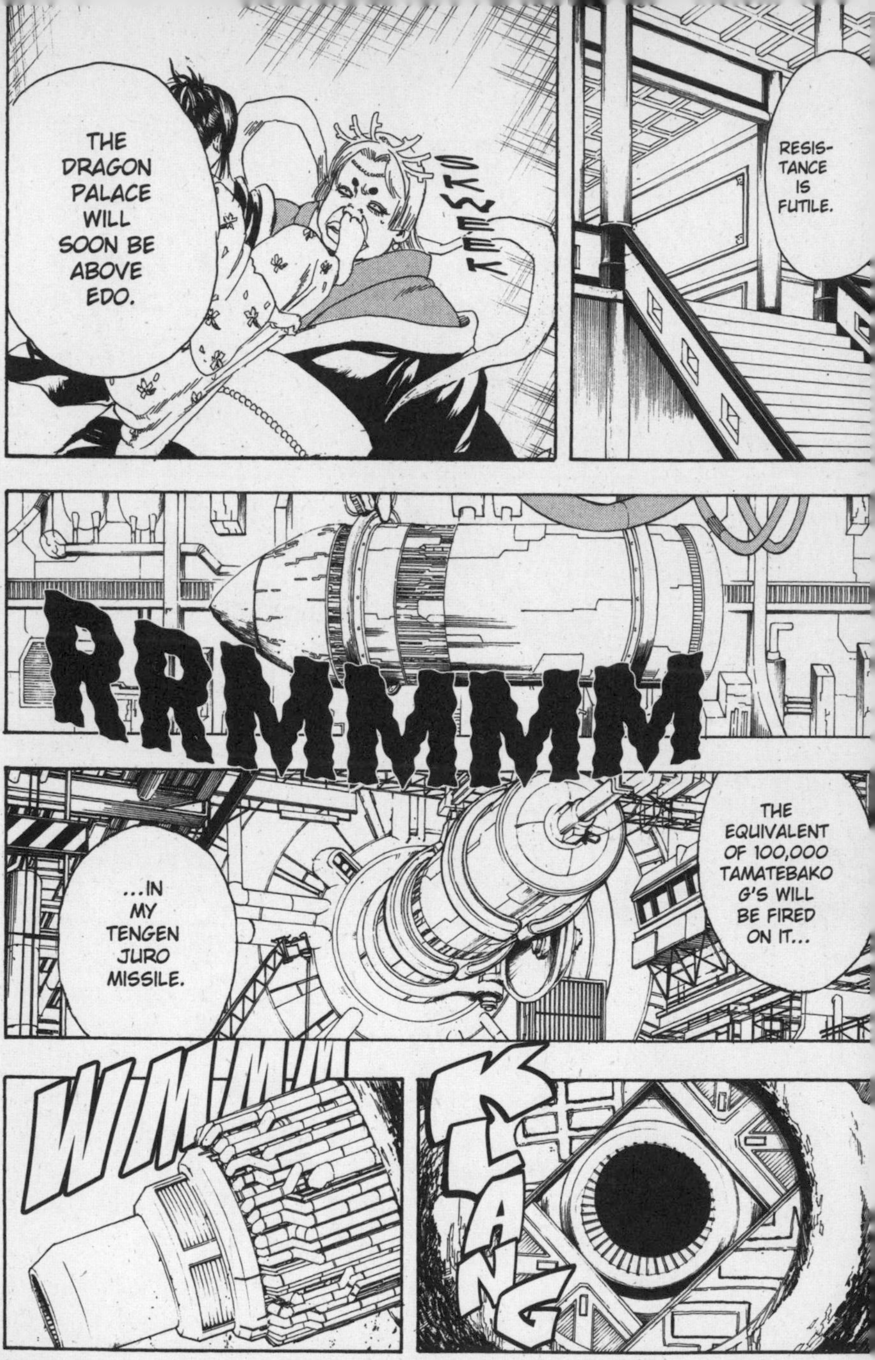
RESIS-TANCE IS FUTILE.
THE DRAGON PALACE WILL SOON BE ABOVE EDO.
SKWEEK
RRMMMM
THE EQUIVALENT OF 100,000 TAMATEBAKO G'S WILL BE FIRED ON IT...
...IN MY TENGEN JURO MISSILE.
KLANG
WMMM

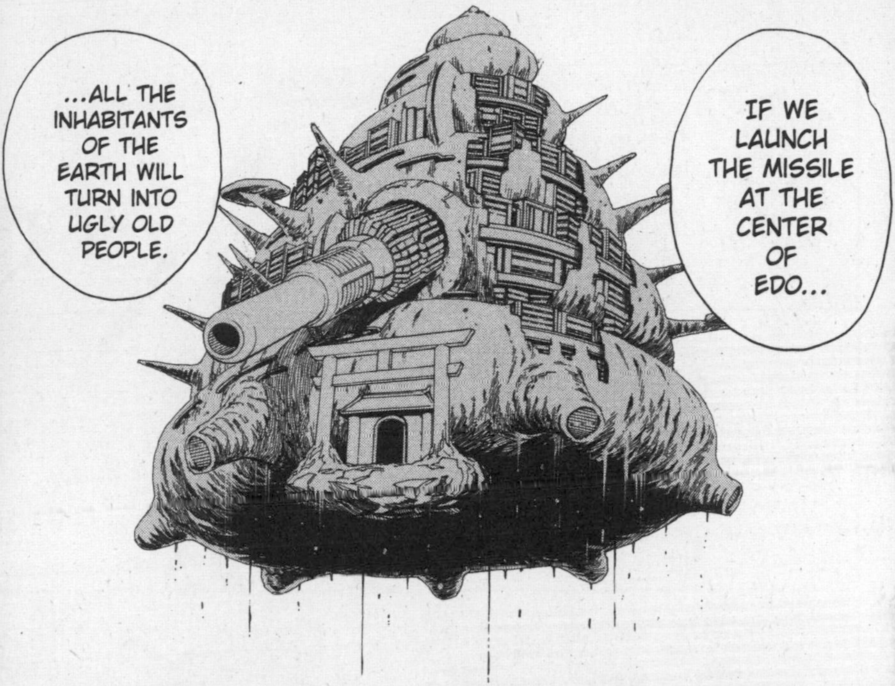
IF WE LAUNCH THE MISSILE AT THE CENTER OF EDO...
...ALL THE INHABITANTS OF THE EARTH WILL TURN INTO UGLY OLD PEOPLE.

Lesson 180 Go Straight Even If You're Bent With Age

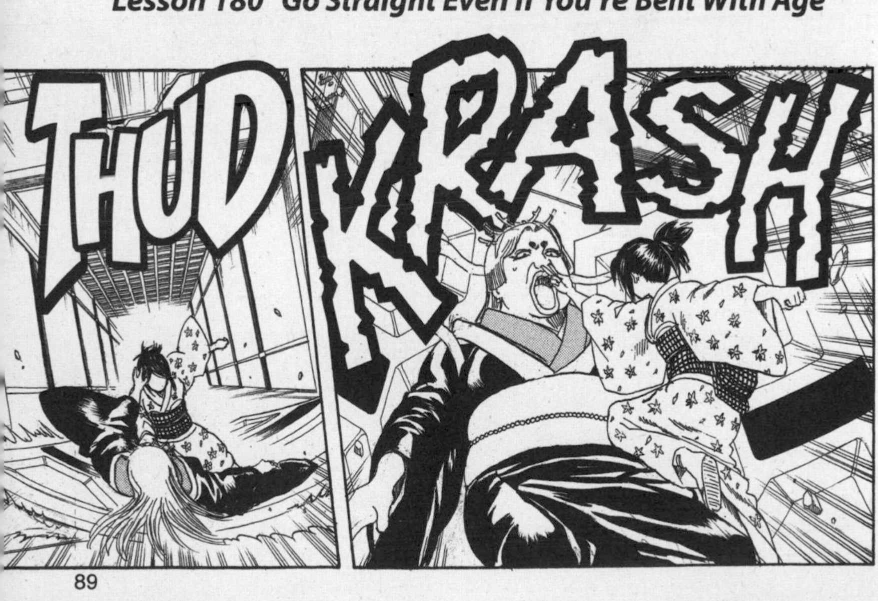
KRASH
THUD

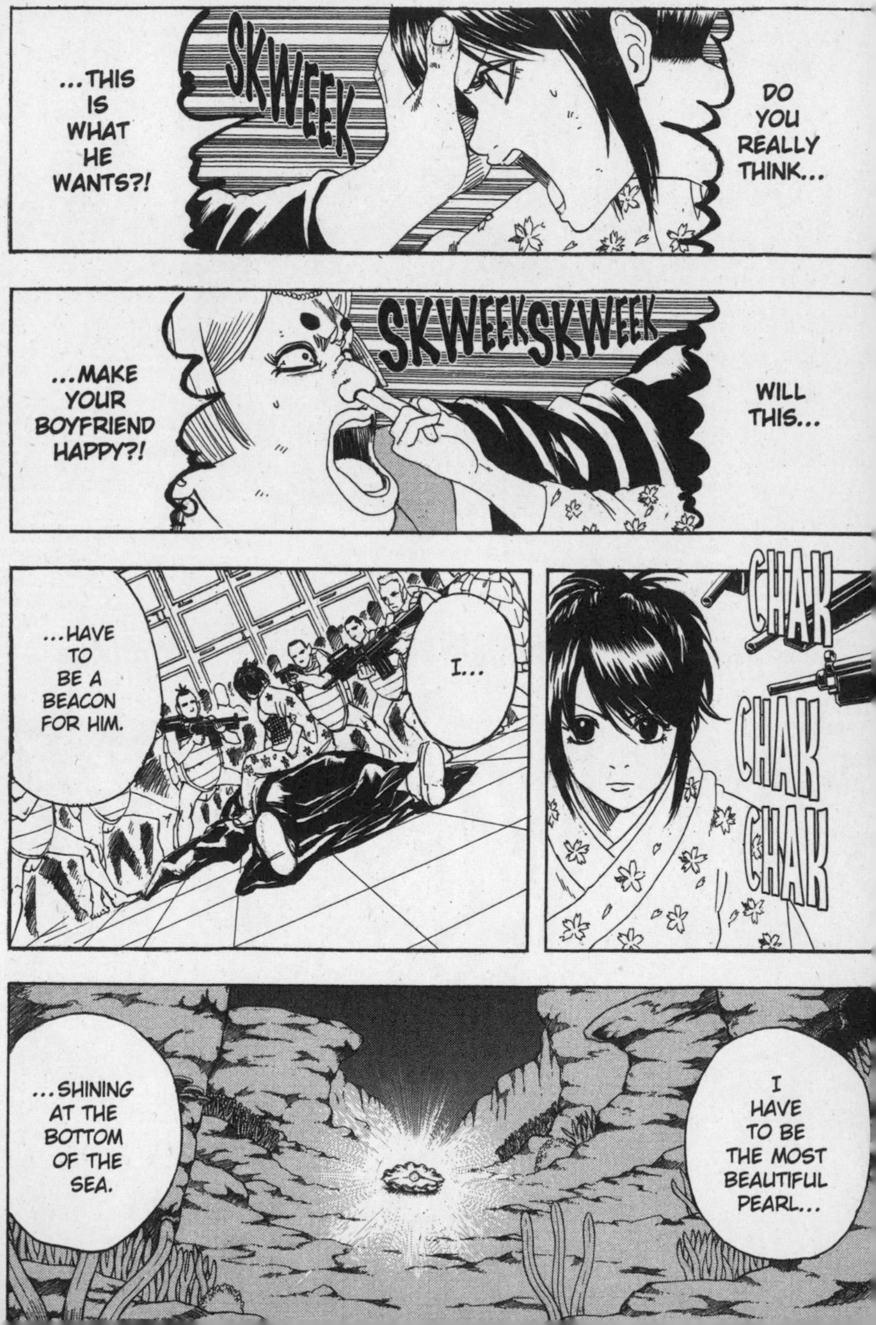
DO YOU REALLY THINK...
SKWEEK
...THIS IS WHAT HE WANTS?!
WILL THIS...
SKWEEKSKWEEK
...MAKE YOUR BOYFRIEND HAPPY?!
CHAK
CHAK
CHAK
I...
...HAVE TO BE A BEACON FOR HIM.
I HAVE TO BE THE MOST BEAUTIFUL PEARL...
...SHINING AT THE BOTTOM OF THE SEA.

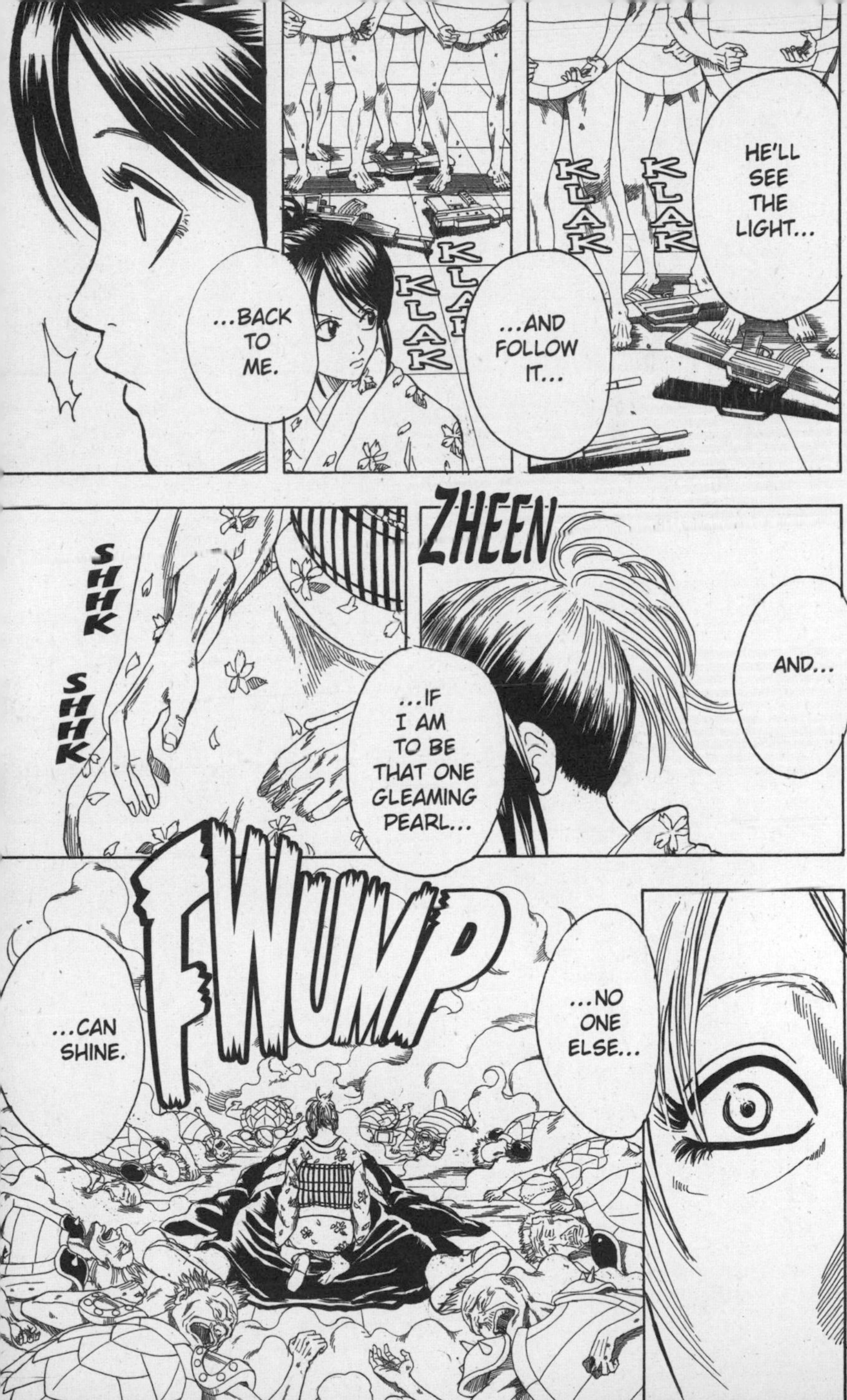
HE'LL SEE THE LIGHT...
KLAK KLAK
...AND FOLLOW IT...
KLAK KLAK
...BACK TO ME.
ZHEEN
AND...
...IF I AM TO BE THAT ONE GLEAMING PEARL...
SHHK SHHK
...NO ONE ELSE...
FWUMP
...CAN SHINE.

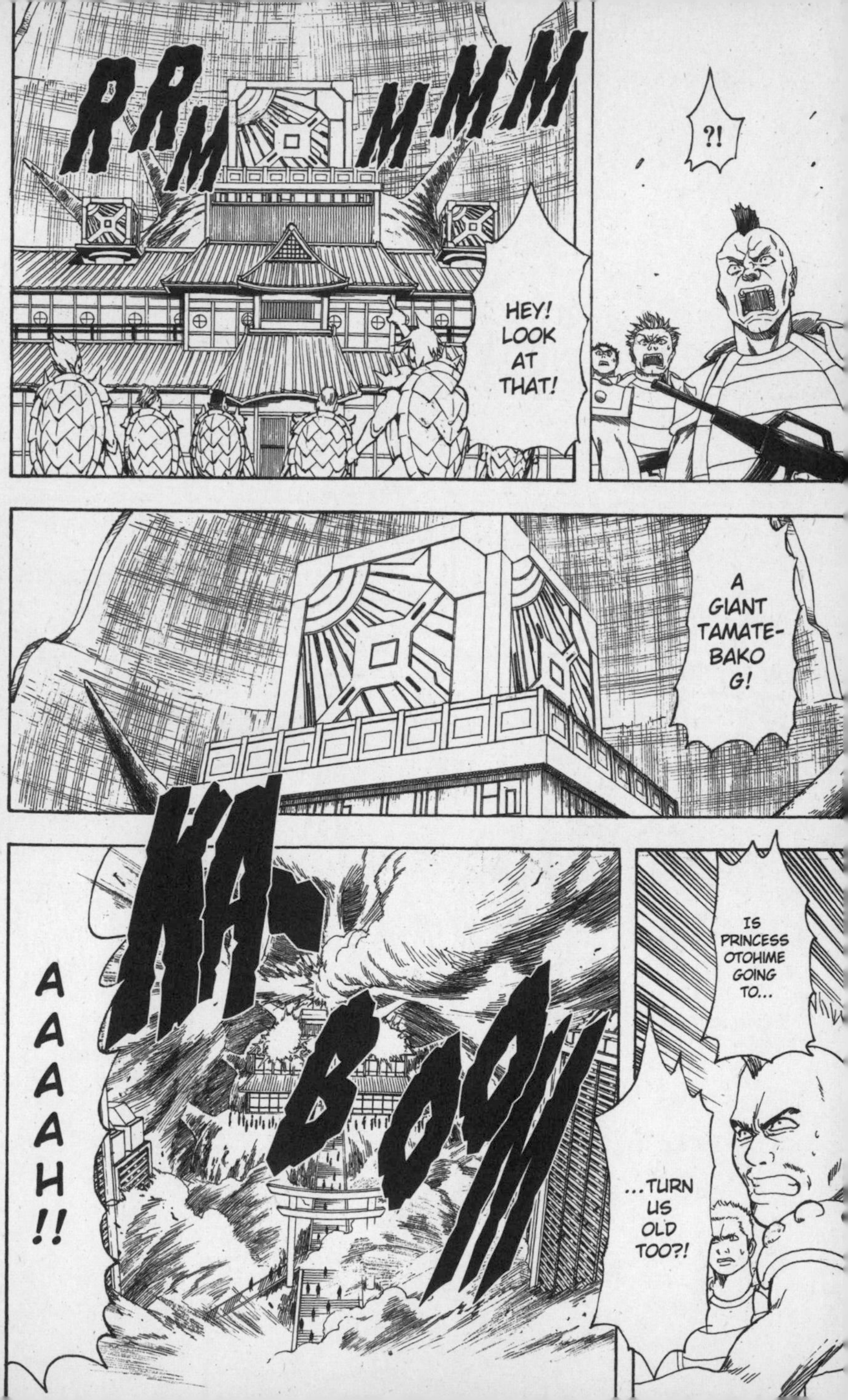
?!
RRMMMM
HEY! LOOK AT THAT!
A GIANT TAMATE-BAKO G!
IS PRINCESS OTOHIME GOING TO...
...TURN US OLD TOO?!
KA-BOOM
AAAAAH!!

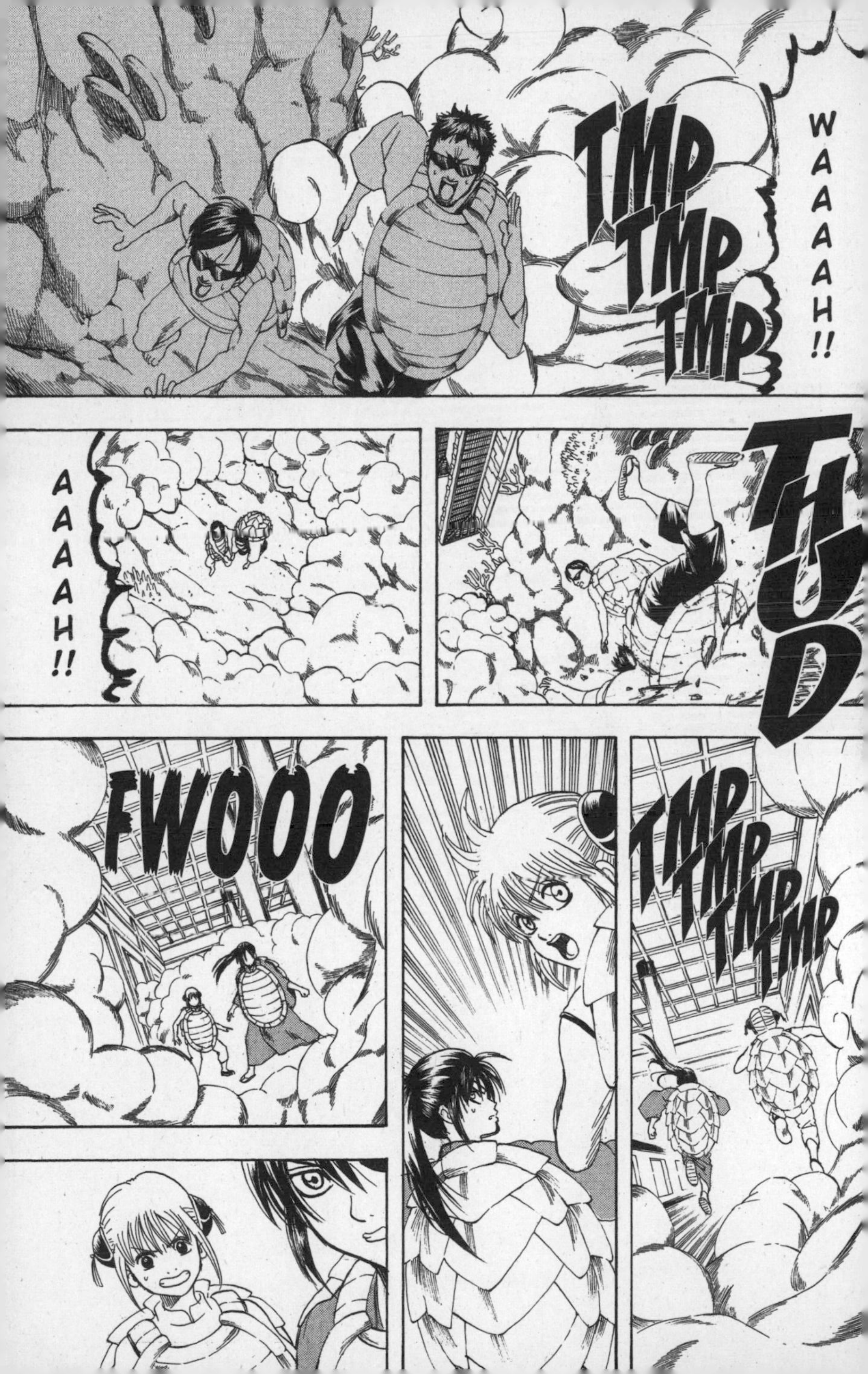
WAAAAAH!!
TMP TMP TMP TMP
THUD
AAAAAH!!
TMP TMP TMP TMP
FWOOO

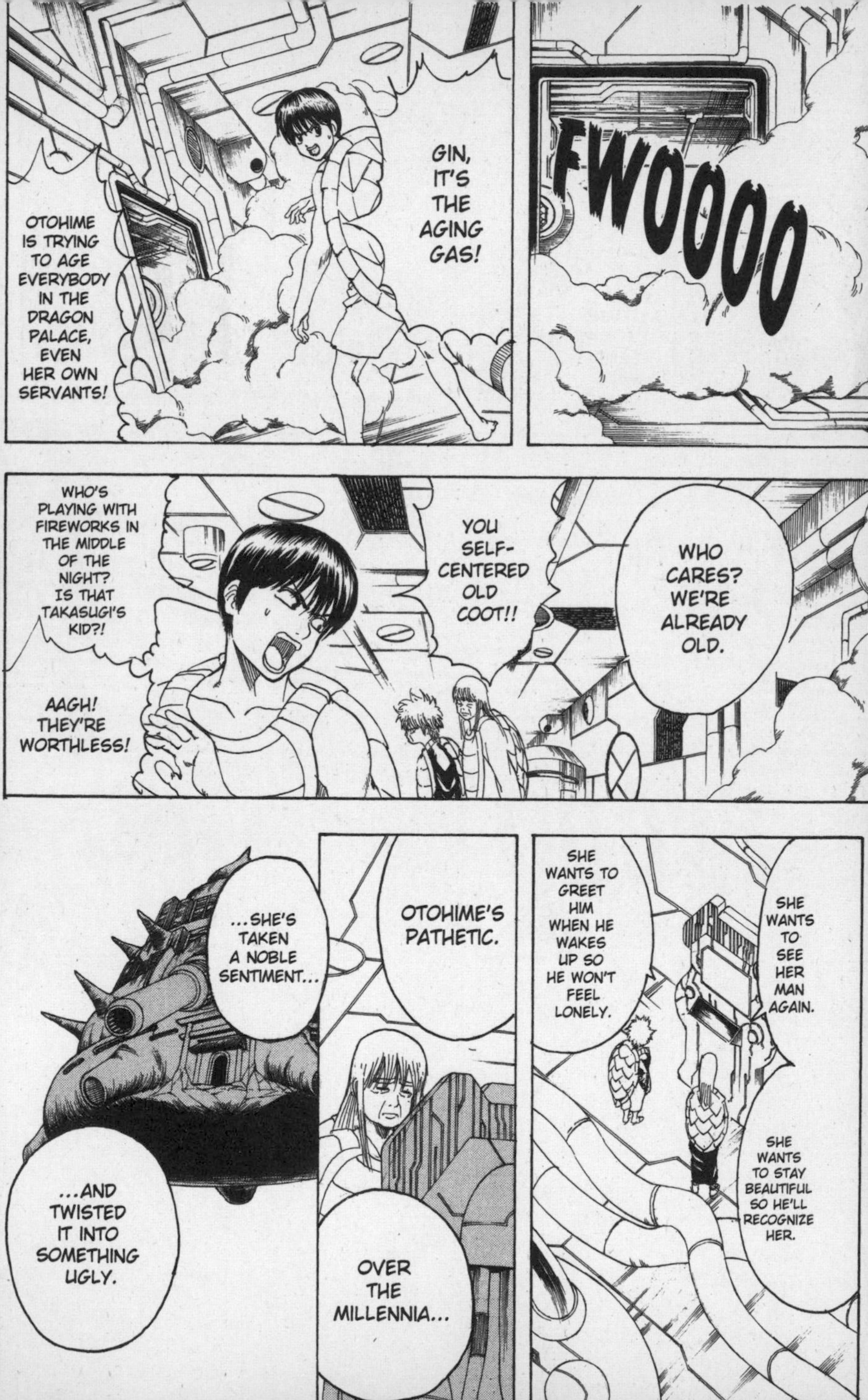
FWOOOO
GIN, IT'S THE AGING GAS!
OTOHIME IS TRYING TO AGE EVERYBODY IN THE DRAGON PALACE, EVEN HER OWN SERVANTS!
WHO CARES? WE'RE ALREADY OLD.
YOU SELF-CENTERED OLD COOT!!
WHO'S PLAYING WITH FIREWORKS IN THE MIDDLE OF THE NIGHT? IS THAT TAKASUGI'S KID?!
AAGH! THEY'RE WORTHLESS!
SHE WANTS TO SEE HER MAN AGAIN.
SHE WANTS TO GREET HIM WHEN HE WAKES UP SO HE WON'T FEEL LONELY.
SHE WANTS TO STAY BEAUTIFUL SO HE'LL RECOGNIZE HER.
OTOHIME'S PATHETIC.
OVER THE MILLENNIA...
...SHE'S TAKEN A NOBLE SENTIMENT...
...AND TWISTED IT INTO SOMETHING UGLY.

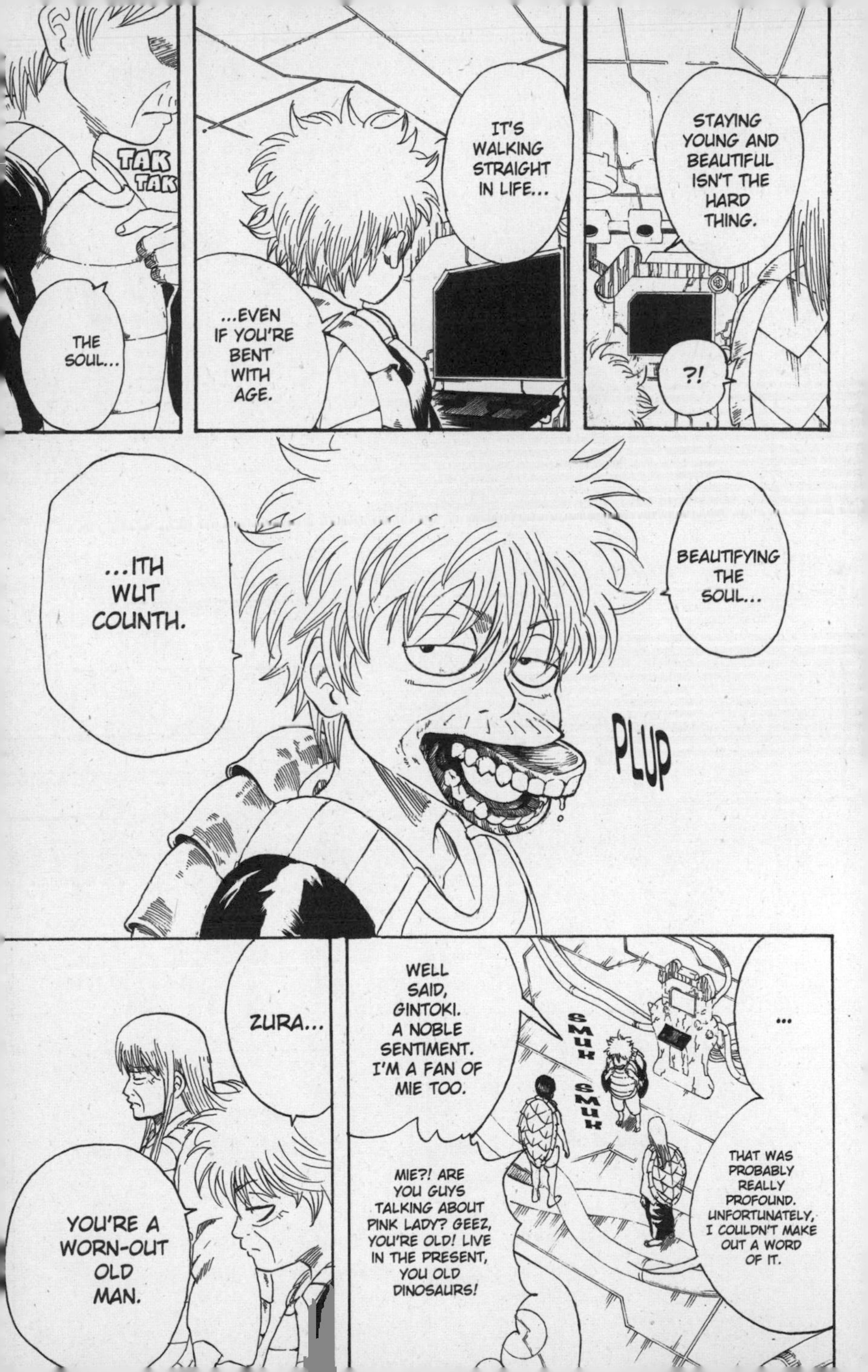
STAYING YOUNG AND BEAUTIFUL ISN'T THE HARD THING.
?!
IT'S WALKING STRAIGHT IN LIFE...
...EVEN IF YOU'RE BENT WITH AGE.
TAK TAK
THE SOUL...
BEAUTIFYING THE SOUL...
PLUP
...ITH WUT COUNTH.
...
WELL SAID, GINTOKI. A NOBLE SENTIMENT. I'M A FAN OF MIE TOO.
SMUK SMUK
THAT WAS PROBABLY REALLY PROFOUND. UNFORTUNATELY, I COULDN'T MAKE OUT A WORD OF IT.
MIE?! ARE YOU GUYS TALKING ABOUT PINK LADY? GEEZ, YOU'RE OLD! LIVE IN THE PRESENT, YOU OLD DINOSAURS!
ZURA...
YOU'RE A WORN-OUT OLD MAN.

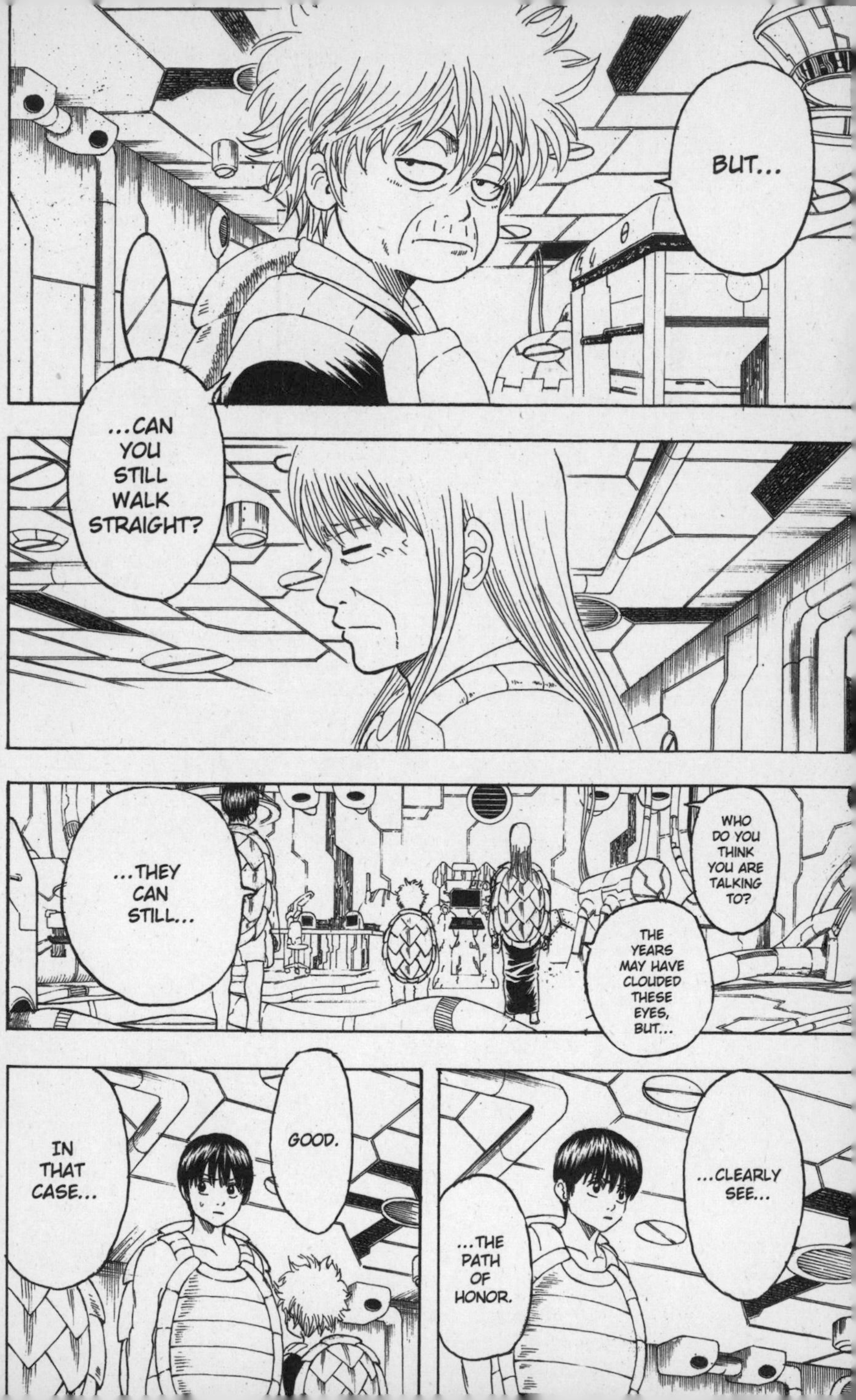
BUT...
...CAN YOU STILL WALK STRAIGHT?
WHO DO YOU THINK YOU ARE TALKING TO?
THE YEARS MAY HAVE CLOUDED THESE EYES, BUT...
...THEY CAN STILL...
...CLEARLY SEE...
...THE PATH OF HONOR.
GOOD.
IN THAT CASE...

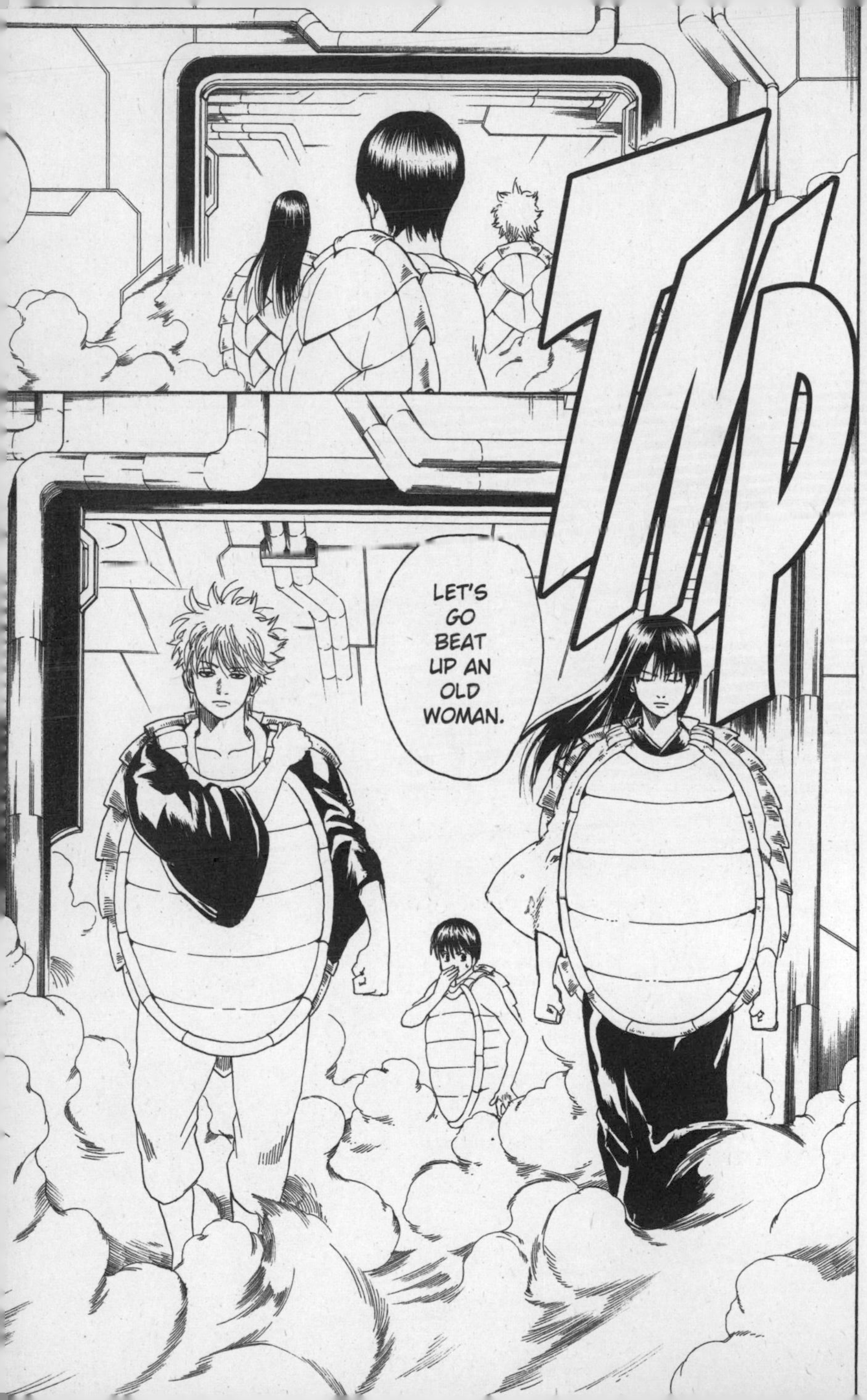
TMP
LET'S GO BEAT UP AN OLD WOMAN.

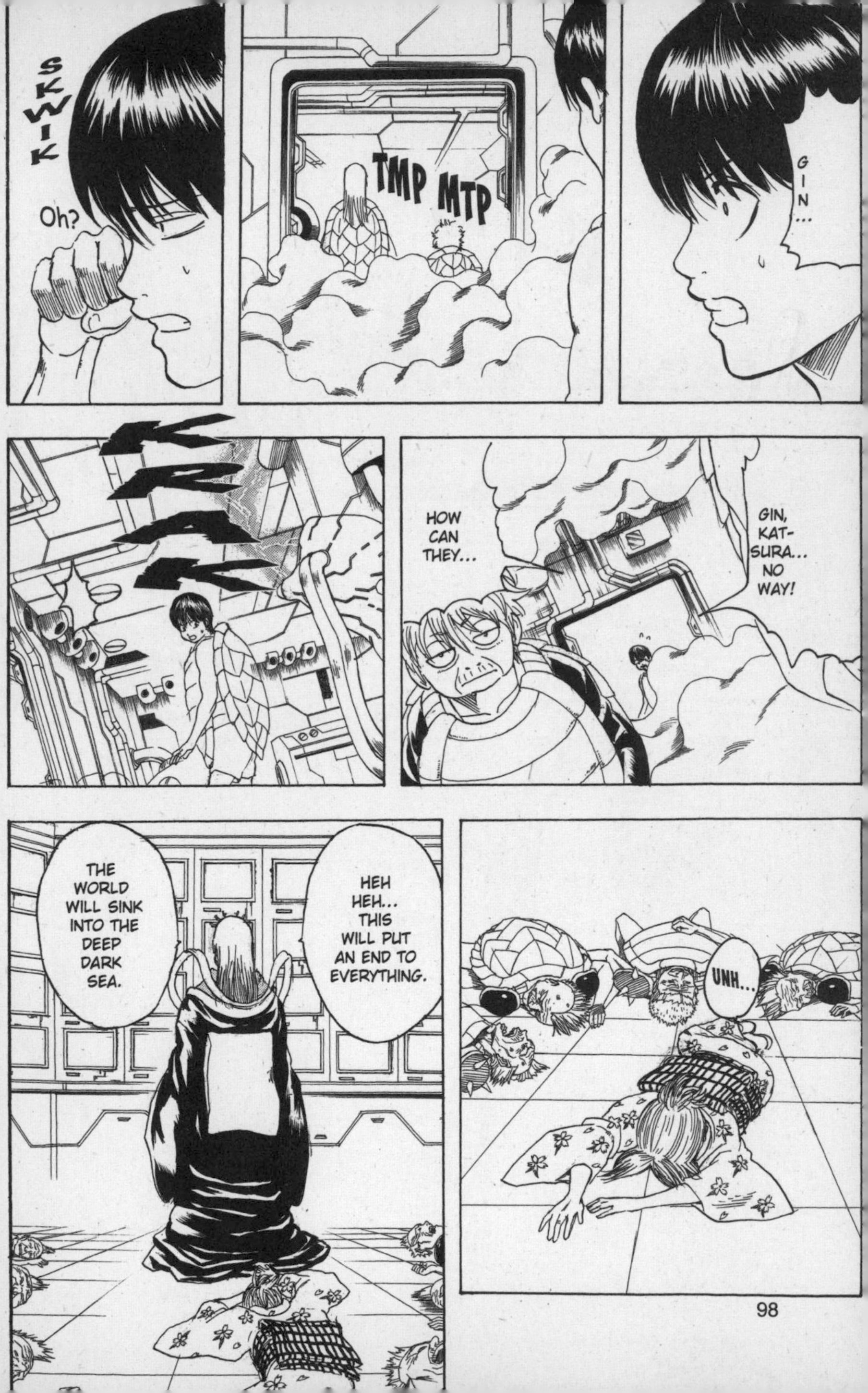
GIN...
TMP MTP
SKWIK
Oh?
GIN, KATSURA... NO WAY!
HOW CAN THEY...
KRAK
UNH...
HEH HEH... THIS WILL PUT AN END TO EVERYTHING.
THE WORLD WILL SINK INTO THE DEEP DARK SEA.

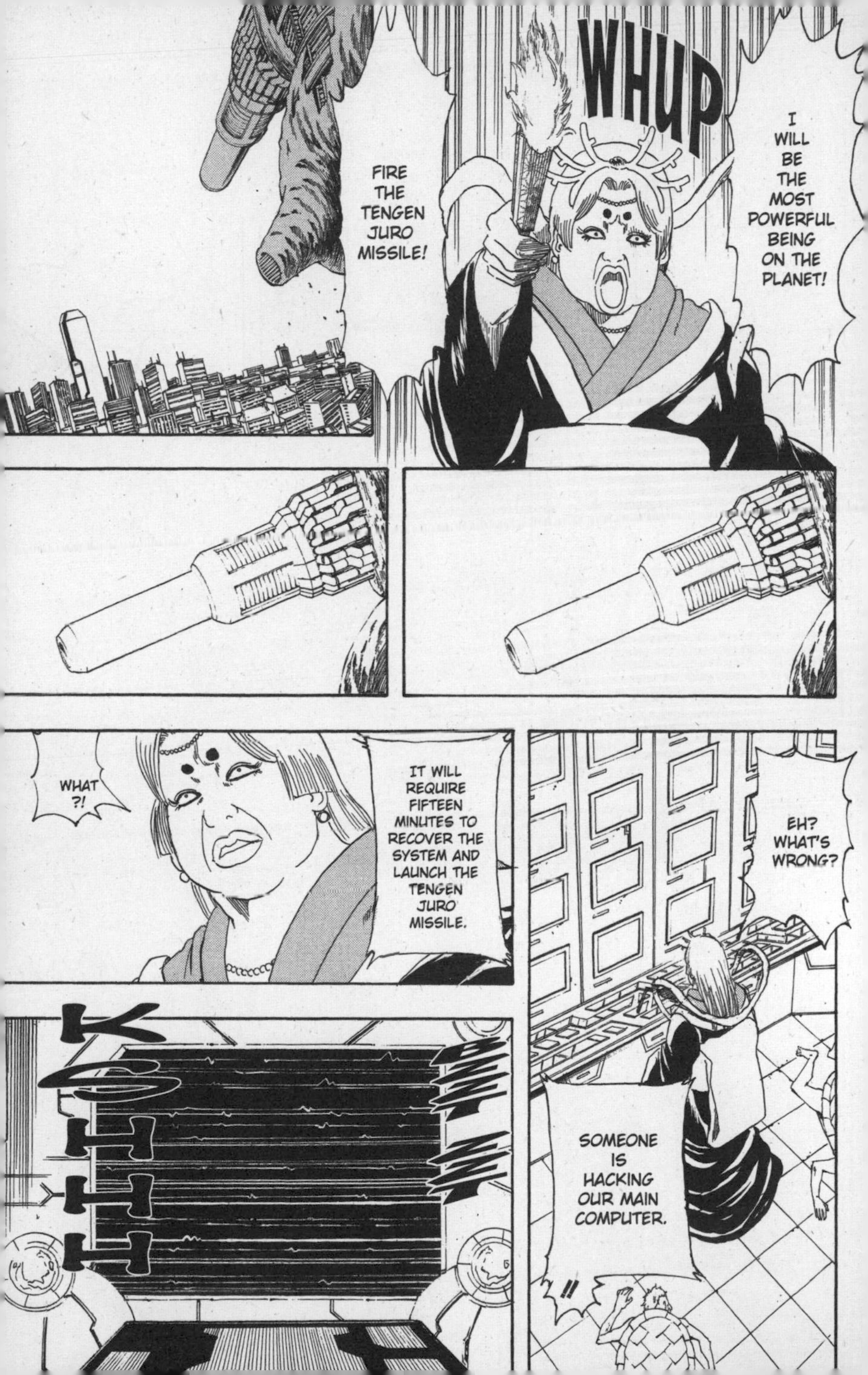
WHUP
I WILL BE THE MOST POWERFUL BEING ON THE PLANET!
FIRE THE TENGEN JURO MISSILE!
EH? WHAT'S WRONG?
SOMEONE IS HACKING OUR MAIN COMPUTER.
!!
IT WILL REQUIRE FIFTEEN MINUTES TO RECOVER THE SYSTEM AND LAUNCH THE TENGEN JURO MISSILE.
WHAT?!
KSHHH

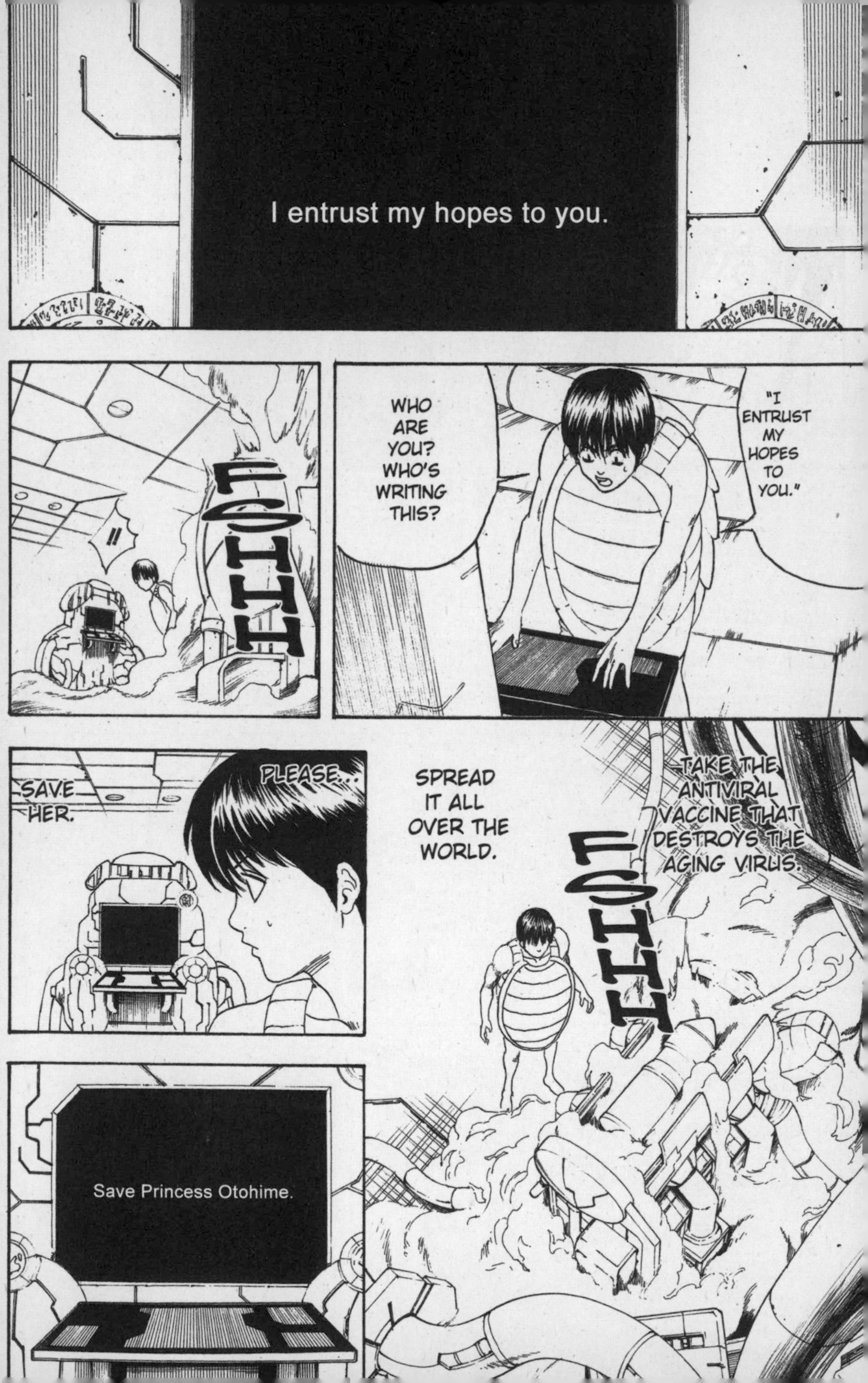
I entrust my hopes to you.
"I ENTRUST MY HOPES TO YOU."
WHO ARE YOU? WHO'S WRITING THIS?
FSHHH
!!
TAKE THE ANTIVIRAL VACCINE THAT DESTROYS THE AGING VIRUS.
SPREAD IT ALL OVER THE WORLD.
FSHHH
PLEASE...
SAVE HER.
Save Princess Otohime.

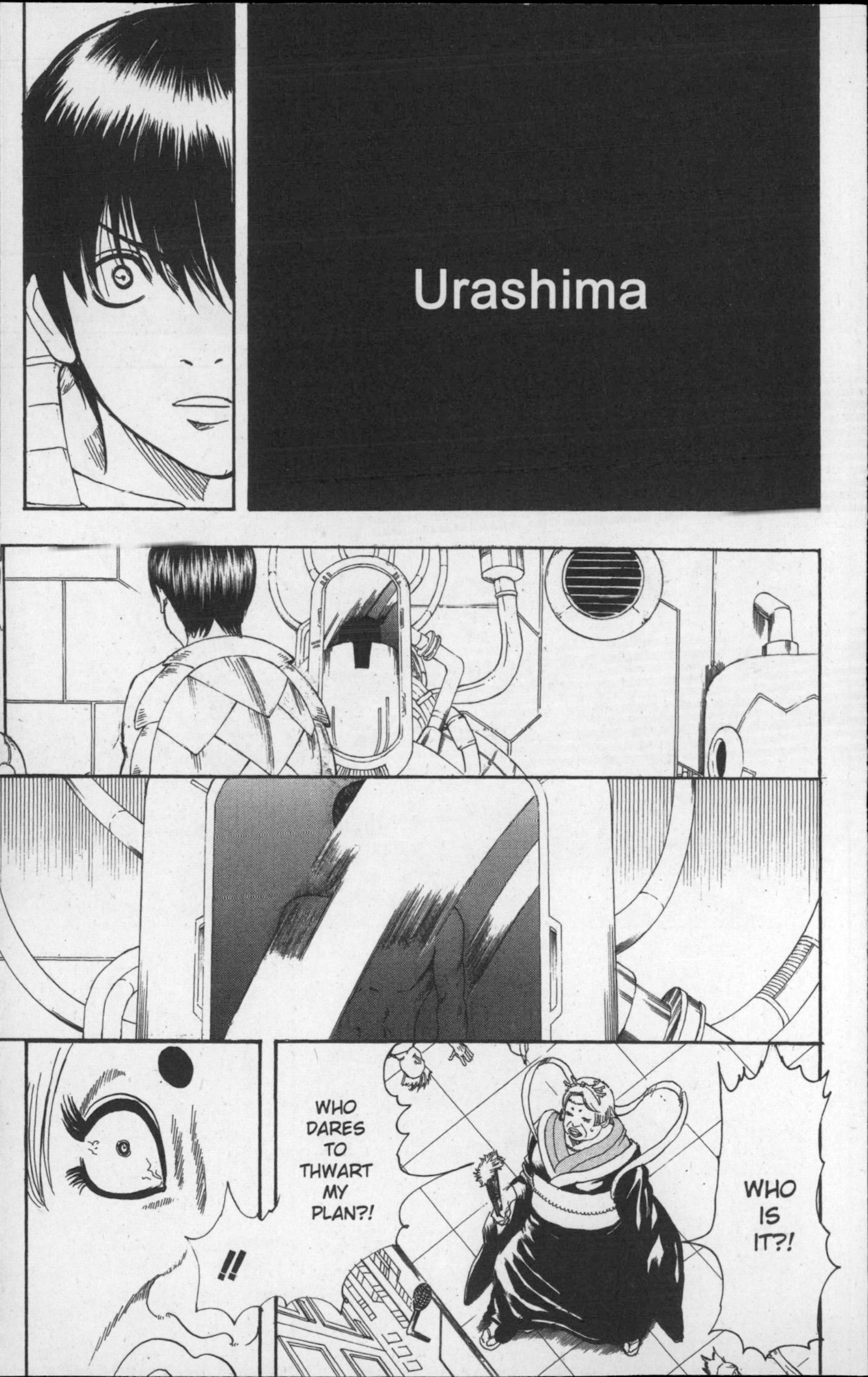
Urashima
WHO IS IT?!
WHO DARES TO THWART MY PLAN?!
!!

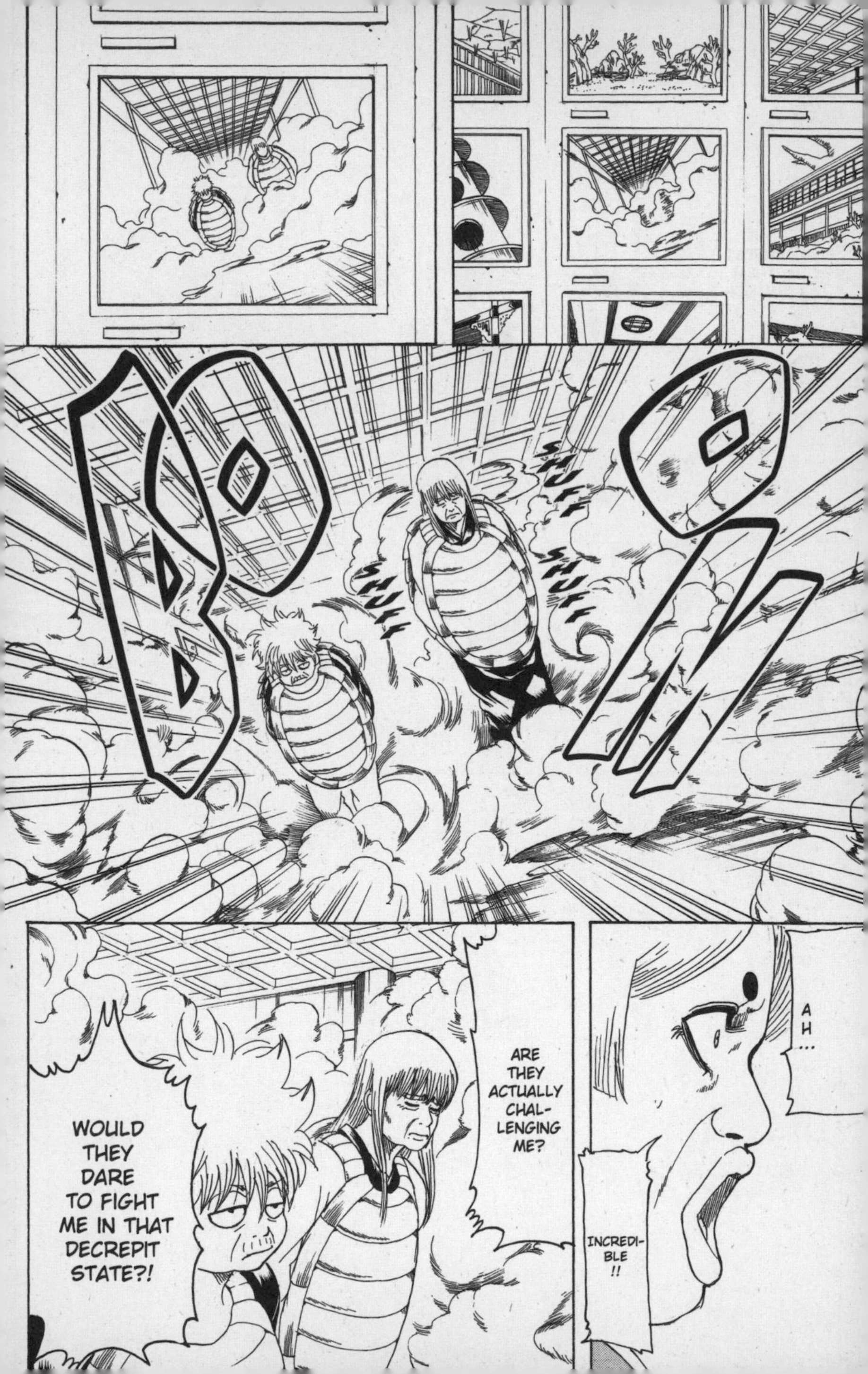
SHUFF SHUFF
SHUFF
AH...
INCREDIBLE!!
ARE THEY ACTUALLY CHALLENGING ME?
WOULD THEY DARE TO FIGHT ME IN THAT DECREPIT STATE?!

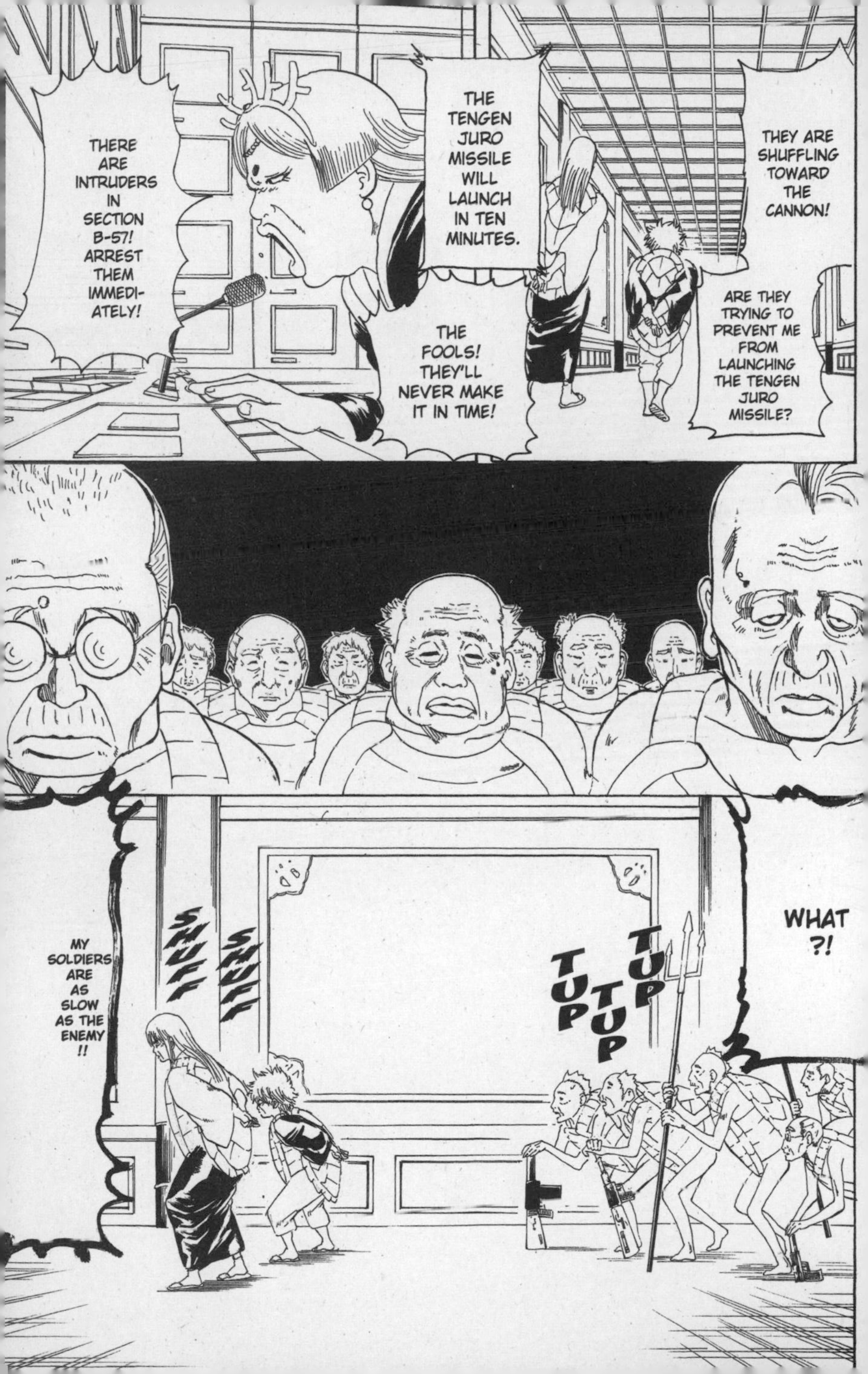
THEY ARE SHUFFLING TOWARD THE CANNON!
ARE THEY TRYING TO PREVENT ME FROM LAUNCHING THE TENGEN JURO MISSILE?
THE TENGEN JURO MISSILE WILL LAUNCH IN TEN MINUTES.
THE FOOLS! THEY'LL NEVER MAKE IT IN TIME!
THERE ARE INTRUDERS IN SECTION B-57! ARREST THEM IMMEDI-ATELY!
WHAT ?!
TUP TUP TUP
SHUFF SHUFF
MY SOLDIERS ARE AS SLOW AS THE ENEMY !!

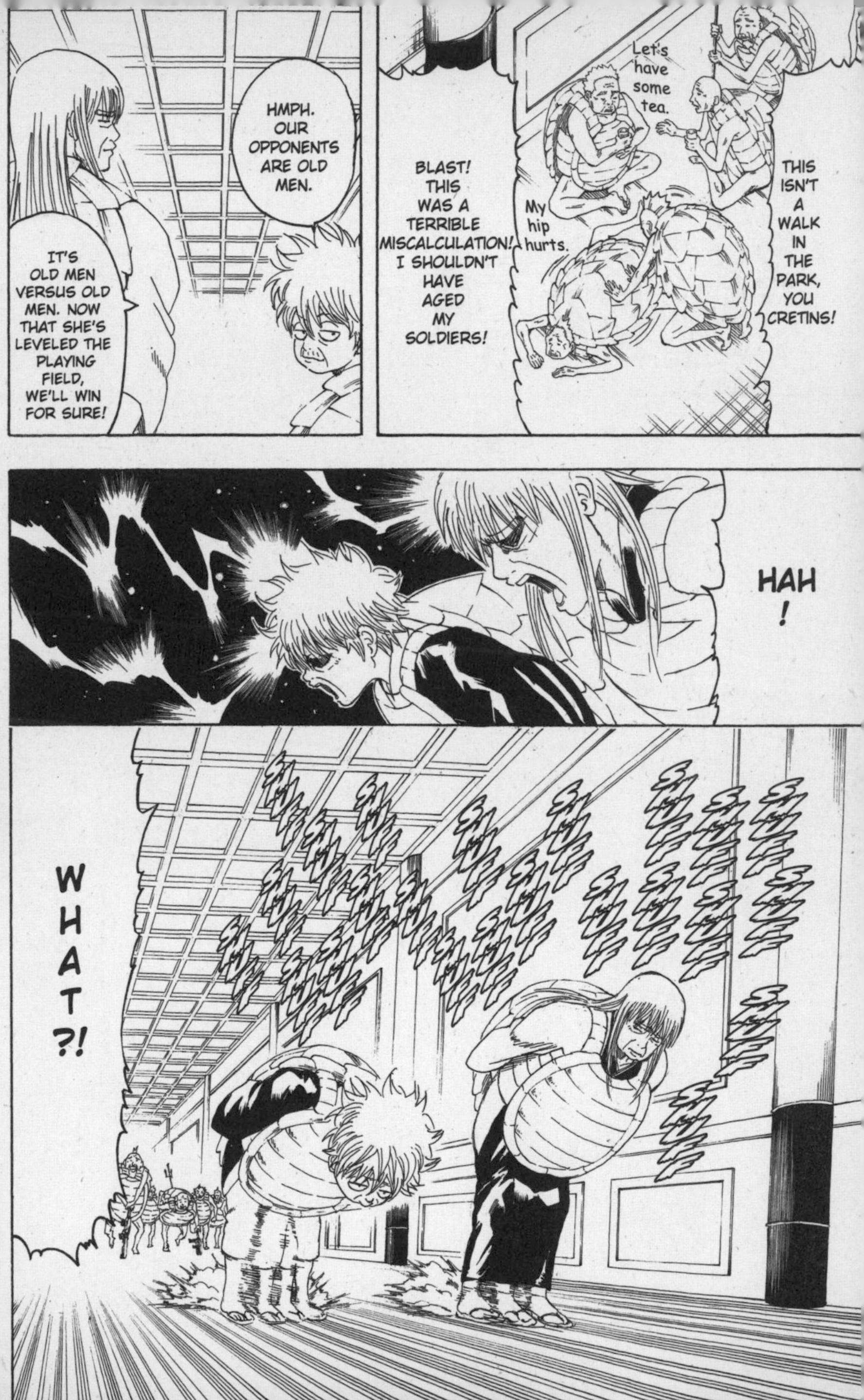
Let's have some tea.
THIS ISN'T A WALK IN THE PARK, YOU CRETINS!
My hip hurts.
BLAST! THIS WAS A TERRIBLE MISCALCULATION! I SHOULDN'T HAVE AGED MY SOLDIERS!
HMPH. OUR OPPONENTS ARE OLD MEN.
IT'S OLD MEN VERSUS OLD MEN. NOW THAT SHE'S LEVELED THE PLAYING FIELD, WE'LL WIN FOR SURE!
HAH!
SHUFF
WHAT?!

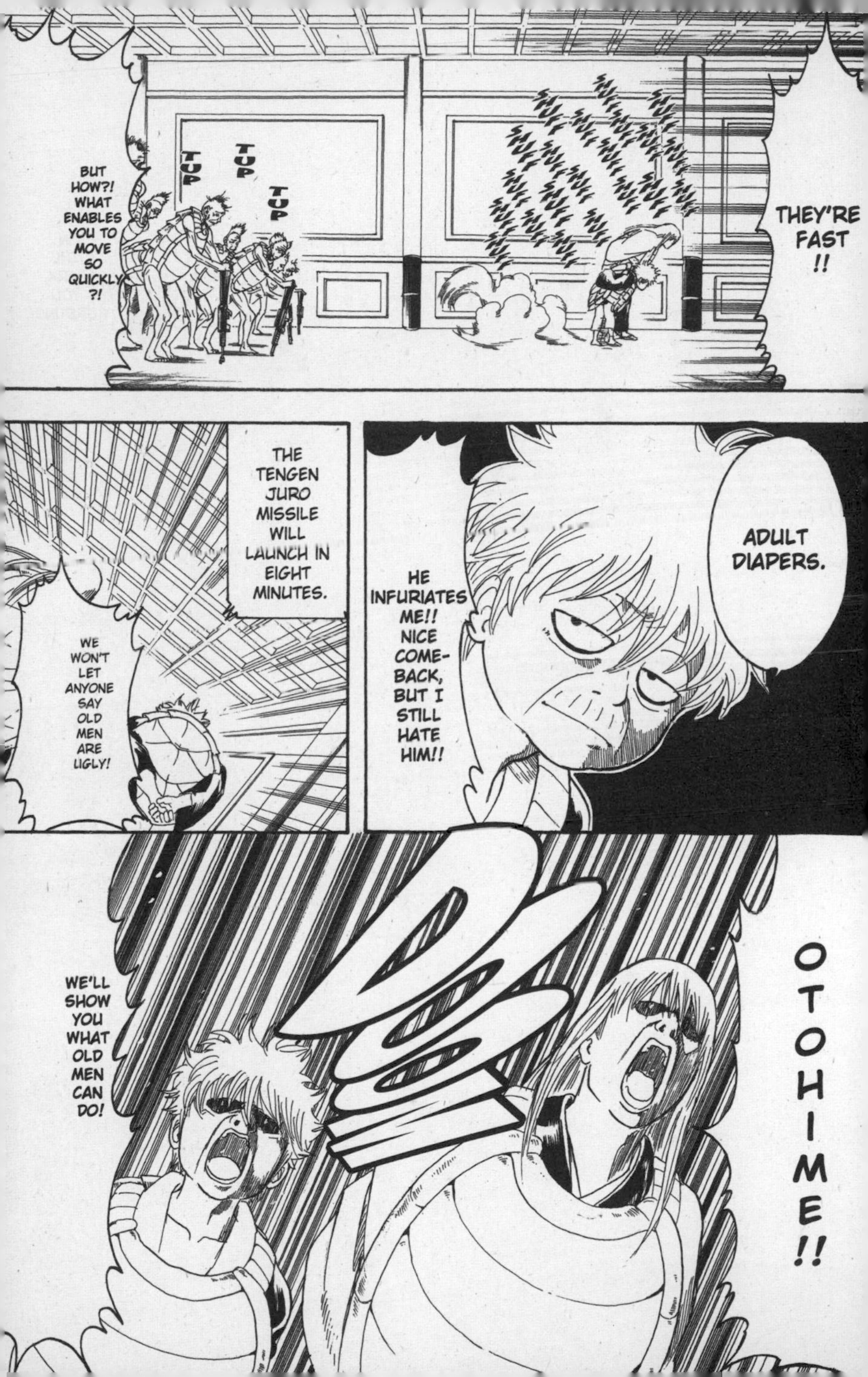
THEY'RE FAST!!
SHUFF SHUFF SHUFF
TUP TUP TUP
BUT HOW?! WHAT ENABLES YOU TO MOVE SO QUICKLY?!
ADULT DIAPERS.
HE INFURIATES ME!! NICE COMEBACK, BUT I STILL HATE HIM!!
THE TENGEN JURO MISSILE WILL LAUNCH IN EIGHT MINUTES.
WE WON'T LET ANYONE SAY OLD MEN ARE UGLY!
OTOHIME!!
WE'LL SHOW YOU WHAT OLD MEN CAN DO!

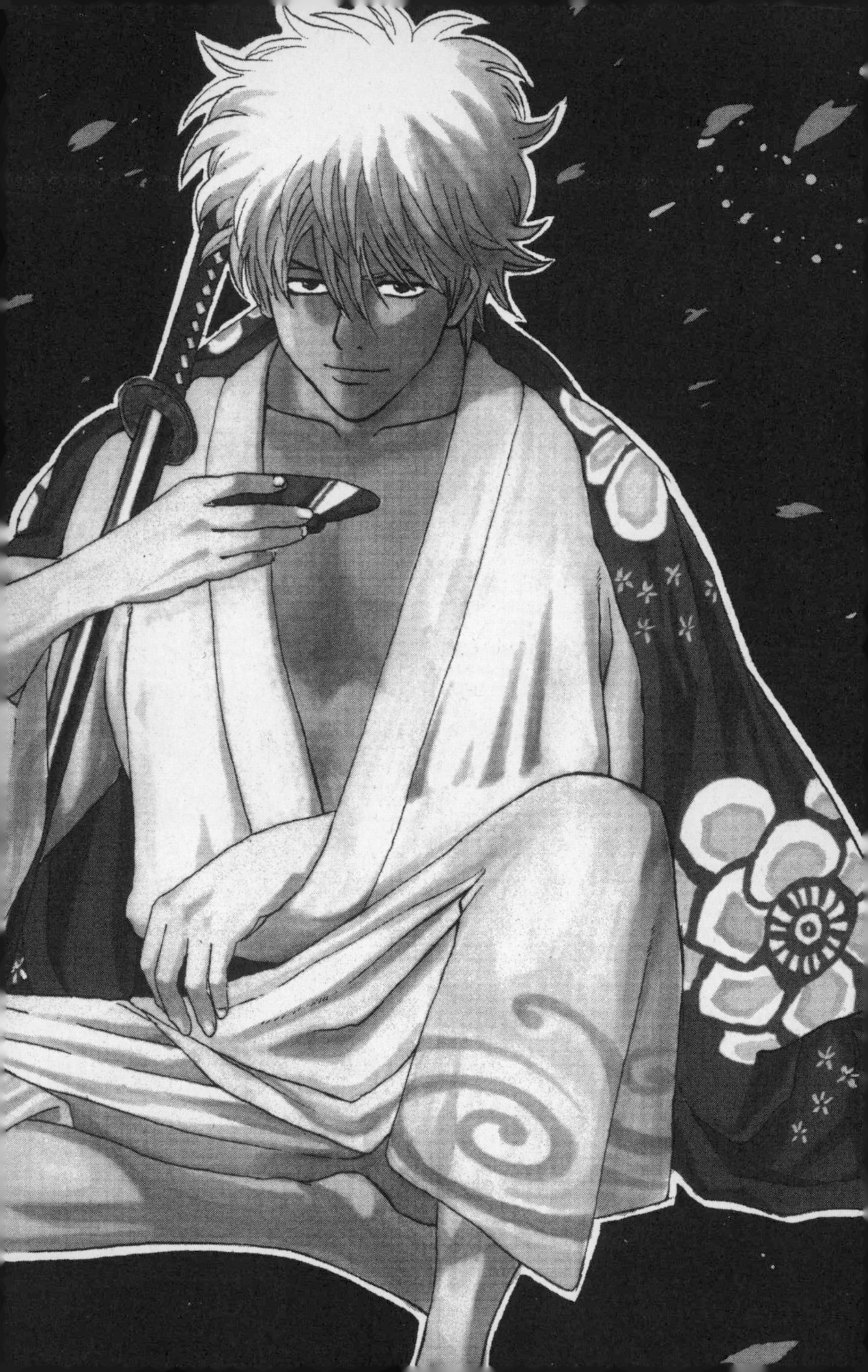

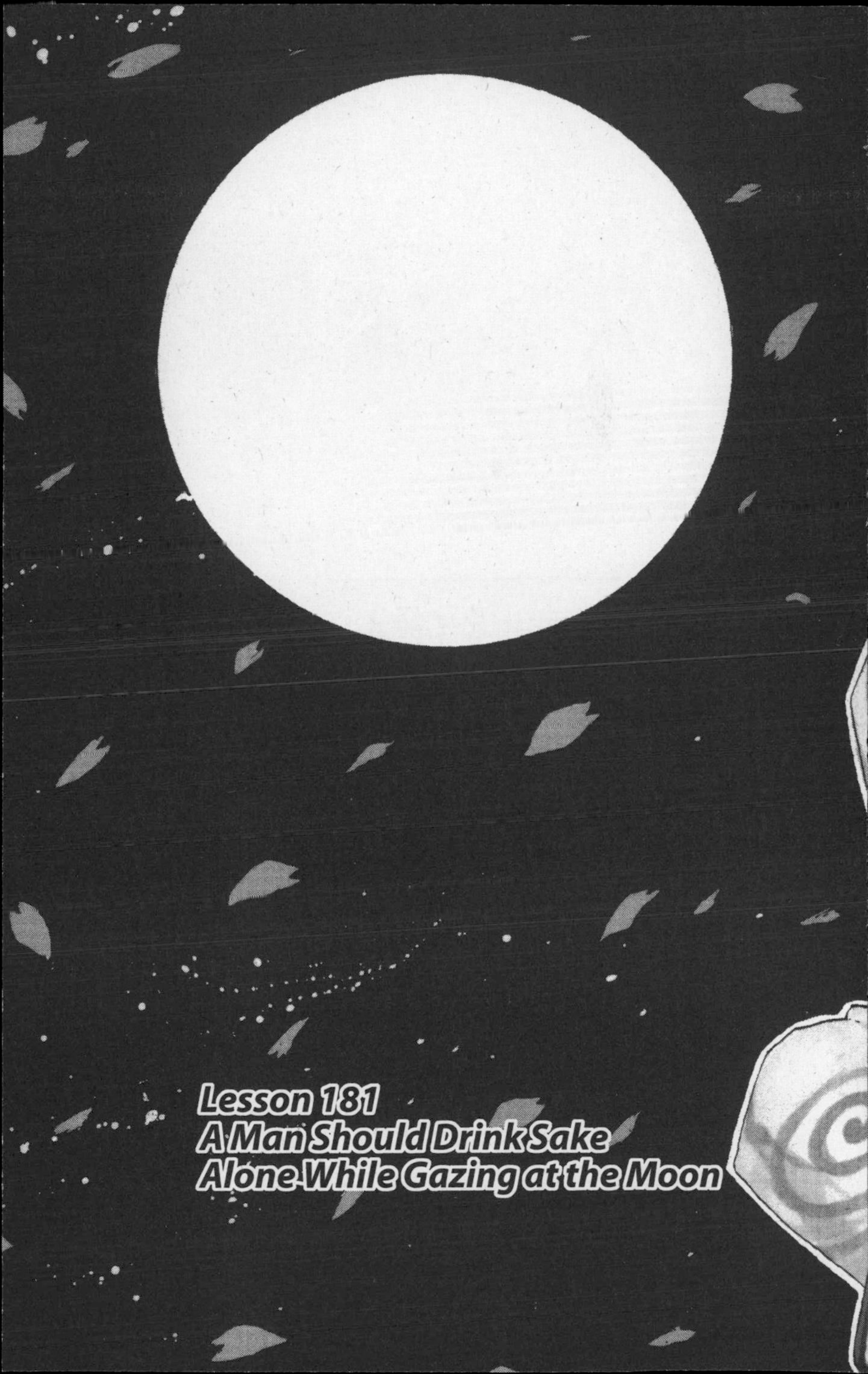
Lesson 181
A Man Should Drink Sake
Alone While Gazing at the Moon

Congratulations on the release of *Jump Square!*

● Published in *Weekly Shonen Jump*, 2007 Volume 47

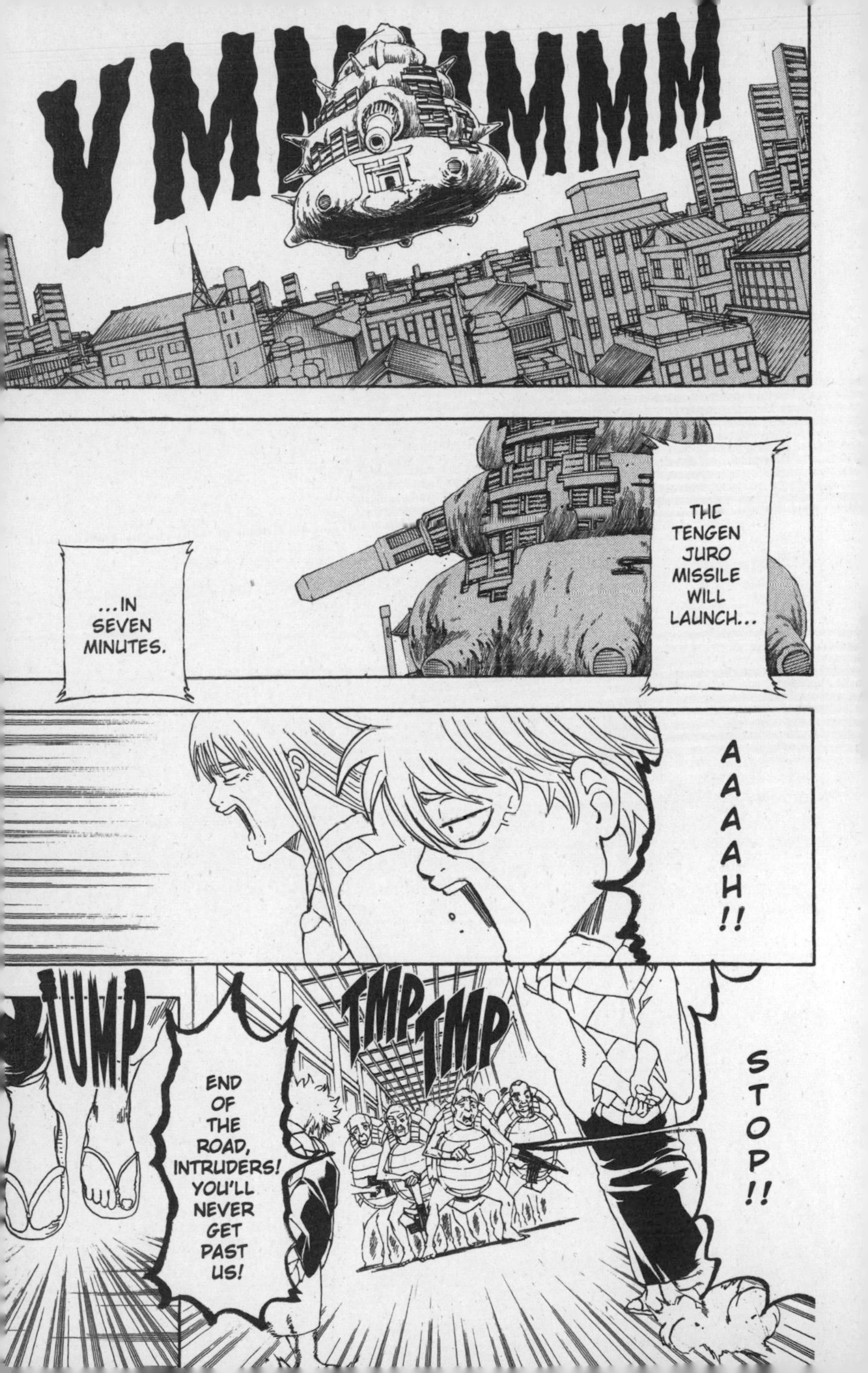
VMMMMMMM
THE TENGEN JURO MISSILE WILL LAUNCH...
...IN SEVEN MINUTES.
AAAAAH!!
STOP!!
TMP TMP
END OF THE ROAD, INTRUDERS! YOU'LL NEVER GET PAST US!
TUMP

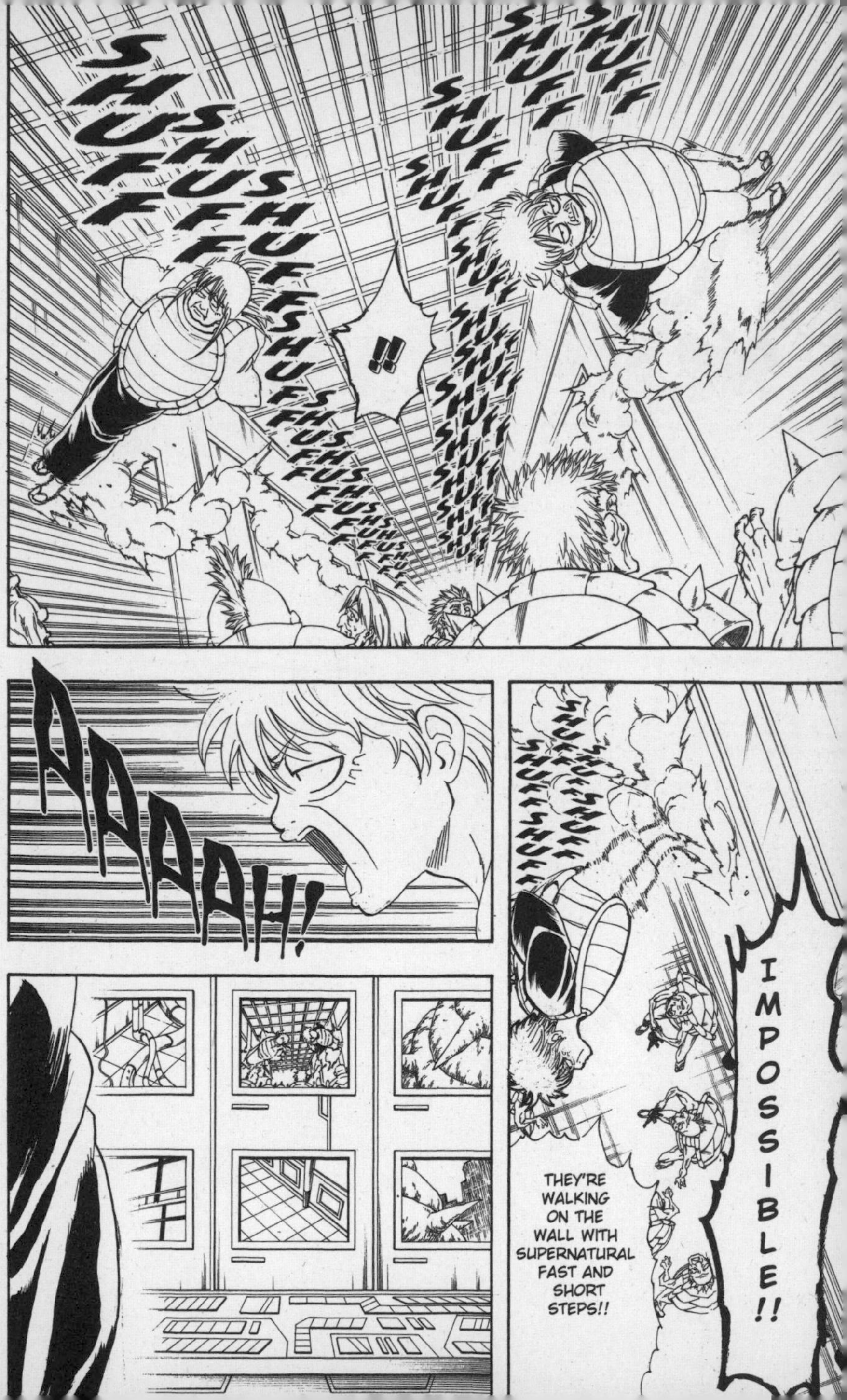
SHUFF SHUFF SHUFF SHUFF
SHUFF SHUFF SHUFF SHUFF
!!
SHUFF SHUFF SHUFF SHUFF
SHUFF SHUFF
IMPOSSIBLE!!
THEY'RE WALKING ON THE WALL WITH SUPERNATURAL FAST AND SHORT STEPS!!
AAAAH!

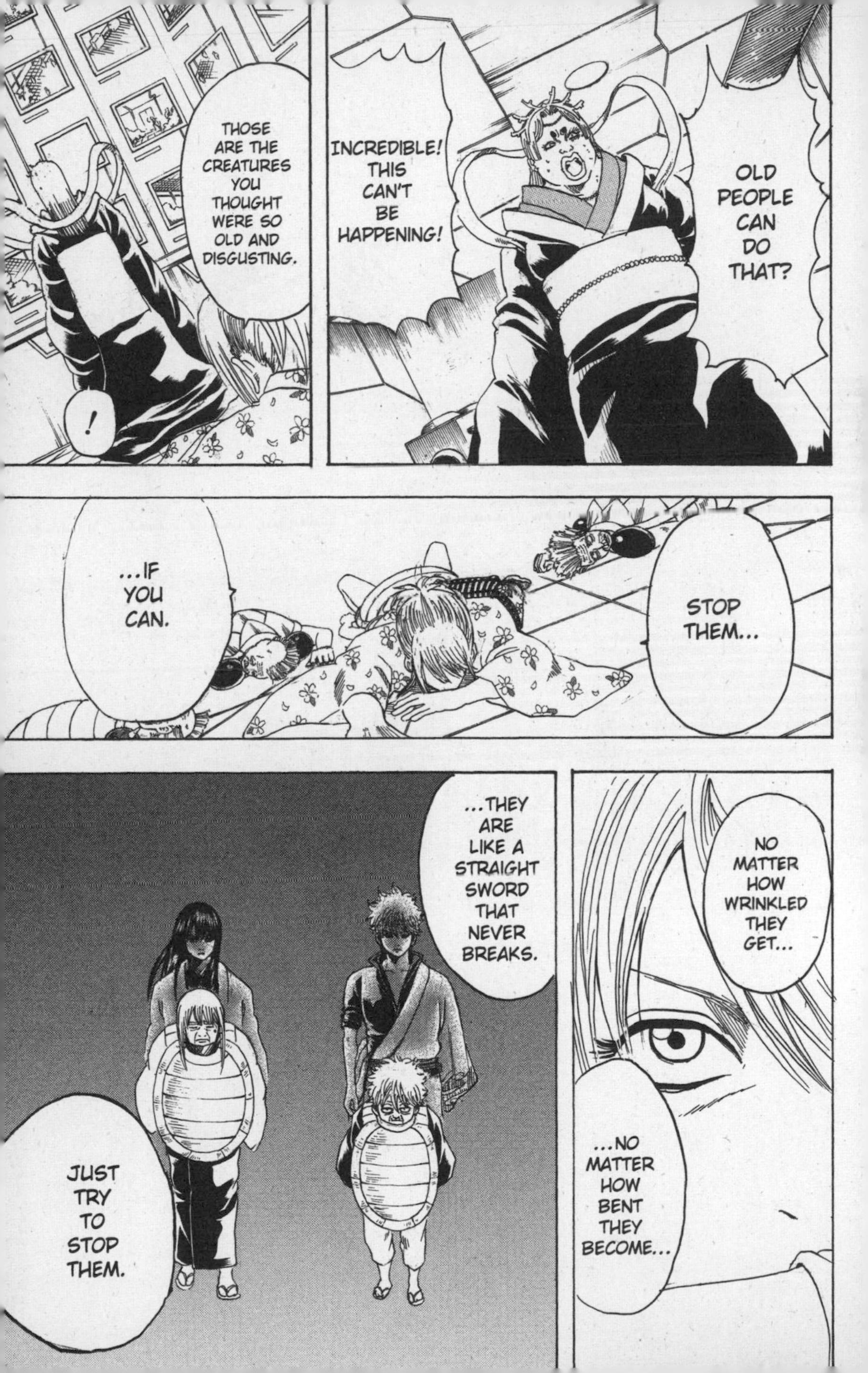
OLD PEOPLE CAN DO THAT?
INCREDIBLE! THIS CAN'T BE HAPPENING!
THOSE ARE THE CREATURES YOU THOUGHT WERE SO OLD AND DISGUSTING.
!
STOP THEM...
...IF YOU CAN.
NO MATTER HOW WRINKLED THEY GET...
...NO MATTER HOW BENT THEY BECOME...
...THEY ARE LIKE A STRAIGHT SWORD THAT NEVER BREAKS.
JUST TRY TO STOP THEM.

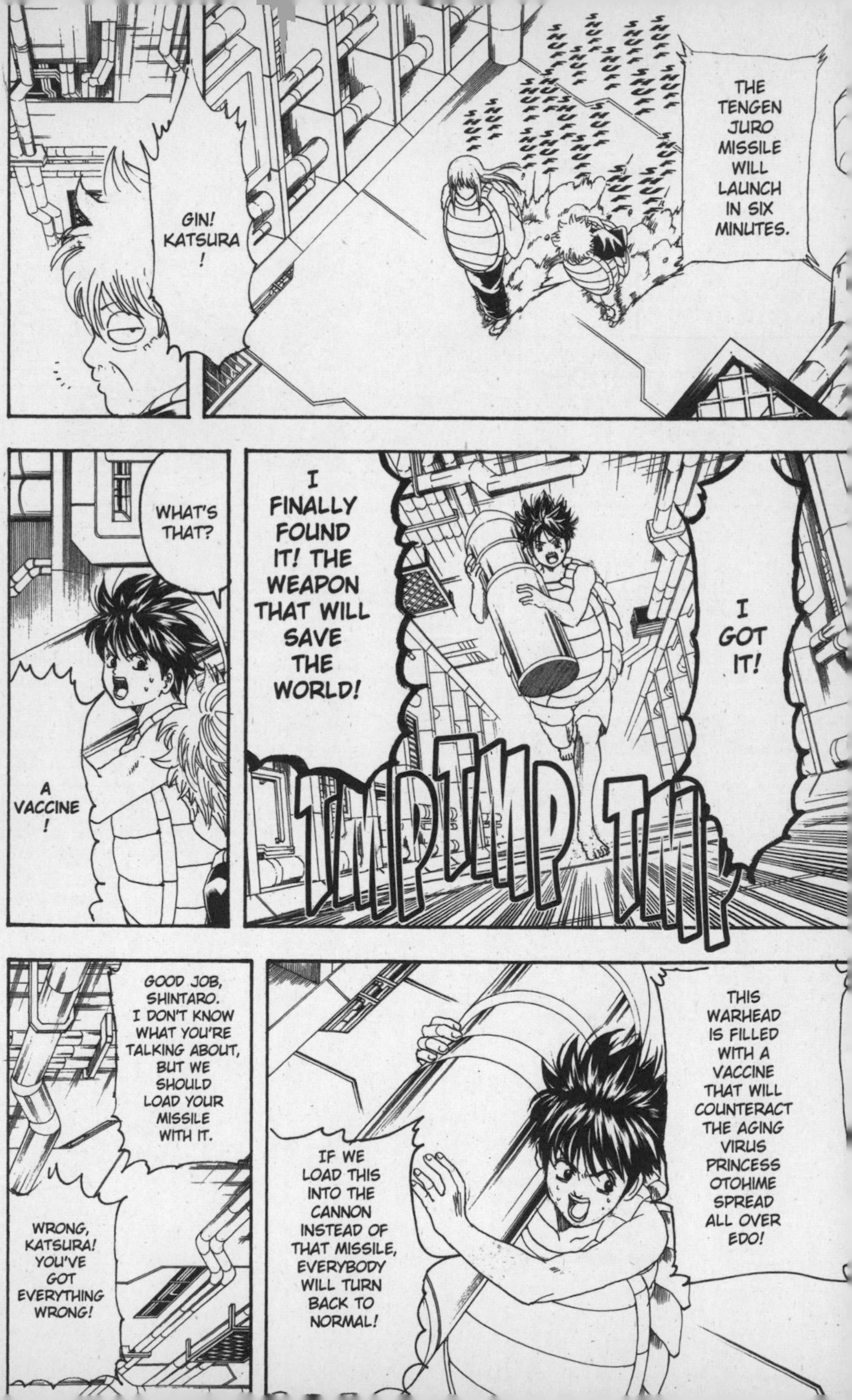
SHUFF SHUFF SHUFF
THE TENGEN JURO MISSILE WILL LAUNCH IN SIX MINUTES.
GIN! KATSURA!
I GOT IT!
I FINALLY FOUND IT! THE WEAPON THAT WILL SAVE THE WORLD!
TMP TMP TMP
WHAT'S THAT?
A VACCINE!
THIS WARHEAD IS FILLED WITH A VACCINE THAT WILL COUNTERACT THE AGING VIRUS PRINCESS OTOHIME SPREAD ALL OVER EDO!
IF WE LOAD THIS INTO THE CANNON INSTEAD OF THAT MISSILE, EVERYBODY WILL TURN BACK TO NORMAL!
GOOD JOB, SHINTARO. I DON'T KNOW WHAT YOU'RE TALKING ABOUT, BUT WE SHOULD LOAD YOUR MISSILE WITH IT.
WRONG, KATSURA! YOU'VE GOT EVERYTHING WRONG!

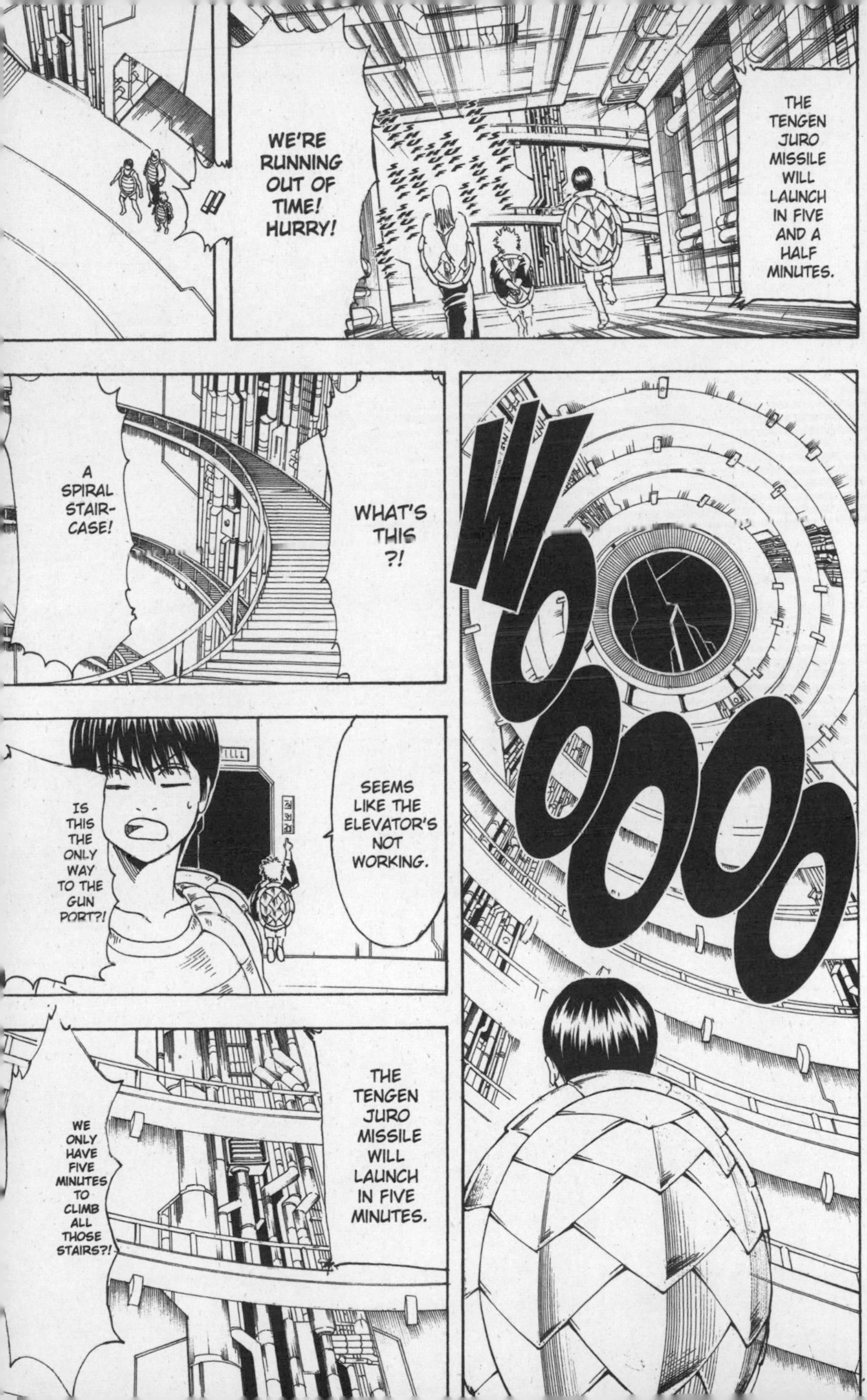
THE TENGEN JURO MISSILE WILL LAUNCH IN FIVE AND A HALF MINUTES.
WE'RE RUNNING OUT OF TIME! HURRY!
SHUFF SHUFF SHUFF SHUFF
WOOOOO
WHAT'S THIS ?!
A SPIRAL STAIR-CASE!
SEEMS LIKE THE ELEVATOR'S NOT WORKING.
IS THIS THE ONLY WAY TO THE GUN PORT?!
THE TENGEN JURO MISSILE WILL LAUNCH IN FIVE MINUTES.
WE ONLY HAVE FIVE MINUTES TO CLIMB ALL THOSE STAIRS?!

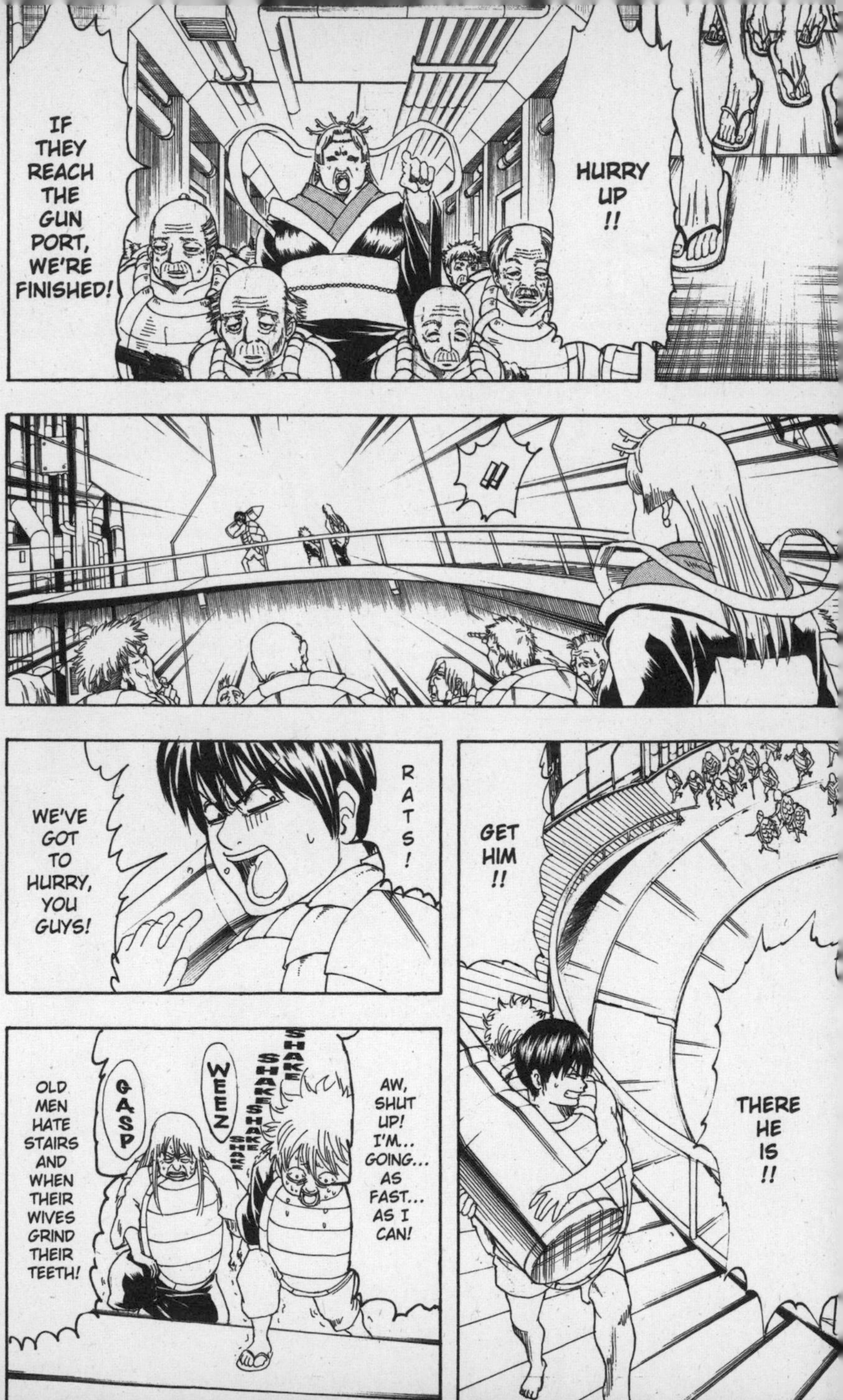
HURRY UP!!
IF THEY REACH THE GUN PORT, WE'RE FINISHED!
!!
GET HIM!!
THERE HE IS!!
RATS!
WE'VE GOT TO HURRY, YOU GUYS!
AW, SHUT UP! I'M... GOING... AS FAST... AS I CAN!
SHAKE SHAKE SHAKE SHAKE
WEEZ
GASP
OLD MEN HATE STAIRS AND WHEN THEIR WIVES GRIND THEIR TEETH!

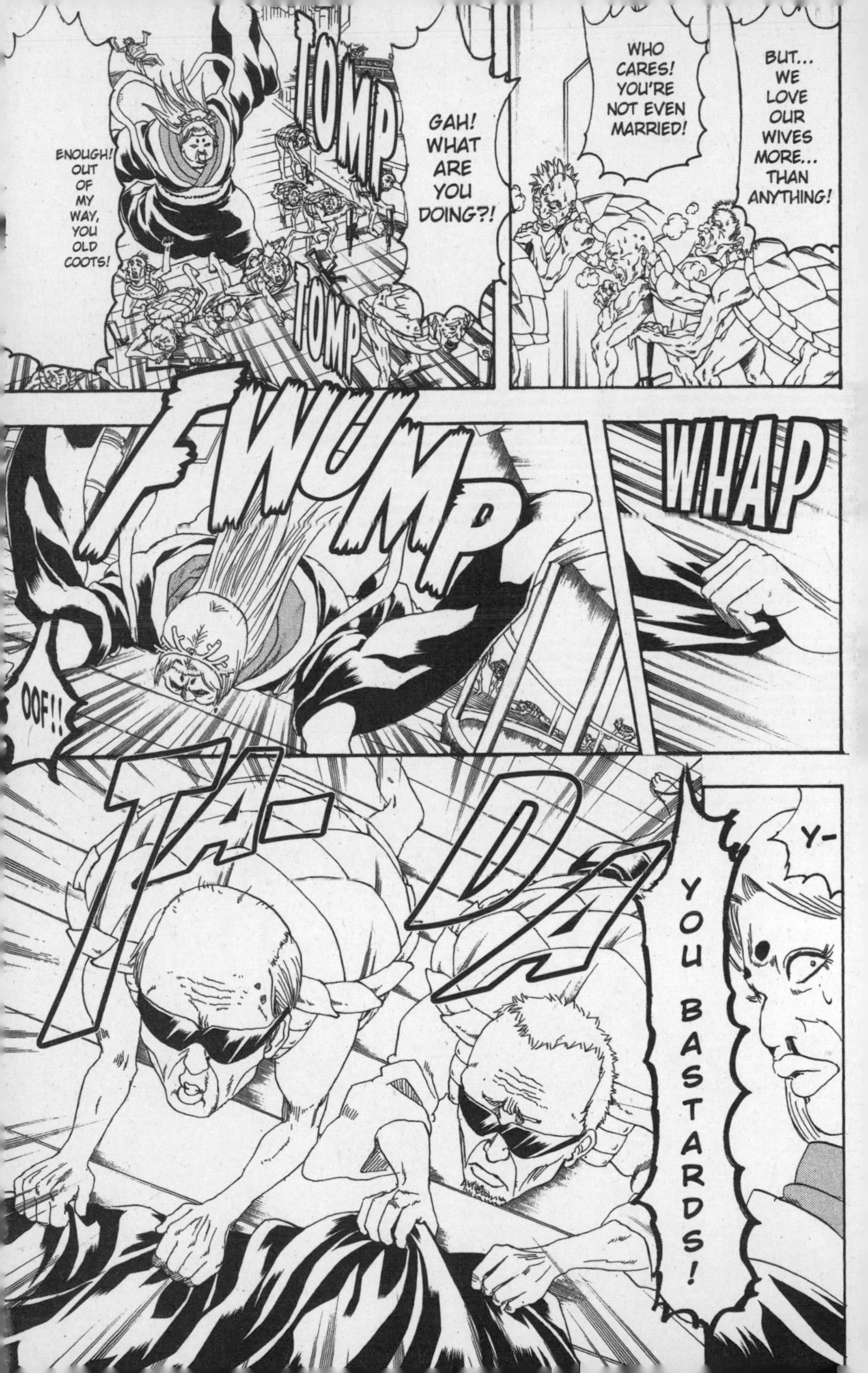
BUT... WE LOVE OUR WIVES MORE... THAN ANYTHING!
WHO CARES! YOU'RE NOT EVEN MARRIED!
GAH! WHAT ARE YOU DOING?!
TOMP
TOMP
ENOUGH! OUT OF MY WAY, YOU OLD COOTS!
WHAP
FWUMP
OOF!!
Y-
YOU BASTARDS!
TA-DA

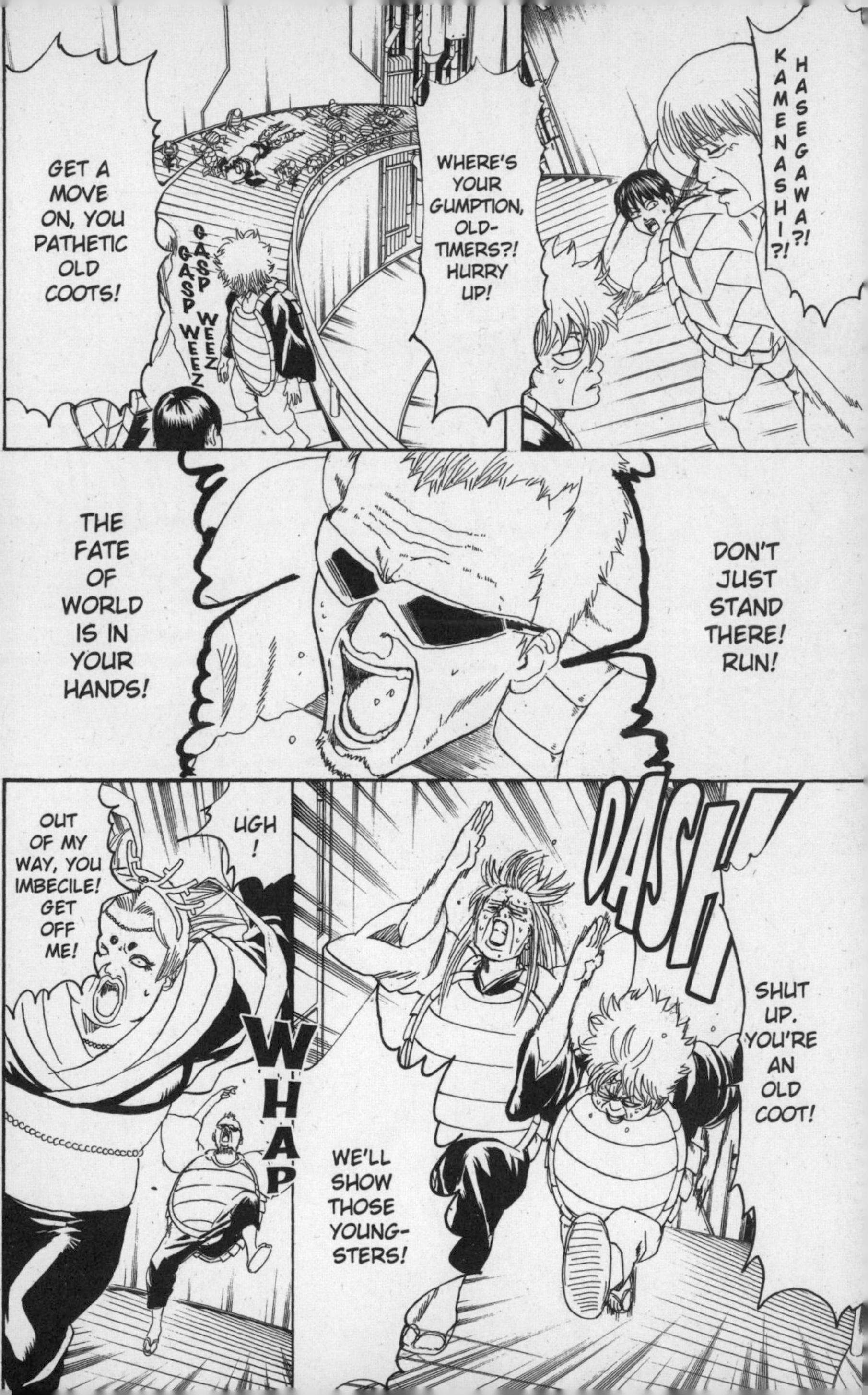
HASEGAWA?!
KAMENASHI?!
WHERE'S YOUR GUMPTION, OLD-TIMERS?! HURRY UP!
GASP WEEZ
GASP WEEZ
GET A MOVE ON, YOU PATHETIC OLD COOTS!
DON'T JUST STAND THERE! RUN!
THE FATE OF WORLD IS IN YOUR HANDS!
DASH
SHUT UP. YOU'RE AN OLD COOT!
WE'LL SHOW THOSE YOUNG-STERS!
UGH!
OUT OF MY WAY, YOU IMBECILE! GET OFF ME!
WHAP

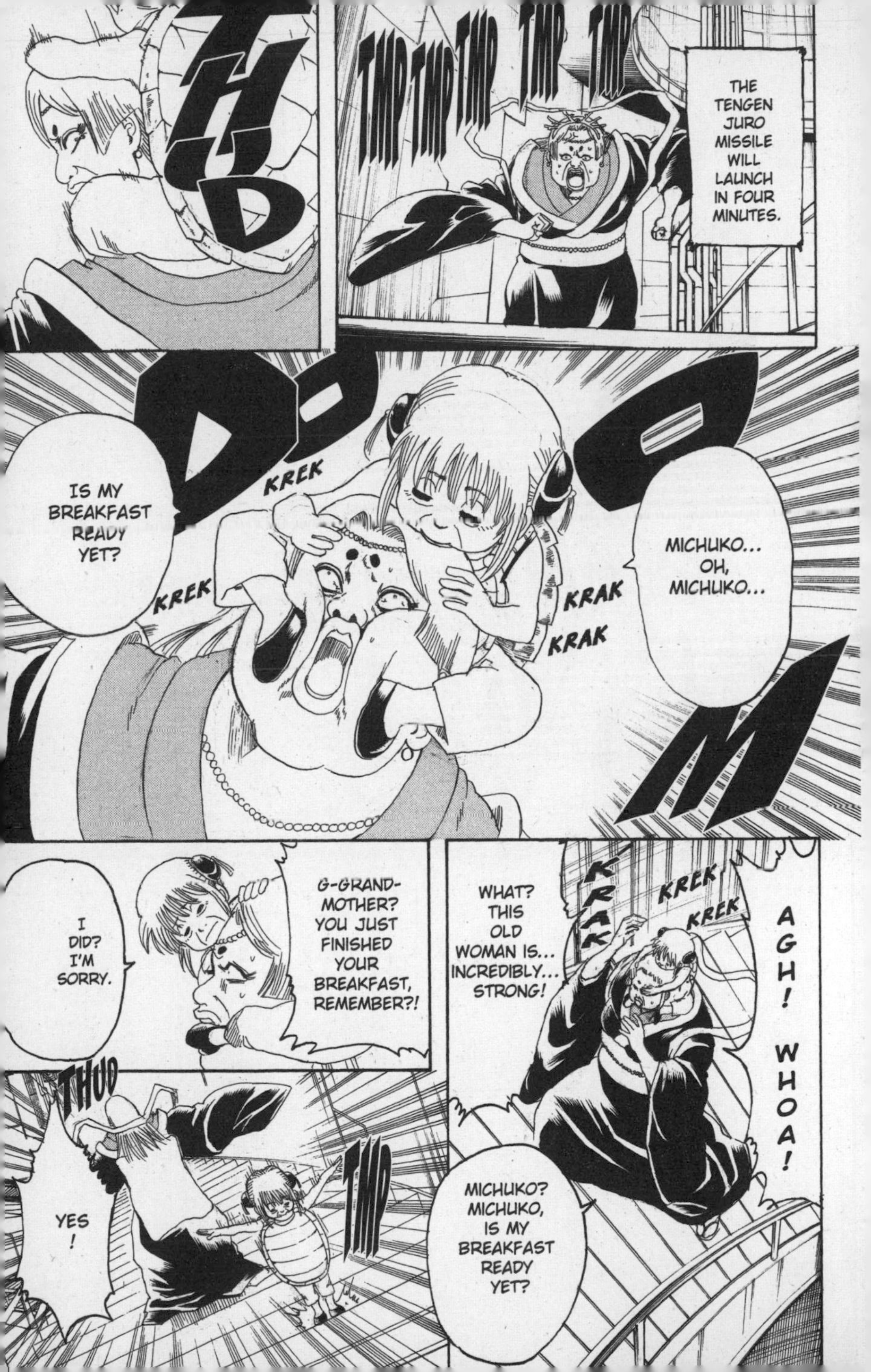
TMP TMP TMP TMP TMP
THE TENGEN JURO MISSILE WILL LAUNCH IN FOUR MINUTES.
MICHUKO... OH, MICHUKO...
KRAK KRAK
KREK KREK
IS MY BREAKFAST READY YET?
KRAK KREK KREK
AGH! WHOA!
WHAT? THIS OLD WOMAN IS... INCREDIBLY... STRONG!
MICHUKO? MICHUKO, IS MY BREAKFAST READY YET?
G-GRANDMOTHER? YOU JUST FINISHED YOUR BREAKFAST, REMEMBER?!
I DID? I'M SORRY.
THUD
TMP
YES!

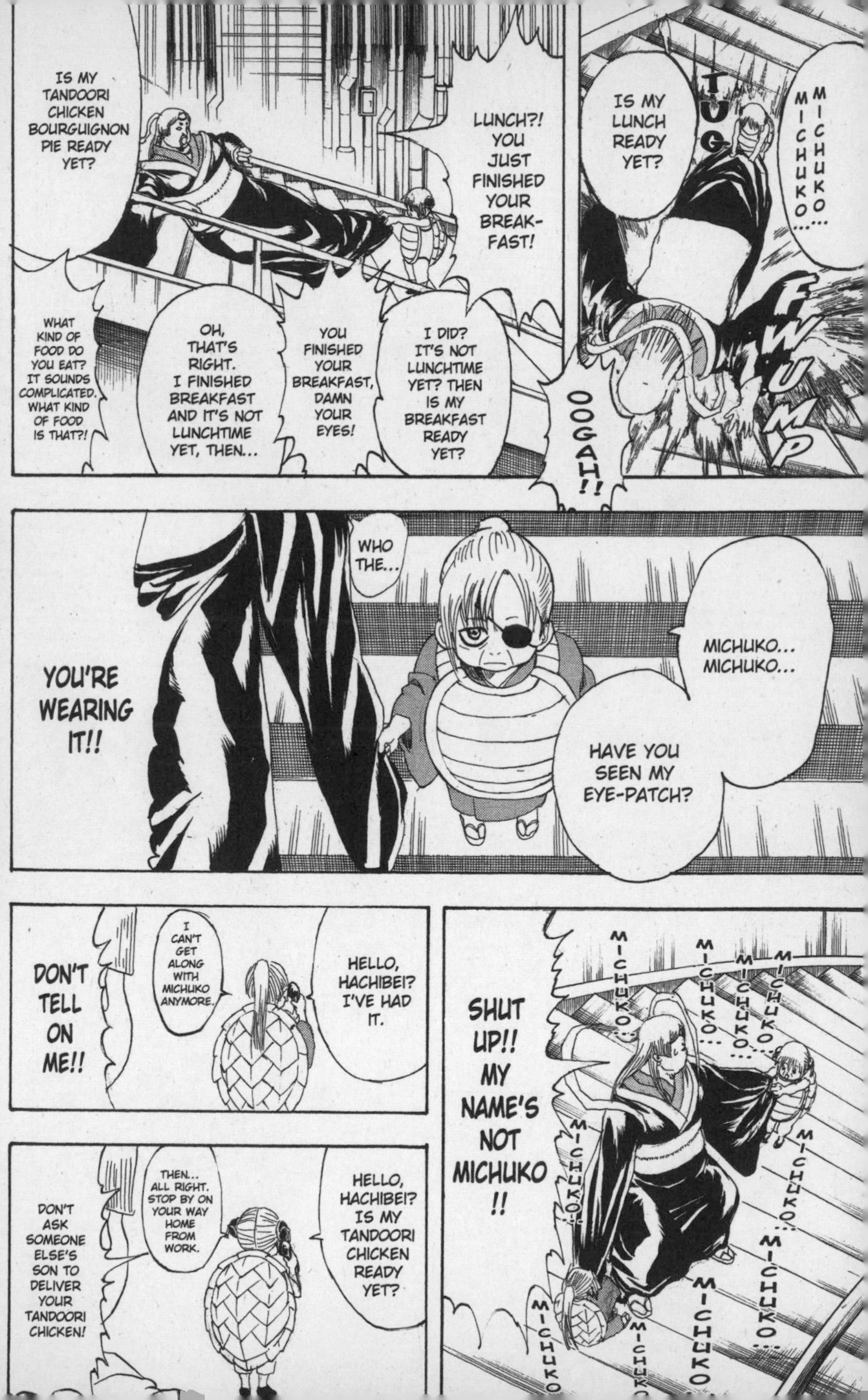
MICHUKO... MICHUKO...
IS MY LUNCH READY YET?
TUG
FWUMP
OOGAH!!
LUNCH?! YOU JUST FINISHED YOUR BREAK-FAST!
I DID? IT'S NOT LUNCHTIME YET? THEN IS MY BREAKFAST READY YET?
YOU FINISHED YOUR BREAKFAST, DAMN YOUR EYES!
OH, THAT'S RIGHT. I FINISHED BREAKFAST AND IT'S NOT LUNCHTIME YET, THEN...
IS MY TANDOORI CHICKEN BOURGUIGNON PIE READY YET?
WHAT KIND OF FOOD DO YOU EAT? IT SOUNDS COMPLICATED. WHAT KIND OF FOOD IS THAT?!
MICHUKO... MICHUKO...
HAVE YOU SEEN MY EYE-PATCH?
WHO THE...
YOU'RE WEARING IT!!
MICHUKO... MICHUKO... MICHUKO... MICHUKO...
MICHUKO... MICHUKO... MICHUKO... MICHUKO... MICHUKO... MICHUKO...
SHUT UP!! MY NAME'S NOT MICHUKO!!
HELLO, HACHIBEI? I'VE HAD IT.
I CAN'T GET ALONG WITH MICHUKO ANYMORE.
DON'T TELL ON ME!!
HELLO, HACHIBEI? IS MY TANDOORI CHICKEN READY YET?
THEN... ALL RIGHT. STOP BY ON YOUR WAY HOME FROM WORK.
DON'T ASK SOMEONE ELSE'S SON TO DELIVER YOUR TANDOORI CHICKEN!

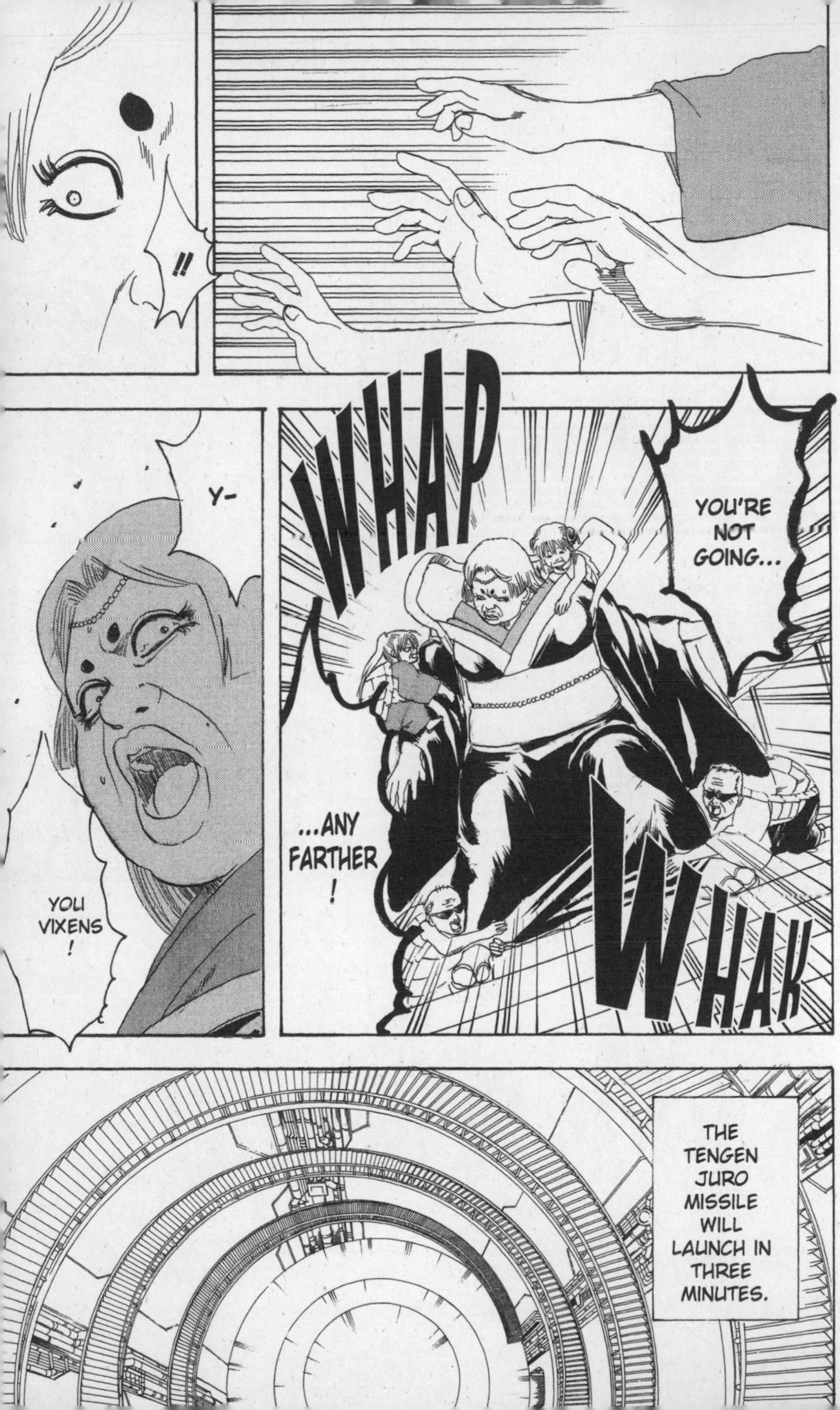
!!
YOU'RE NOT GOING...
WHAP
...ANY FARTHER!
WHAK
Y-
YOU VIXENS!
THE TENGEN JURO MISSILE WILL LAUNCH IN THREE MINUTES.

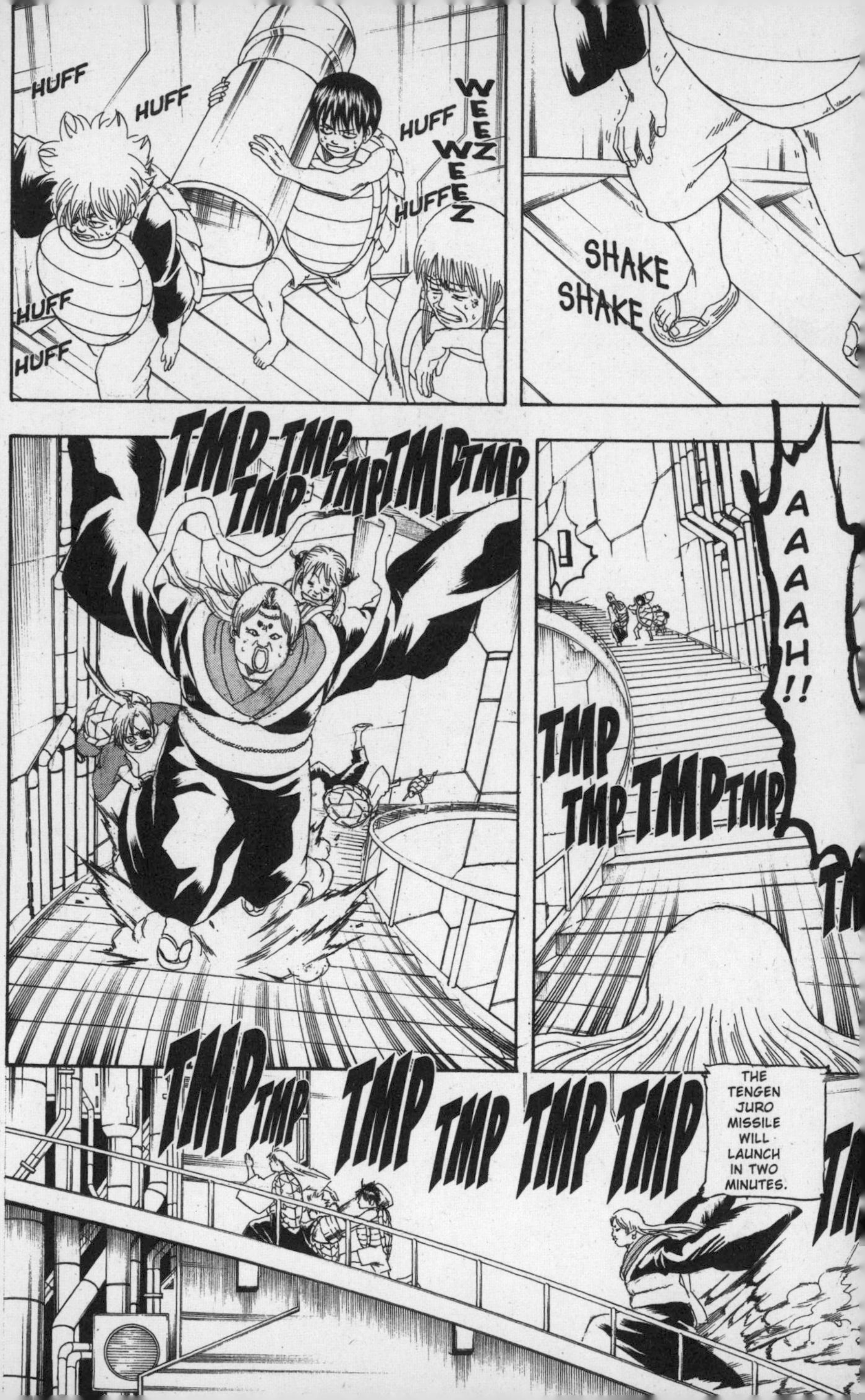
SHAKE SHAKE
WEEZ
WEEZ
HUFF
HUFF
HUFF
HUFF
HUFF
HUFF
AAAAAH!!
!
TMP TMP TMP TMP
TMP TMP TMP TMP TMP TMP
THE TENGEN JURO MISSILE WILL LAUNCH IN TWO MINUTES.
TMP TMP TMP TMP
TMP TMP

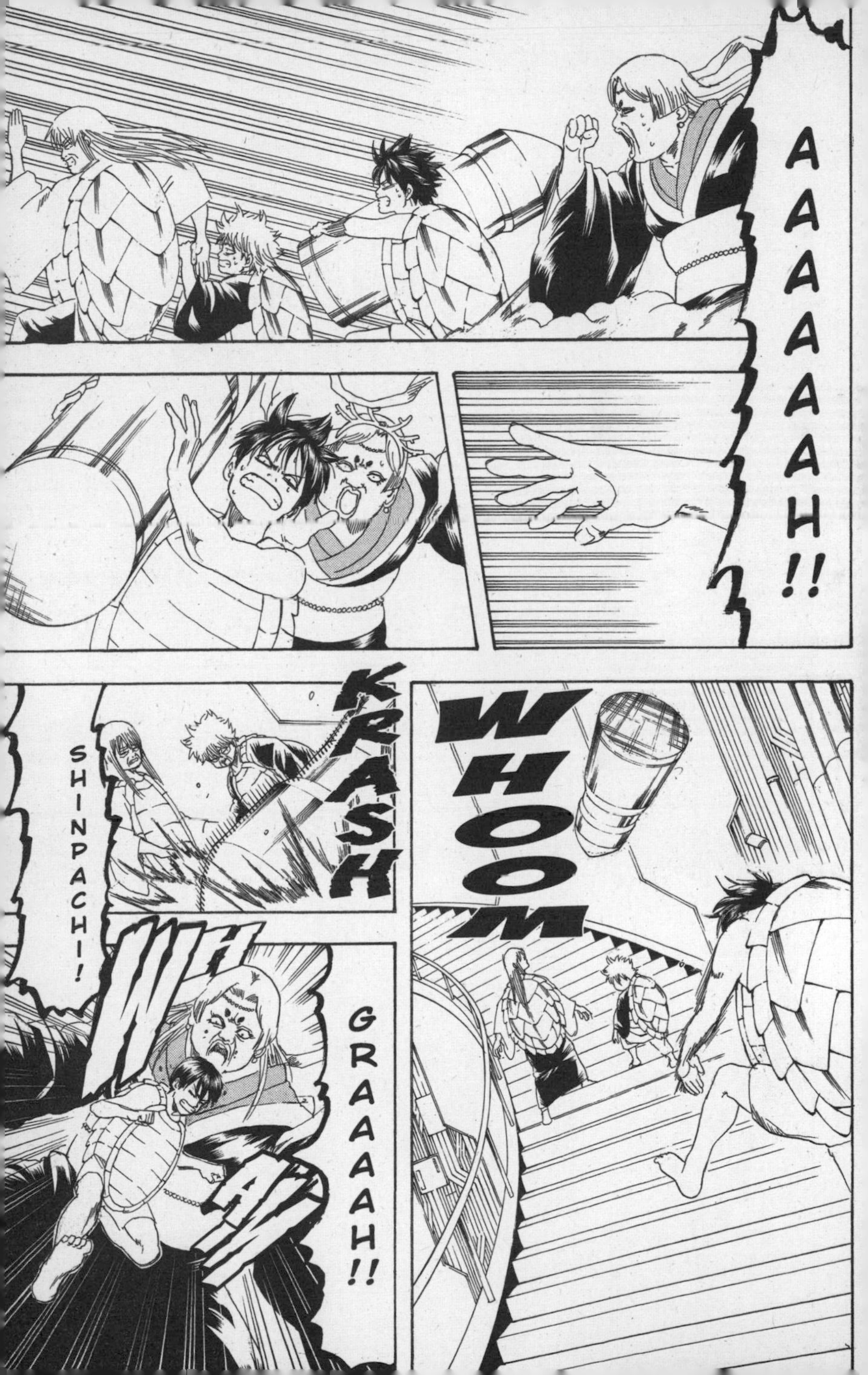
AAAAAAH!!
WHOOM
KRASH
SHINPACHI!
GRAAAAAH!!

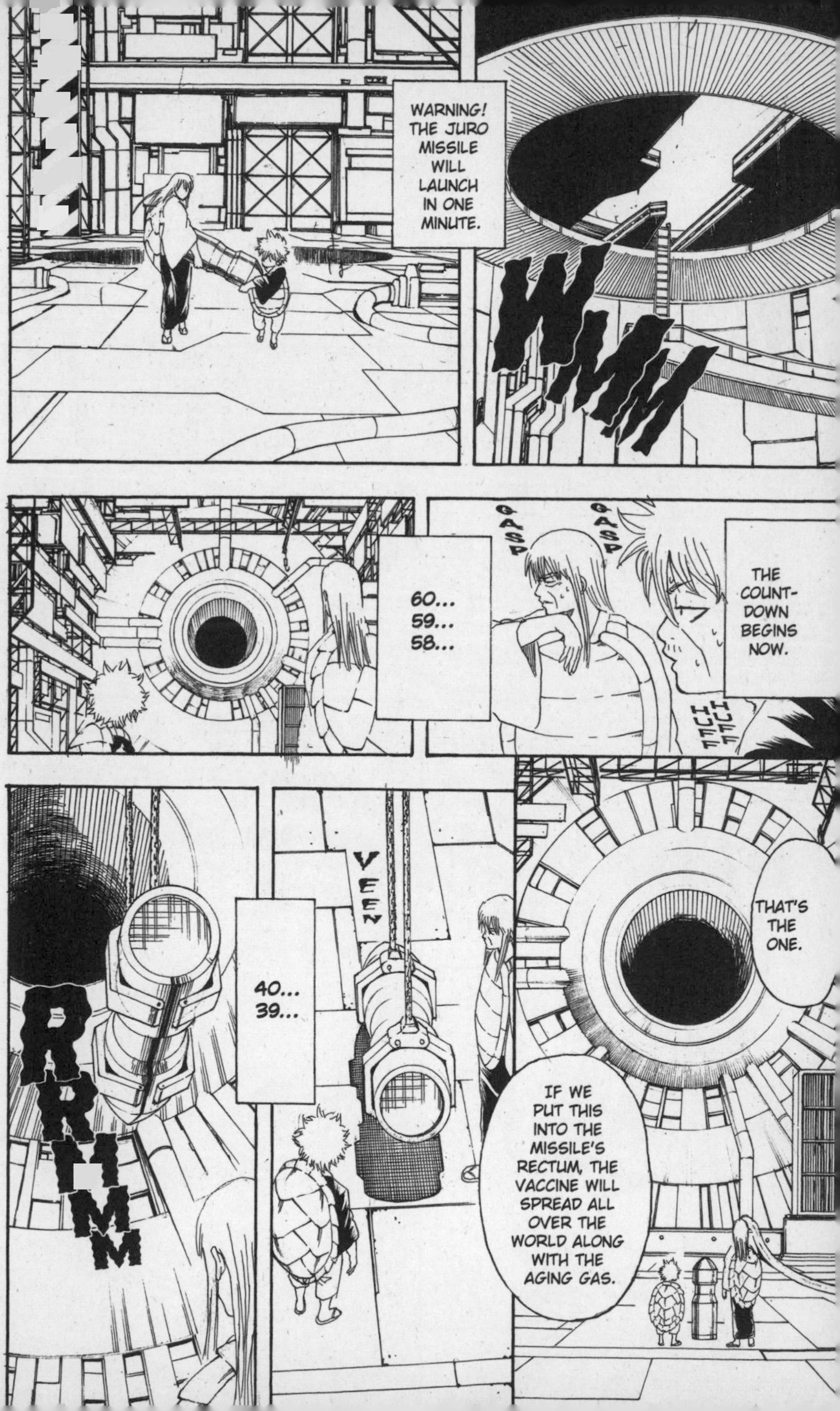
WARNING! THE JURO MISSILE WILL LAUNCH IN ONE MINUTE.
WMM
GASP
GASP
THE COUNT-DOWN BEGINS NOW.
HUFF HUFF
60... 59... 58...
THAT'S THE ONE.
IF WE PUT THIS INTO THE MISSILE'S RECTUM, THE VACCINE WILL SPREAD ALL OVER THE WORLD ALONG WITH THE AGING GAS.
VEEN
40... 39...
RRMMM

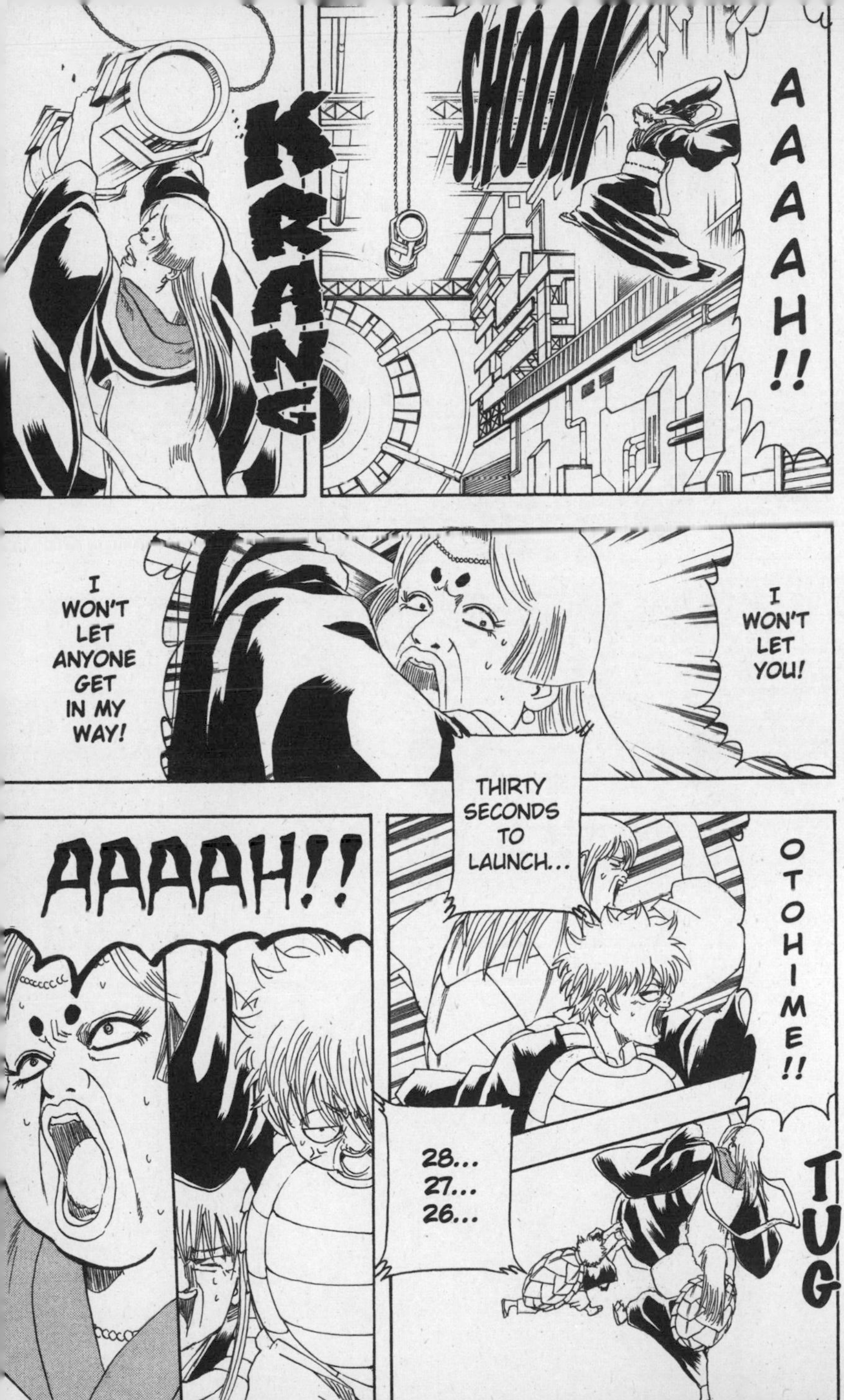
SHOOM
AAAAH!!
KRANG
I WON'T LET YOU!
I WON'T LET ANYONE GET IN MY WAY!
THIRTY SECONDS TO LAUNCH...
OTOHIME!!
28...
27...
26...
TUG
AAAAH!!

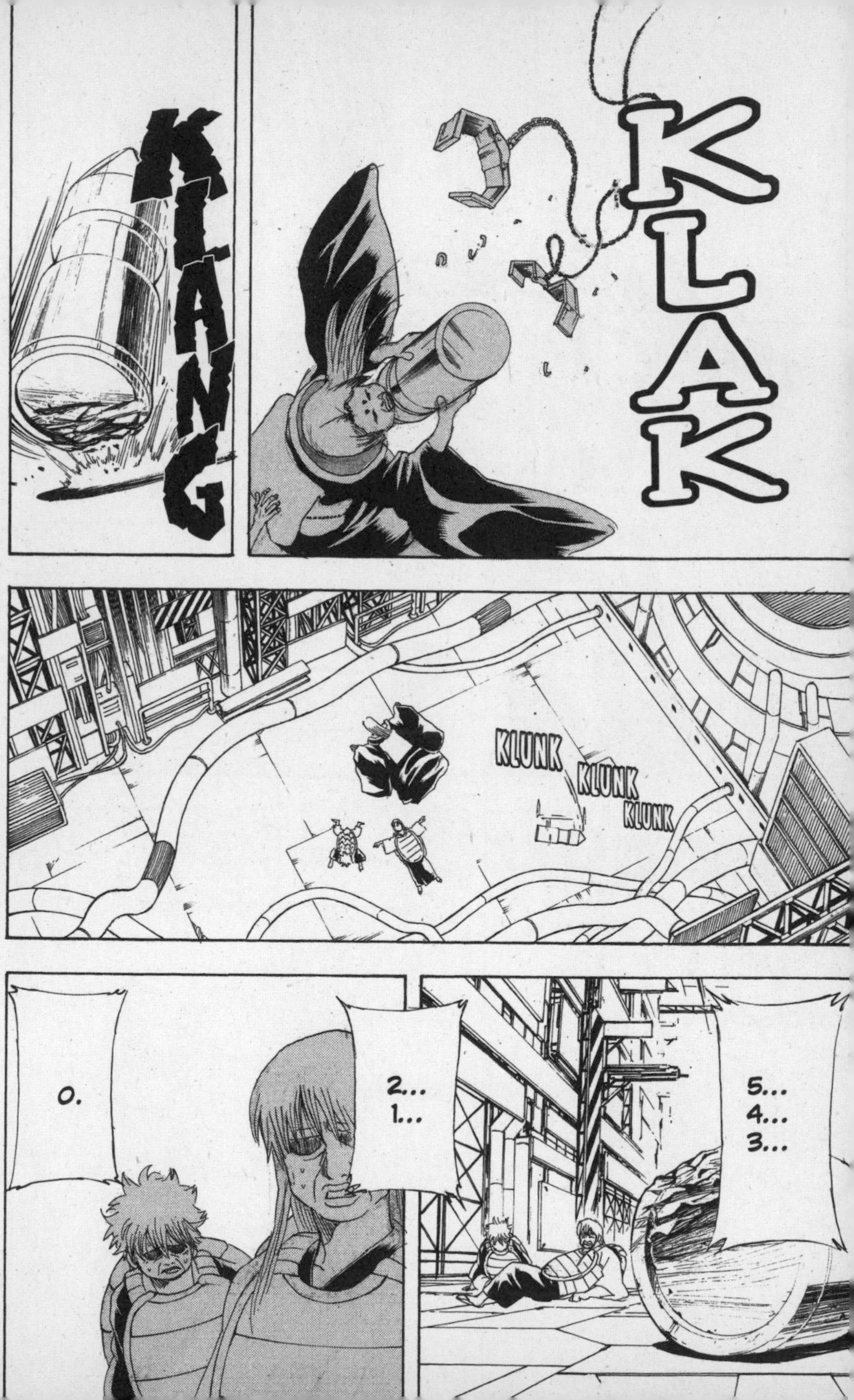
KLAK
KLANG
KLUNK
KLUNK
KLUNK
5... 4... 3...
2... 1...
0.

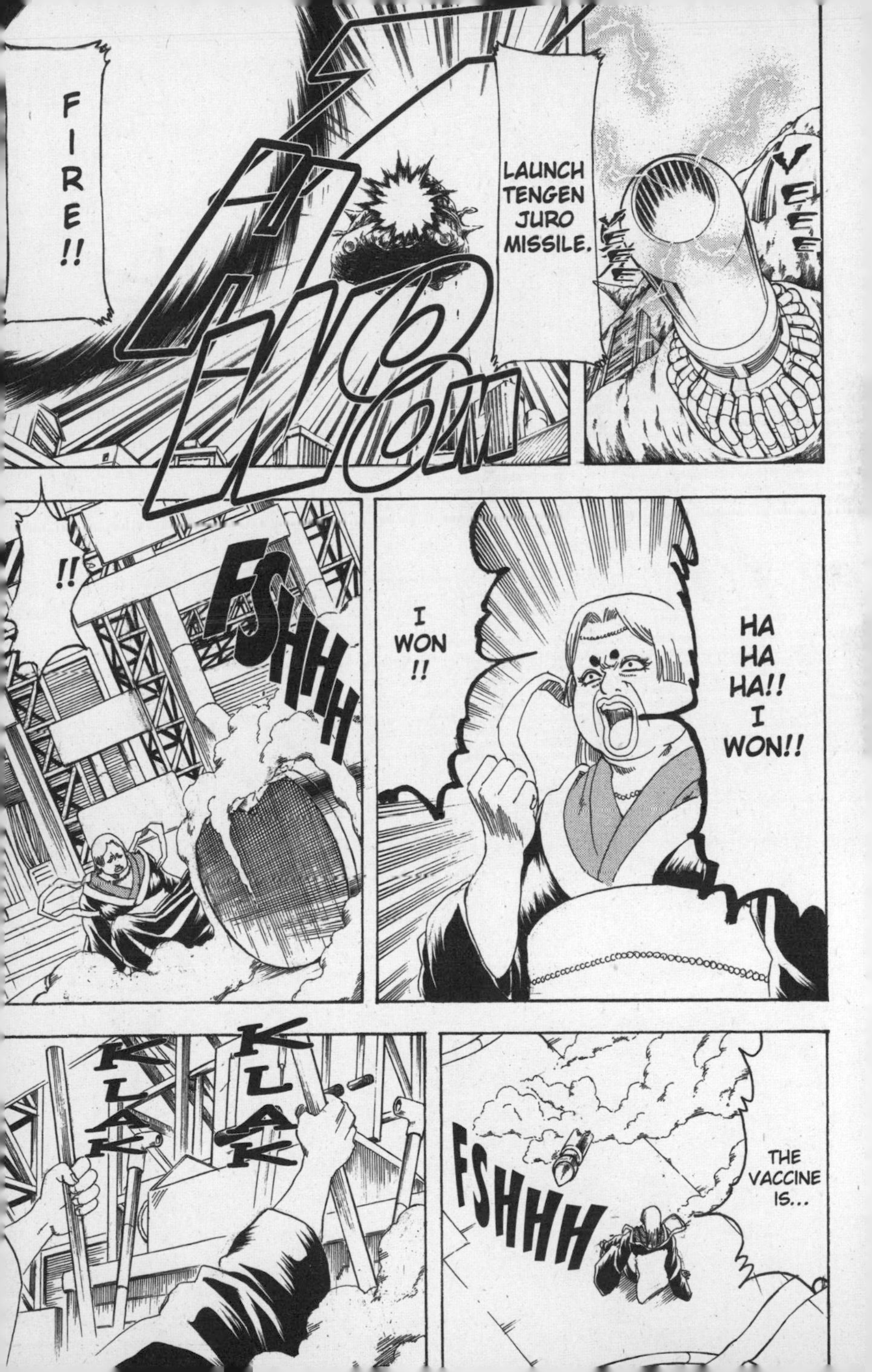
VEEE
VEEE
LAUNCH TENGEN JURO MISSILE.
FIRE!!
HA HA HA!! I WON!!
I WON !!
FSHHH
!!
THE VACCINE IS...
FSHHH
KLAK
KLAK

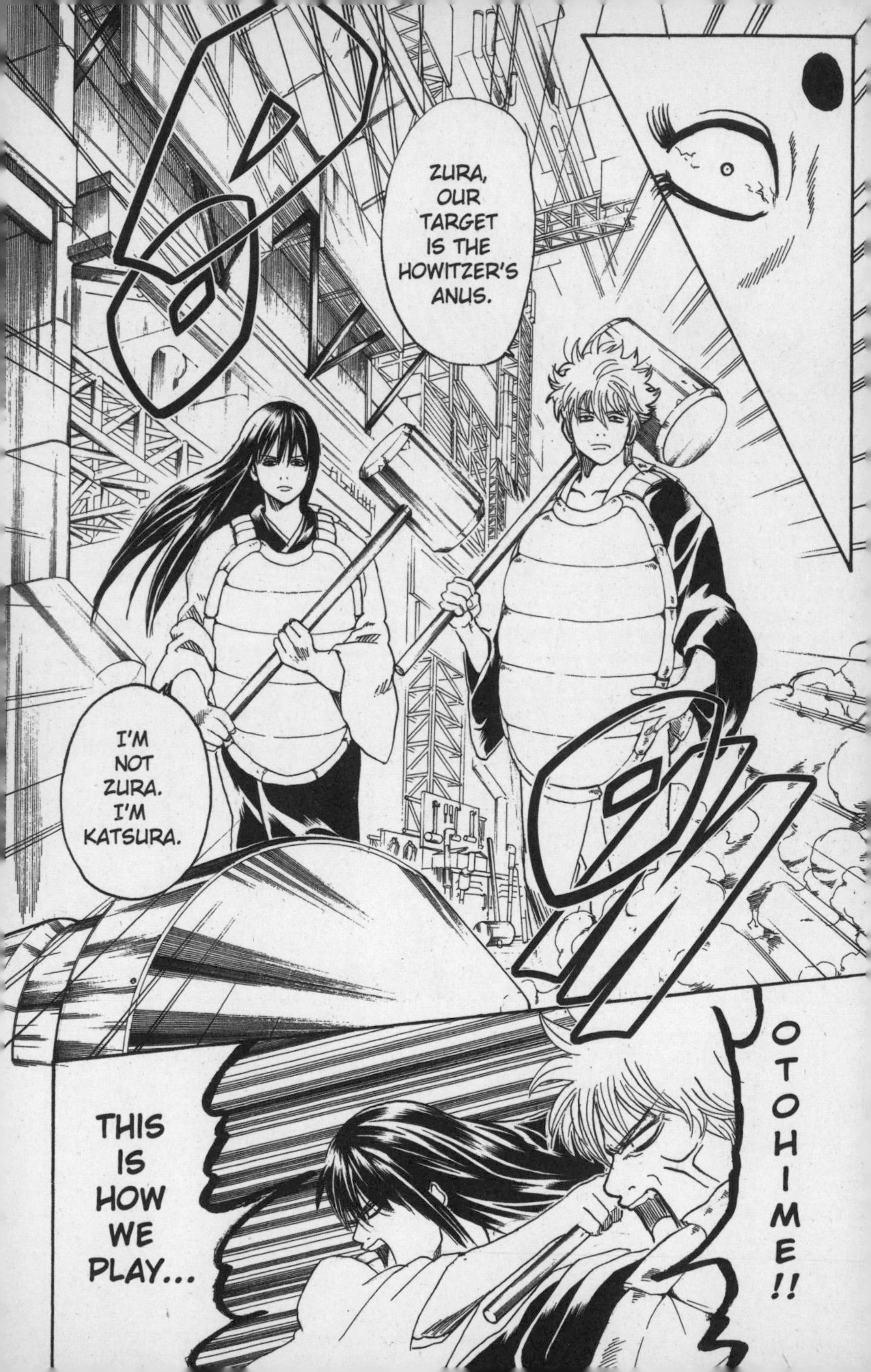
ZURA, OUR TARGET IS THE HOWITZER'S ANUS.
I'M NOT ZURA. I'M KATSURA.
OTOHIME!!
THIS IS HOW WE PLAY...

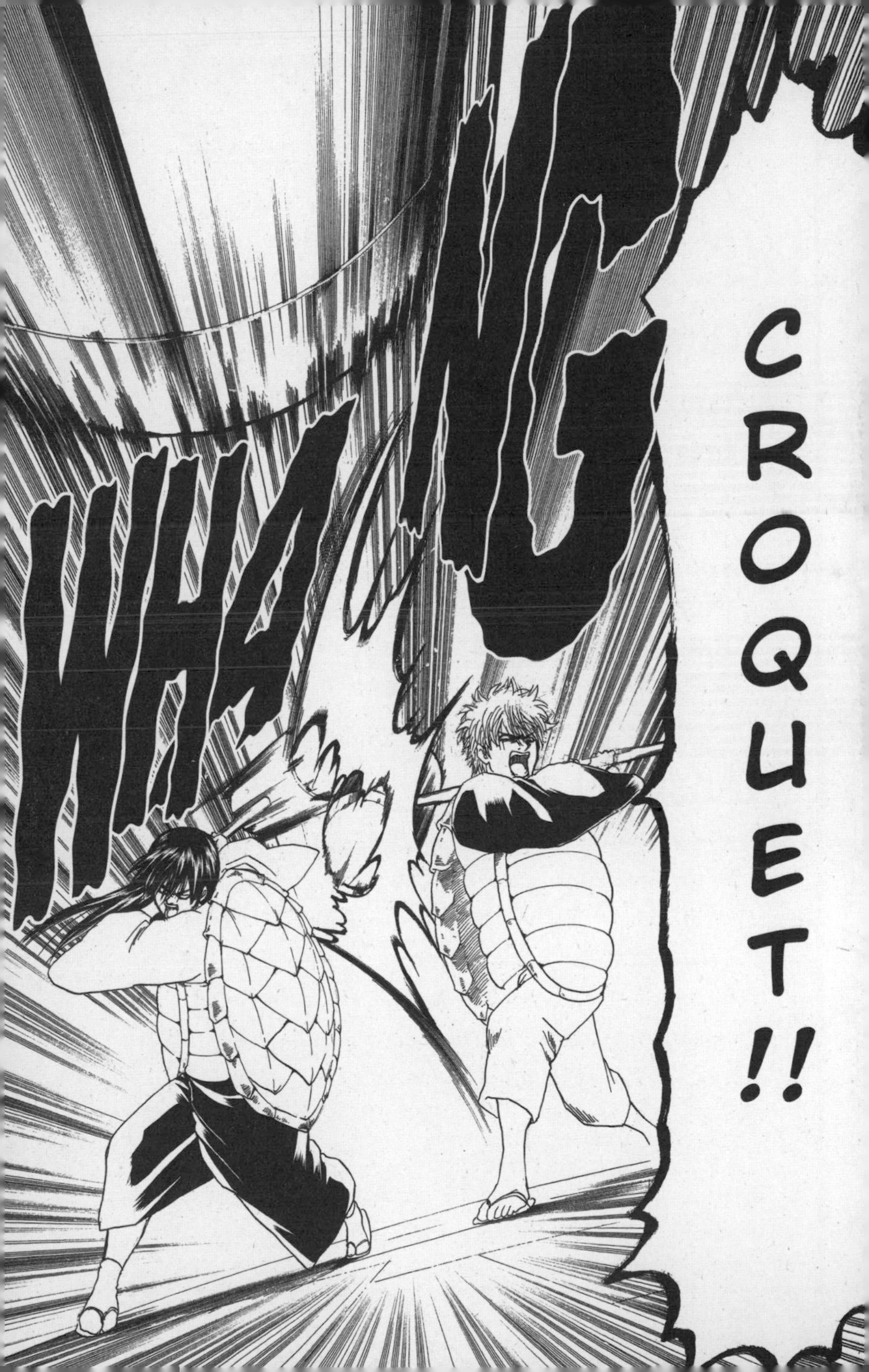
WHANG
CROQUET!!

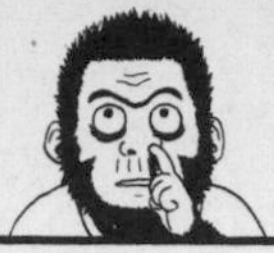

Sorachi's Q&A
Hanging with the Readers #59

(Question from Gin Sekai)

How many Shinsengumi members are there? In Lesson 33, 18 men represented over half of the Shinsengumi, which is comprised of 10 units. So, if we exclude Yamazaki who works alone, then each unit would have only 2 to 3 members. Are there really only around 35 Shinsengumi members?

(Answer)

Shinsengumi periodically recruits new officers. It has grown into a large organization. In volume 19, Kondo is heading to his hometown, where he does his recruiting. Currently, each unit has about 10 members.

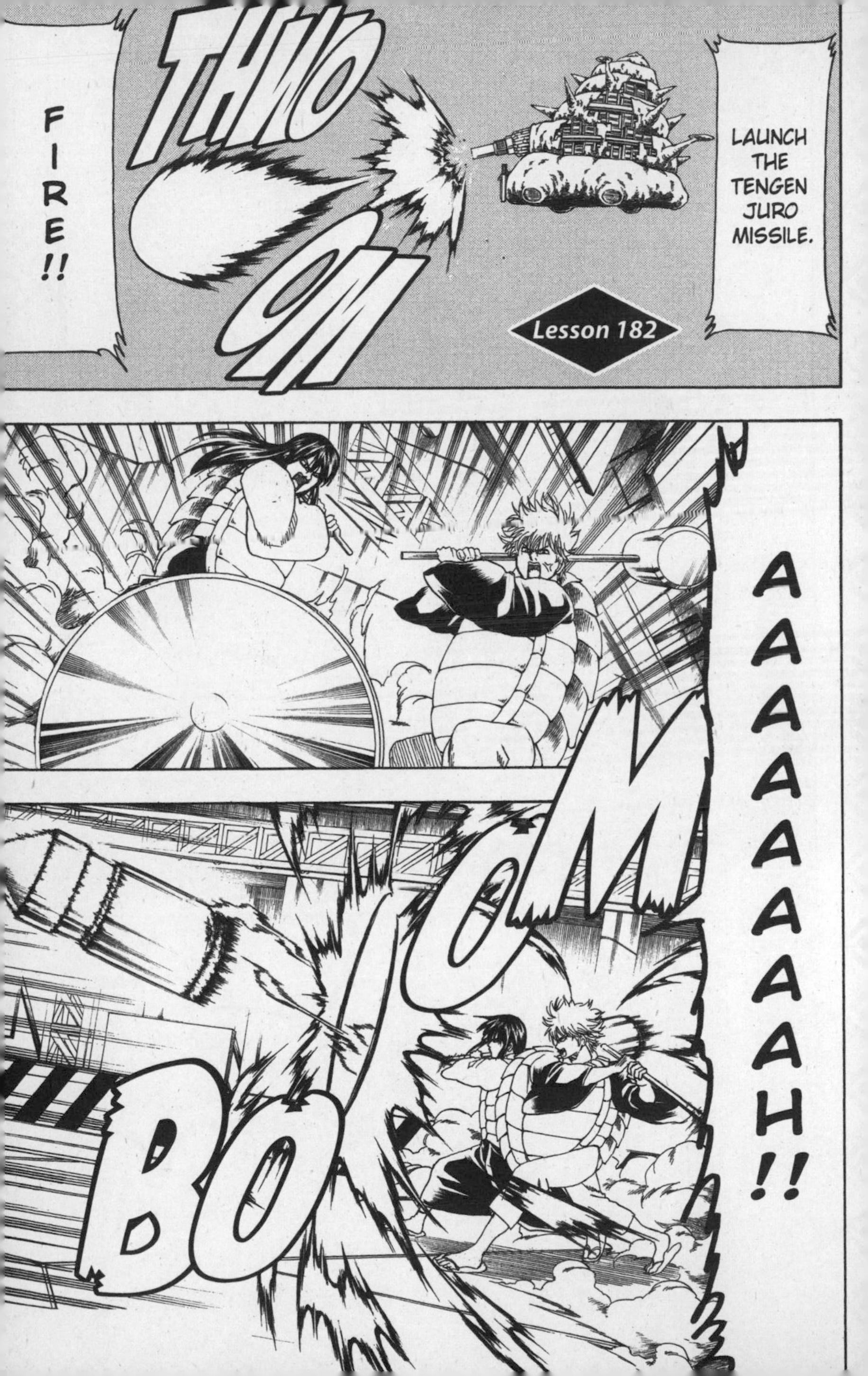
LAUNCH THE TENGEN JURO MISSILE.
Lesson 182
FIRE!!
THWOOM
AAAAAAAAH!!
BOOM

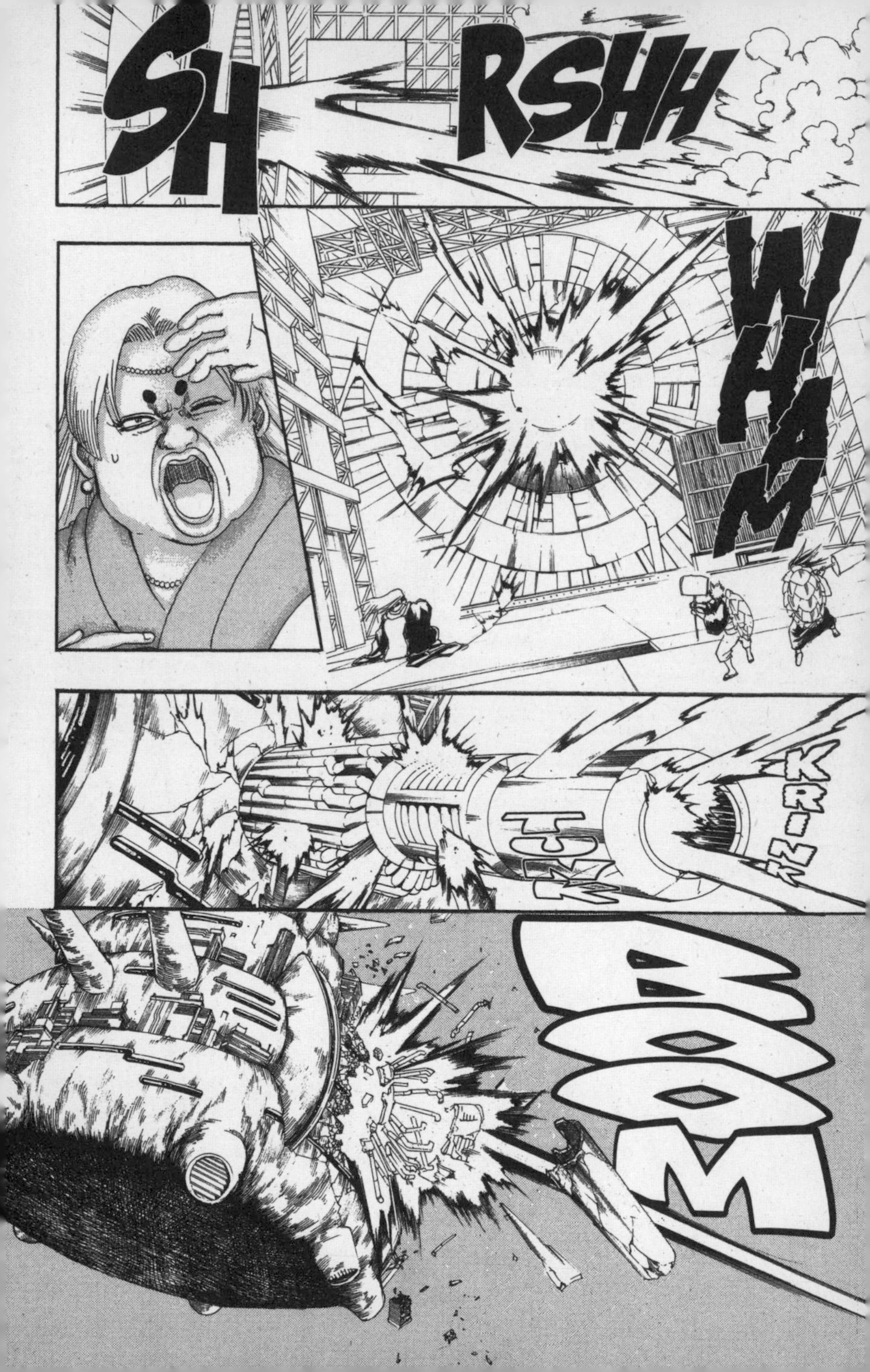
SH RSHH
WHAM
KRINK
TUNK
BOOM

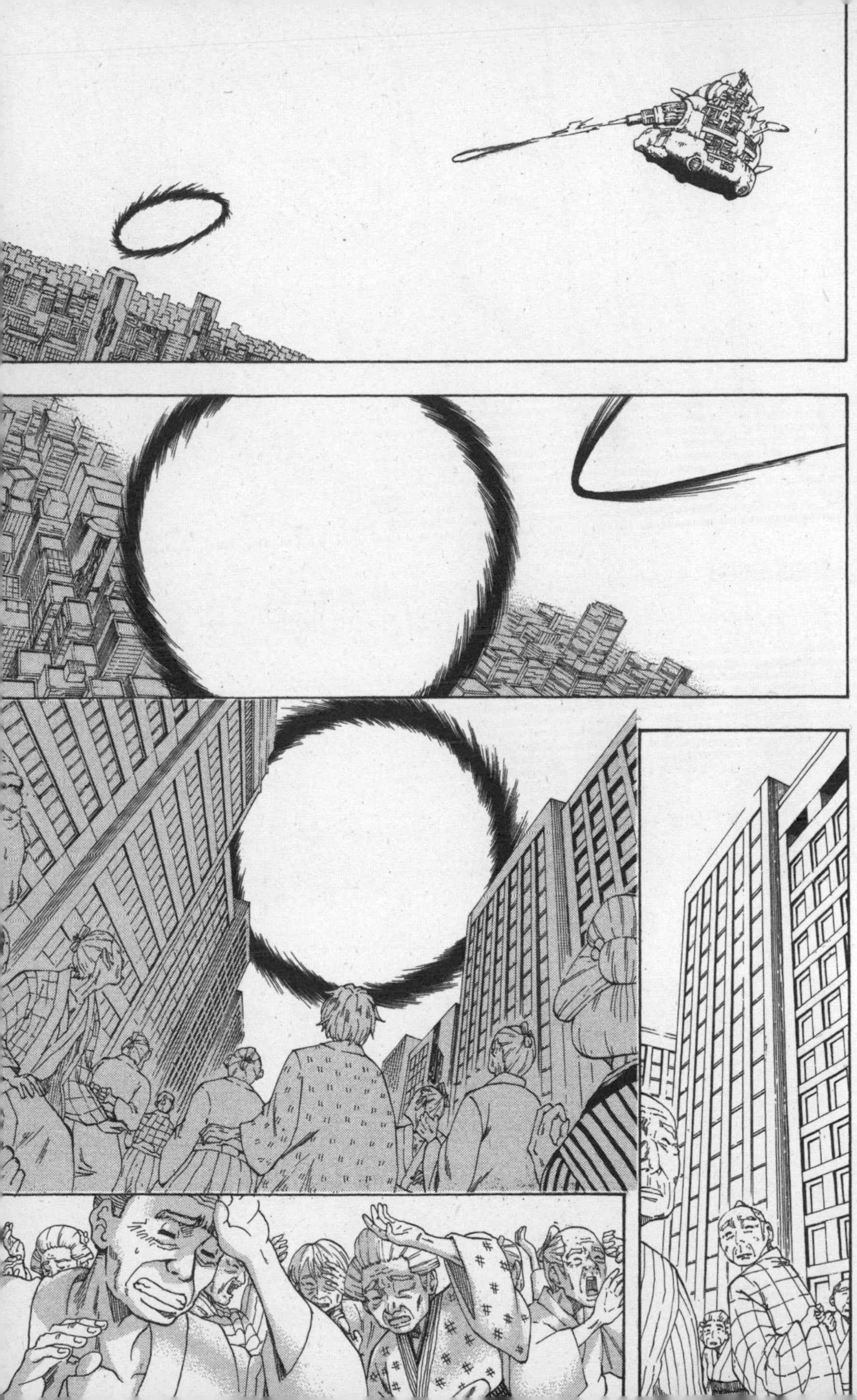

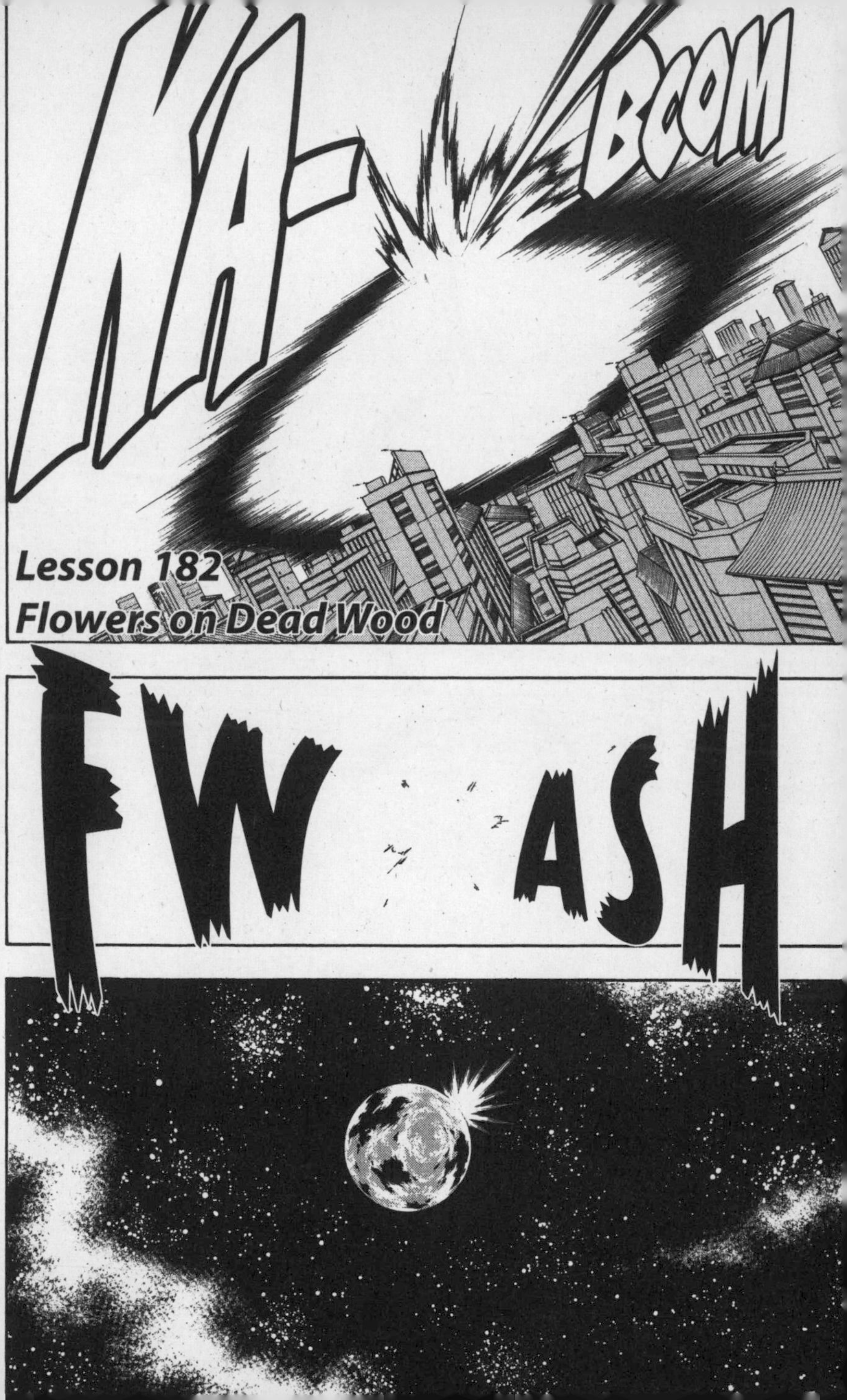
KA-BOOM
Lesson 182
Flowers on Dead Wood
FWASH

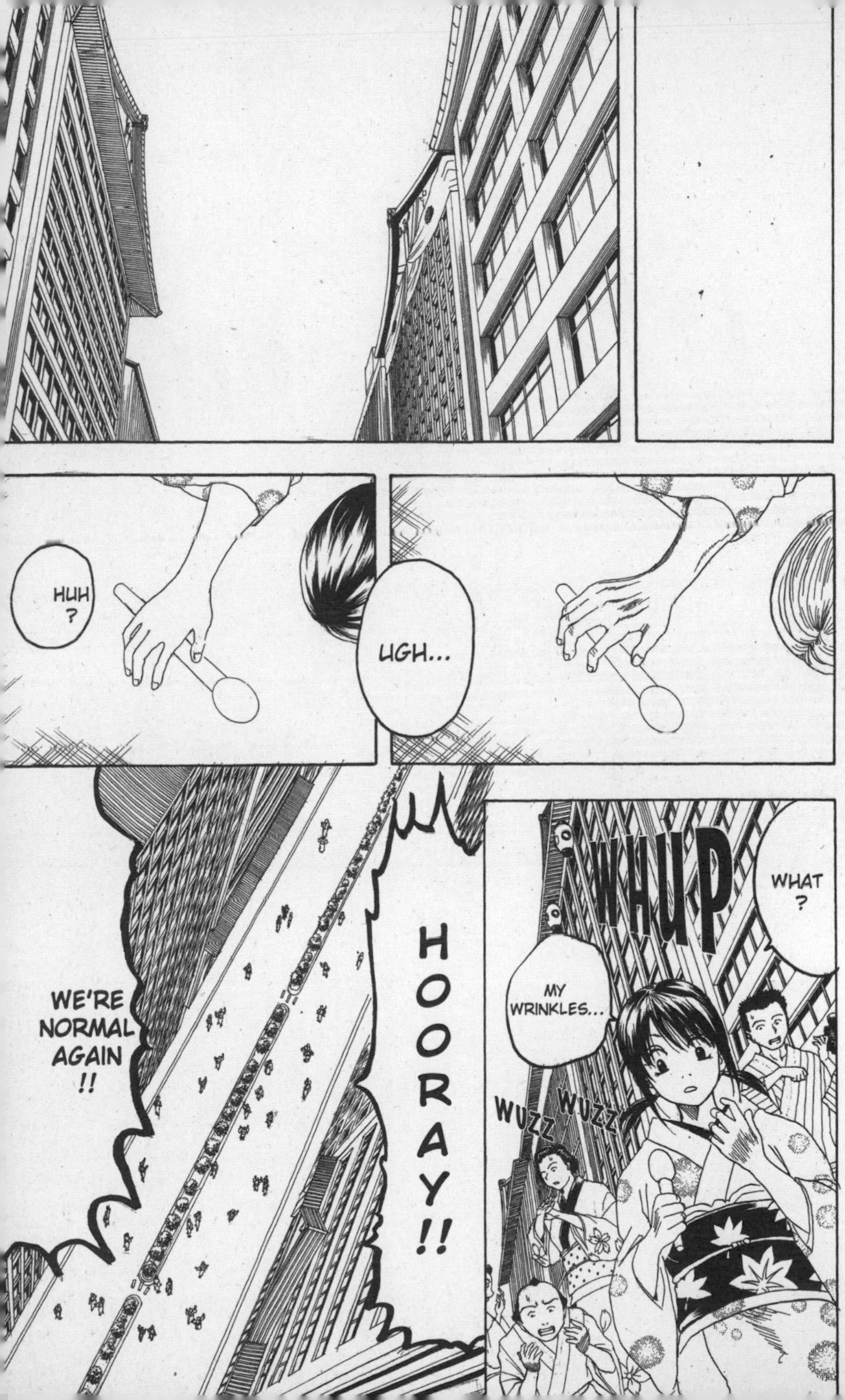
UGH...
HUH ?
WHAT ?
WHUP
MY WRINKLES...
WUZZ
WUZZ
HOORAY!!
WE'RE NORMAL AGAIN !!

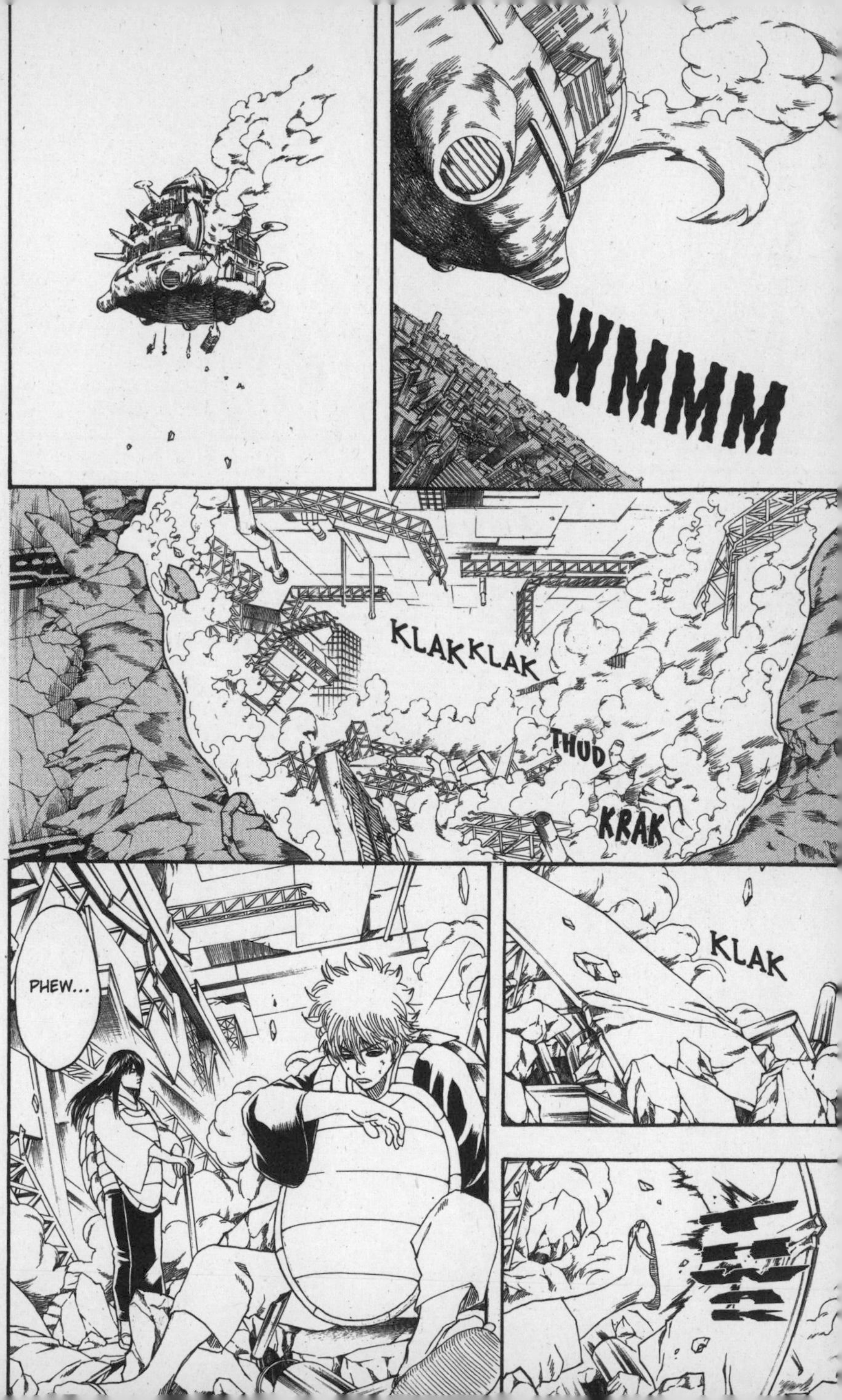
WMMM
KLAKKLAK
THUD
KRAK
KLAK
PHEW...

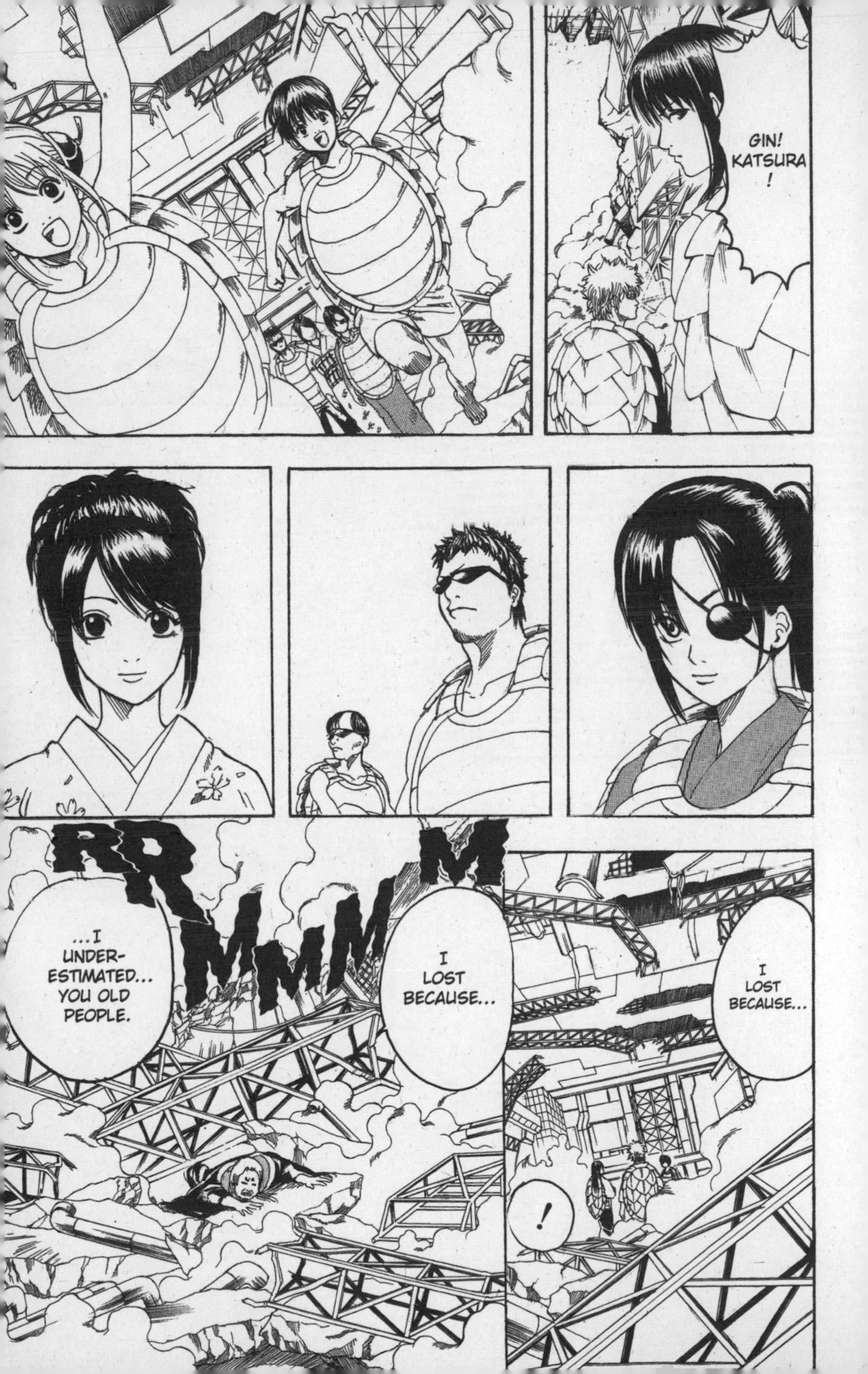
GIN! KATSURA !
I LOST BECAUSE...
!
RRMMMM
I LOST BECAUSE...
...I UNDER-ESTIMATED... YOU OLD PEOPLE.

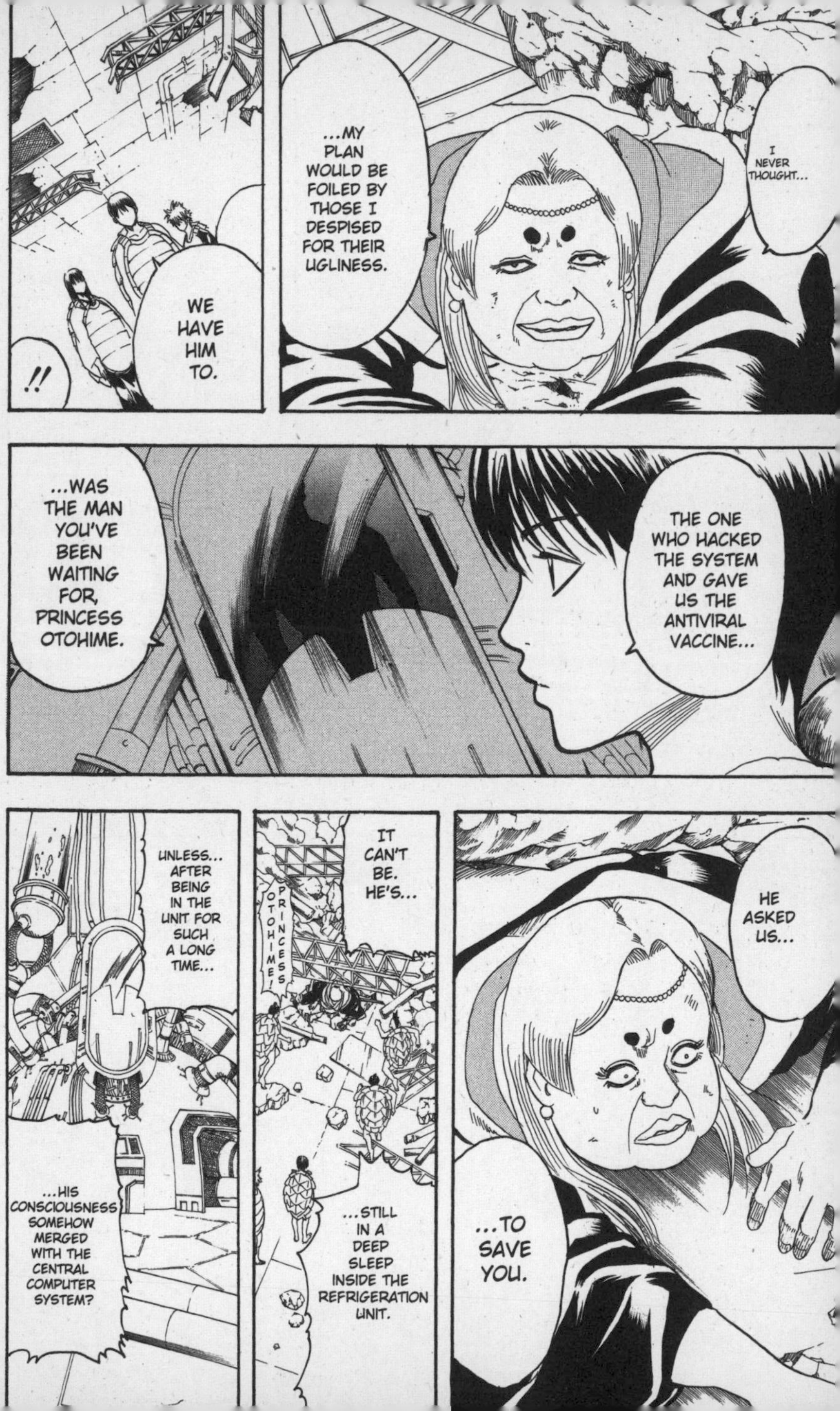
I NEVER THOUGHT...
...MY PLAN WOULD BE FOILED BY THOSE I DESPISED FOR THEIR UGLINESS.
WE HAVE HIM TO.
!!
THE ONE WHO HACKED THE SYSTEM AND GAVE US THE ANTIVIRAL VACCINE...
...WAS THE MAN YOU'VE BEEN WAITING FOR, PRINCESS OTOHIME.
HE ASKED US...
...TO SAVE YOU.
IT CAN'T BE. HE'S...
PRINCESS OTOHIME!
...STILL IN A DEEP SLEEP INSIDE THE REFRIGERATION UNIT.
UNLESS... AFTER BEING IN THE UNIT FOR SUCH A LONG TIME...
...HIS CONSCIOUSNESS SOMEHOW MERGED WITH THE CENTRAL COMPUTER SYSTEM?

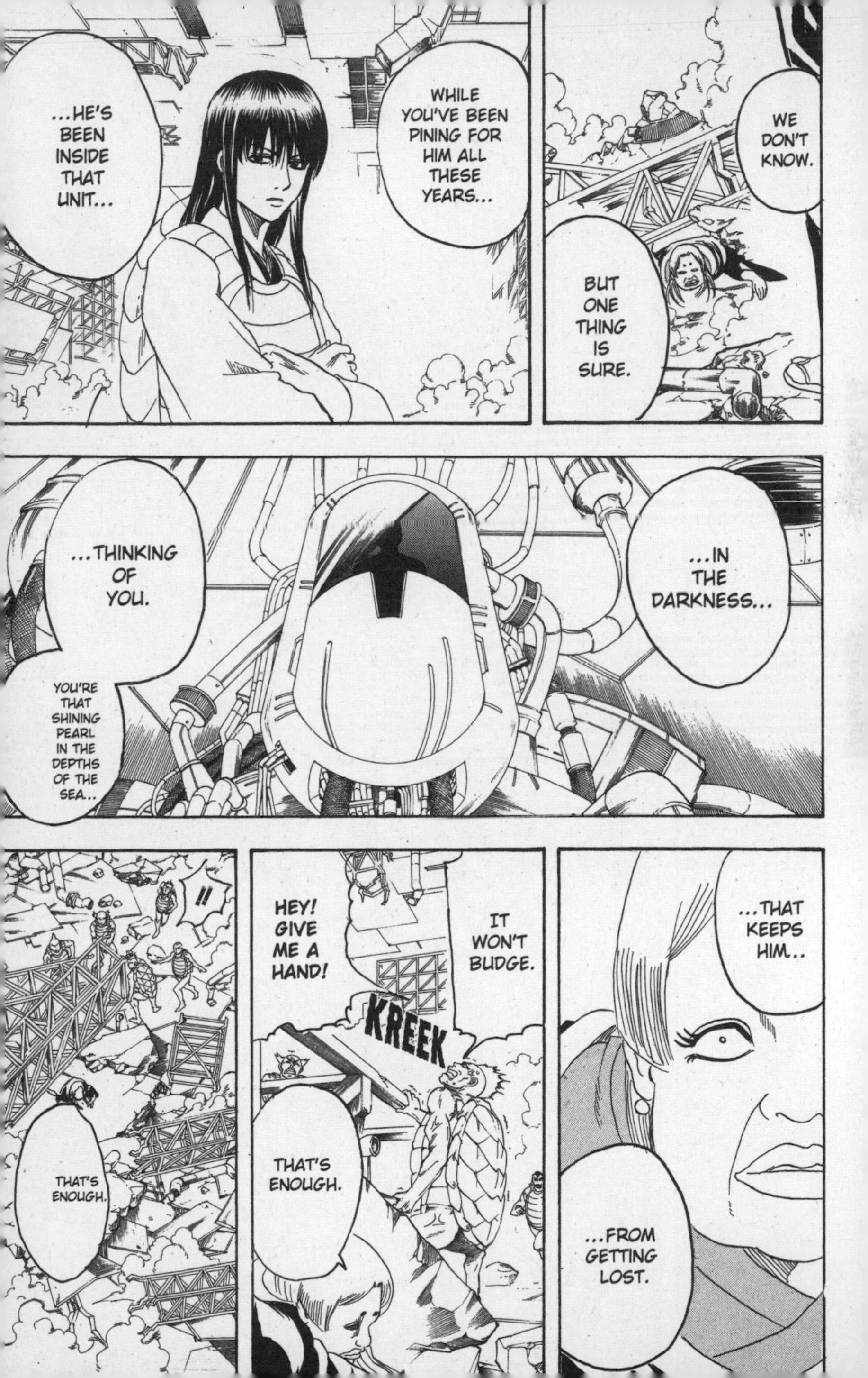
WE DON'T KNOW.
BUT ONE THING IS SURE.
WHILE YOU'VE BEEN PINING FOR HIM ALL THESE YEARS...
...HE'S BEEN INSIDE THAT UNIT...
...IN THE DARKNESS...
...THINKING OF YOU.
YOU'RE THAT SHINING PEARL IN THE DEPTHS OF THE SEA...
...THAT KEEPS HIM...
...FROM GETTING LOST.
IT WON'T BUDGE.
HEY! GIVE ME A HAND!
KREEK
THAT'S ENOUGH.
!!
THAT'S ENOUGH.

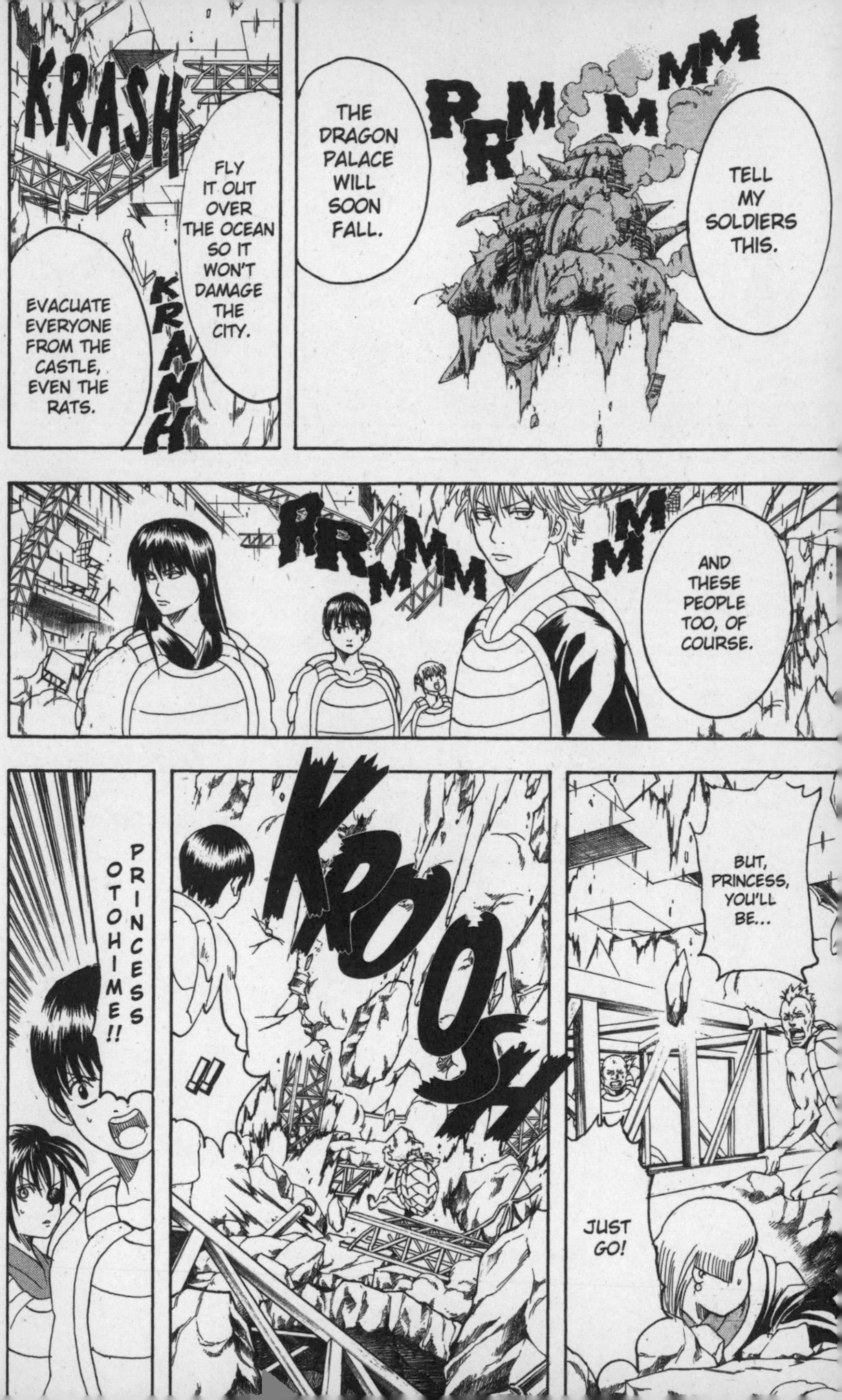
RRMMMMM
TELL MY SOLDIERS THIS.
THE DRAGON PALACE WILL SOON FALL.
KRASH
FLY IT OUT OVER THE OCEAN SO IT WON'T DAMAGE THE CITY.
EVACUATE EVERYONE FROM THE CASTLE, EVEN THE RATS.
KRANH
AND THESE PEOPLE TOO, OF COURSE.
RRMMMMM
BUT, PRINCESS, YOU'LL BE...
JUST GO!
KROOSH
!!
PRINCESS OTOHIME!!

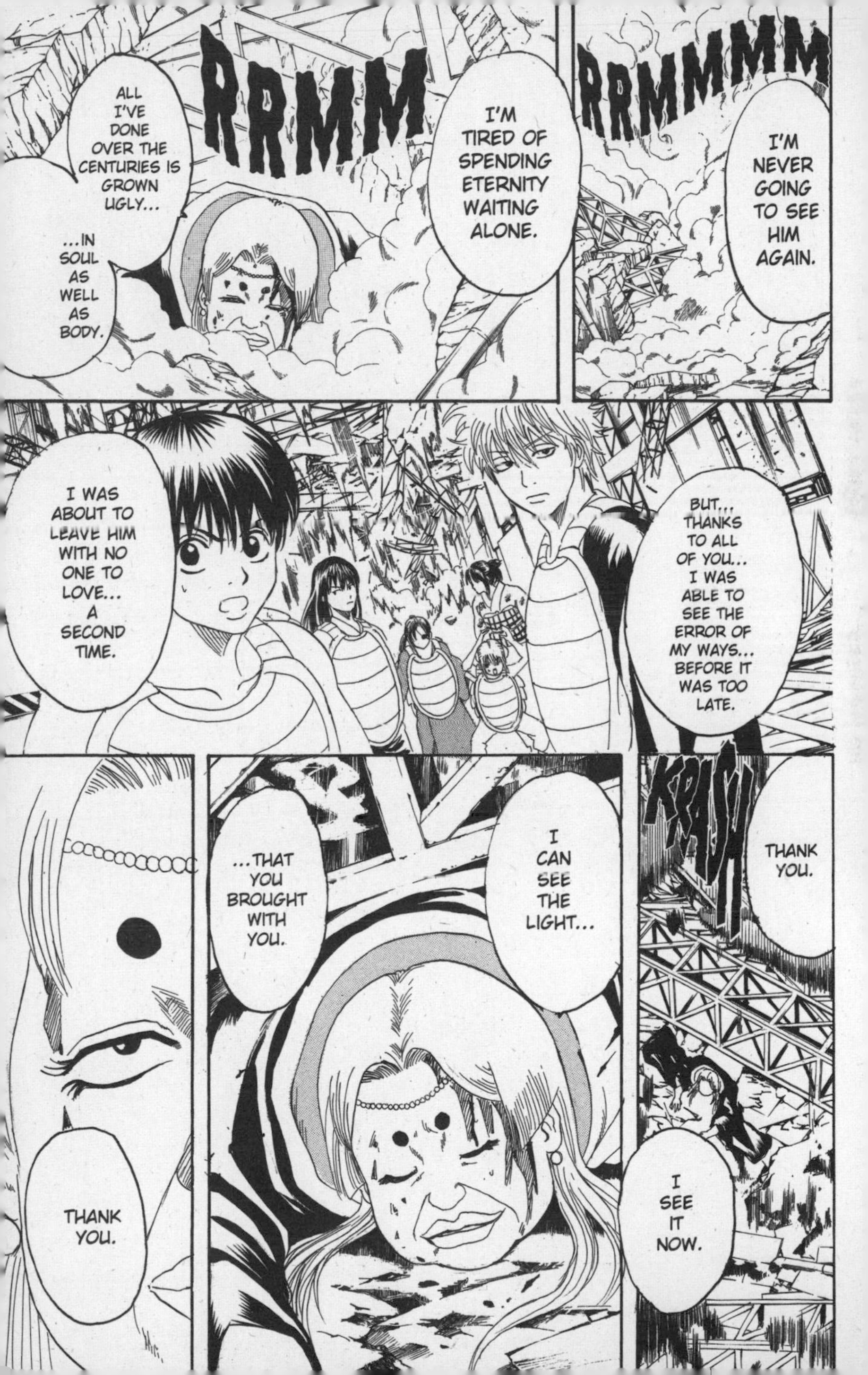
RRMMMMM
I'M NEVER GOING TO SEE HIM AGAIN.
RRMM
I'M TIRED OF SPENDING ETERNITY WAITING ALONE.
ALL I'VE DONE OVER THE CENTURIES IS GROWN UGLY...
...IN SOUL AS WELL AS BODY.
I WAS ABOUT TO LEAVE HIM WITH NO ONE TO LOVE... A SECOND TIME.
BUT... THANKS TO ALL OF YOU... I WAS ABLE TO SEE THE ERROR OF MY WAYS... BEFORE IT WAS TOO LATE.
KRASH
THANK YOU.
I SEE IT NOW.
I CAN SEE THE LIGHT...
...THAT YOU BROUGHT WITH YOU.
THANK YOU.

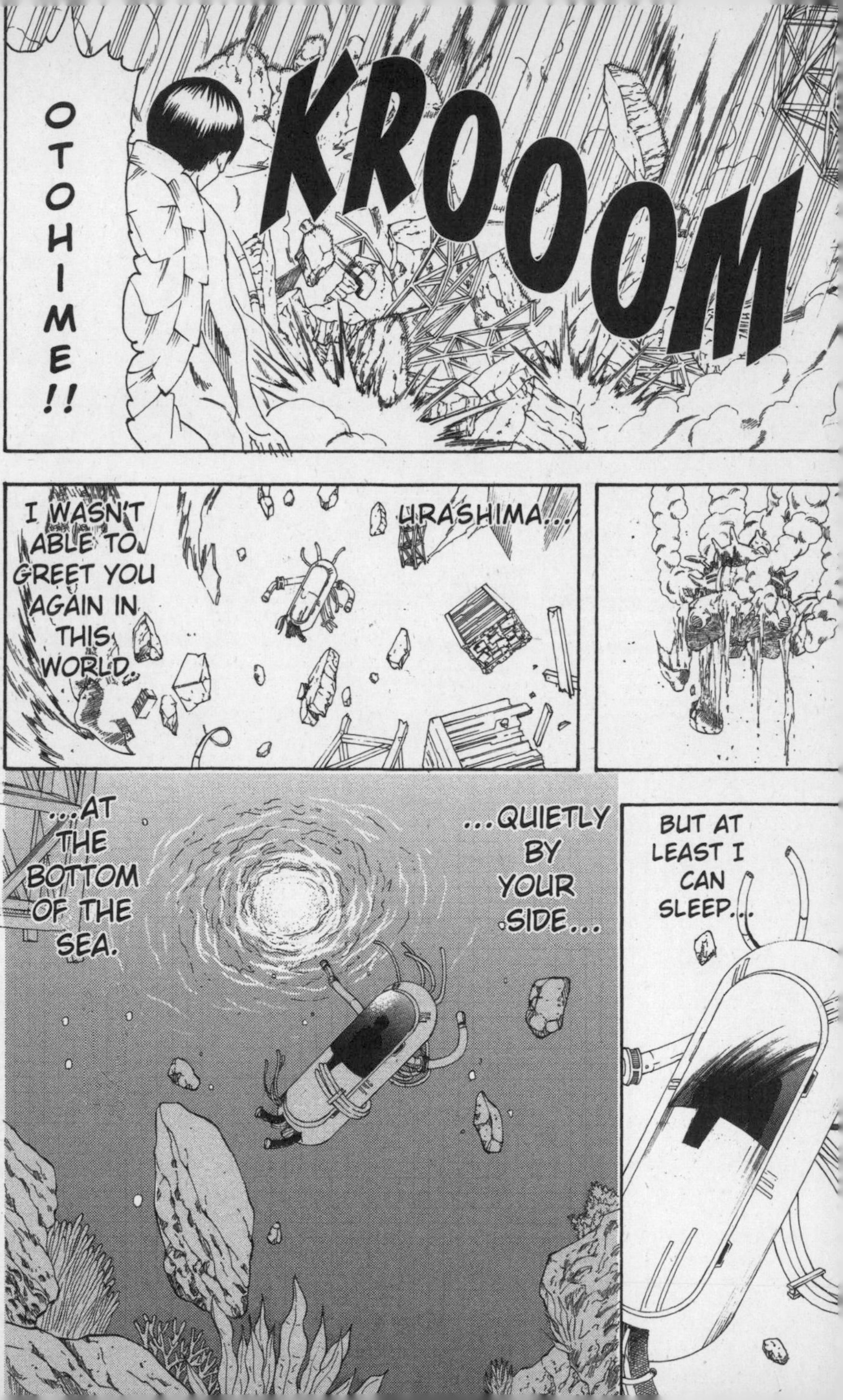
KROOOM
OTOHIME!!
URASHIMA...
I WASN'T ABLE TO GREET YOU AGAIN IN THIS WORLD.
BUT AT LEAST I CAN SLEEP...
...QUIETLY BY YOUR SIDE...
...AT THE BOTTOM OF THE SEA.

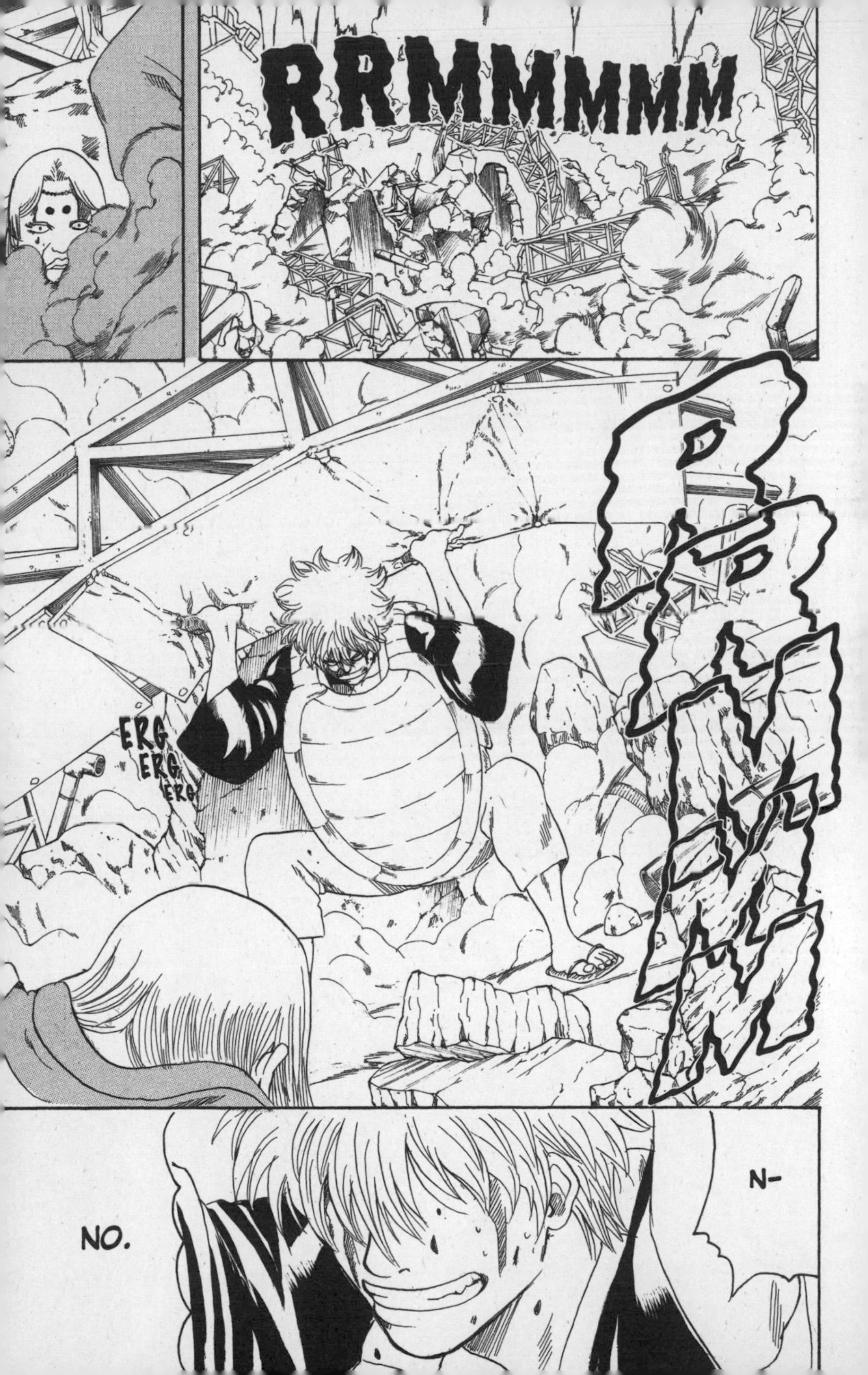
RRMMMMM
ERG
ERG
ERG
N-
NO.

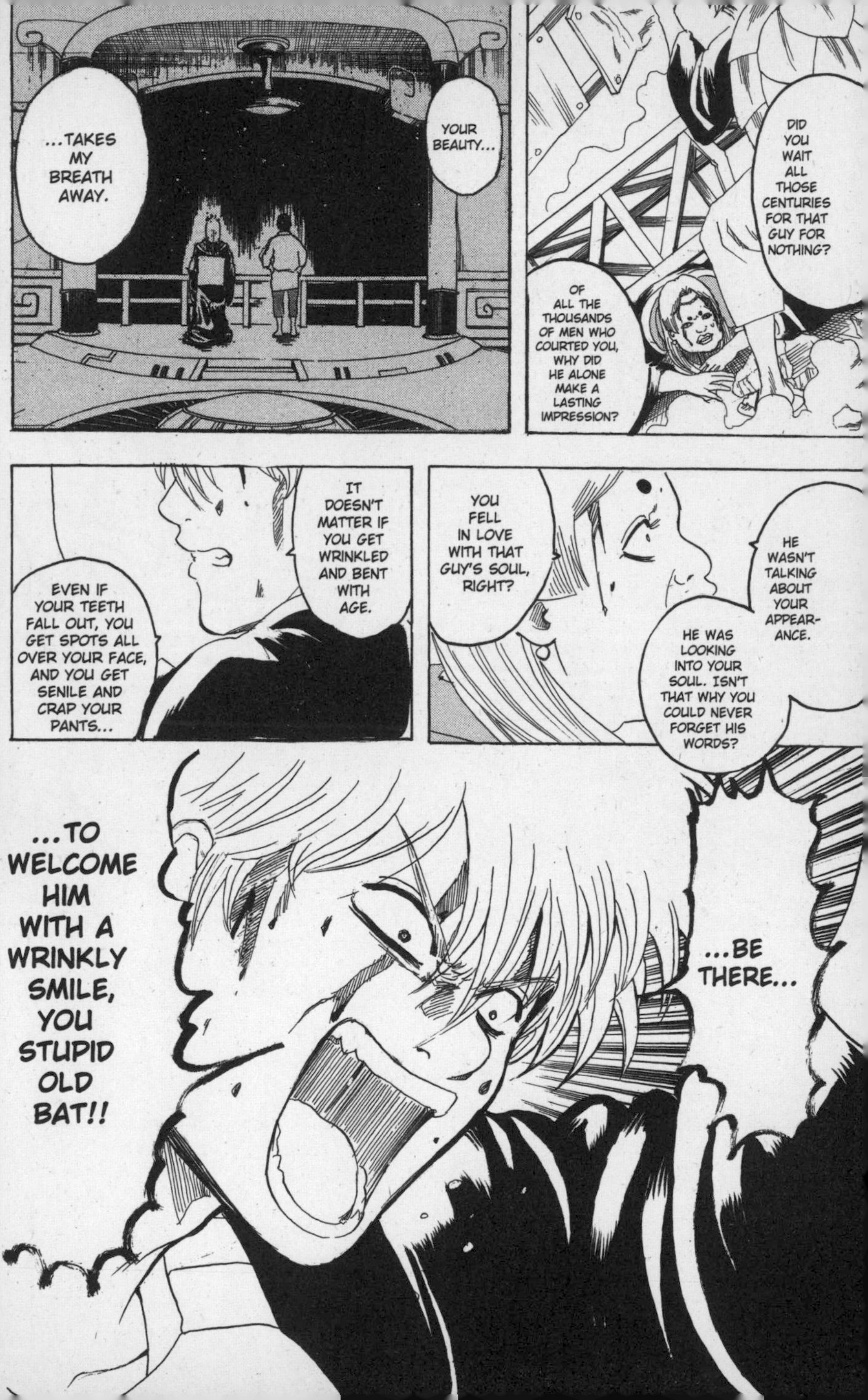
DID YOU WAIT ALL THOSE CENTURIES FOR THAT GUY FOR NOTHING?
OF ALL THE THOUSANDS OF MEN WHO COURTED YOU, WHY DID HE ALONE MAKE A LASTING IMPRESSION?
YOUR BEAUTY...
...TAKES MY BREATH AWAY.
HE WASN'T TALKING ABOUT YOUR APPEAR-ANCE.
HE WAS LOOKING INTO YOUR SOUL. ISN'T THAT WHY YOU COULD NEVER FORGET HIS WORDS?
YOU FELL IN LOVE WITH THAT GUY'S SOUL, RIGHT?
IT DOESN'T MATTER IF YOU GET WRINKLED AND BENT WITH AGE.
EVEN IF YOUR TEETH FALL OUT, YOU GET SPOTS ALL OVER YOUR FACE, AND YOU GET SENILE AND CRAP YOUR PANTS...
...BE THERE...
...TO WELCOME HIM WITH A WRINKLY SMILE, YOU STUPID OLD BAT!!

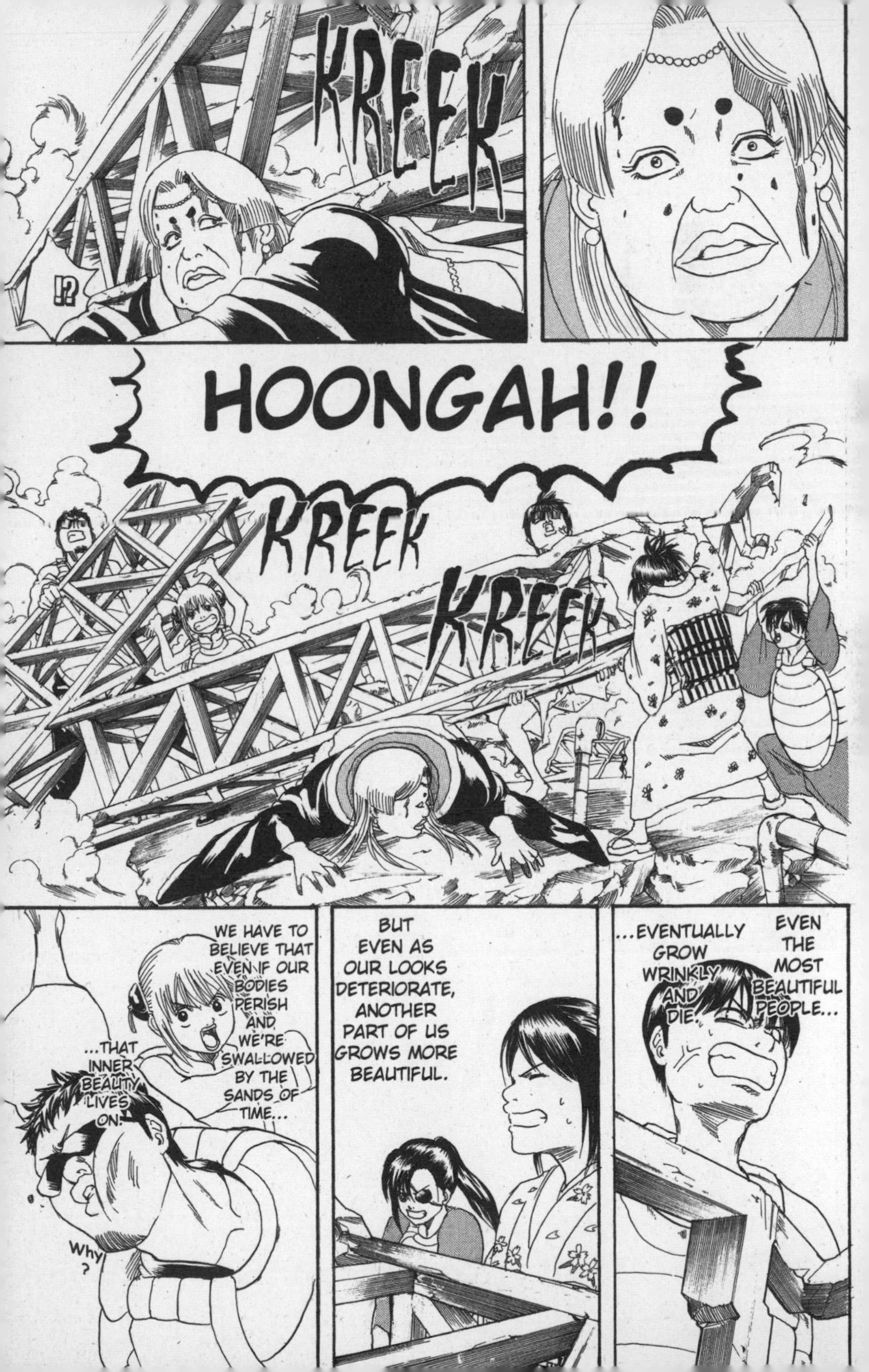
KREEK
!?
HOONGAH!!
KREEK
KREEK
EVEN THE MOST BEAUTIFUL PEOPLE...
...EVENTUALLY GROW WRINKLY AND DIE.
BUT EVEN AS OUR LOOKS DETERIORATE, ANOTHER PART OF US GROWS MORE BEAUTIFUL.
WE HAVE TO BELIEVE THAT EVEN IF OUR BODIES PERISH AND WE'RE SWALLOWED BY THE SANDS OF TIME...
...THAT INNER BEAUTY LIVES ON.
Why?

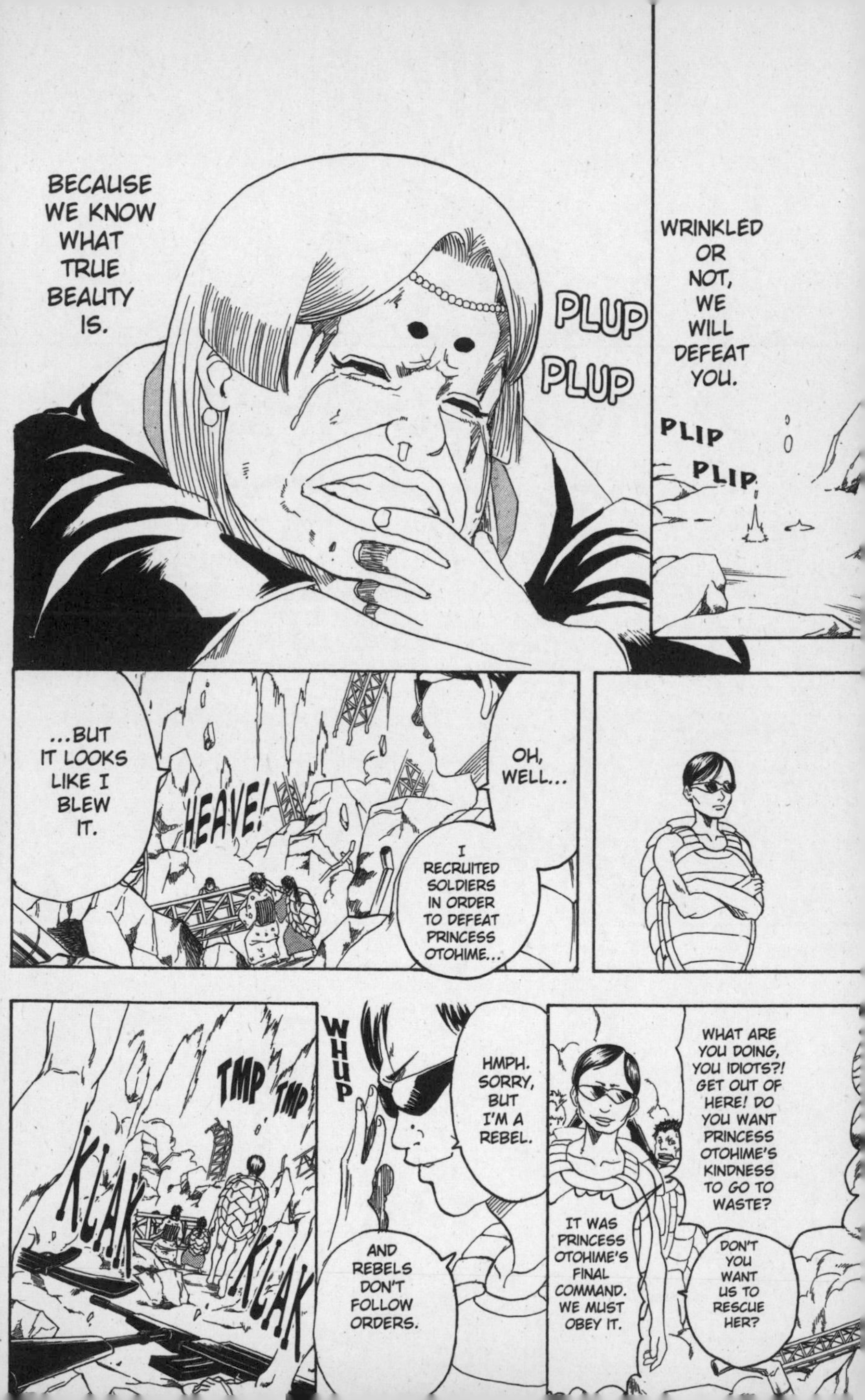
WRINKLED OR NOT, WE WILL DEFEAT YOU.
PLIP
PLIP
PLUP
PLUP
BECAUSE WE KNOW WHAT TRUE BEAUTY IS.
OH, WELL...
I RECRUITED SOLDIERS IN ORDER TO DEFEAT PRINCESS OTOHIME...
...BUT IT LOOKS LIKE I BLEW IT.
HEAVE!
WHAT ARE YOU DOING, YOU IDIOTS?! GET OUT OF HERE! DO YOU WANT PRINCESS OTOHIME'S KINDNESS TO GO TO WASTE?
DON'T YOU WANT US TO RESCUE HER?
IT WAS PRINCESS OTOHIME'S FINAL COMMAND. WE MUST OBEY IT.
WHUP
HMPH. SORRY, BUT I'M A REBEL.
AND REBELS DON'T FOLLOW ORDERS.
TMP
TMP
KLAK
KLAK

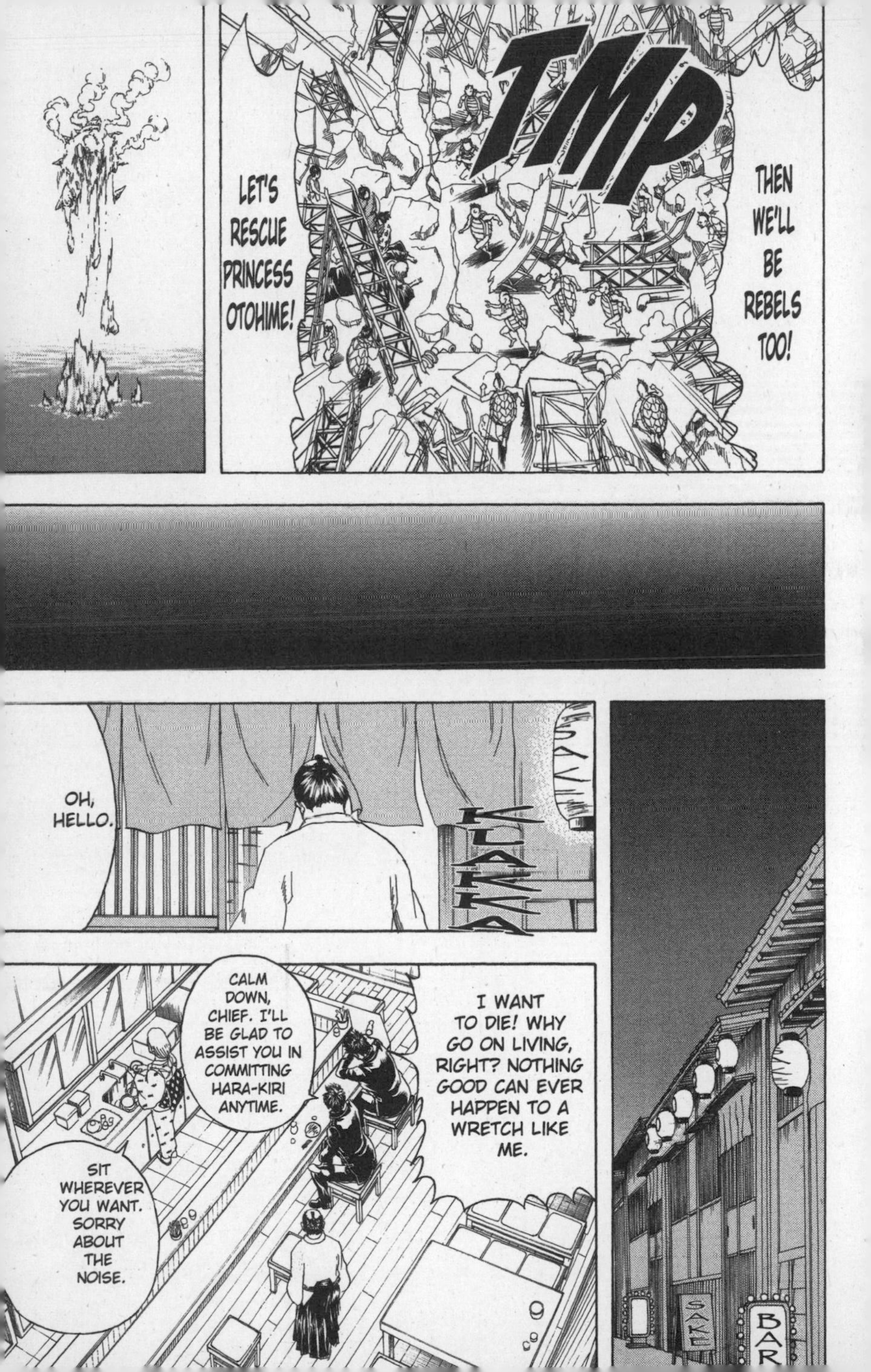
THEN WE'LL BE REBELS TOO!
TMP
LET'S RESCUE PRINCESS OTOHIME!
SAKE
BAR
KLAKKA
OH, HELLO.
I WANT TO DIE! WHY GO ON LIVING, RIGHT? NOTHING GOOD CAN EVER HAPPEN TO A WRETCH LIKE ME.
CALM DOWN, CHIEF. I'LL BE GLAD TO ASSIST YOU IN COMMITTING HARA-KIRI ANYTIME.
SIT WHEREVER YOU WANT. SORRY ABOUT THE NOISE.

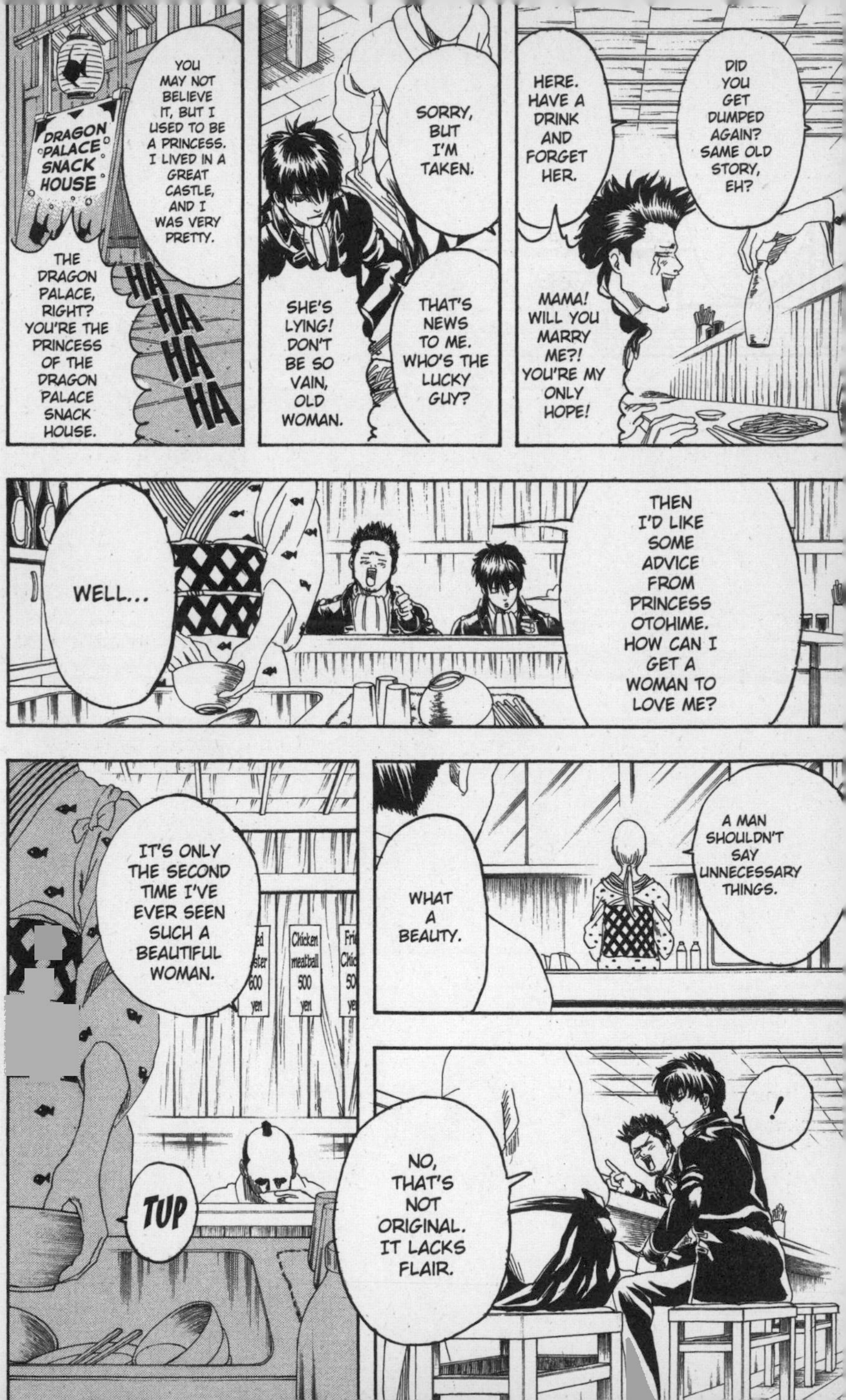
DID YOU GET DUMPED AGAIN? SAME OLD STORY, EH?
HERE. HAVE A DRINK AND FORGET HER.
MAMA! WILL YOU MARRY ME?! YOU'RE MY ONLY HOPE!
SORRY, BUT I'M TAKEN.
THAT'S NEWS TO ME. WHO'S THE LUCKY GUY?
SHE'S LYING! DON'T BE SO VAIN, OLD WOMAN.
YOU MAY NOT BELIEVE IT, BUT I USED TO BE A PRINCESS. I LIVED IN A GREAT CASTLE, AND I WAS VERY PRETTY.
DRAGON PALACE SNACK HOUSE
HA HA HA HA
THE DRAGON PALACE, RIGHT? YOU'RE THE PRINCESS OF THE DRAGON PALACE SNACK HOUSE.
THEN I'D LIKE SOME ADVICE FROM PRINCESS OTOHIME. HOW CAN I GET A WOMAN TO LOVE ME?
WELL...
A MAN SHOULDN'T SAY UNNECESSARY THINGS.
WHAT A BEAUTY.
!
NO, THAT'S NOT ORIGINAL. IT LACKS FLAIR.
IT'S ONLY THE SECOND TIME I'VE EVER SEEN SUCH A BEAUTIFUL WOMAN.
Chicken meatball 500 yen
TUP

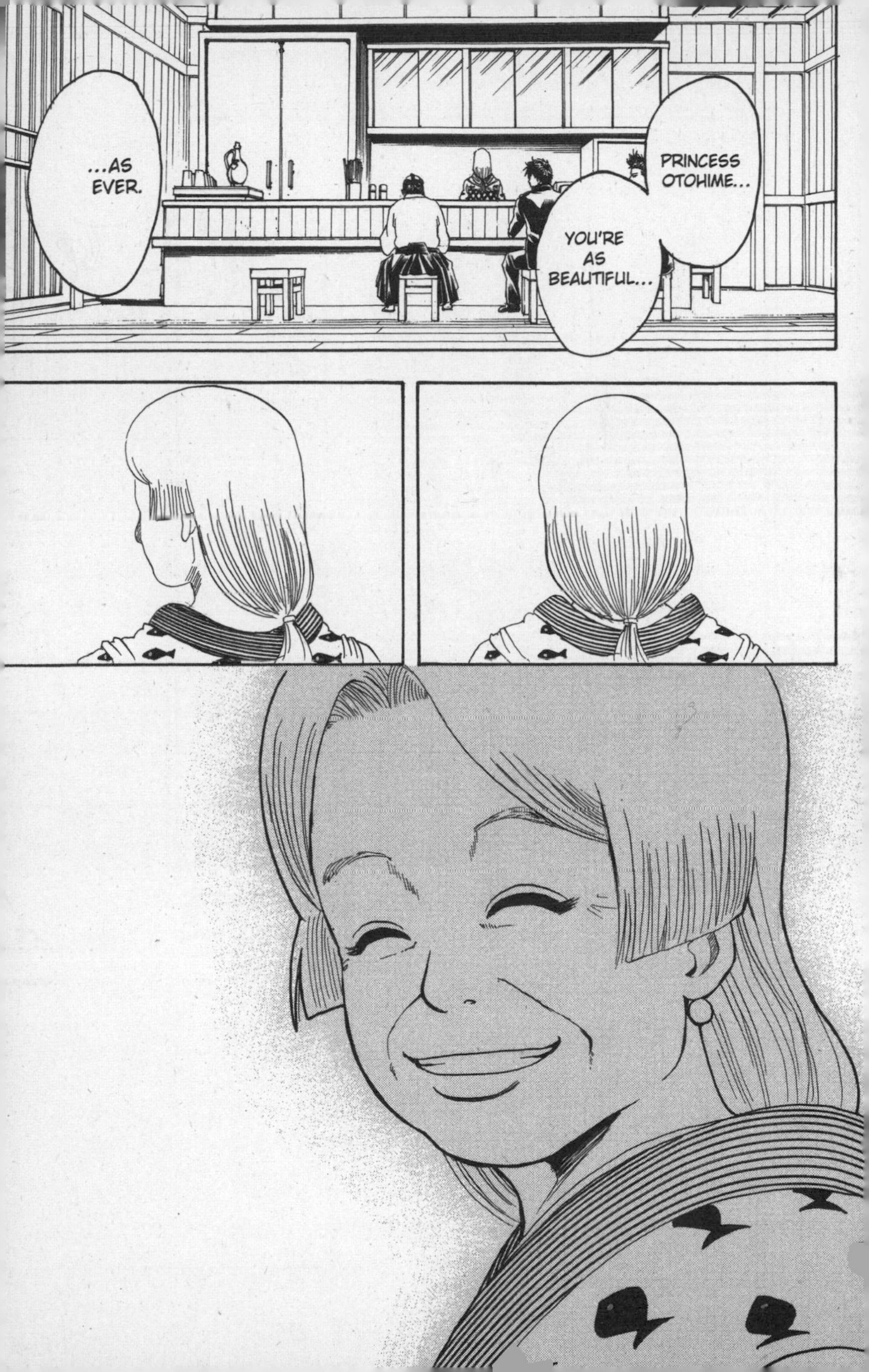
PRINCESS OTOHIME...
YOU'RE AS BEAUTIFUL...
...AS EVER.

FABULOUS FAN ART!

ric T. in California sent us this drawing of Gin looking cool. Gin would surely be pleased.
Now draw us some pictures of Shinpachi and Kagura!

end your fan art to:

VIZ Media
Attn: Mike Montesa, Editor
295 Bay St.
San Francisco, CA 94133

e sure to include the signed release form available here:
ttp://www.shonenjump.com/fanart/Fan_Art_Release.pdf
ubmissions will not be returned. Submissions without a signed release form will
e fed to the Amanto sea lions at Fisherman's Wharf...

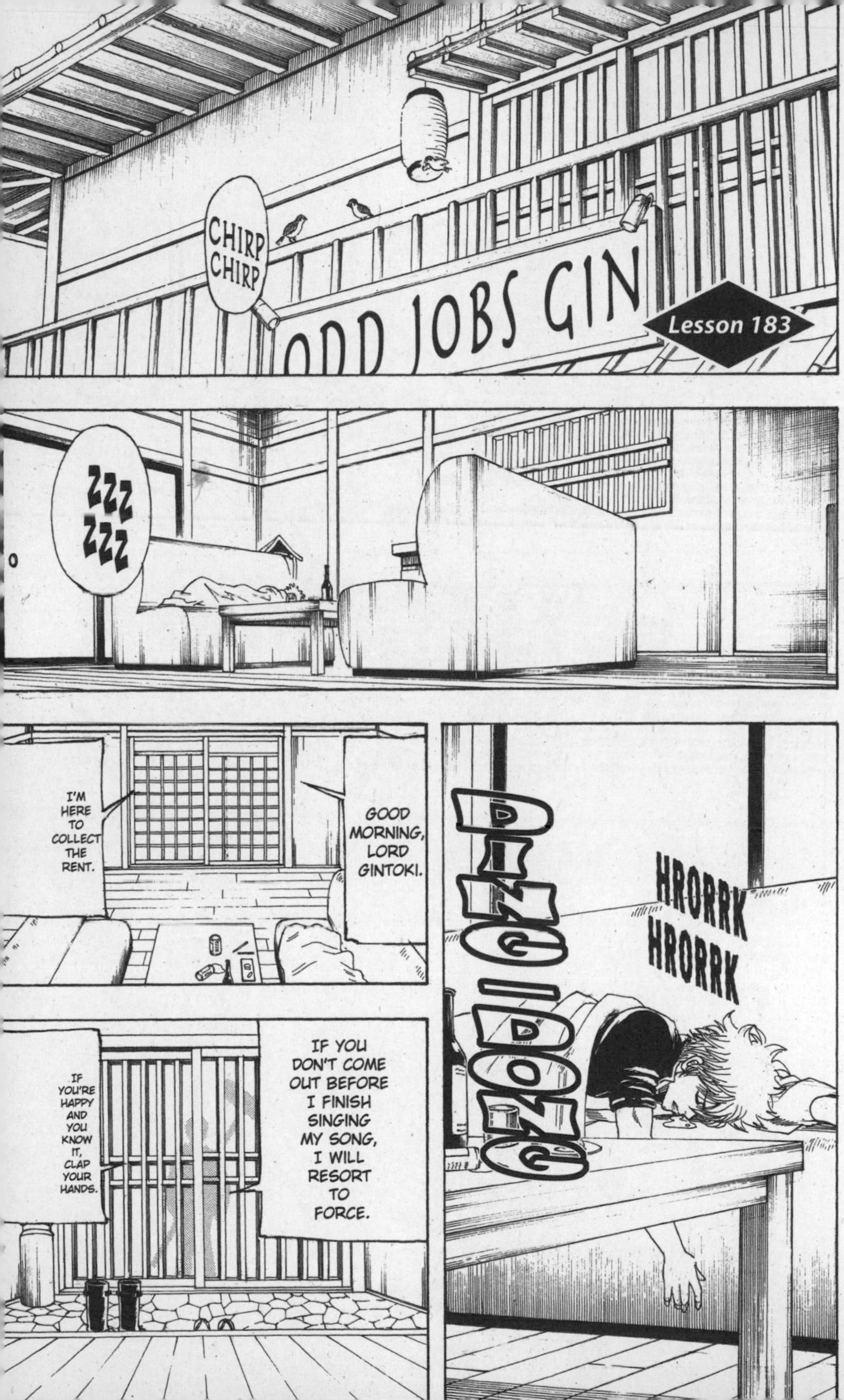
Lesson 183
ODD JOBS GIN
CHIRP CHIRP
ZZZ ZZZ
HRORRK HRORRK
DING DONG
GOOD MORNING, LORD GINTOKI.
I'M HERE TO COLLECT THE RENT.
IF YOU DON'T COME OUT BEFORE I FINISH SINGING MY SONG, I WILL RESORT TO FORCE.
IF YOU'RE HAPPY AND YOU KNOW IT, CLAP YOUR HANDS.

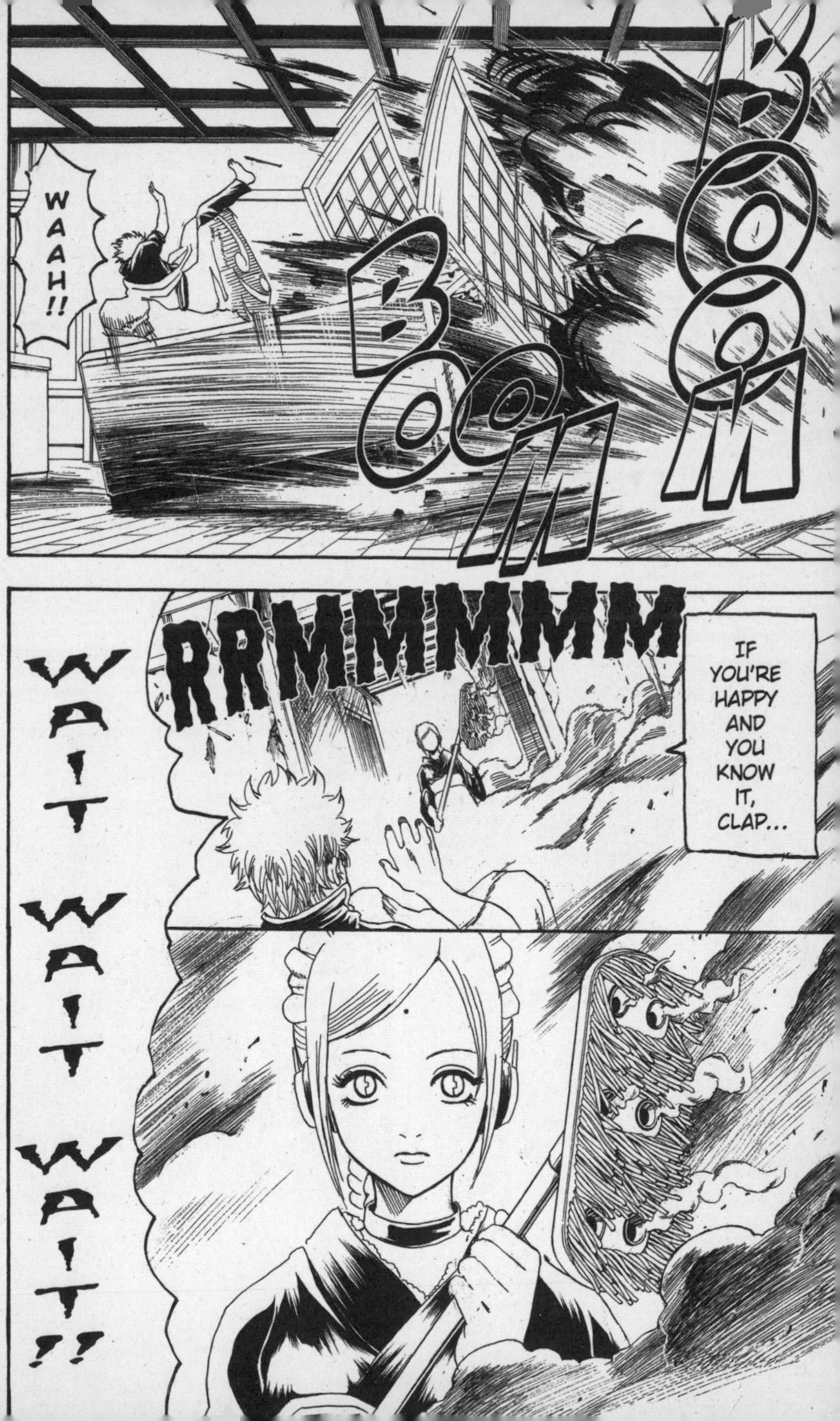
BOOOM
BOOOM
WAAAH!!
IF YOU'RE HAPPY AND YOU KNOW IT, CLAP...
RRMMMMMM
WAIT WAIT WAIT WAIT?!

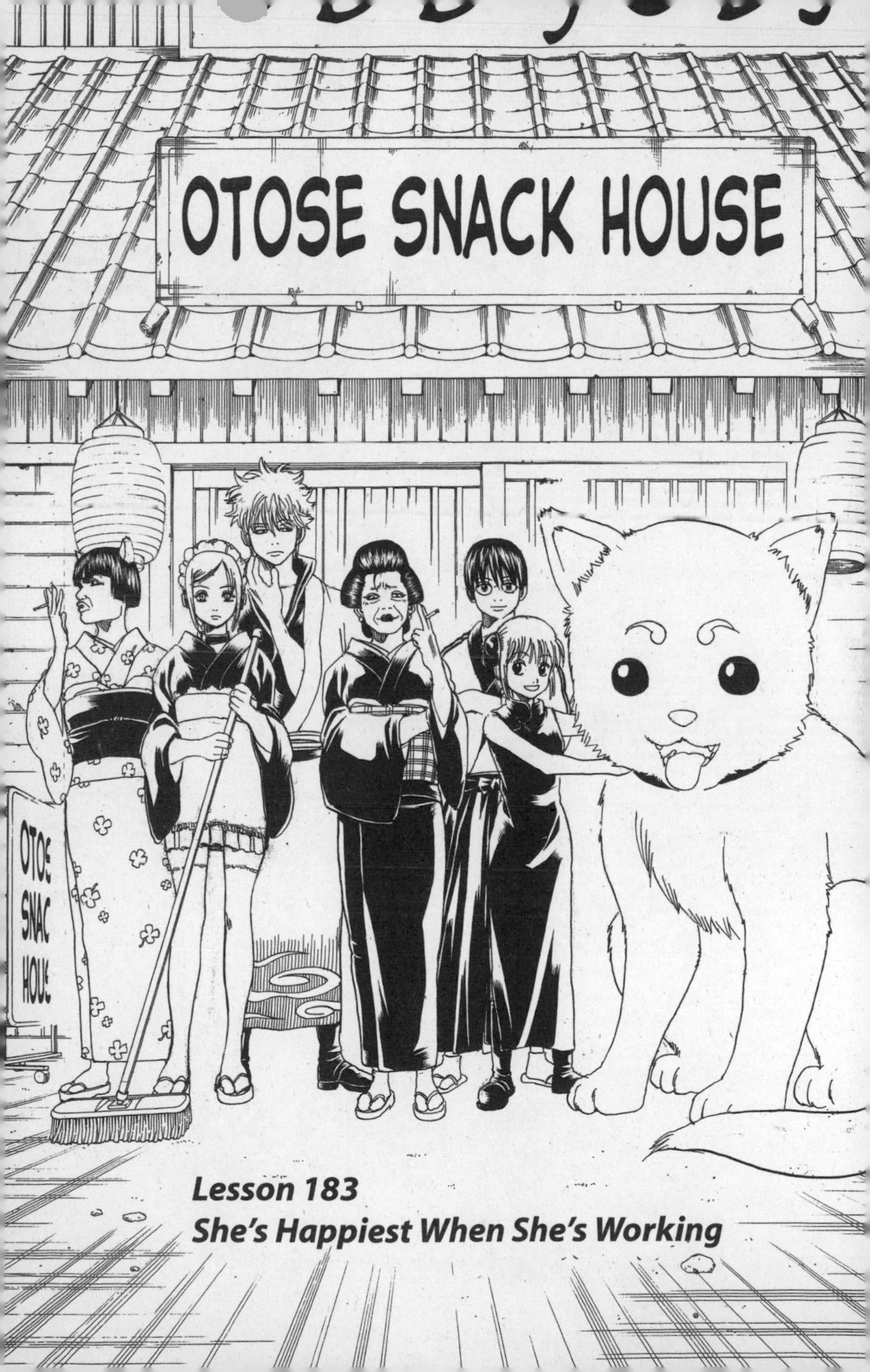
OTOSE SNACK HOUSE
OTOSE SNAC HOUS

Lesson 183
She's Happiest When She's Working

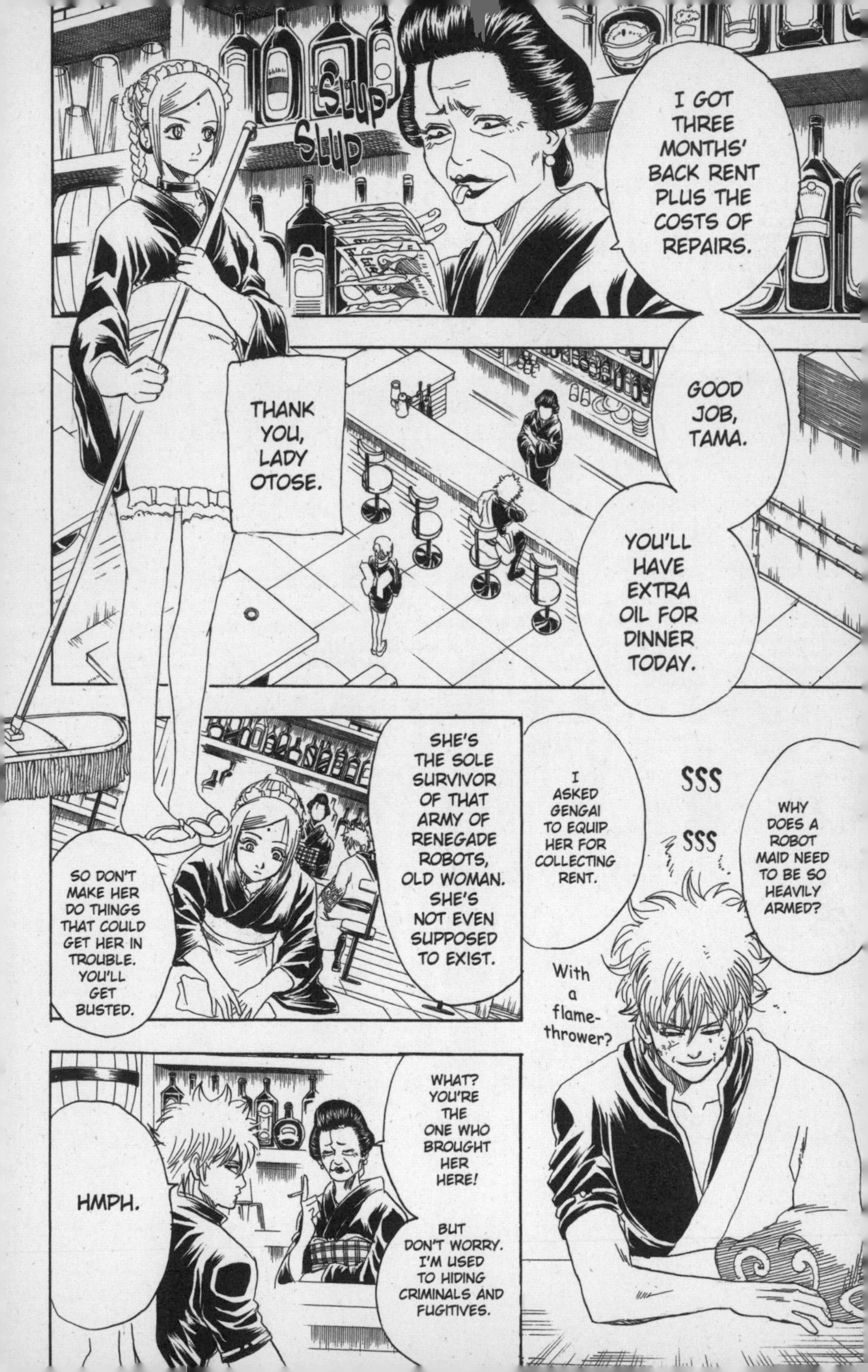
SLUP SLUP
I GOT THREE MONTHS' BACK RENT PLUS THE COSTS OF REPAIRS.
GOOD JOB, TAMA.
YOU'LL HAVE EXTRA OIL FOR DINNER TODAY.
THANK YOU, LADY OTOSE.
WHY DOES A ROBOT MAID NEED TO BE SO HEAVILY ARMED?
SSS SSS
I ASKED GENGAI TO EQUIP HER FOR COLLECTING RENT.
With a flame-thrower?
SHE'S THE SOLE SURVIVOR OF THAT ARMY OF RENEGADE ROBOTS, OLD WOMAN. SHE'S NOT EVEN SUPPOSED TO EXIST.
SO DON'T MAKE HER DO THINGS THAT COULD GET HER IN TROUBLE. YOU'LL GET BUSTED.
WHAT? YOU'RE THE ONE WHO BROUGHT HER HERE!
BUT DON'T WORRY. I'M USED TO HIDING CRIMINALS AND FUGITIVES.
HMPH.

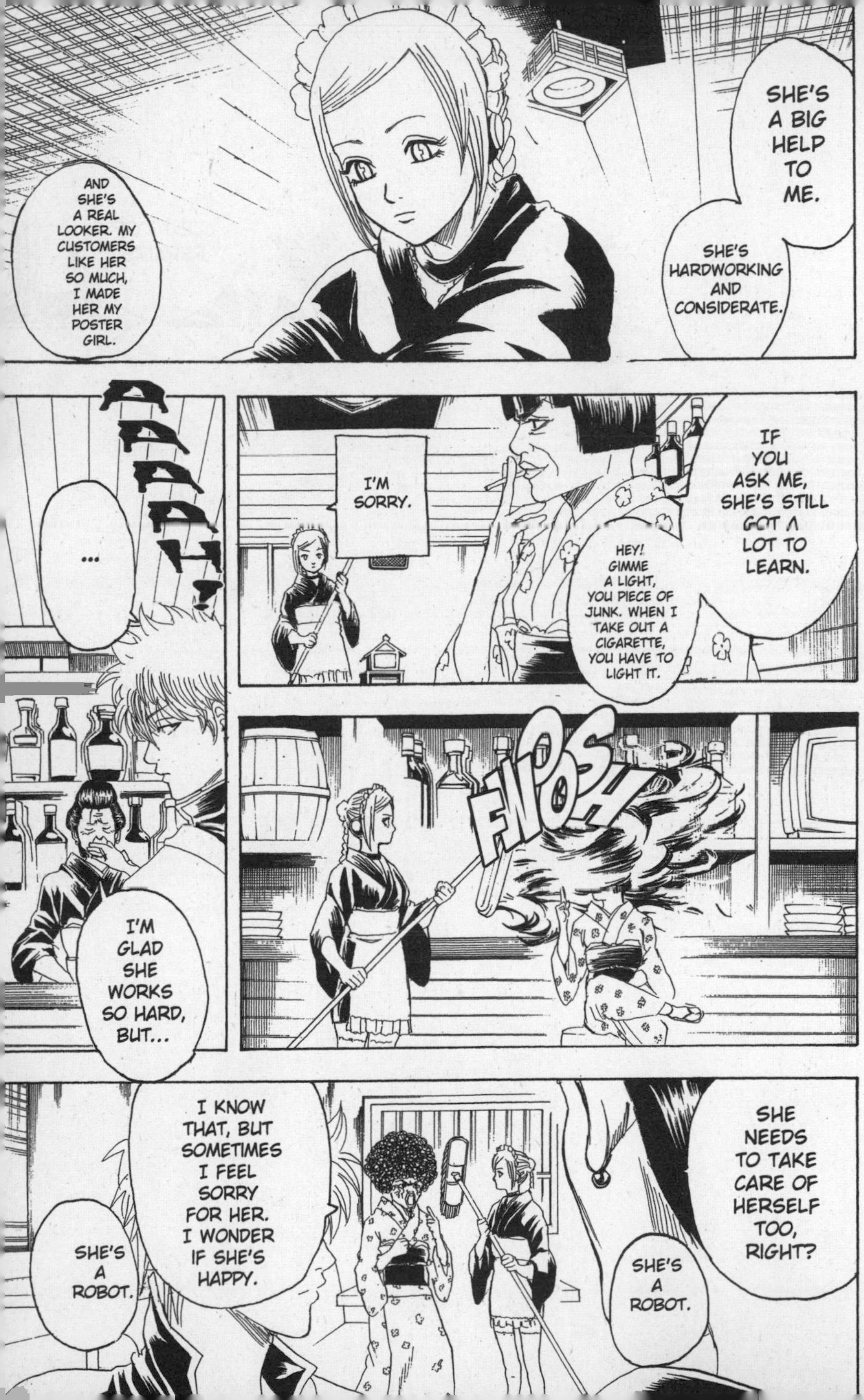
SHE'S A BIG HELP TO ME.
SHE'S HARDWORKING AND CONSIDERATE.
AND SHE'S A REAL LOOKER. MY CUSTOMERS LIKE HER SO MUCH, I MADE HER MY POSTER GIRL.
IF YOU ASK ME, SHE'S STILL GOT A LOT TO LEARN.
HEY! GIMME A LIGHT, YOU PIECE OF JUNK. WHEN I TAKE OUT A CIGARETTE, YOU HAVE TO LIGHT IT.
I'M SORRY.
FWOOSH
AAAAH!?
...
I'M GLAD SHE WORKS SO HARD, BUT...
SHE NEEDS TO TAKE CARE OF HERSELF TOO, RIGHT?
SHE'S A ROBOT.
I KNOW THAT, BUT SOMETIMES I FEEL SORRY FOR HER. I WONDER IF SHE'S HAPPY.
SHE'S A ROBOT.

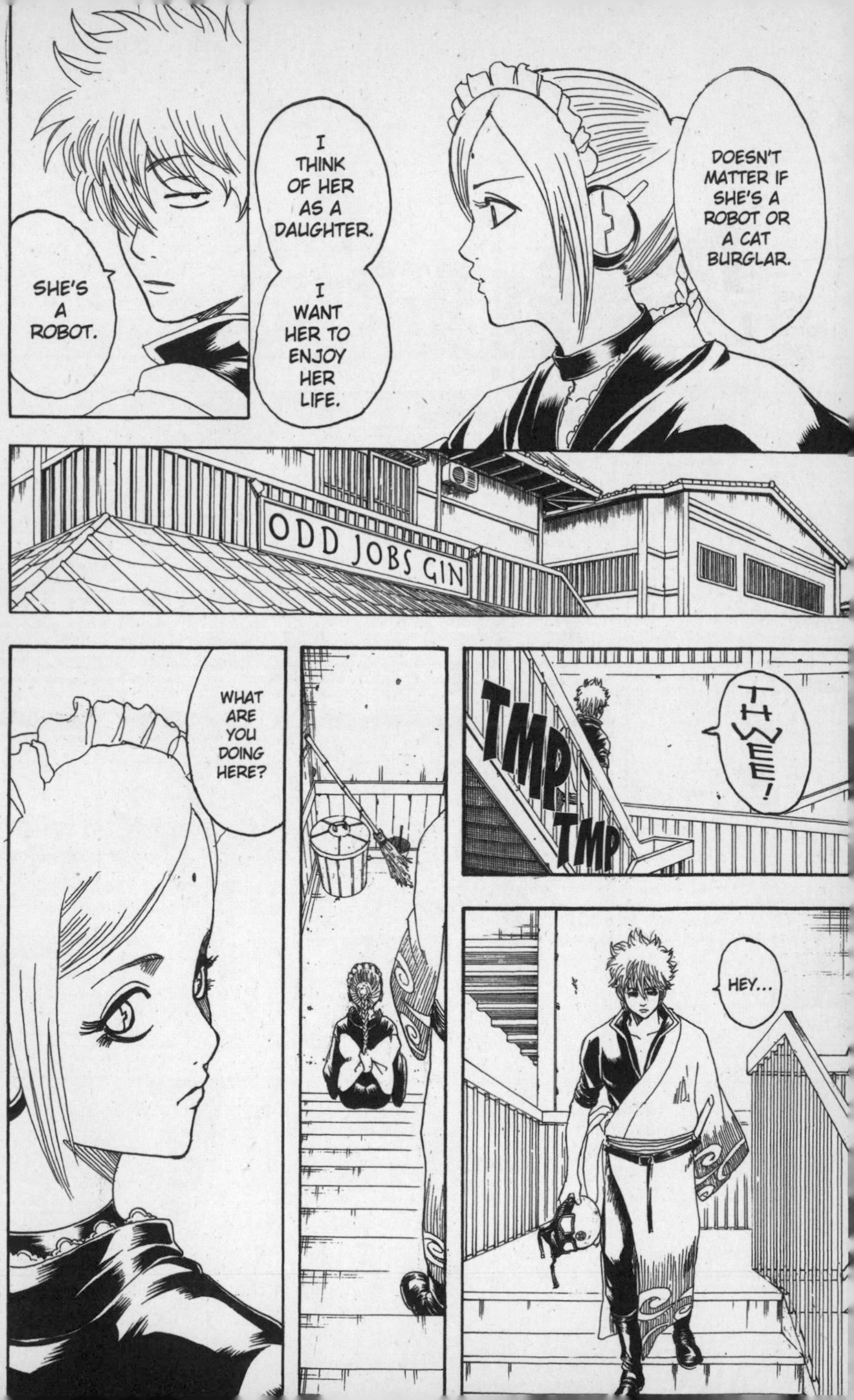
DOESN'T MATTER IF SHE'S A ROBOT OR A CAT BURGLAR.
I THINK OF HER AS A DAUGHTER.
I WANT HER TO ENJOY HER LIFE.
SHE'S A ROBOT.
ODD JOBS GIN
THWEE!
TMP
TMP
HEY...
WHAT ARE YOU DOING HERE?

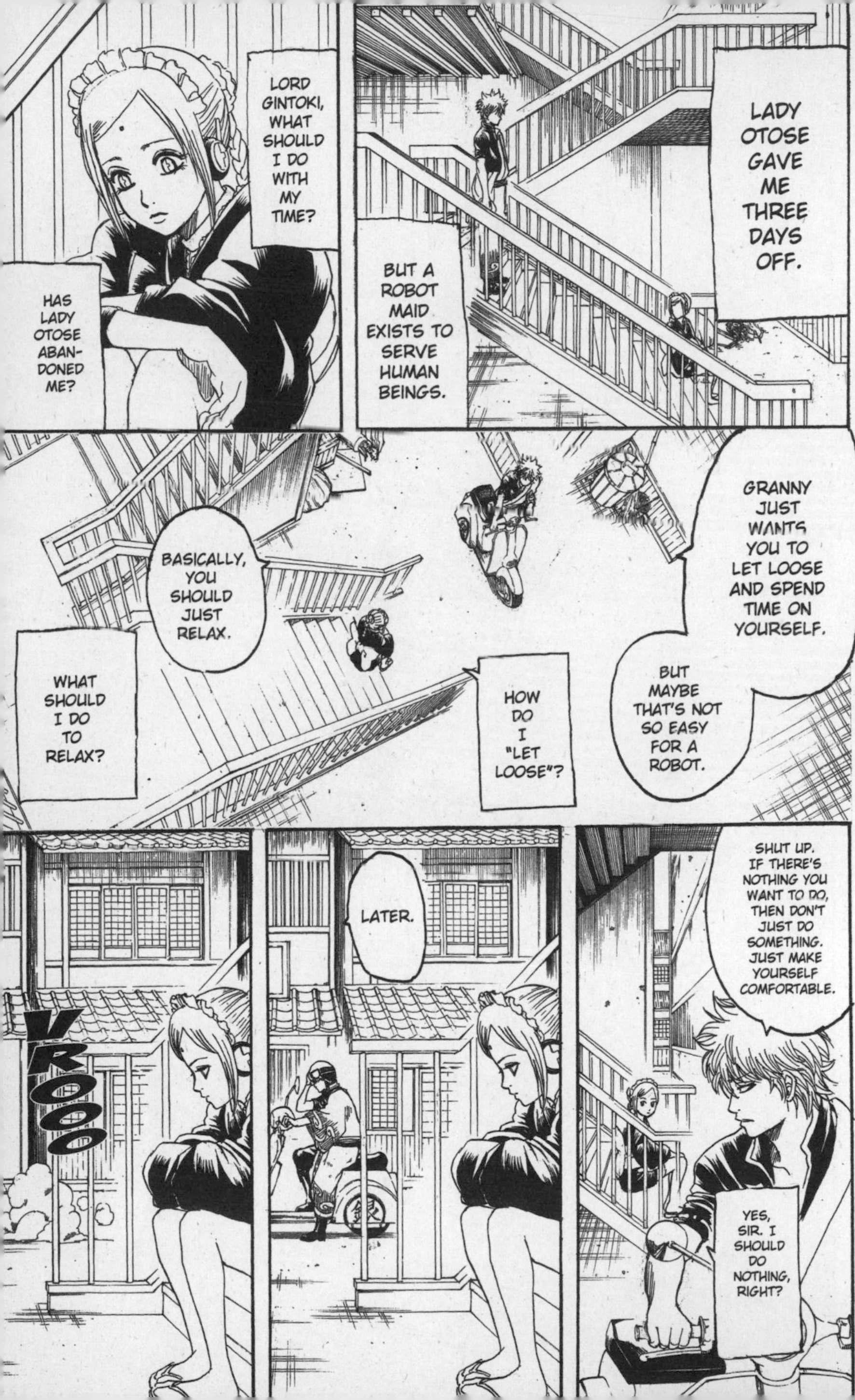
LADY OTOSE GAVE ME THREE DAYS OFF.
BUT A ROBOT MAID EXISTS TO SERVE HUMAN BEINGS.
LORD GINTOKI, WHAT SHOULD I DO WITH MY TIME?
HAS LADY OTOSE ABANDONED ME?
GRANNY JUST WANTS YOU TO LET LOOSE AND SPEND TIME ON YOURSELF.
BUT MAYBE THAT'S NOT SO EASY FOR A ROBOT.
HOW DO I "LET LOOSE"?
BASICALLY, YOU SHOULD JUST RELAX.
WHAT SHOULD I DO TO RELAX?
SHUT UP. IF THERE'S NOTHING YOU WANT TO DO, THEN DON'T JUST DO SOMETHING. JUST MAKE YOURSELF COMFORTABLE.
YES, SIR. I SHOULD DO NOTHING, RIGHT?
LATER.
VROOO

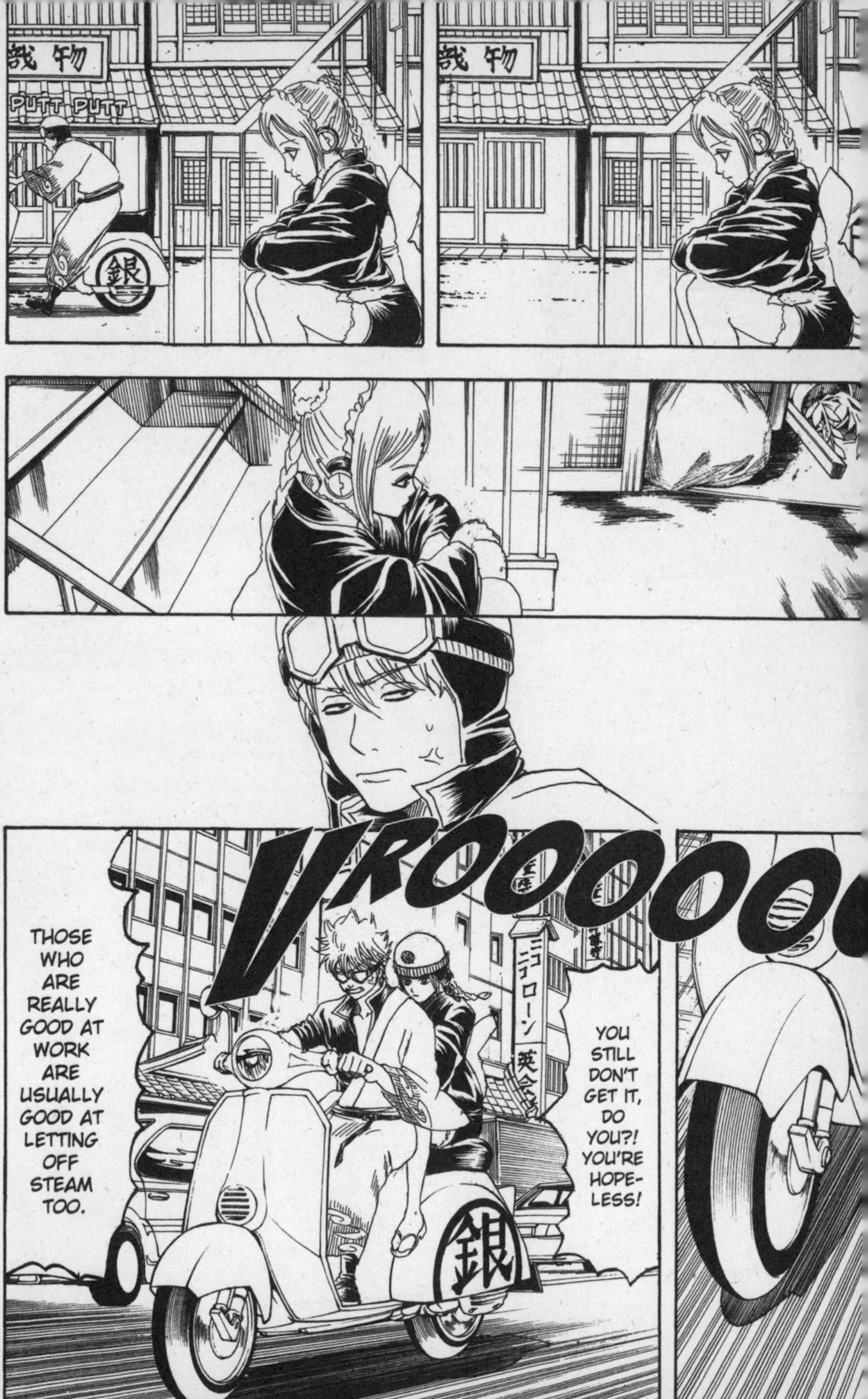
PUTT PUTT
銀
VROOOOOO
YOU STILL DON'T GET IT, DO YOU?! YOU'RE HOPELESS!
THOSE WHO ARE REALLY GOOD AT WORK ARE USUALLY GOOD AT LETTING OFF STEAM TOO.
銀

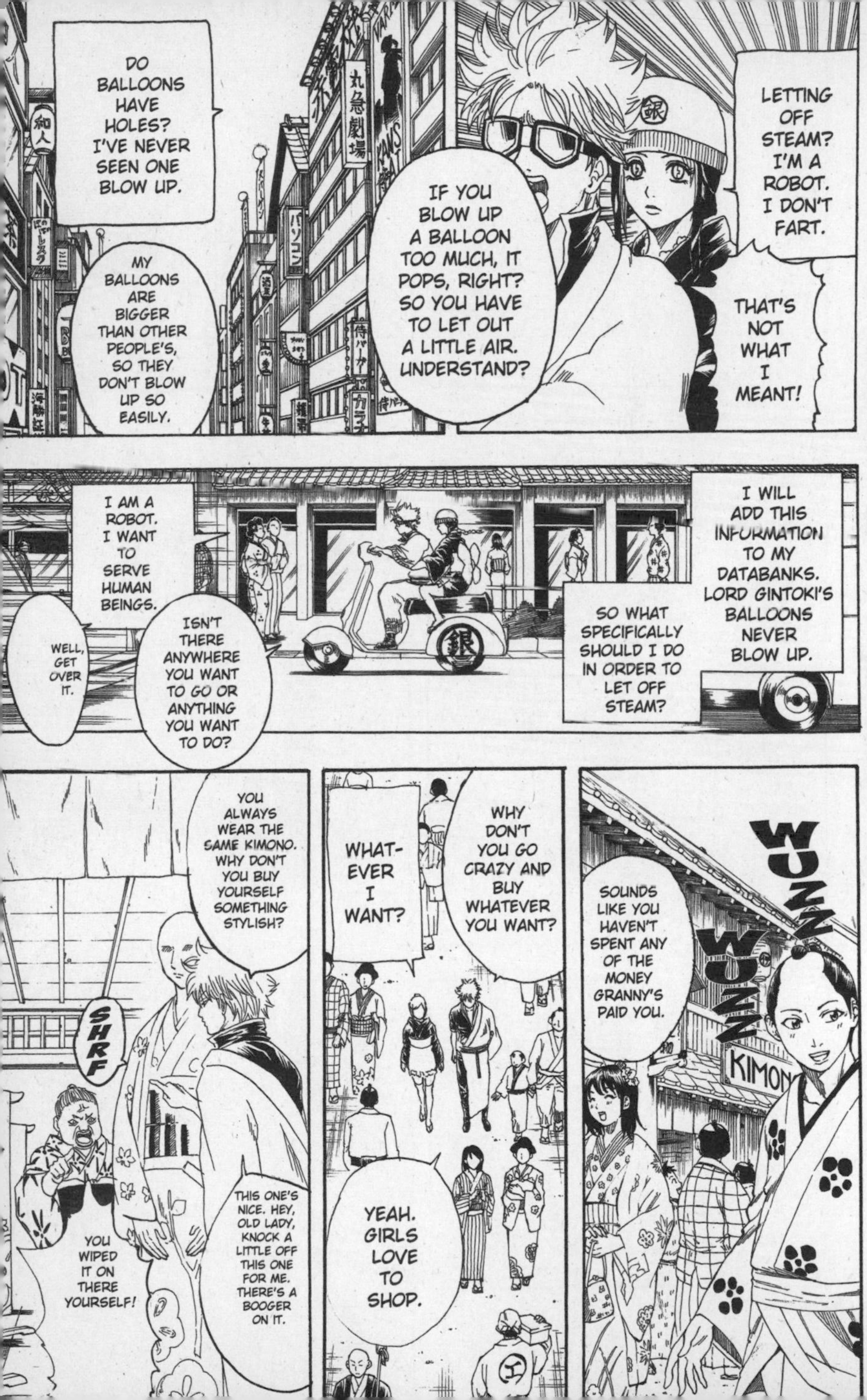
LETTING OFF STEAM? I'M A ROBOT. I DON'T FART.
THAT'S NOT WHAT I MEANT!
IF YOU BLOW UP A BALLOON TOO MUCH, IT POPS, RIGHT? SO YOU HAVE TO LET OUT A LITTLE AIR. UNDERSTAND?
DO BALLOONS HAVE HOLES? I'VE NEVER SEEN ONE BLOW UP.
MY BALLOONS ARE BIGGER THAN OTHER PEOPLE'S, SO THEY DON'T BLOW UP SO EASILY.
I WILL ADD THIS INFORMATION TO MY DATABANKS. LORD GINTOKI'S BALLOONS NEVER BLOW UP.
SO WHAT SPECIFICALLY SHOULD I DO IN ORDER TO LET OFF STEAM?
ISN'T THERE ANYWHERE YOU WANT TO GO OR ANYTHING YOU WANT TO DO?
I AM A ROBOT. I WANT TO SERVE HUMAN BEINGS.
WELL, GET OVER IT.
WUZN
WUZN
SOUNDS LIKE YOU HAVEN'T SPENT ANY OF THE MONEY GRANNY'S PAID YOU.
KIMON
WHY DON'T YOU GO CRAZY AND BUY WHATEVER YOU WANT?
WHAT-EVER I WANT?
YEAH. GIRLS LOVE TO SHOP.
YOU ALWAYS WEAR THE SAME KIMONO. WHY DON'T YOU BUY YOURSELF SOMETHING STYLISH?
SHRF
THIS ONE'S NICE. HEY, OLD LADY, KNOCK A LITTLE OFF THIS ONE FOR ME. THERE'S A BOOGER ON IT.
YOU WIPED IT ON THERE YOURSELF!

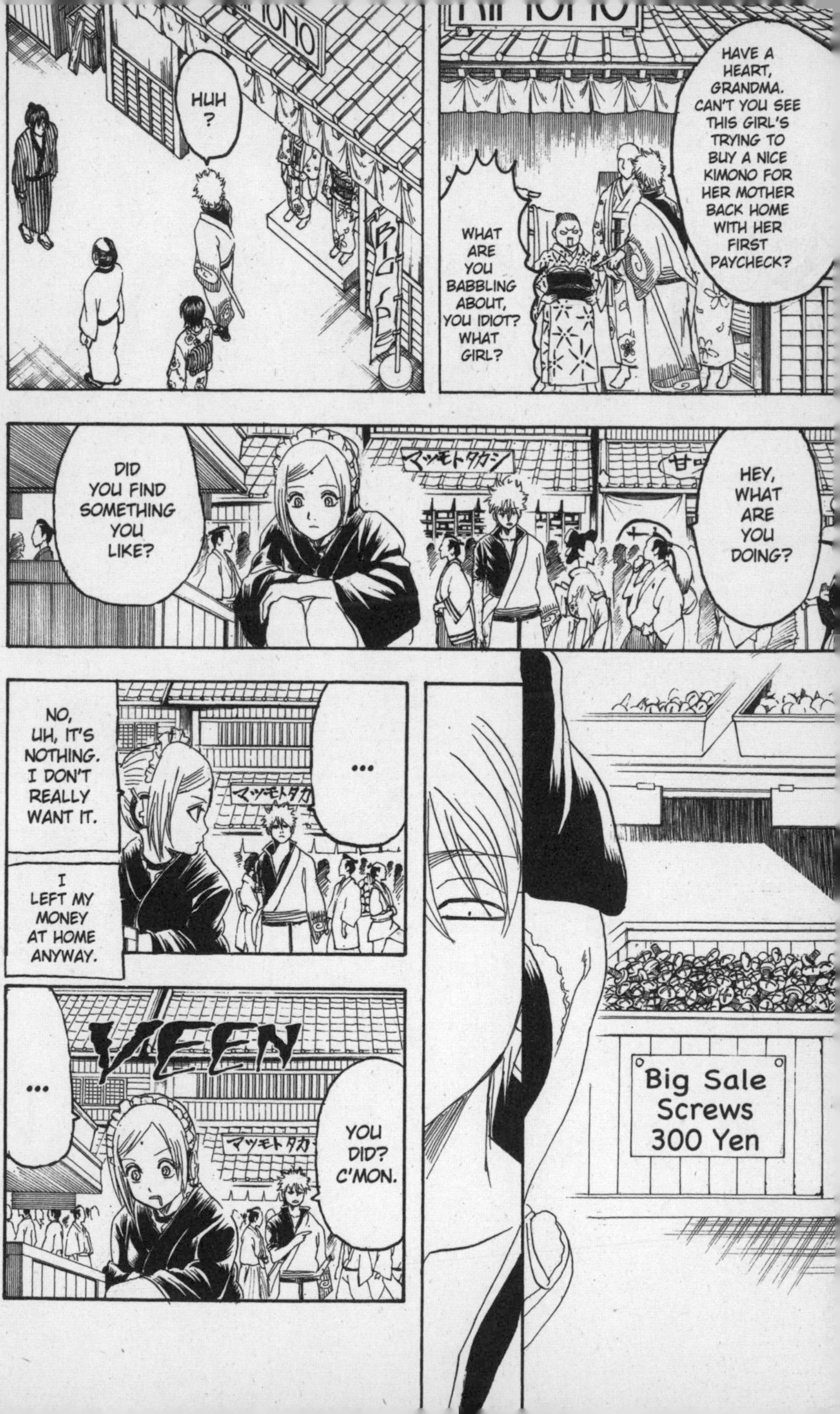
HAVE A HEART, GRANDMA. CAN'T YOU SEE THIS GIRL'S TRYING TO BUY A NICE KIMONO FOR HER MOTHER BACK HOME WITH HER FIRST PAYCHECK?
WHAT ARE YOU BABBLING ABOUT, YOU IDIOT? WHAT GIRL?
HUH?
HEY, WHAT ARE YOU DOING?
マツモトタカシ
DID YOU FIND SOMETHING YOU LIKE?
Big Sale Screws 300 Yen
...
NO, UH, IT'S NOTHING. I DON'T REALLY WANT IT.
I LEFT MY MONEY AT HOME ANYWAY.
YOU DID? C'MON.
VEEN
...

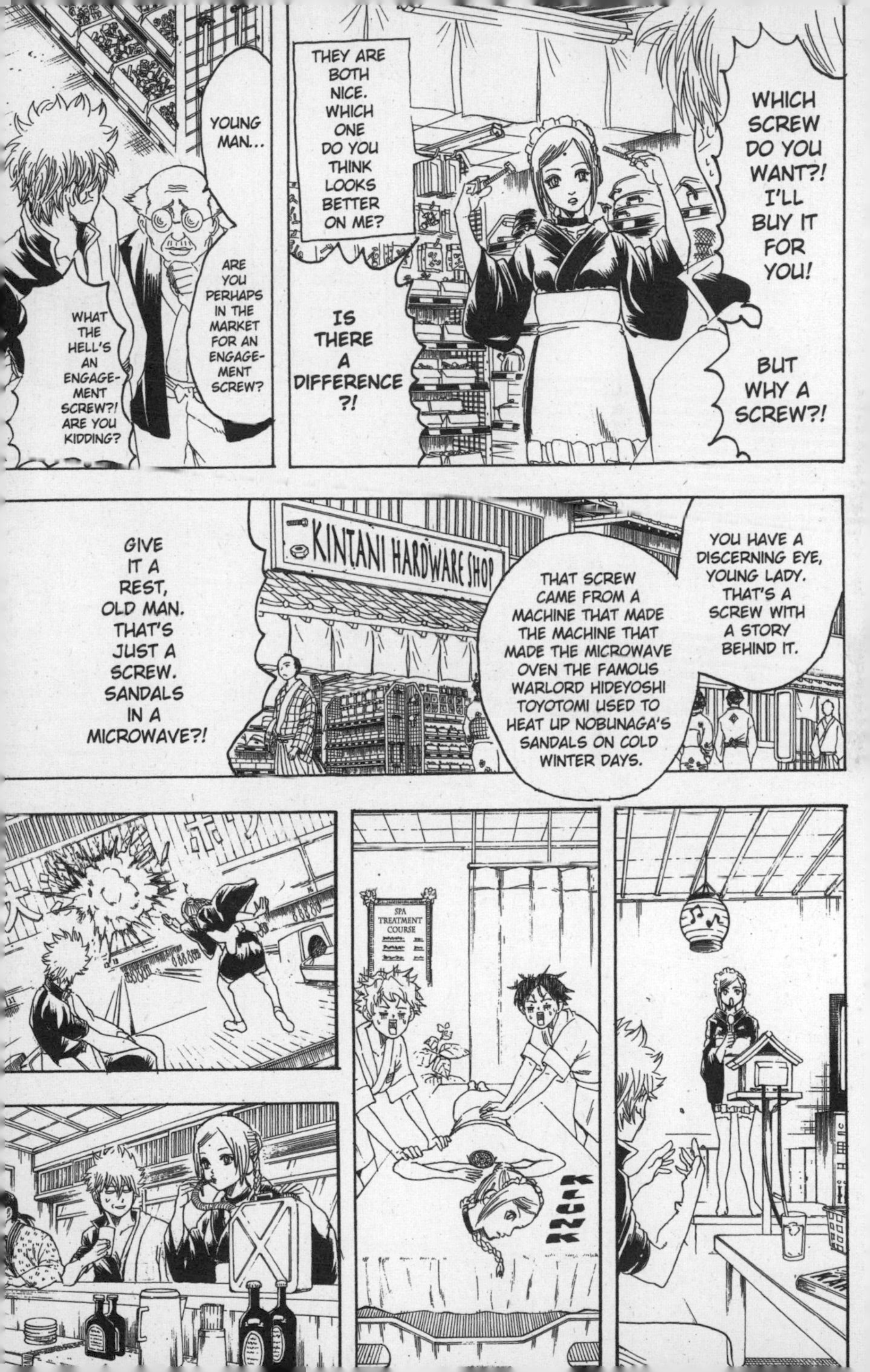
WHICH SCREW DO YOU WANT?! I'LL BUY IT FOR YOU!
THEY ARE BOTH NICE. WHICH ONE DO YOU THINK LOOKS BETTER ON ME?
BUT WHY A SCREW?!
IS THERE A DIFFERENCE?!
YOUNG MAN...
ARE YOU PERHAPS IN THE MARKET FOR AN ENGAGEMENT SCREW?
WHAT THE HELL'S AN ENGAGEMENT SCREW?! ARE YOU KIDDING?
YOU HAVE A DISCERNING EYE, YOUNG LADY. THAT'S A SCREW WITH A STORY BEHIND IT.
THAT SCREW CAME FROM A MACHINE THAT MADE THE MACHINE THAT MADE THE MICROWAVE OVEN THE FAMOUS WARLORD HIDEYOSHI TOYOTOMI USED TO HEAT UP NOBUNAGA'S SANDALS ON COLD WINTER DAYS.
KINTANI HARDWARE SHOP
GIVE IT A REST, OLD MAN. THAT'S JUST A SCREW. SANDALS IN A MICROWAVE?!
SPA TREATMENT COURSE
KLUNK

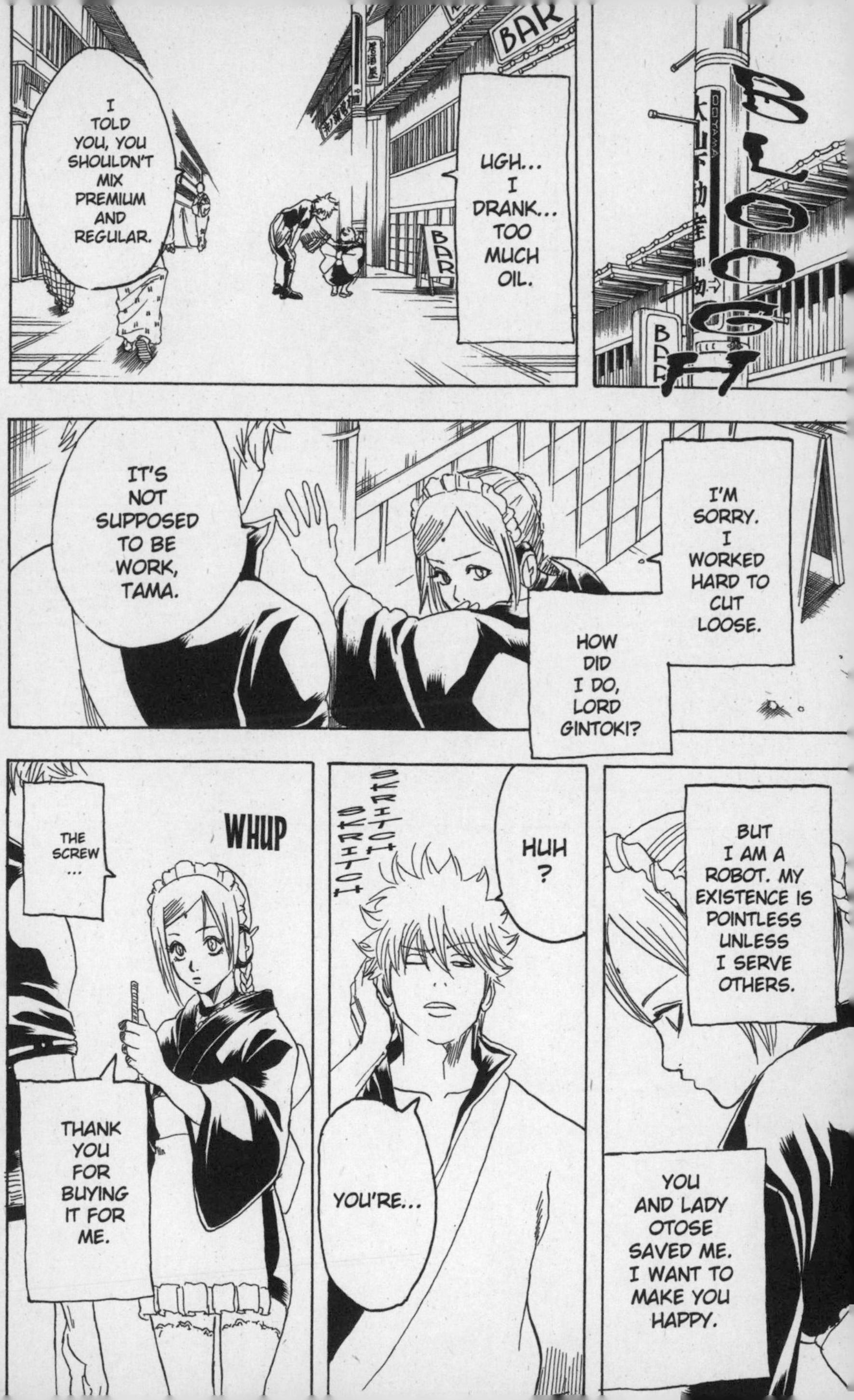

BLOOGH
UGH... I DRANK... TOO MUCH OIL.
I TOLD YOU, YOU SHOULDN'T MIX PREMIUM AND REGULAR.
I'M SORRY. I WORKED HARD TO CUT LOOSE.
HOW DID I DO, LORD GINTOKI?
IT'S NOT SUPPOSED TO BE WORK, TAMA.
BUT I AM A ROBOT. MY EXISTENCE IS POINTLESS UNLESS I SERVE OTHERS.
YOU AND LADY OTOSE SAVED ME. I WANT TO MAKE YOU HAPPY.
SKRITCH SKRITCH
HUH?
YOU'RE...
WHUP
THE SCREW...
THANK YOU FOR BUYING IT FOR ME.

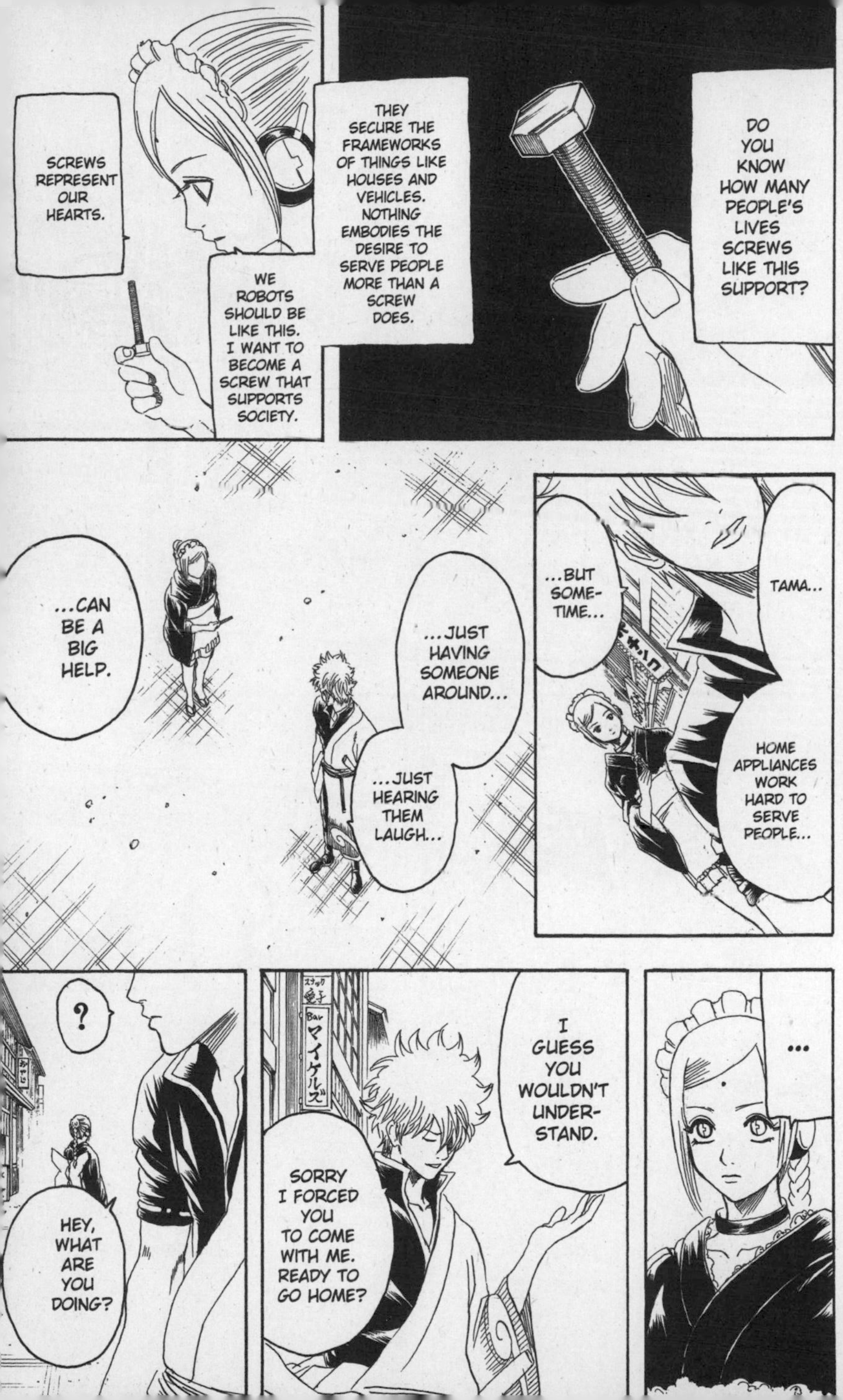
DO YOU KNOW HOW MANY PEOPLE'S LIVES SCREWS LIKE THIS SUPPORT?
THEY SECURE THE FRAMEWORKS OF THINGS LIKE HOUSES AND VEHICLES. NOTHING EMBODIES THE DESIRE TO SERVE PEOPLE MORE THAN A SCREW DOES.
SCREWS REPRESENT OUR HEARTS.
WE ROBOTS SHOULD BE LIKE THIS. I WANT TO BECOME A SCREW THAT SUPPORTS SOCIETY.
TAMA...
HOME APPLIANCES WORK HARD TO SERVE PEOPLE...
...BUT SOME-TIME...
...JUST HAVING SOMEONE AROUND...
...JUST HEARING THEM LAUGH...
...CAN BE A BIG HELP.
...
I GUESS YOU WOULDN'T UNDER-STAND.
Bar マイケルズ
SORRY I FORCED YOU TO COME WITH ME. READY TO GO HOME?
?
HEY, WHAT ARE YOU DOING?

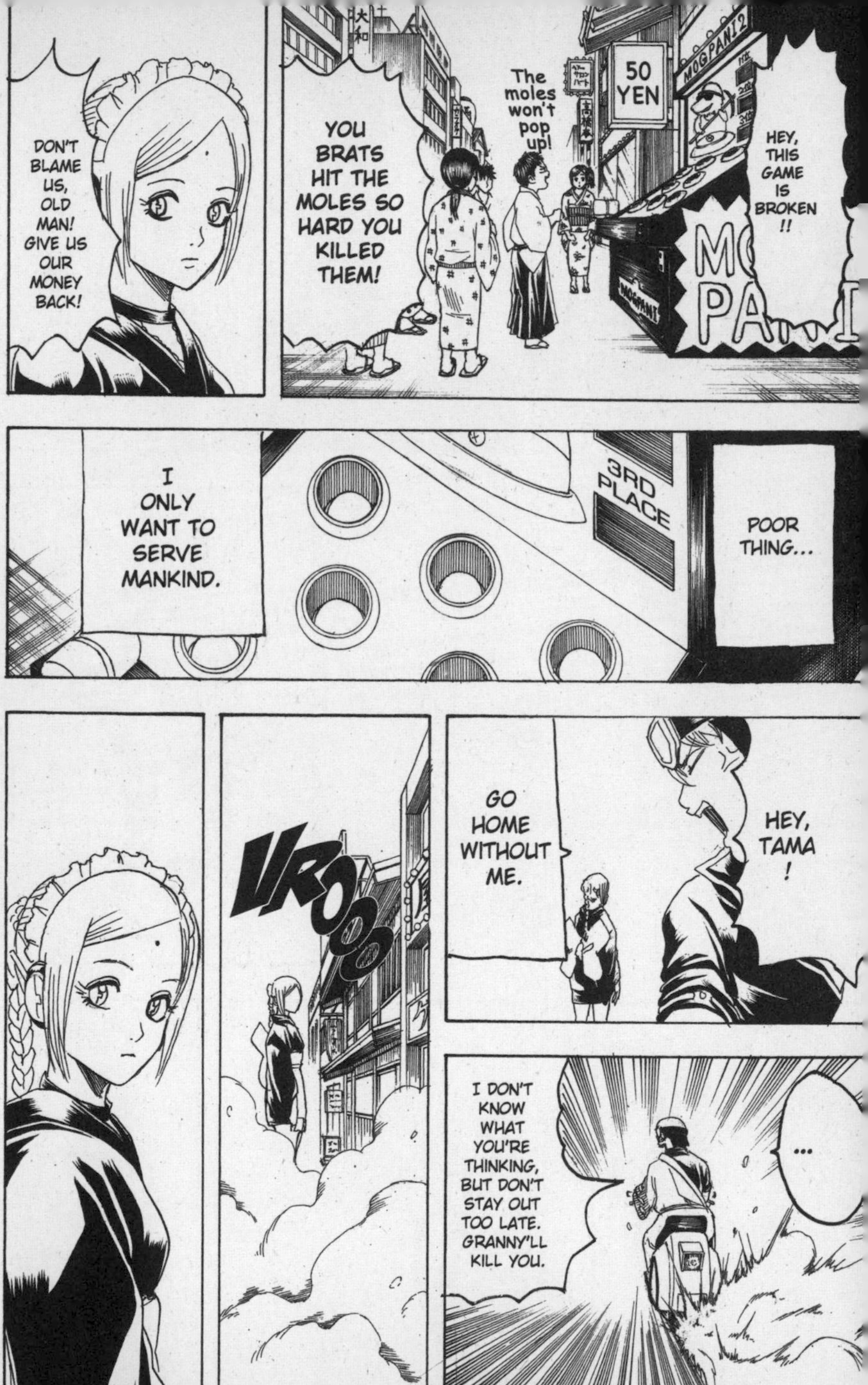
MOGPANI2
50 YEN
HEY, THIS GAME IS BROKEN!!
MOGPANI
The moles won't pop up!
YOU BRATS HIT THE MOLES SO HARD YOU KILLED THEM!
DON'T BLAME US, OLD MAN! GIVE US OUR MONEY BACK!
POOR THING...
3RD PLACE
I ONLY WANT TO SERVE MANKIND.
HEY, TAMA!
GO HOME WITHOUT ME.
...
I DON'T KNOW WHAT YOU'RE THINKING, BUT DON'T STAY OUT TOO LATE. GRANNY'LL KILL YOU.
VROOO

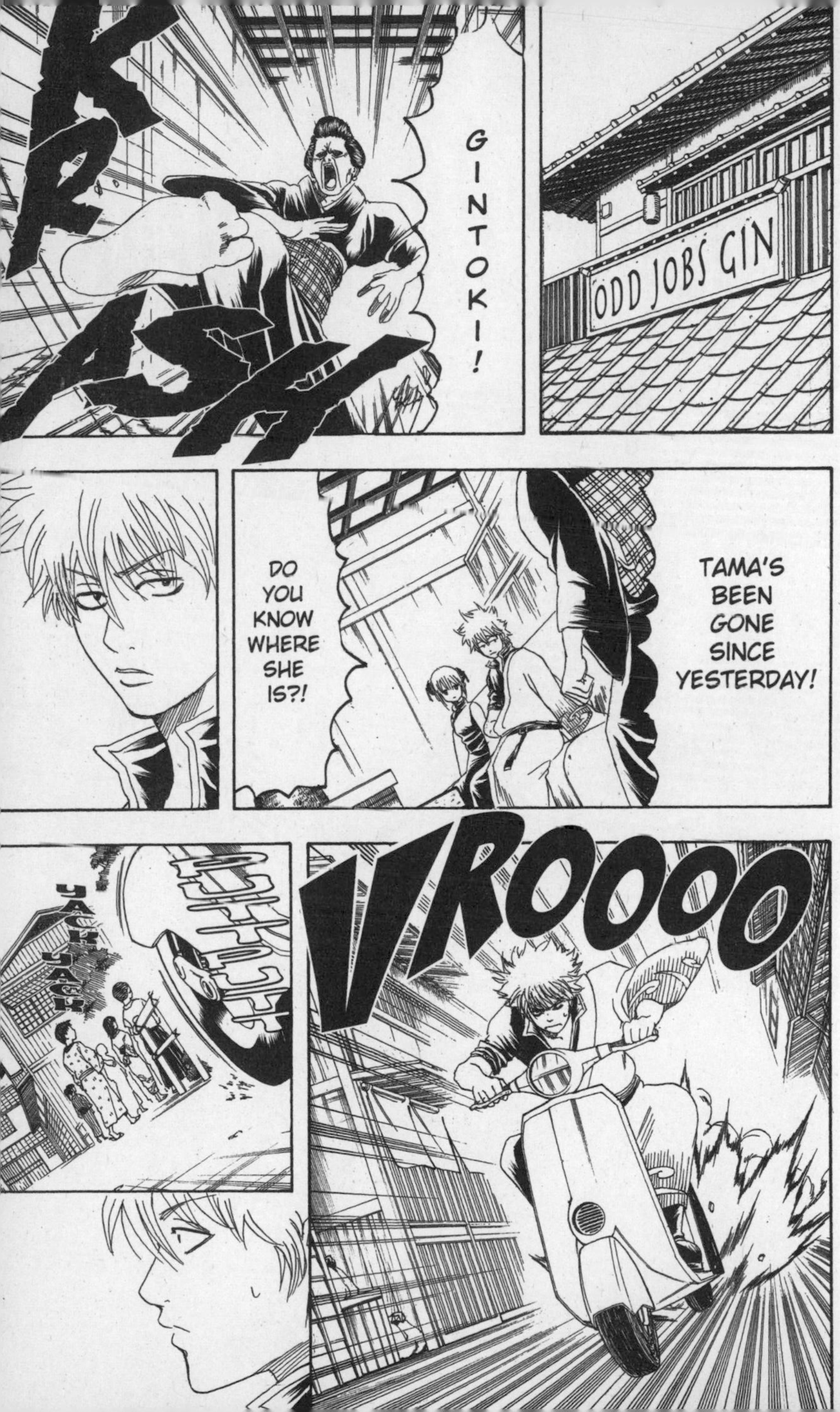
ODD JOBS GIN
GINTOKI!
KRASH
TAMA'S BEEN GONE SINCE YESTERDAY!
DO YOU KNOW WHERE SHE IS?!
VROOOO
YACH YACH

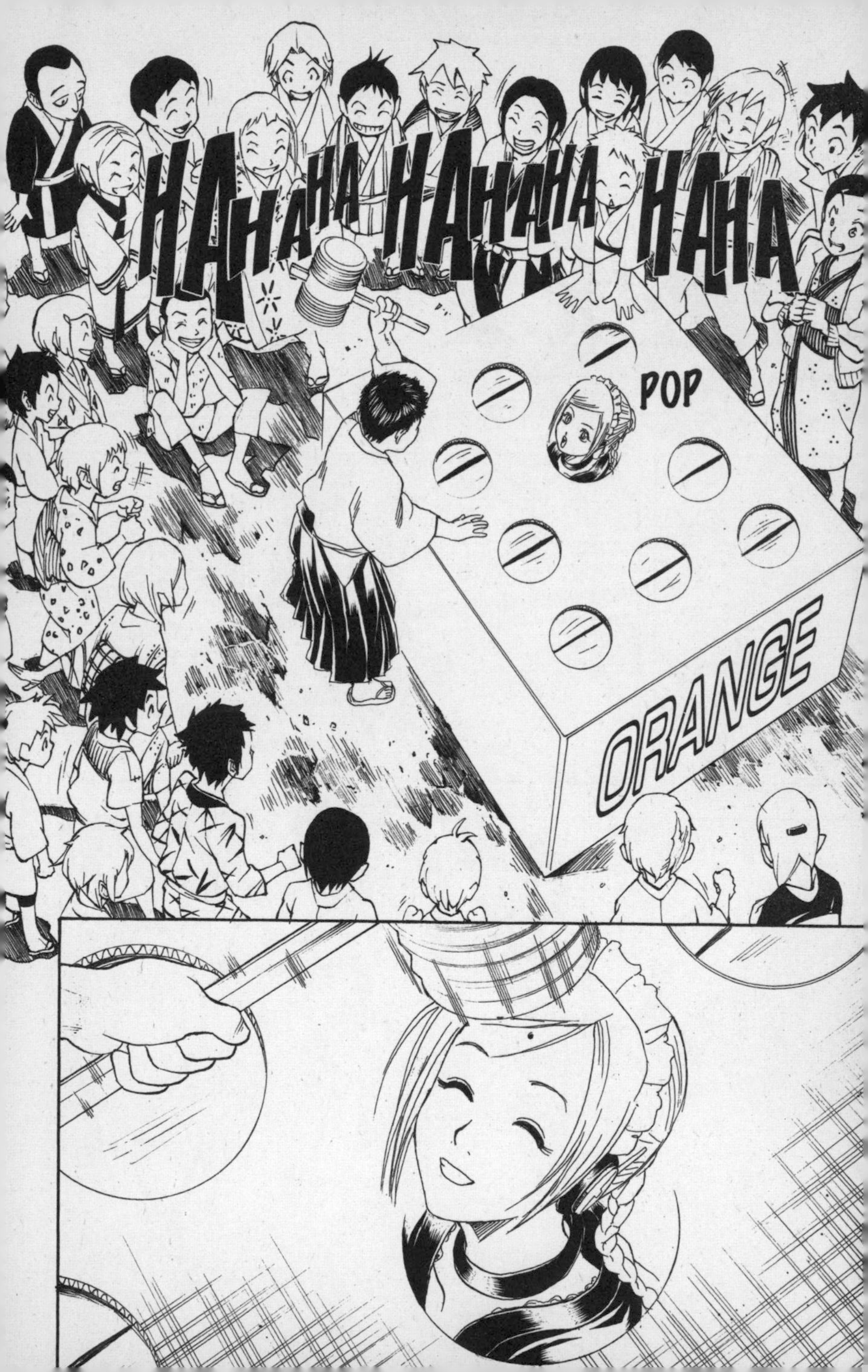
HAHAHAHA HAHAHAHA HAHA
POP
ORANGE

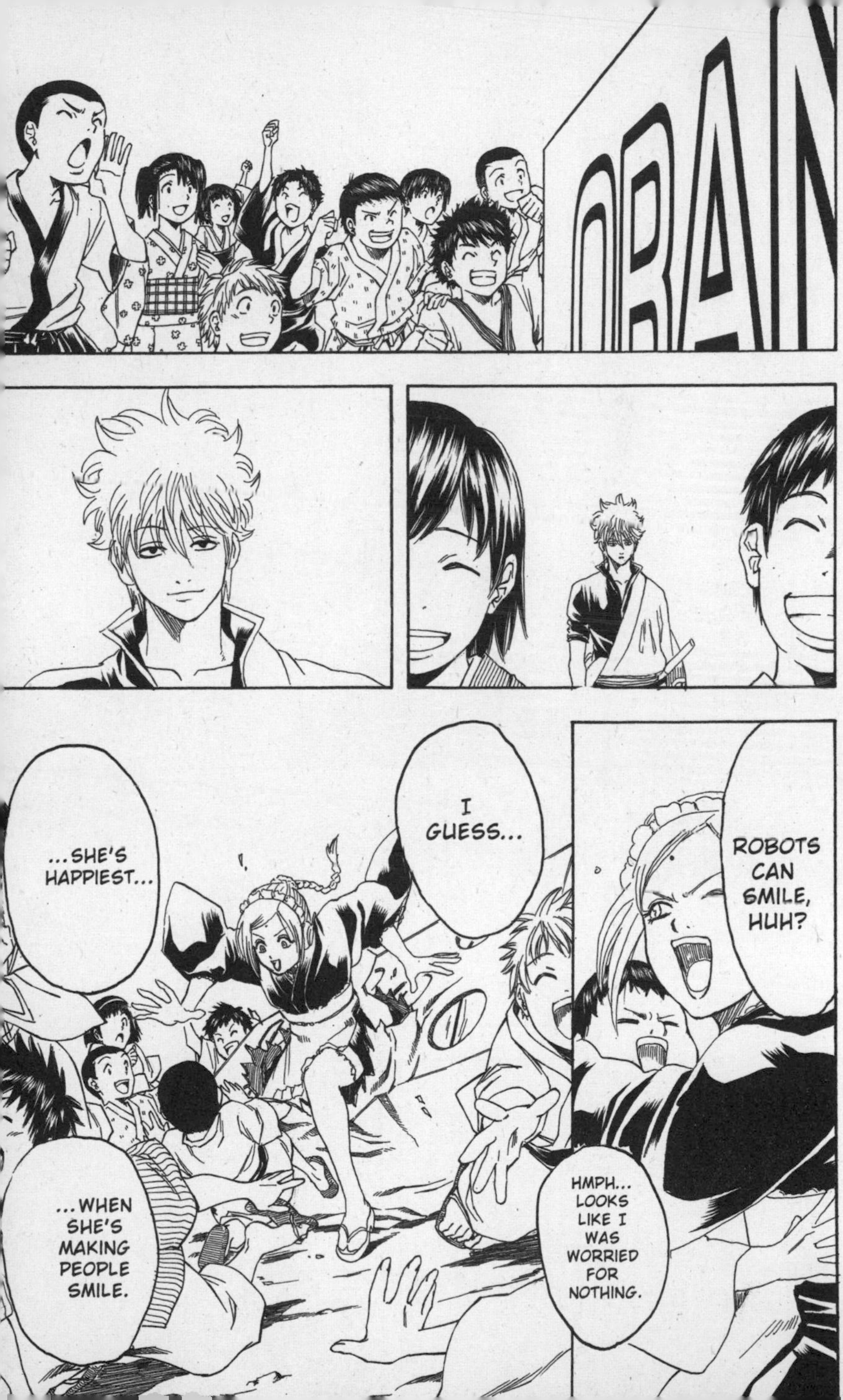
ORAN
ROBOTS CAN SMILE, HUH?
HMPH... LOOKS LIKE I WAS WORRIED FOR NOTHING.
I GUESS...
...SHE'S HAPPIEST...
...WHEN SHE'S MAKING PEOPLE SMILE.

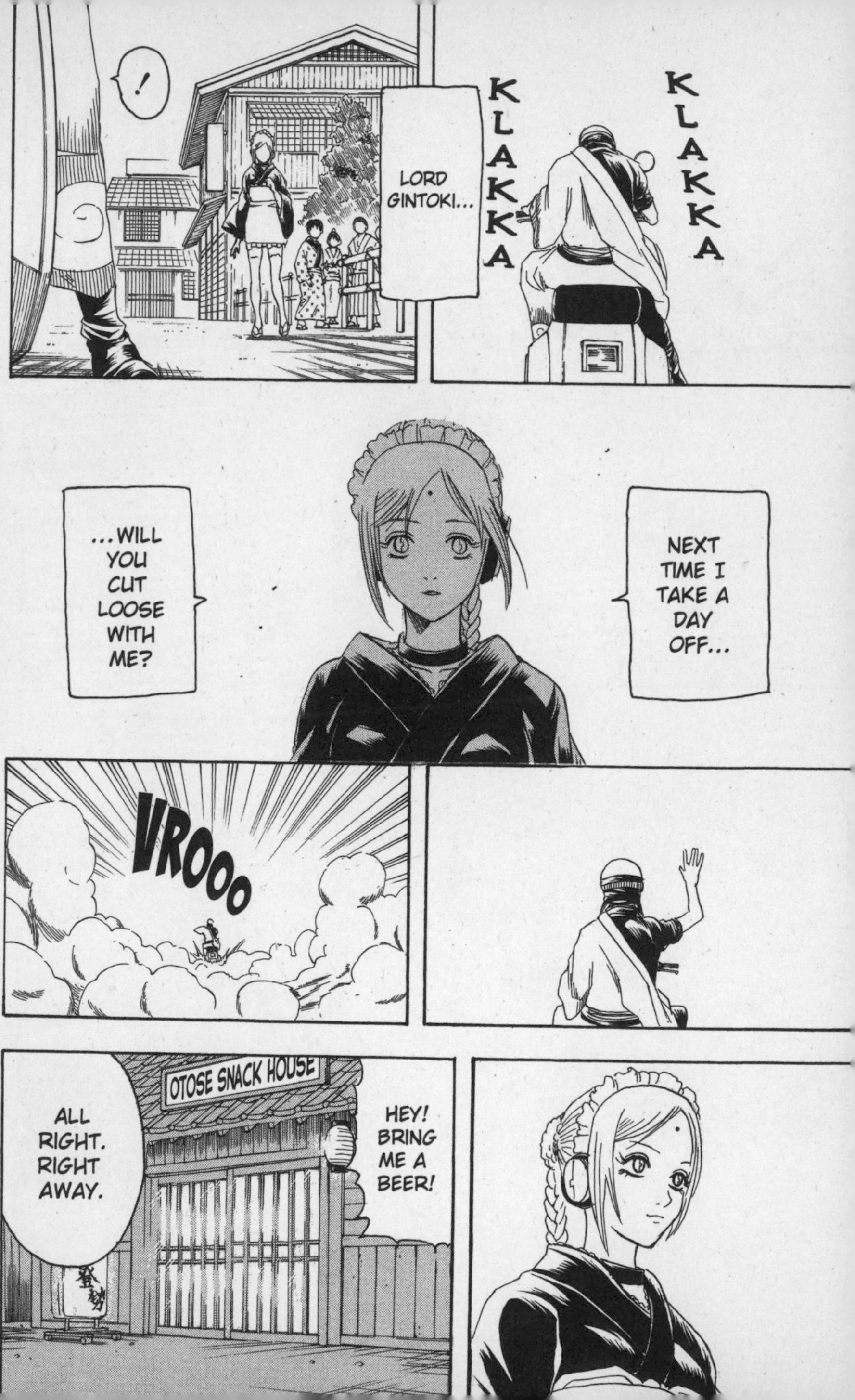
KLAKKA
KLAKKA
LORD GINTOKI...
!
NEXT TIME I TAKE A DAY OFF...
...WILL YOU CUT LOOSE WITH ME?
VROOO
OTOSE SNACK HOUSE
HEY! BRING ME A BEER!
ALL RIGHT. RIGHT AWAY.

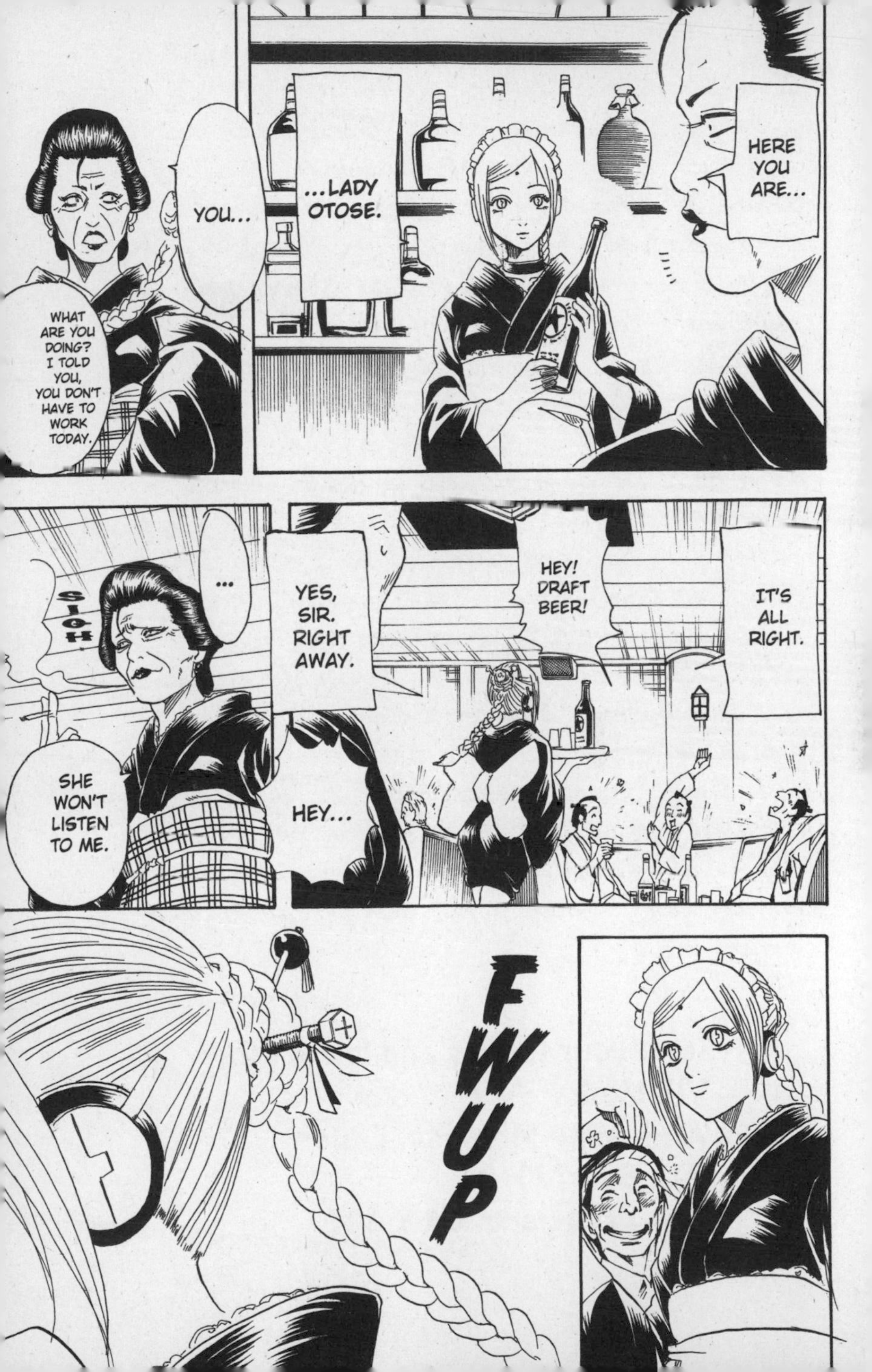
HERE YOU ARE...
...LADY OTOSE.
YOU...
WHAT ARE YOU DOING? I TOLD YOU, YOU DON'T HAVE TO WORK TODAY.
IT'S ALL RIGHT.
HEY! DRAFT BEER!
YES, SIR. RIGHT AWAY.
HEY...
...
SIGH
SHE WON'T LISTEN TO ME.
FWUP

I've been writing at some length, but I just want to say these words: Thank you for six years of hard work, Mr. Oonishi. We had our share of shouting matches and I've said and written rude things about you, but it is thanks to you that I've had the wonderful experience of being a manga artist. Thanks for coming all the way to Hokkaido when I was a rookie and kicking my butt and saying, "Come to Tokyo." I used to think of Tokyo as a nest of demons, so I never would've come here if not for him. We shook each other's hands and half-jokingly said, "Let's conquer the world." That memory has given me the strength to keep working despite the difficulties of producing a weekly manga. Unfortunately, I haven't conquered the world yet—there's no way I ever could—but I will continue to work hard to become a manga artist Mr. Oonishi can be proud to say he nurtured. Thank you very much for all you've done, and...don't touch your dinger.

Send your letters and fan art to:
VIZ Media
Attn: Mike Montesa, Editor
P.O. Box 77010
San Francisco, CA 94107

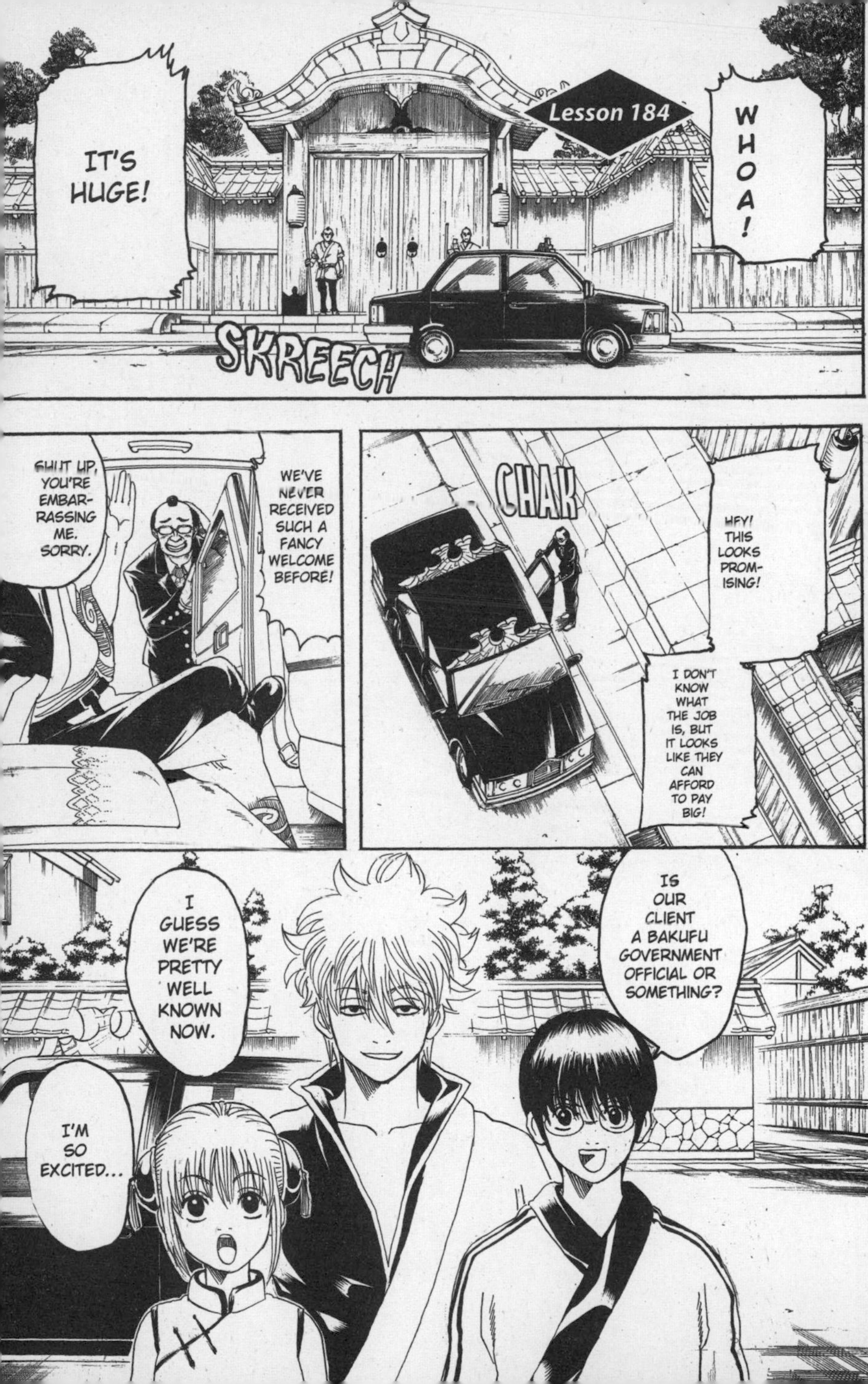
Lesson 184
WHOA!
IT'S HUGE!
SKREECH
CHAK
HEY! THIS LOOKS PROMISING!
I DON'T KNOW WHAT THE JOB IS, BUT IT LOOKS LIKE THEY CAN AFFORD TO PAY BIG!
WE'VE NEVER RECEIVED SUCH A FANCY WELCOME BEFORE!
SHUT UP, YOU'RE EMBARRASSING ME. SORRY.
IS OUR CLIENT A BAKUFU GOVERNMENT OFFICIAL OR SOMETHING?
I GUESS WE'RE PRETTY WELL KNOWN NOW.
I'M SO EXCITED...

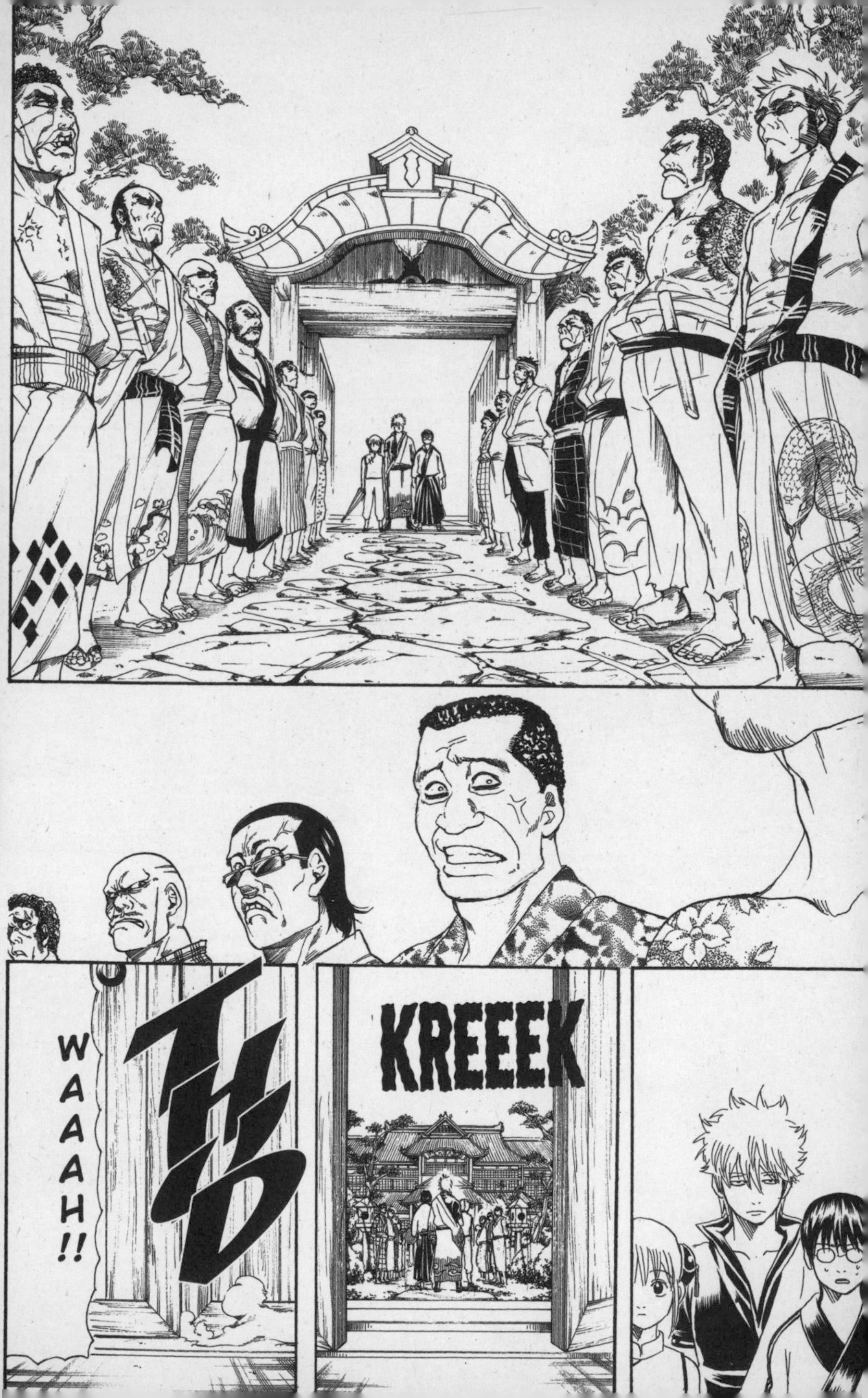
KREEK
THUD
WAAAH!!

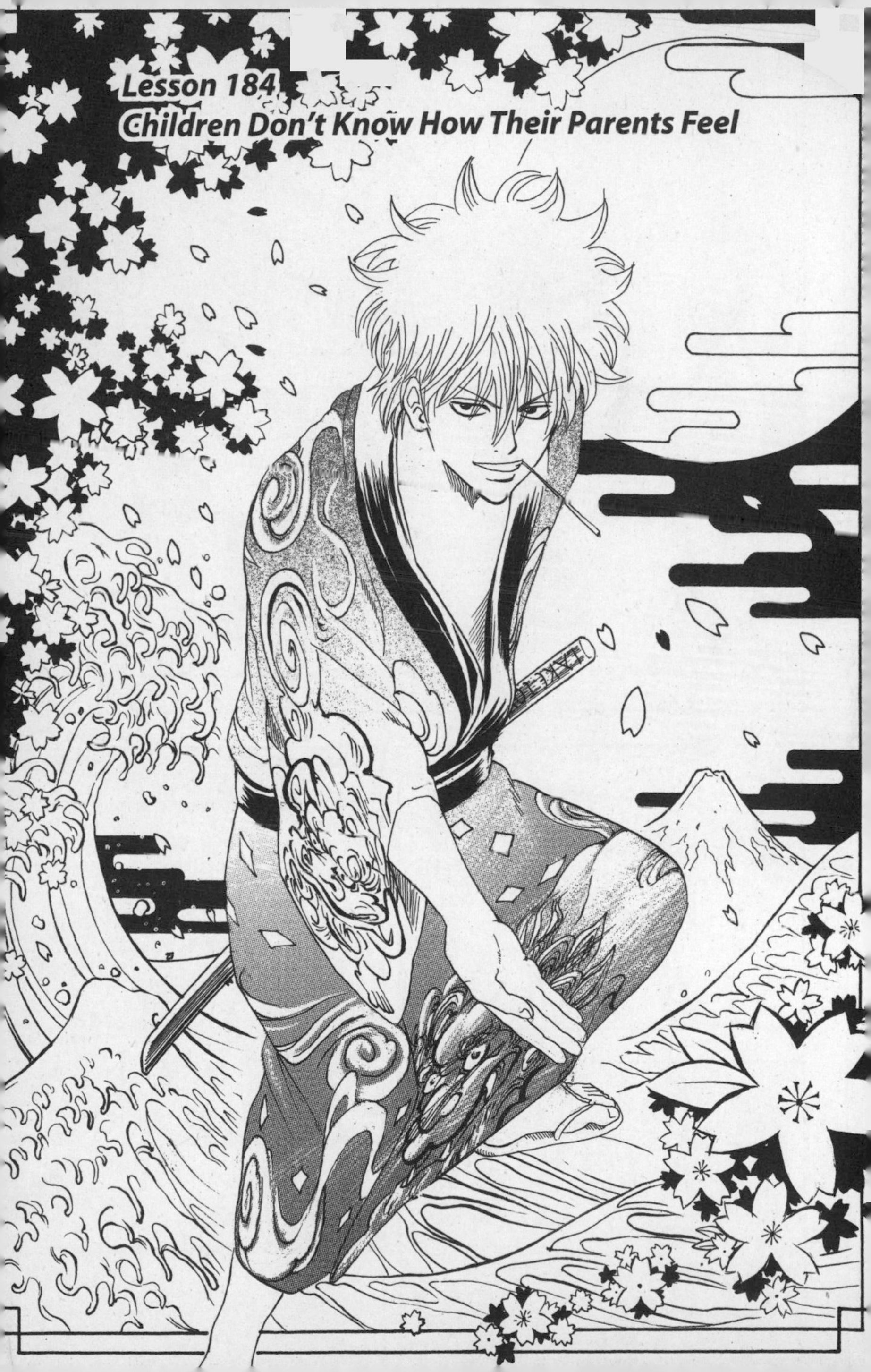
Lesson 184
Children Don't Know How Their Parents Feel

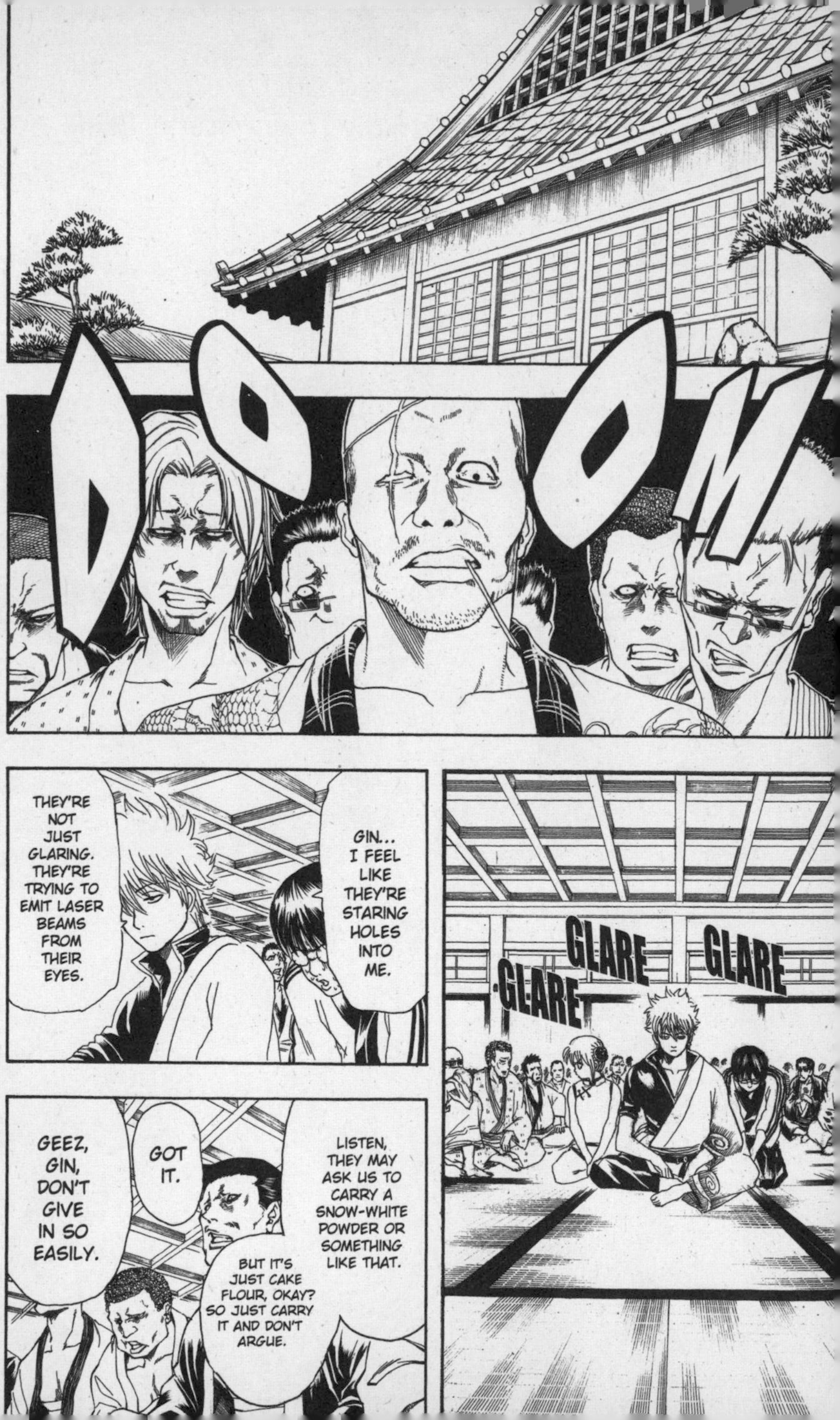
DOOM
GLARE
GLARE
GLARE
GIN... I FEEL LIKE THEY'RE STARING HOLES INTO ME.
THEY'RE NOT JUST GLARING. THEY'RE TRYING TO EMIT LASER BEAMS FROM THEIR EYES.
LISTEN, THEY MAY ASK US TO CARRY A SNOW-WHITE POWDER OR SOMETHING LIKE THAT.
BUT IT'S JUST CAKE FLOUR, OKAY? SO JUST CARRY IT AND DON'T ARGUE.
GOT IT.
GEEZ, GIN, DON'T GIVE IN SO EASILY.

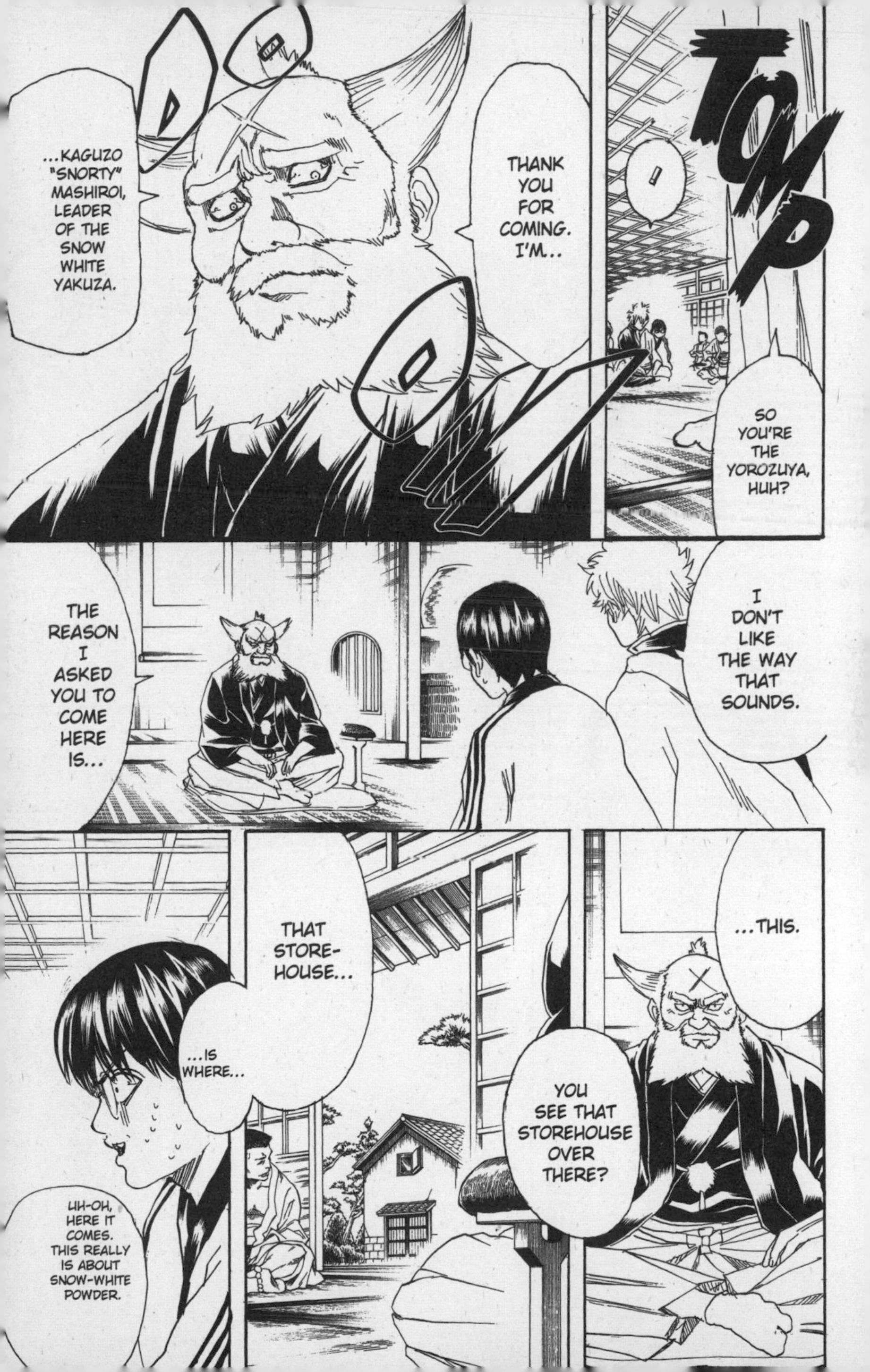
TOMP
!
SO YOU'RE THE YOROZUYA, HUH?
THANK YOU FOR COMING. I'M...
...KAGUZO "SNORTY" MASHIROI, LEADER OF THE SNOW WHITE YAKUZA.
I DON'T LIKE THE WAY THAT SOUNDS.
THE REASON I ASKED YOU TO COME HERE IS...
...THIS.
YOU SEE THAT STOREHOUSE OVER THERE?
THAT STORE-HOUSE...
...IS WHERE...
UH-OH, HERE IT COMES. THIS REALLY IS ABOUT SNOW-WHITE POWDER.

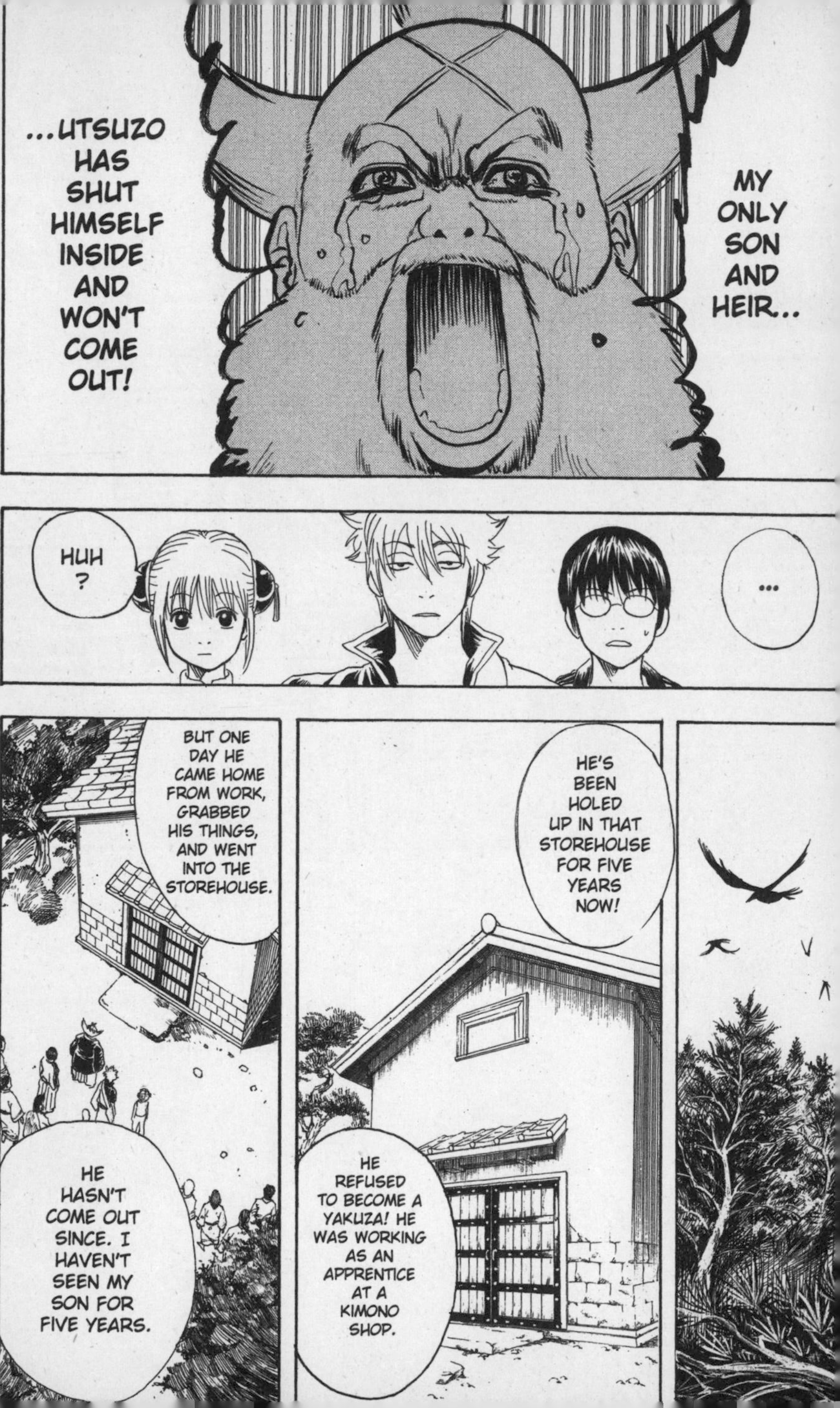
MY ONLY SON AND HEIR...
...UTSUZO HAS SHUT HIMSELF INSIDE AND WON'T COME OUT!
...
HUH?
HE'S BEEN HOLED UP IN THAT STOREHOUSE FOR FIVE YEARS NOW!
HE REFUSED TO BECOME A YAKUZA! HE WAS WORKING AS AN APPRENTICE AT A KIMONO SHOP.
BUT ONE DAY HE CAME HOME FROM WORK, GRABBED HIS THINGS, AND WENT INTO THE STOREHOUSE.
HE HASN'T COME OUT SINCE. I HAVEN'T SEEN MY SON FOR FIVE YEARS.

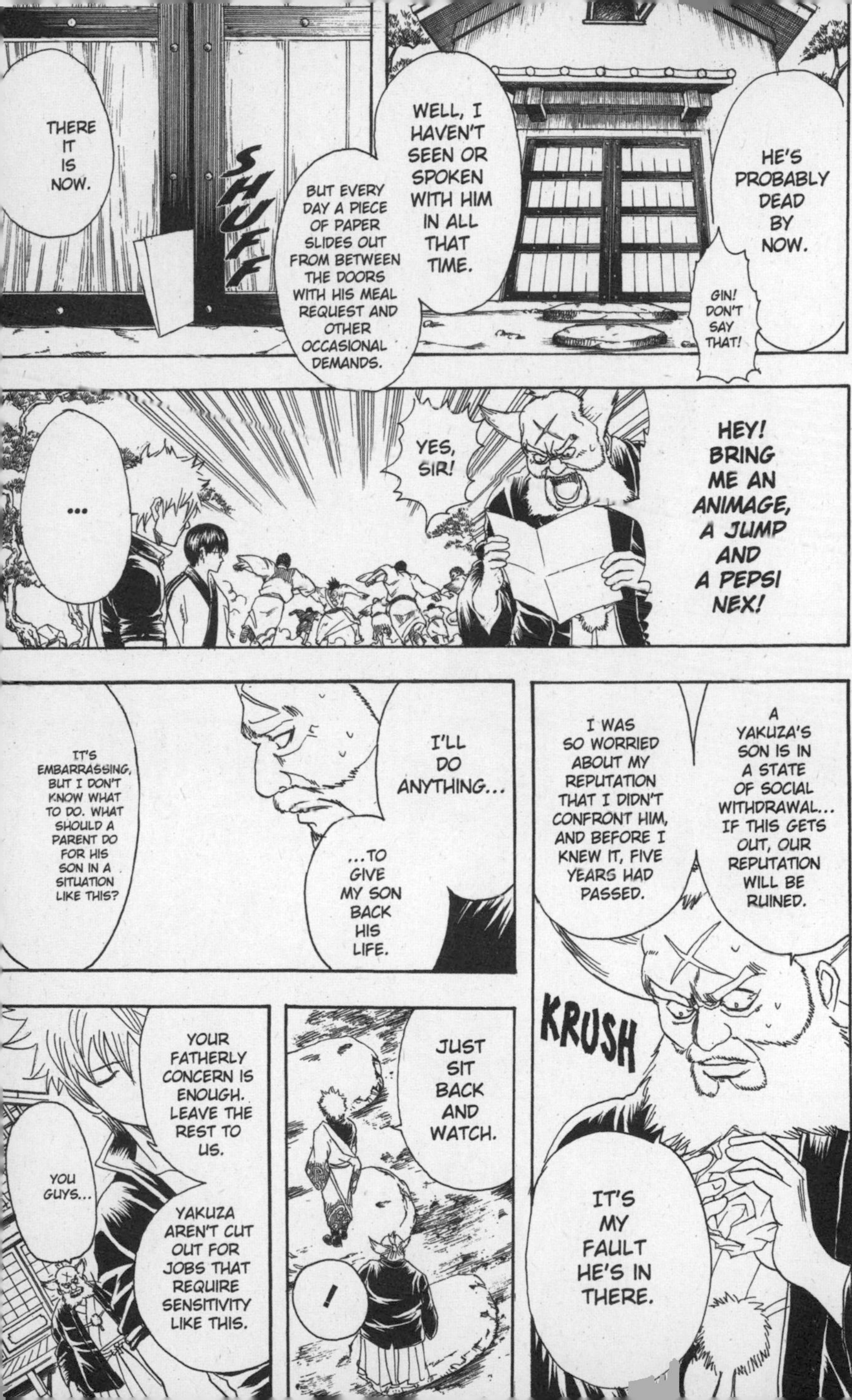
HE'S PROBABLY DEAD BY NOW.
GIN! DON'T SAY THAT!
WELL, I HAVEN'T SEEN OR SPOKEN WITH HIM IN ALL THAT TIME.
BUT EVERY DAY A PIECE OF PAPER SLIDES OUT FROM BETWEEN THE DOORS WITH HIS MEAL REQUEST AND OTHER OCCASIONAL DEMANDS.
SHUFF
THERE IT IS NOW.
HEY! BRING ME AN ANIMAGE, A JUMP AND A PEPSI NEX!
YES, SIR!
...
A YAKUZA'S SON IS IN A STATE OF SOCIAL WITHDRAWAL... IF THIS GETS OUT, OUR REPUTATION WILL BE RUINED.
I WAS SO WORRIED ABOUT MY REPUTATION THAT I DIDN'T CONFRONT HIM, AND BEFORE I KNEW IT, FIVE YEARS HAD PASSED.
KRUSH
IT'S MY FAULT HE'S IN THERE.
I'LL DO ANYTHING...
...TO GIVE MY SON BACK HIS LIFE.
IT'S EMBARRASSING, BUT I DON'T KNOW WHAT TO DO. WHAT SHOULD A PARENT DO FOR HIS SON IN A SITUATION LIKE THIS?
JUST SIT BACK AND WATCH.
!
YOUR FATHERLY CONCERN IS ENOUGH. LEAVE THE REST TO US.
YAKUZA AREN'T CUT OUT FOR JOBS THAT REQUIRE SENSITIVITY LIKE THIS.
YOU GUYS...

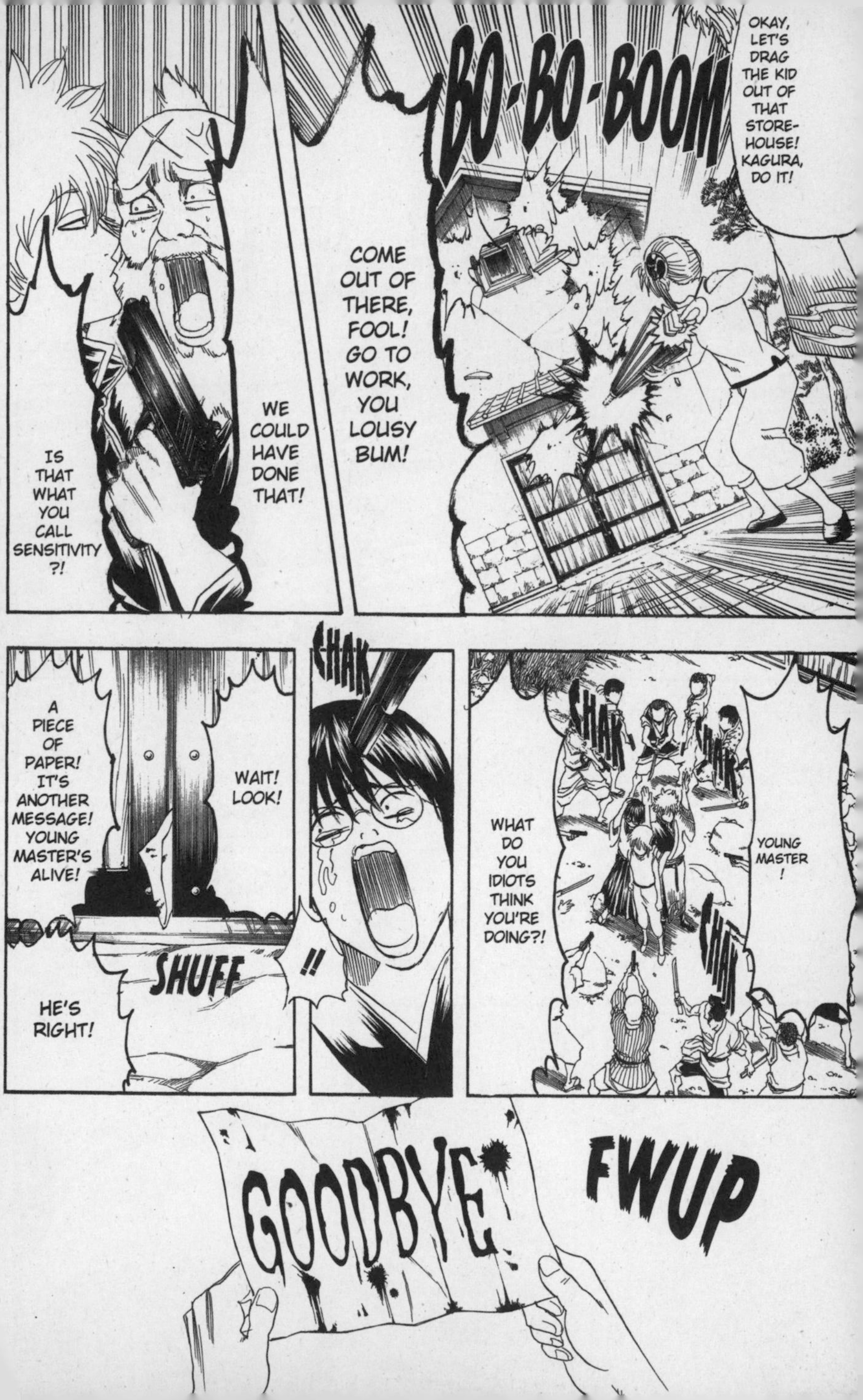
OKAY, LET'S DRAG THE KID OUT OF THAT STOREHOUSE! KAGURA, DO IT!
BO-BO-BOOM
COME OUT OF THERE, FOOL! GO TO WORK, YOU LOUSY BUM!
WE COULD HAVE DONE THAT!
IS THAT WHAT YOU CALL SENSITIVITY?!
YOUNG MASTER!
SHAK
SHAK
WHAT DO YOU IDIOTS THINK YOU'RE DOING?!
CHAK
SHAK
WAIT! LOOK!
!!
A PIECE OF PAPER! IT'S ANOTHER MESSAGE! YOUNG MASTER'S ALIVE!
SHUFF
HE'S RIGHT!
FWUP
GOODBYE

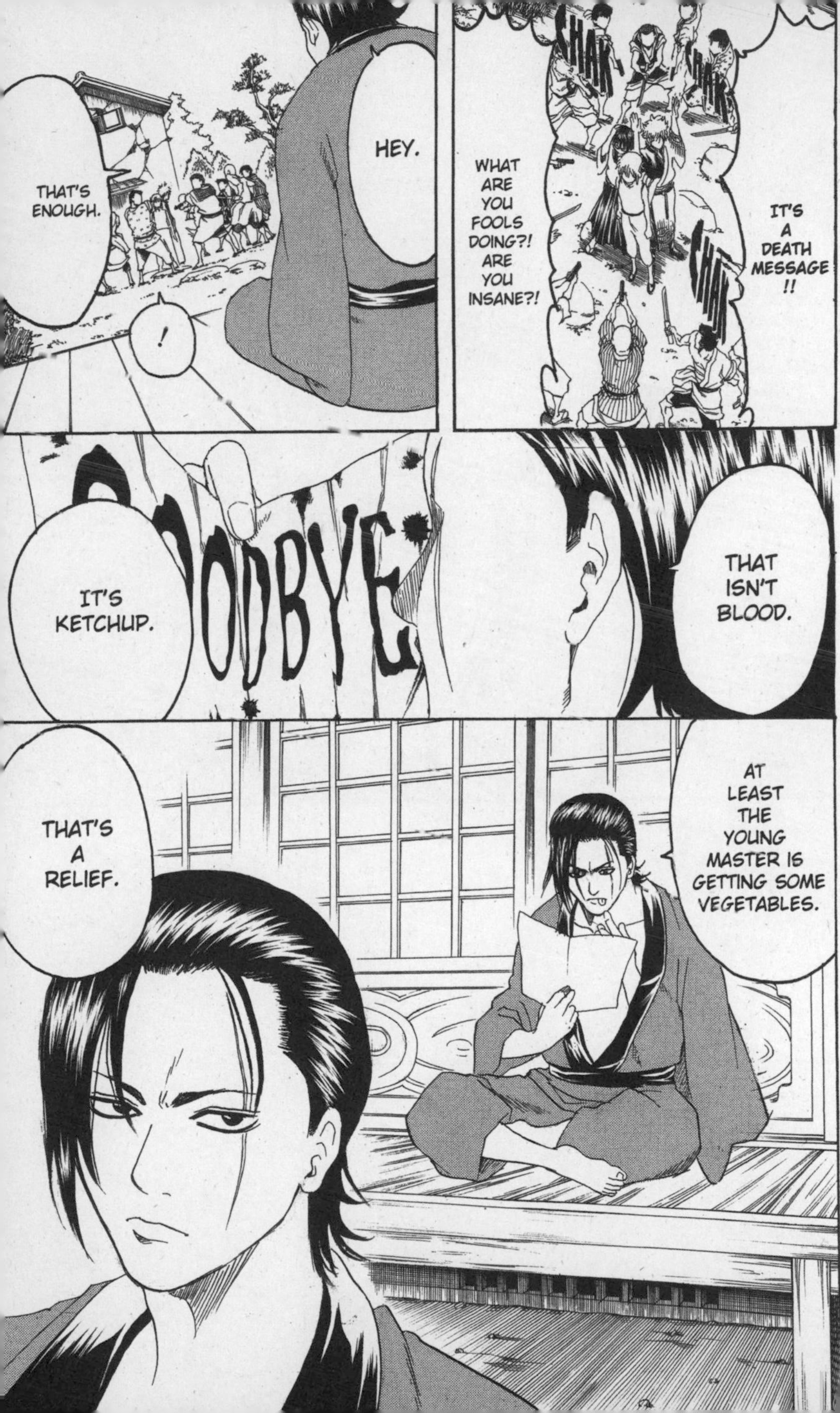
SHAK
SHAK
SHAK
IT'S A DEATH MESSAGE!!
WHAT ARE YOU FOOLS DOING?! ARE YOU INSANE?!
HEY.
!
THAT'S ENOUGH.
THAT ISN'T BLOOD.
IT'S KETCHUP.
AT LEAST THE YOUNG MASTER IS GETTING SOME VEGETABLES.
THAT'S A RELIEF.

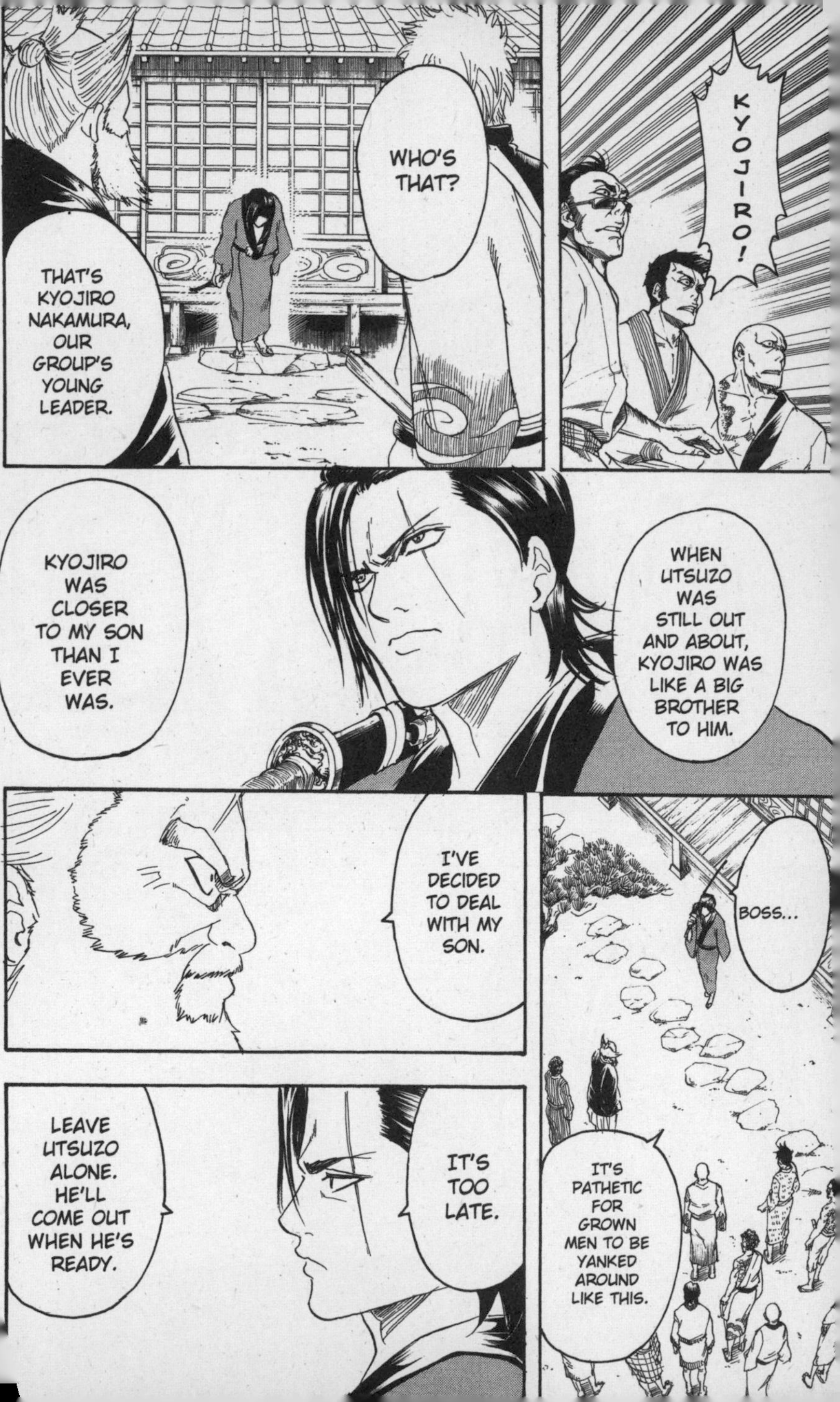
KYOJIRO!
WHO'S THAT?
THAT'S KYOJIRO NAKAMURA, OUR GROUP'S YOUNG LEADER.
WHEN UTSUZO WAS STILL OUT AND ABOUT, KYOJIRO WAS LIKE A BIG BROTHER TO HIM.
KYOJIRO WAS CLOSER TO MY SON THAN I EVER WAS.
BOSS...
IT'S PATHETIC FOR GROWN MEN TO BE YANKED AROUND LIKE THIS.
I'VE DECIDED TO DEAL WITH MY SON.
IT'S TOO LATE.
LEAVE UTSUZO ALONE. HE'LL COME OUT WHEN HE'S READY.

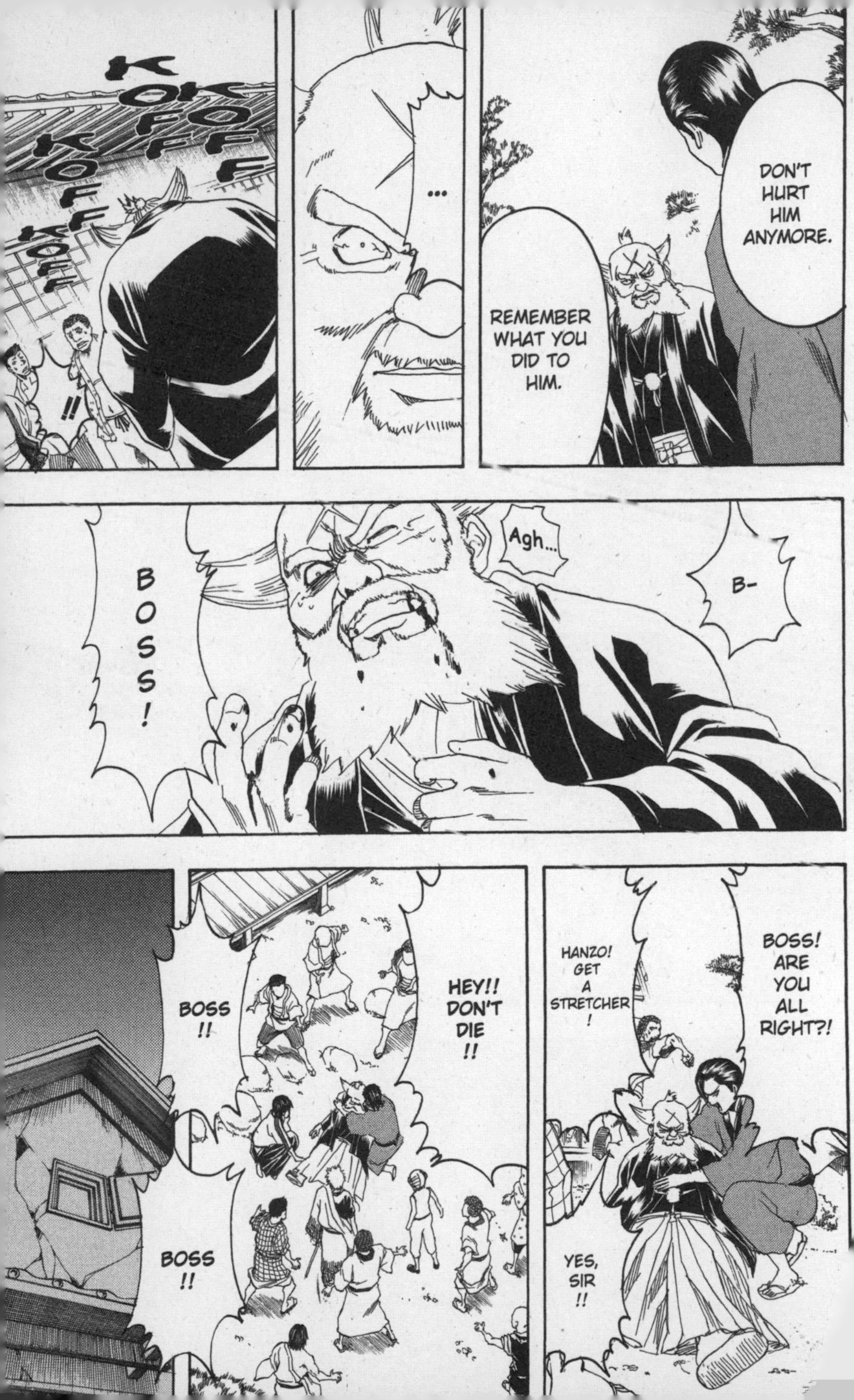
DON'T HURT HIM ANYMORE.
REMEMBER WHAT YOU DID TO HIM.
...
KOFF KOFF
KOFF KOFF
!!
B-
Agh...
BOSS!
BOSS! ARE YOU ALL RIGHT?!
HANZO! GET A STRETCHER!
YES, SIR!!
HEY!! DON'T DIE!!
BOSS!!
BOSS!!

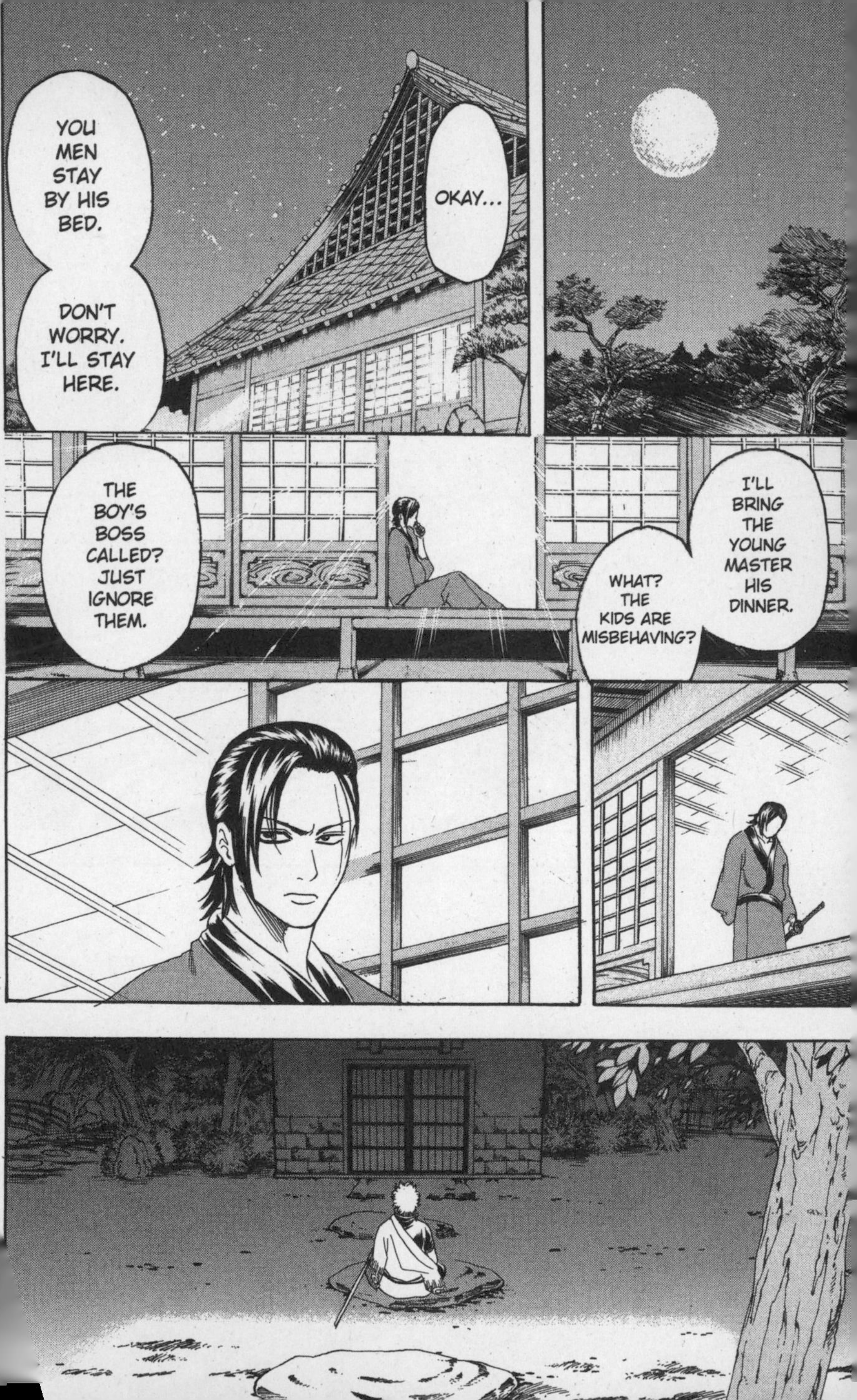
YOU MEN STAY BY HIS BED.
DON'T WORRY. I'LL STAY HERE.
OKAY...
I'LL BRING THE YOUNG MASTER HIS DINNER.
WHAT? THE KIDS ARE MISBEHAVING?
THE BOY'S BOSS CALLED? JUST IGNORE THEM.

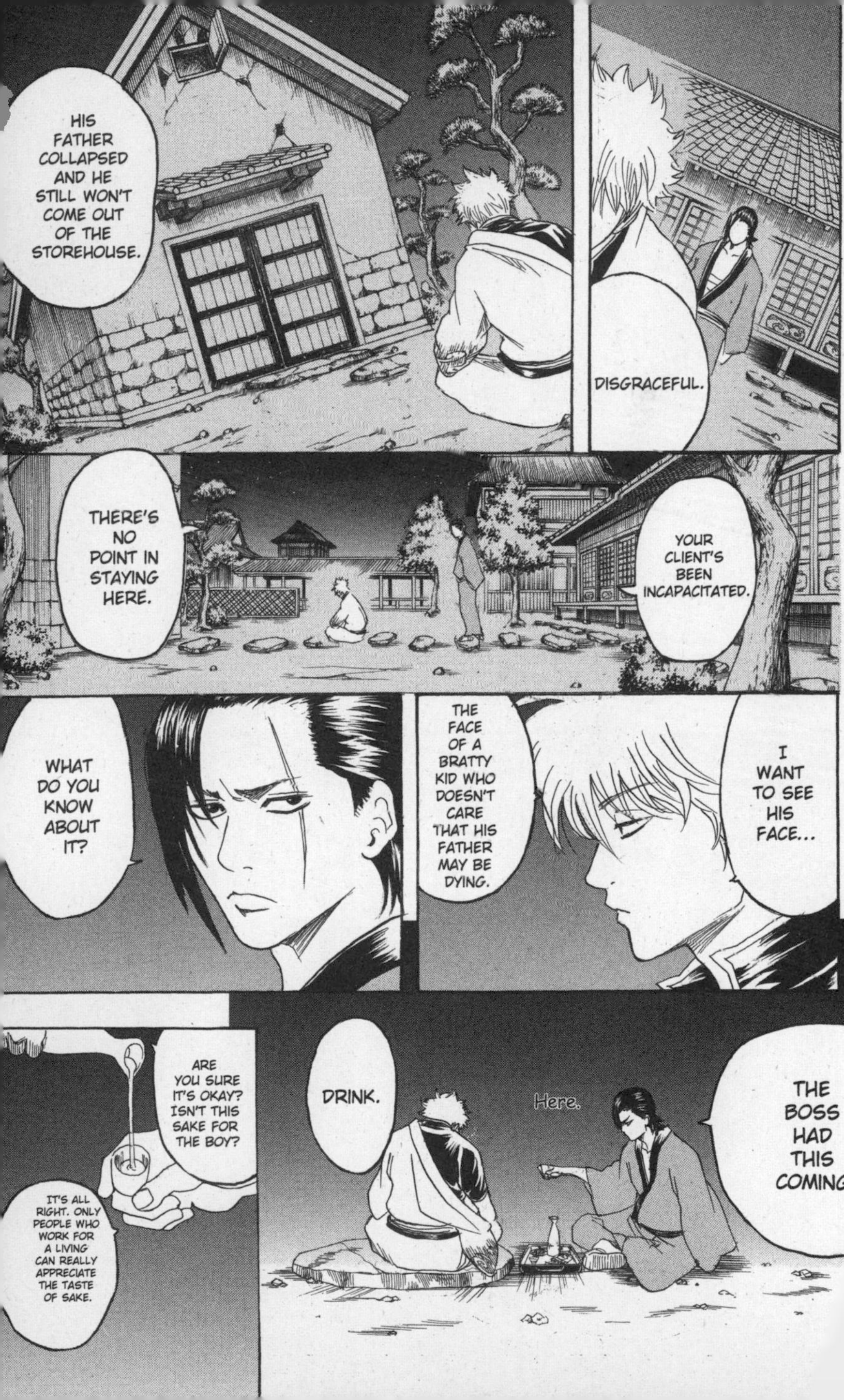
DISGRACEFUL.
HIS FATHER COLLAPSED AND HE STILL WON'T COME OUT OF THE STOREHOUSE.
YOUR CLIENT'S BEEN INCAPACITATED.
THERE'S NO POINT IN STAYING HERE.
I WANT TO SEE HIS FACE...
THE FACE OF A BRATTY KID WHO DOESN'T CARE THAT HIS FATHER MAY BE DYING.
WHAT DO YOU KNOW ABOUT IT?
THE BOSS HAD THIS COMING.
Here.
DRINK.
ARE YOU SURE IT'S OKAY? ISN'T THIS SAKE FOR THE BOY?
IT'S ALL RIGHT. ONLY PEOPLE WHO WORK FOR A LIVING CAN REALLY APPRECIATE THE TASTE OF SAKE.

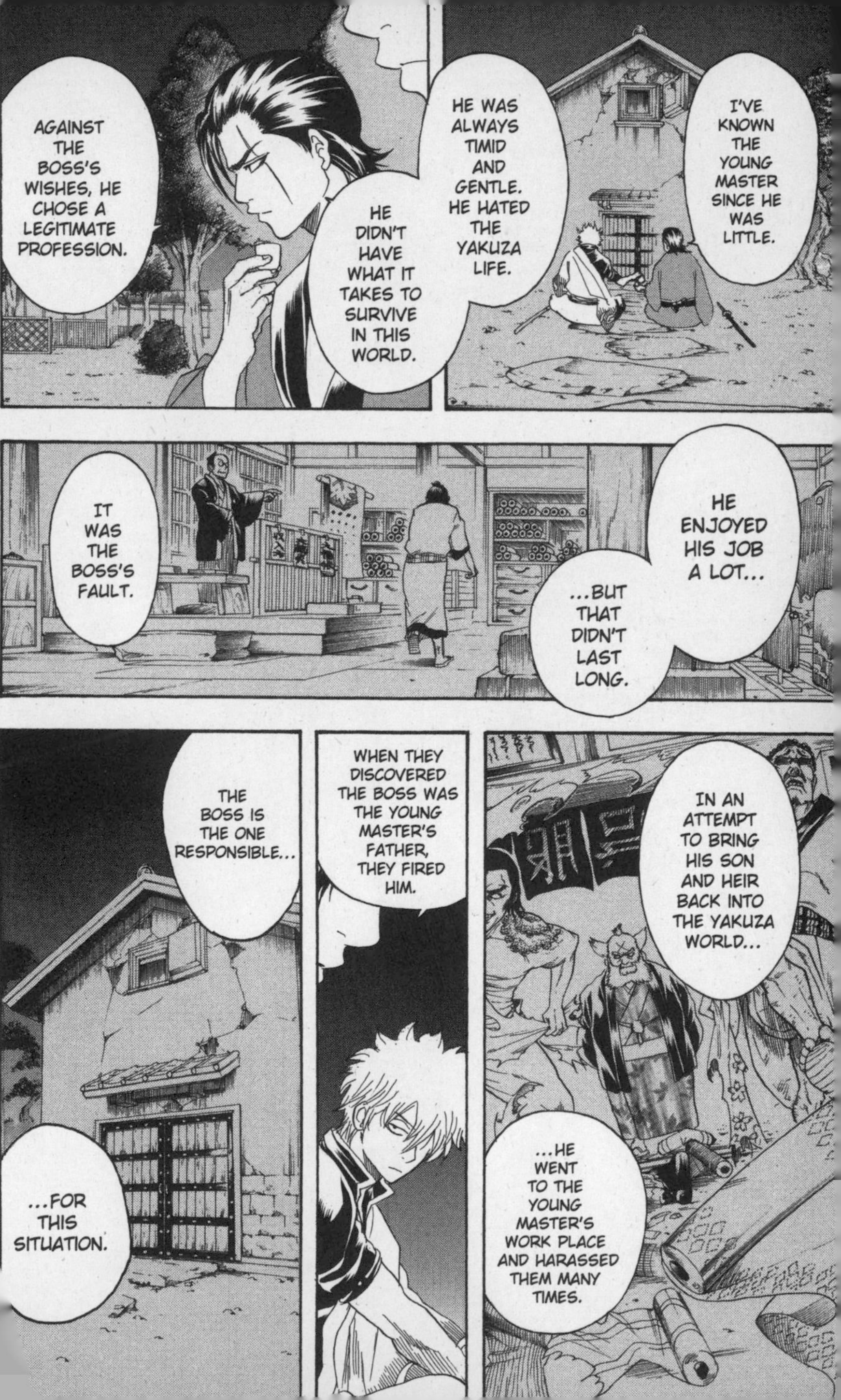

I'VE KNOWN THE YOUNG MASTER SINCE HE WAS LITTLE.
HE WAS ALWAYS TIMID AND GENTLE. HE HATED THE YAKUZA LIFE.
HE DIDN'T HAVE WHAT IT TAKES TO SURVIVE IN THIS WORLD.
AGAINST THE BOSS'S WISHES, HE CHOSE A LEGITIMATE PROFESSION.
HE ENJOYED HIS JOB A LOT...
...BUT THAT DIDN'T LAST LONG.
IT WAS THE BOSS'S FAULT.
IN AN ATTEMPT TO BRING HIS SON AND HEIR BACK INTO THE YAKUZA WORLD...
...HE WENT TO THE YOUNG MASTER'S WORK PLACE AND HARASSED THEM MANY TIMES.
WHEN THEY DISCOVERED THE BOSS WAS THE YOUNG MASTER'S FATHER, THEY FIRED HIM.
THE BOSS IS THE ONE RESPONSIBLE...
...FOR THIS SITUATION.

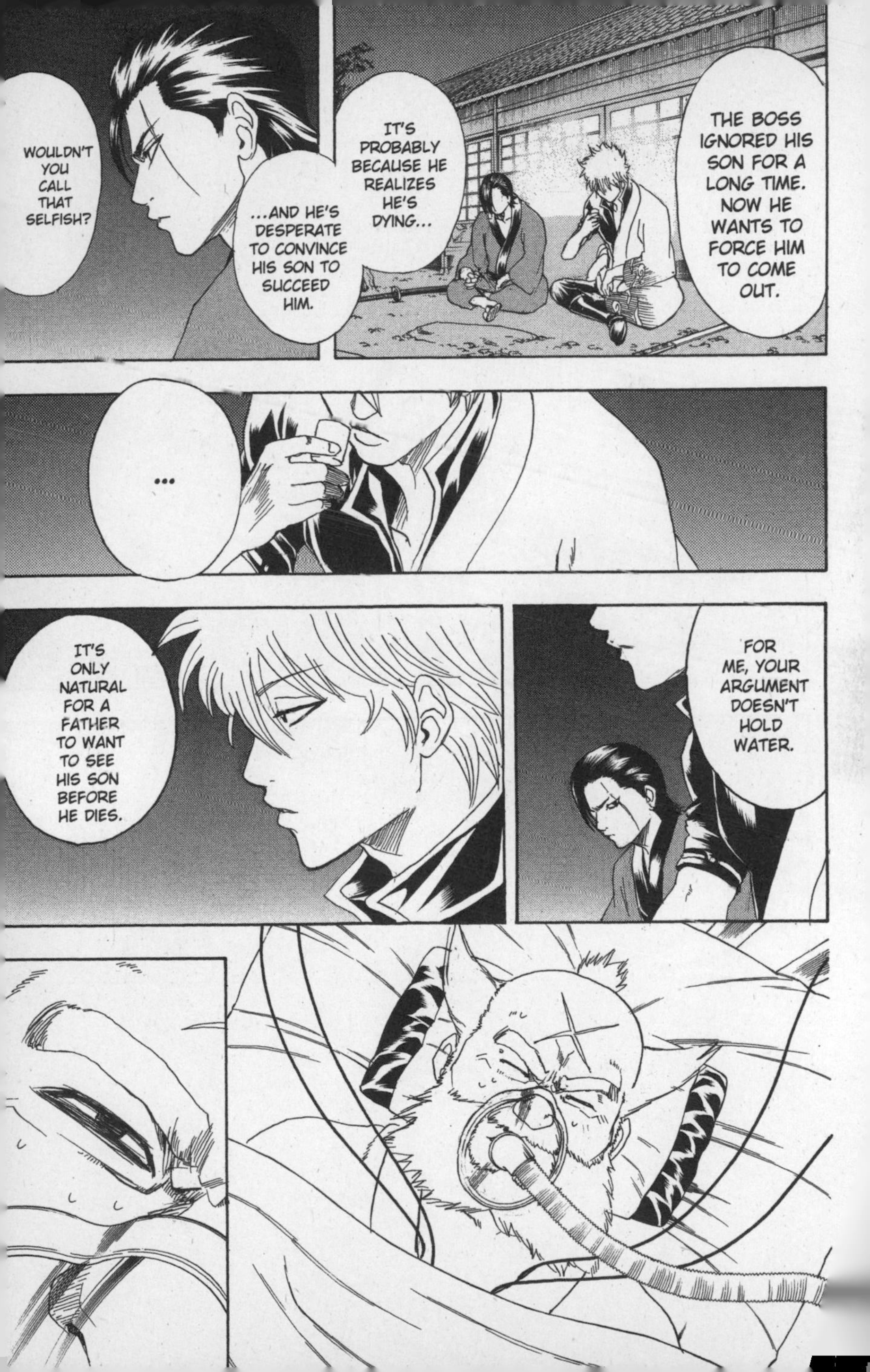
THE BOSS IGNORED HIS SON FOR A LONG TIME. NOW HE WANTS TO FORCE HIM TO COME OUT.
IT'S PROBABLY BECAUSE HE REALIZES HE'S DYING...
...AND HE'S DESPERATE TO CONVINCE HIS SON TO SUCCEED HIM.
WOULDN'T YOU CALL THAT SELFISH?
...
FOR ME, YOUR ARGUMENT DOESN'T HOLD WATER.
IT'S ONLY NATURAL FOR A FATHER TO WANT TO SEE HIS SON BEFORE HE DIES.

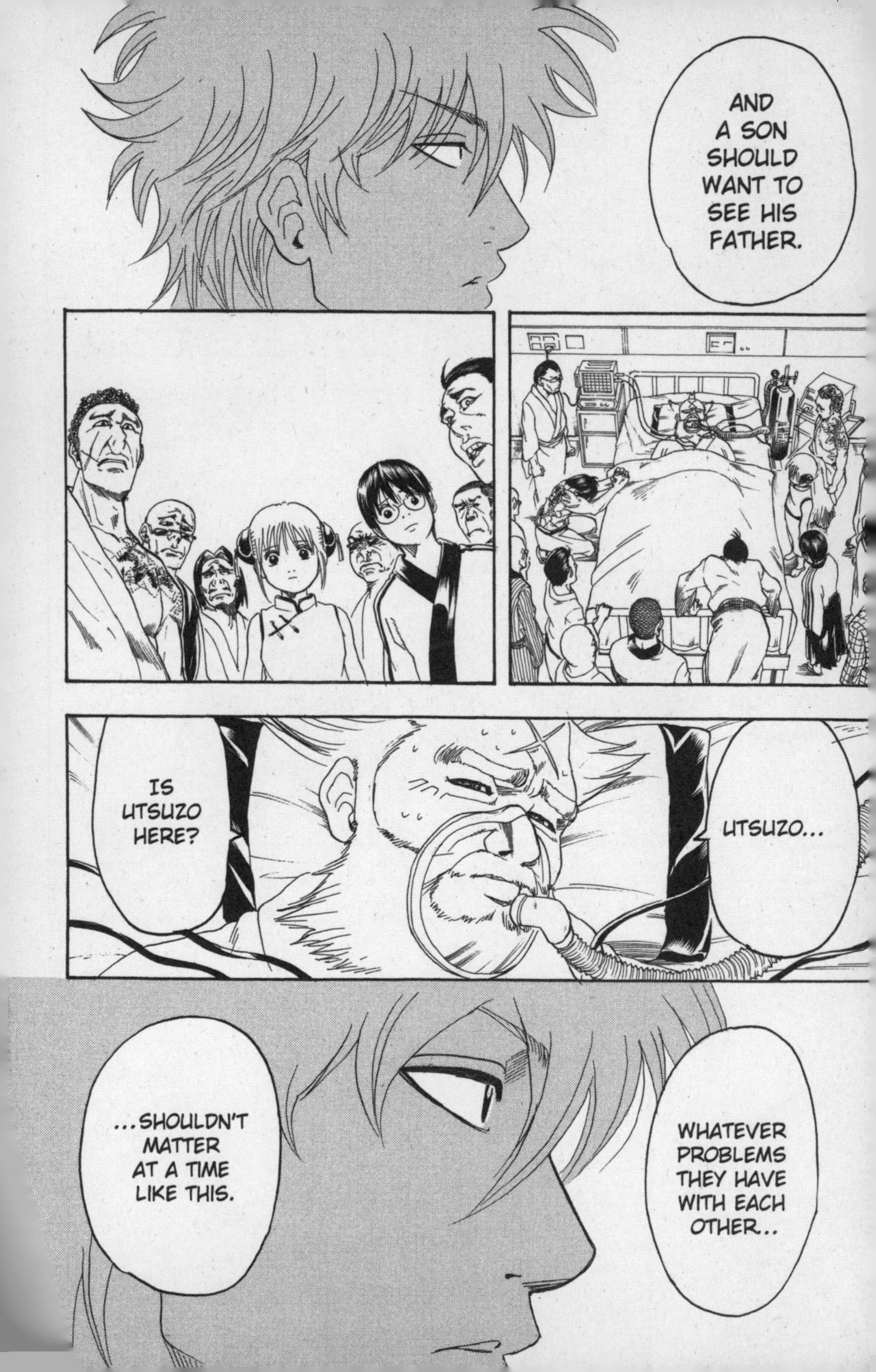
AND A SON SHOULD WANT TO SEE HIS FATHER.
UTSUZO...
IS UTSUZO HERE?
WHATEVER PROBLEMS THEY HAVE WITH EACH OTHER..
...SHOULDN'T MATTER AT A TIME LIKE THIS.

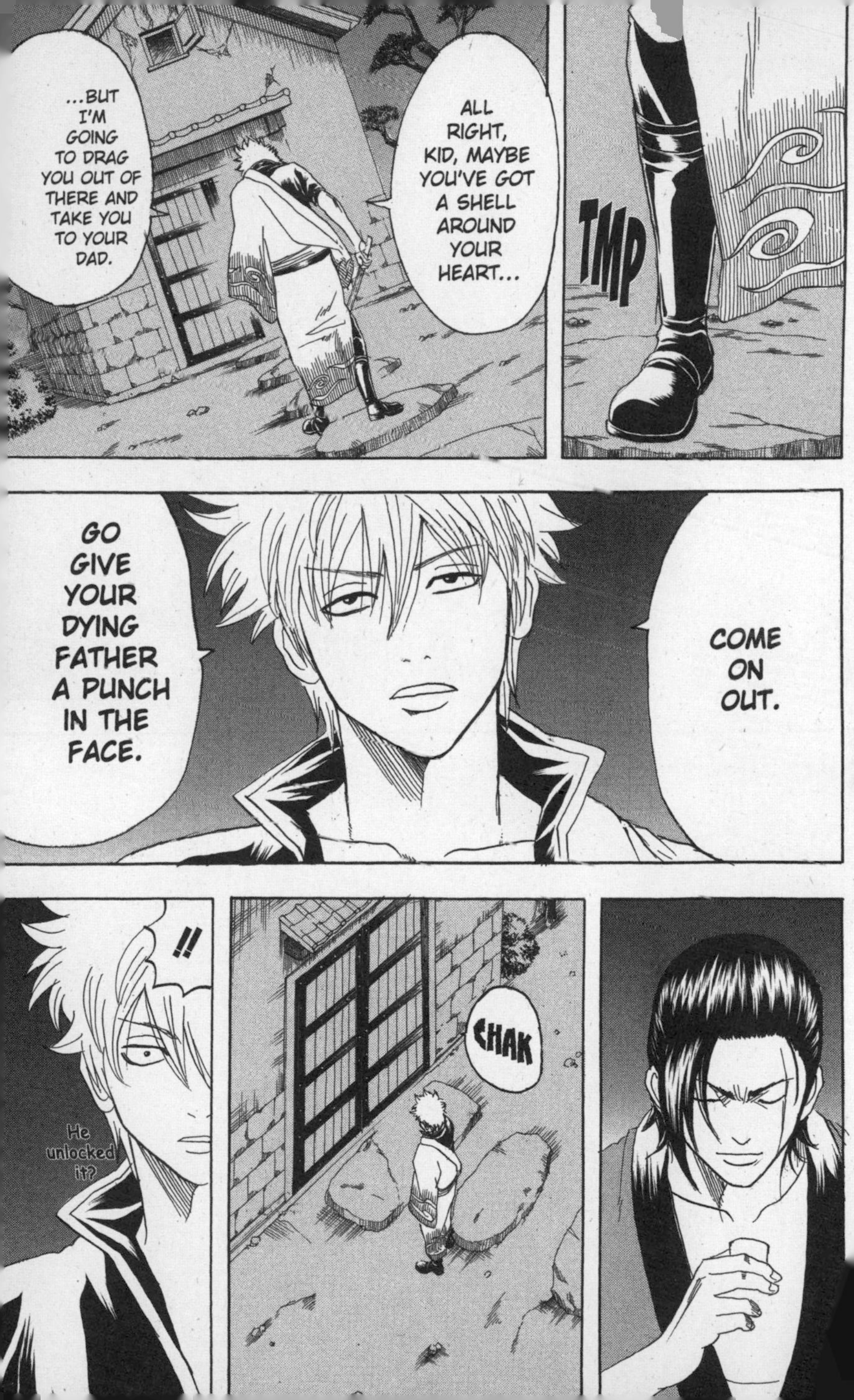
TMP
ALL RIGHT, KID, MAYBE YOU'VE GOT A SHELL AROUND YOUR HEART...
...BUT I'M GOING TO DRAG YOU OUT OF THERE AND TAKE YOU TO YOUR DAD.
COME ON OUT.
GO GIVE YOUR DYING FATHER A PUNCH IN THE FACE.
CHAK
!!
He unlocked it?

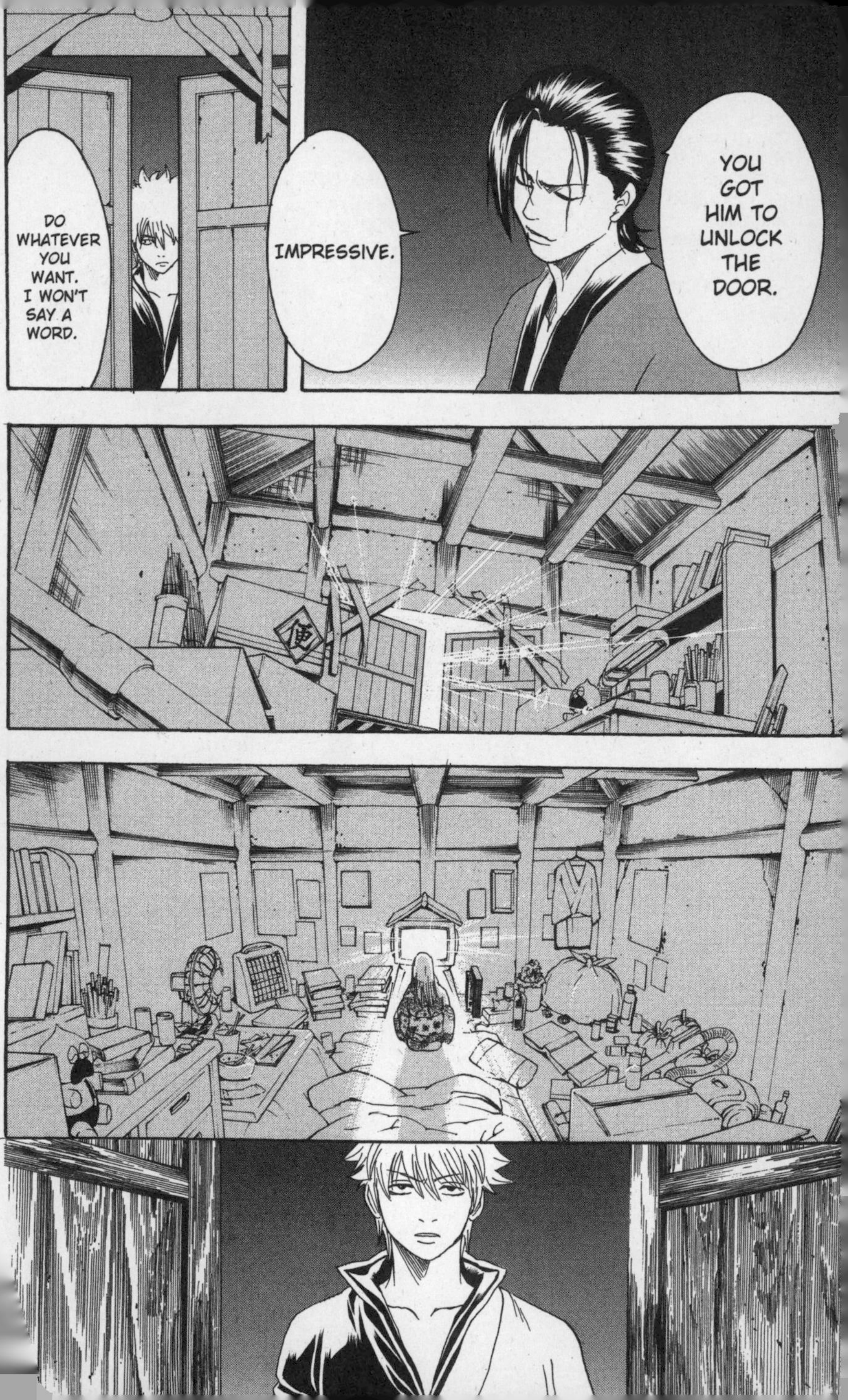
YOU GOT HIM TO UNLOCK THE DOOR.
IMPRESSIVE.
DO WHATEVER YOU WANT. I WON'T SAY A WORD.
便

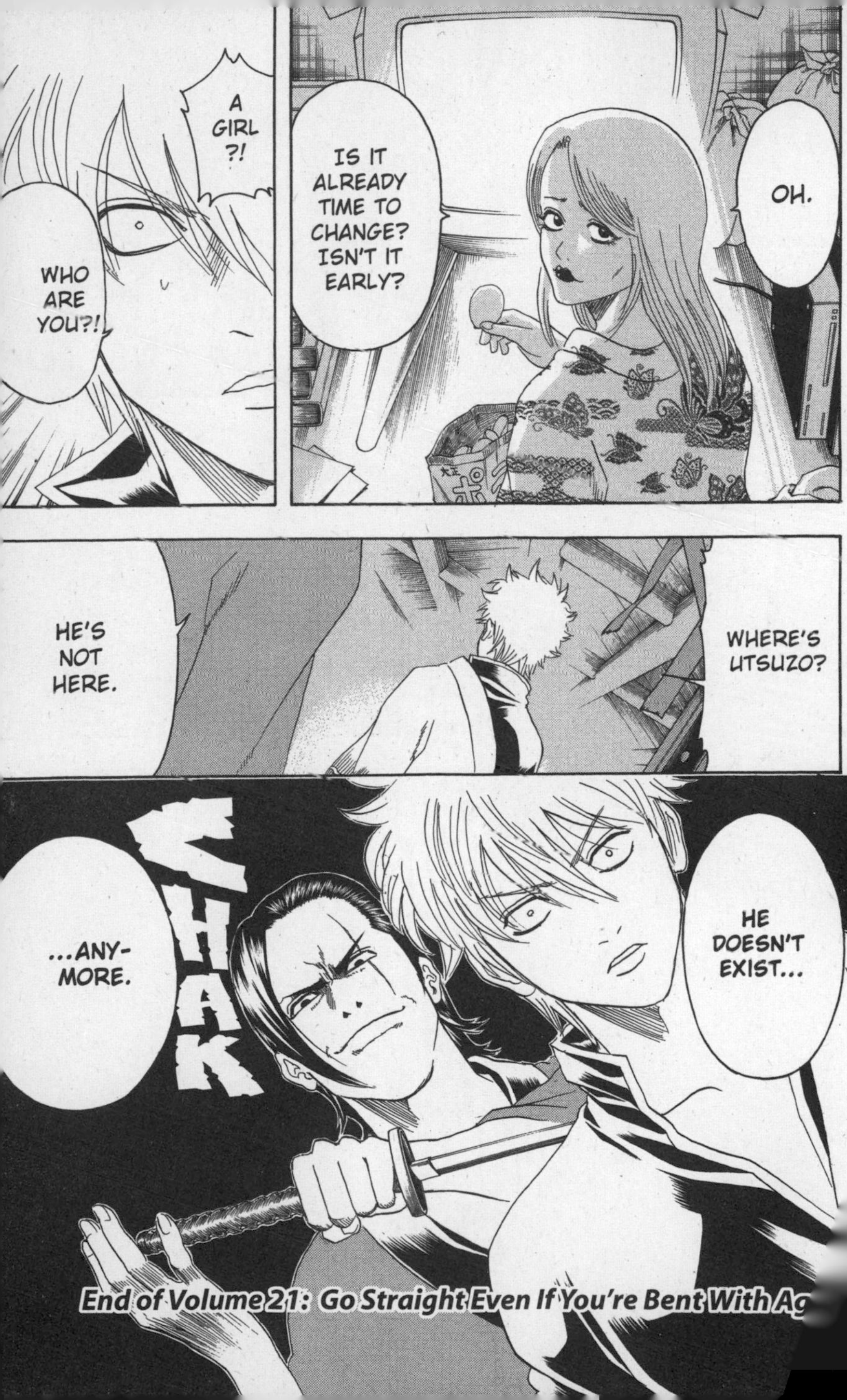
OH.
IS IT ALREADY TIME TO CHANGE? ISN'T IT EARLY?
A GIRL ?!
WHO ARE YOU?!
WHERE'S UTSUZO?
HE'S NOT HERE.
HE DOESN'T EXIST...
SHAK
...ANY-MORE.
End of Volume 21: Go Straight Even If You're Bent With Ag

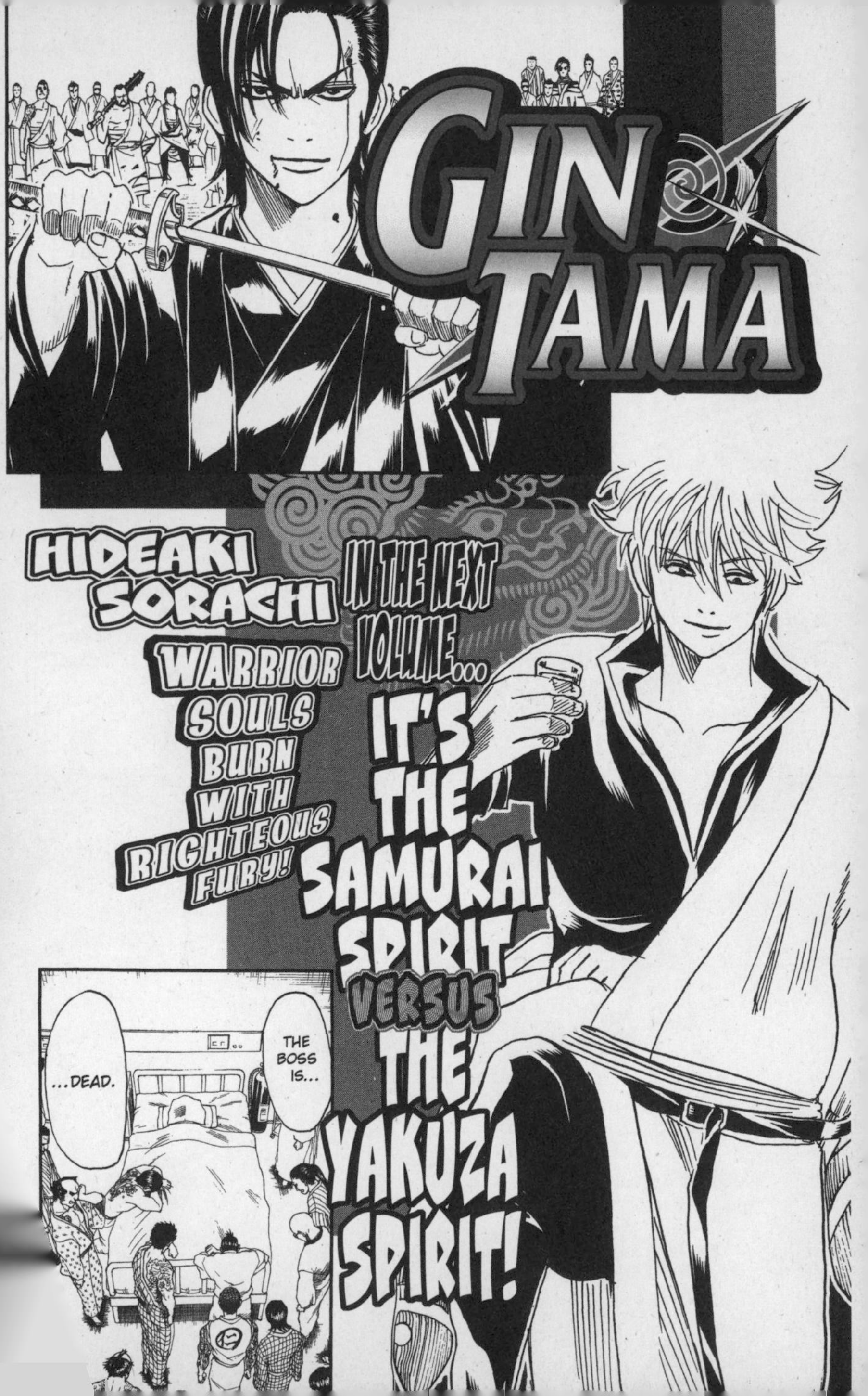
GIN TAMA
HIDEAKI SORACHI
IN THE NEXT VOLUME...
WARRIOR SOULS BURN WITH RIGHTEOUS FURY!
IT'S THE SAMURAI SPIRIT VERSUS THE YAKUZA SPIRIT!
THE BOSS IS...
...DEAD.

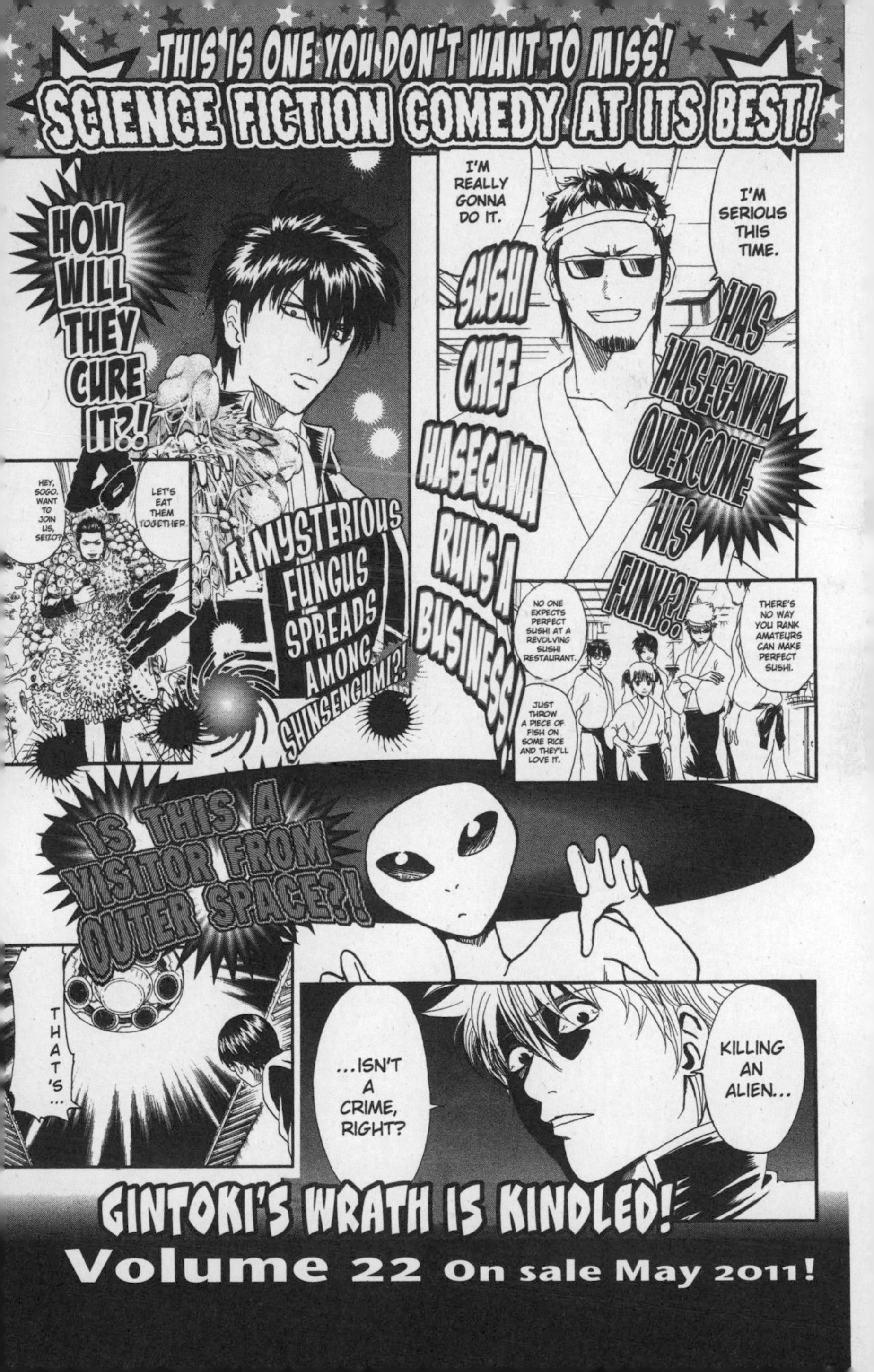

THIS IS ONE YOU DON'T WANT TO MISS!
SCIENCE FICTION COMEDY AT ITS BEST!
I'M SERIOUS THIS TIME.
I'M REALLY GONNA DO IT.
HAS HASEGAWA OVERCOME HIS FUNK?!
SUSHI CHEF HASEGAWA RUNS A BUSINESS!
HOW WILL THEY CURE IT?!
A MYSTERIOUS FUNGUS SPREADS AMONG SHINSENGUMI?!
THERE'S NO WAY YOU RANK AMATEURS CAN MAKE PERFECT SUSHI.
NO ONE EXPECTS PERFECT SUSHI AT A REVOLVING SUSHI RESTAURANT.
JUST THROW A PIECE OF FISH ON SOME RICE AND THEY'LL LOVE IT.
LET'S EAT THEM TOGETHER.
HEY, SOGO. WANT TO JOIN US, SEIZO?
IS THIS A VISITOR FROM OUTER SPACE?!
KILLING AN ALIEN...
...ISN'T A CRIME, RIGHT?
THAT'S...
GINTOKI'S WRATH IS KINDLED!
Volume 22 On sale May 2011!